D0705371

Good Night Officially

MBC $19.95

HISTORY AND WARFARE

Arther Ferrill, *Series Editor*

GOOD NIGHT OFFICIALLY: The Pacific War Letters of a
Destroyer Sailor   *William M. McBride*

CRETE: THE BATTLE AND THE RESISTANCE   *Antony Beevor*

THE HUNDRED YEARS WAR FOR MOROCCO:
Gunpowder and the Military Revolution in the Early Modern
Muslim World   *Weston F. Cook, Jr.*

HIPPEIS: The Cavalry of Ancient Greece   *Leslie J. Worley*

FEEDING MARS: Logistics in Western Warfare from the
Middle Ages to the Present   *John Lynn, editor*

THE SEVEN MILITARY CLASSICS OF ANCIENT CHINA
Ralph D. Sawyer, translator

FORTHCOMING

THE HALT IN THE MUD: French Strategic Planning from
Waterloo to Sedan   *Gary P. Cox*

THE BATTLE OF THE ATLANTIC   *Timothy Runyan and
Jan Copes, editors*

ON WATERLOO
The Campaign of 1815 in France by *Carl von Clausewitz*
Memorandum on the Battle of Waterloo by *the Duke of Wellington*
Christopher Bassford, translator

THE ANATOMY OF A LITTLE WAR: A Diplomatic and
Military History of the Gundovald Affair, 567–585
Bernard S. Bachrach

THE GENERAL'S GENERAL: A Biography of Arthur
MacArthur   *Kenneth Ray Young*

WARFARE AND CIVILIZATION IN THE
ISLAMIC MIDDLE EAST, 600–1600   *William J. Hamblin*

ORDERING SOCIETY: A World History of
Military Institutions   *Barton C. Hacker*

Hello, Baby Darling:-

No Baby I don't mind you
letting other people read
my letters occasionally.
Thanks for the compliment.
I hope your friends aren't
bored XXXX by them.

...ay. First of all, I want to apologize
...dney is o.k. I got a letter from him
...t down about five days before that. He
...uartered. They won't tell us of course
...s as secret as possible. I have written
... much information as I could and tried
... letter as asking me to do ...... I'll
... try and write her. H........ is:
..., yes, Sid made ....e may
...t of this. (B........

...e get

MRS. J. O. RAINES
c/o Drs. Cary, Cox & Love
631 Medical Arts Building
Dallas 1, Texas

J. O. RAINES Y2...
U.S.S. HOWORTH (D...
c/o Fleet Post Offic...
San Francisco, Calif.

VIA AIR MAIL

PASSED BY NAVAL CENSOR

...d
... other
... a lot of
...posed to go
...t us because of
...t to a very valuable
... The other can gunned
...s to be knocked off by our
...t them ashore up here. There
...wire. Very neat and efficient.
... tell you about Sid. I sure am glad
...him a lot. (Old in actions I mean).
...onal" letter when I can get those planes off
... night. XXX I came home on leave and met you
...oor and had a great big frown on your face. I
...g and crying. I asked you what was the matter and you
...u later". Darling, is something the matter? Are you
...I've never had such a dream before and I don't want you to
...and tell me how things are, huh? Bye for now Baby Doll, I
...please believe that. God bless you Darling and remember that I am
...ave forever.

Your devoted husband,

P.S. I LOVE YOU!!!

GOOD NIGHT OFFICIALLY

The Pacific War Letters of a Destroyer Sailor

The Letters of
Yeoman James Orvill Raines

Edited with Introductions by
William M. McBride

Westview Press
BOULDER • SAN FRANCISCO • OXFORD

History and Warfare

All rights reserved. No part of this publication may be reproduced or transmitted in any form or by any means, electronic or mechanical, including photocopy, recording, or any information storage and retrieval system, without permission in writing from the publisher.

Copyright © 1994 by Westview Press, Inc.

Published in 1994 in the United States of America by Westview Press, Inc., 5500 Central Avenue, Boulder, Colorado 80301-2877, and in the United Kingdom by Westview Press, 36 Lonsdale Road, Summertown, Oxford OX2 7EW

Library of Congress Cataloging-in-Publication Data
Raines, James Orvill, d. 1945.
  Good night officially : the Pacific War letters of a destroyer
sailor / [edited by] William M. McBride.
      p. cm. — (History and warfare)
  Letters of Yeoman 2/c James Orvill Raines to his wife.
  Includes bibliographical references.
  ISBN 0-8133-1950-1
  1. Raines, James Orvill, d. 1945—Correspondence.   2. Raines, Ray
Ellen—Correspondence.   3. Howorth (Ship)   4. World War, 1939–1945—
Naval operations, American.   5. World War, 1939–1945—Campaigns—
Pacific Area.   6. World War, 1939–1945—personal narratives,
American.   7. Seamen—United States—Correspondence.   I. McBride,
William M.   II. Title.   III. Series.
D774.H68R35   1994
940.54'26'092—dc20
[B]   93-28239
                                                                                  CIP

Printed and bound in the United States of America

The paper used in this publication meets the requirements
of the American National Standard for Permanence of Paper
for Printed Library Materials Z39.48-1984.

10   9   8   7   6   5   4   3   2   1

For all tin can sailors, particularly my snipes, who toughed it out in the thankless arena of the fire and engine rooms in Hamner *(DD 718) two decades ago, especially Machinist's Mate 2/c Jim Bowdon, who helped me to comprehend and thereby command; Machinist's Mate 3/c Robert Schuchardt, blinded in one eye; and Boiler Technician 2/c Ken Schwartz, who, in retrospect, died so young;*

and those who went to war in Howorth *(DD 592) in 1944, including*

Ensign Max Bayless,
Lieutenant Pete Hamner,
Fire Controlman 3/c Morris LeCren,
Fire Controlman 2/c George Nolan,
Yeoman 2/c Orvill Raines,
Fire Controlman 1/c Julius Sanchez, and
Fire Controlman 3/c J. W. Stribling,
none of whom ever came home;

and for my father, sent deep into the Pacific maelstrom from Pearl Harbor in January 1942 with a World War I helmet and a 1903 Springfield.

They hear the sound of the seas that pound
On the half-inch plates of steel
And they close their eyes to the lullabies
Of the creaking sides and keel.

They're a lusty crowd that's vastly proud
Of the slim grey craft they drive
Of the roaring flues and the humming screws
Which make her a thing alive.

They love the lunge of her surging plunge
And the murk of her smokescreen too
As they sail the seas in their dungarees
A grey destroyer's crew.

—"Destroyermen" *(anonymous)*

Contents

THREE: "THE DEVIL'S OWN CREATION"

ILLUSTRATIONS

Preface

My interest in USS *Howorth* originated during my thirty-three months of duty in the Pacific Fleet destroyer *Hamner*, named after *Howorth's* gunnery officer killed at Okinawa, Lieutenant Henry R. "Pete" Hamner. His legacy included the *Reader's Digest* subscriptions his mother presented each year to the wardroom and crew. Later, as executive officer in the hydrofoil *Plainview*, exasperated by the endless stream of logs and records demanded by higher authorities, I peevishly tested the navy's record system and wrote away for information on Lieutenant Hamner and *Howorth*. I was surprised by the magnitude of the material documenting *Howorth's* Pacific War, ranging from hourly barometric readings and seawater injection temperatures to ammunition effectiveness reports.

As I pursued *Howorth's* history over the years, I came into contact with several of her crew as well as family members of some of those who never returned from the Western Pacific. I am especially indebted to Commander Patrick H. Arnold, U.S. Navy (Retired), who served as fire control and plotting room officer prior to the kamikaze attack on April 6, 1945. A soft-spoken, almost shy individual, Pat left the Virginia Tidewater and enlisted in the navy in 1934. As a fire controlman 1/c, he fired a machine gun at Japanese planes at Pearl Harbor from the destroyer *Selfridge*. Promoted to chief petty officer and later to warrant officer and chief warrant officer, he served in *Selfridge* during the early, desperate battles in the Southwest Pacific. He was later commissioned an ensign and transferred to the new destroyer *Howorth* in April 1944. In *Howorth*, Pat Arnold shared a stateroom with Lieutenant (junior grade) Jim Ellis, who was badly burned at Okinawa, and Pete Hamner, who had a "most pleasant personality, a ready smile, a pleasant soft voice, loved his family dearly, and was dedicated to the service." For over forty years, Pat kept the mangled .45-caliber pistol Pete Hamner was wearing when a Japanese suicide plane ended his life at the age of twenty-three. Along with that pistol, Pat retained strong memories of the Pacific destroyer war. Four decades later he could still "feel the vibration of *Howorth* at high speed, hear the gunfire, and feel the ship shudder when struck."

I also owe a great deal to Harold D. Middleton, former machinist's mate 2/c, who was kind enough to share his unauthorized diary and snapshots from his wartime duty in *Howorth*. Harold was a driving force behind the creation of the USS *Howorth* Veterans Association in 1988 and the monumental search for former *Howorth* sailors. I am indebted as well to Larry Nelson, former radioman 3/c and the *Howorth* Veterans Association's energetic secretary-treasurer, who undertook his own research into the history of his ship by extracting *Howorth's War Diary* from the federal archives; and to Karen Sue Nelson, who retyped the diary for dissemination to the *Howorth* veterans. When the association made contact with the widow of Yeoman 2/c James Orvill Raines, the core of this book came to light. A portion of Orvill Raines's letters to his wife were among the reminiscences retyped by Ed Severson and privately distributed by the association in 1991. Ed's efforts in producing the association's booklets, "War Diary" and "Letters/Memories," were prodigious and made my task much easier.

I am most grateful to Ray Ellen Dewey for her generosity in allowing me complete access to the voluminous correspondence of her late husband, Orvill. I am also indebted to Joan Hamner Tuthill for allowing me to consult the diary and letters of her brother, Pete Hamner, and to Doris LeCren Wiggins for sharing the letters her brother, Fire Controlman 3/c Morris LeCren, wrote to his family. I also appreciate the assistance of Robert B. Lyons, who manned the starboard Mark 51 40mm gun director on *Howorth's* flying bridge, and of Jay V. Grimm and Jerry Miller, who were also stationed there. They shared their recollections and pertinent correspondence regarding their experiences; all three were badly burned when a kamikaze hit within 10 feet of their positions on April 6, 1945. Grimm was blown overboard and spent two hours in the cold sea before being rescued as darkness fell.

I also thank those who have read parts or all of the manuscript for this book and offered suggestions for improvement, especially Lauren Osborne, Kenneth J. Hagan, Eugene B. Sledge, Philip F. Riley, Michael Galgano, Peter Kracht, and my anonymous reviewers. I appreciate the thoughtful copyediting of Alice Colwell and the work of Michelle S. Asakawa, my production editor.

The goal of the *Howorth* Veterans Association has been remembrance of the formative, and perhaps pivotal, experiences of the crew's lives: the war, the long months at sea, and the loss of their shipmates at Okinawa. *Howorth* fought in more battles than many ships and fewer than others. No admirals trod her decks issuing historic commands, yet she is representative of the U.S. naval experience in the Pacific Ocean War. Most of the time, *Howorth's* crew steamed on and on, trapped in a seemingly endless, boring routine. Entering the combat zone added tension and apprehension, punctuated by moments of pure terror. War consumes innocence and alters, in different ways and in different measures, all those it touches. There is no doubt that service in *Howorth* affected the life of each member of her crew.

Although I served in a destroyer of Second World War vintage, my experience had little in common with that of the crew of *Howorth*, save for hard work, tedium, constant fatigue, and the ever-changing, beautiful sea. In the Marine Corps the phrase *Semper Fi*, drawn from the Corps's motto, *Semper Fidelis*, can be a sardonic comment or an enthusiastic affirmation, depending upon its intonation. In the navy the same variety of meanings holds true for the word *shipmate*. For those who have served in small ships on vast oceans, the term has special meaning. For the crew of *Howorth*, *shipmate* evokes an additional feeling of camaraderie and familial loyalty derived from common wartime experience. I appreciate their extension of that term to me.

William M. McBride
McGaheysville, Virginia

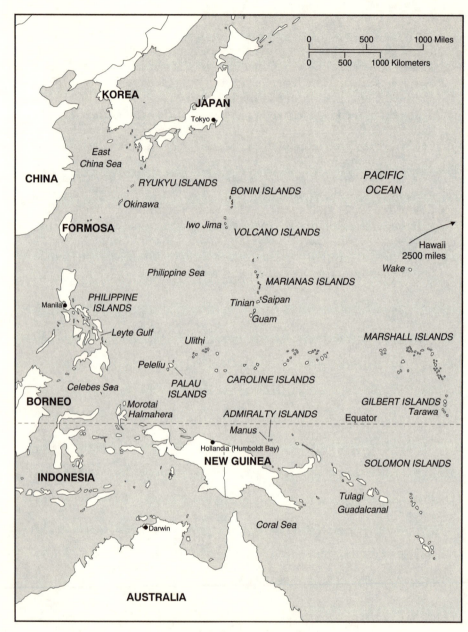

THE WESTERN PACIFIC

Introduction

On the morning of December 7, 1941, the U.S. Navy exchanged one capital ship for another. The battleship-based naval policy, which had dominated U.S. naval strategy for fifty years, was replaced by one centered on the aircraft carrier. War plans required little modification because, as one senior naval officer cogently observed in 1925, the "naval airplane is merely a new sort of projectile, carried by a surface ship."[1] Naval aviation's advantage was its ability to project and concentrate power at a much greater distance than a battleship. Although the aircraft carrier replaced the battleship and the aviation-based naval strategy evolved during the Pacific War, the rest of the navy changed very little. Lesser-valued warships, such as cruisers and destroyers, still acted as the watchdogs of the fleet, constantly patrolling and protecting the navy's capital ships.

Destroyers were derived from ships designed to destroy the torpedo boats that posed a serious threat to battleships at the end of the nineteenth century. By the beginning of World War II, U.S. fleet destroyers had evolved into warships capable of fighting on "three planes": above, on, and under the sea.[2] On the surface of the high seas, destroyers possessed a potent offensive capability with 5-inch guns that delivered a 54-pound explosive projectile out to a range of a little over 9 nautical miles. Although smaller destroyer escorts possessed better submarine detection equipment, fleet destroyers were capable of finding and sinking submarines. In the Second World War, the most dynamic developments in naval warfare occurred above the sea. By the time the Battle of the Coral Sea was fought east of Australia in May 1942, air power had extended the naval battlefield to the point that the U.S. and Japanese

---

1. Captain Yates Stirling, USN, "Some Fundamentals of Sea Power," *U.S. Naval Institute Proceedings* 51 (1925): 889–918; see 913–914.

2. For one of the earliest calls for a "three-plane navy" as well as an overview of the force-structure hierarchy of the pre-1942 navy, see William M. McBride, "Challenging a Strategic Paradigm: Aviation and the U.S. Navy Special Policy Board of 1924," *The Journal of Strategic Studies* 14 (1991): 72–89, especially 82 and 76–77.

fleets were able to engage without coming within visual range of one another.

There is an adage within the U.S. submarine community that the best way to annihilate a submarine is with another submarine. A parallel claim can be applied retroactively to aviation in the 1942–1945 Pacific War. But large fleet and smaller escort aircraft carriers were in short supply, and much of the burden of antiair defense for fleet formations and supply convoys fell to fleet destroyers. The rapid evolution of aircraft during the war forced destroyer designers to upgrade air search radars and gunfire control systems as well as increase the quantity of guns on fleet destroyers. This was difficult given the lack of weight and volume margins available for additional equipment on most U.S. destroyers. The antiaircraft problem was further complicated by Japanese aerial suicide attacks, the kamikazes, which were in effect antiship missiles.

The story covered in this book takes place in one of the 175 fleet destroyers of the *Fletcher* class built by the U.S. Navy between 1942 and 1944. Construction commenced on USS *Howorth* at the Puget Sound Navy Yard in Bremerton, Washington, on November 26, 1941. *Howorth* was commissioned on April 3, 1944, and sent westward to join the war against Japan that summer. *Howorth* was not a famous ship like the battleship *Missouri* or the carrier *Enterprise*; her sailors earned no prestigious Navy Unit Commendation, although these awards went to other crews for doing, and suffering, far less. *Howorth* participated in battles at places with exotic names such as Morotai, Tacloban, Ormoc, Mindoro, Lingayen Gulf, the Volcano Islands, and the Ryukyu Islands—names little known today except by military historians and by those who fought there. In her brief career, *Howorth* carried her cramped, homesick crew more than 105,000 nautical miles; they crossed the equator eight times, conducted eleven shore bombardment campaigns, destroyed twelve Japanese planes, earned five battle stars, and left seven of her crew behind in the cold seas off Okinawa.

Fletcher-class destroyers such as *Howorth* were the largest U.S. destroyers built prior to 1944, but they were still small ships. A sprinter of average ability could run the distance from stem to stern in under fifteen seconds. At its widest point, the hull measured just 40 feet. Within this modest volume, 350 men were jammed into a space originally designed to hold a crew of 250 amid a 60,000-horsepower steam turbine propulsion plant, ammunition magazines, fuel tanks, gun mounts and handling rooms, and all the other equipment that composes a warship. Unlike U.S. warships of the 1960s, designed for habitability to encourage reenlistment, warships of the 1940s were designed for the exigencies of war, not crew comfort. Crew members were berthed in metal-

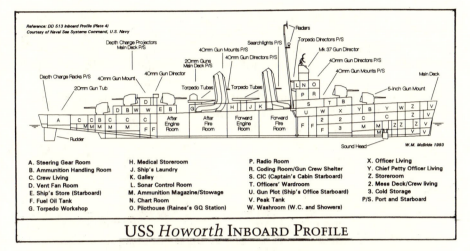

USS *Howorth* Inboard Profile

A. Steering Gear Room
B. Ammunition Handling Room
C. Crew Living
D. Vent Fan Room
E. Ship's Store (Starboard)
F. Fuel Oil Tank
G. Torpedo Workshop

H. Medical Storeroom
J. Ship's Laundry
K. Galley
L. Sonar Control Room
M. Ammunition Magazine/Stowage
N. Chart Room
O. Pilothouse (Raines's GQ Station)

P. Radio Room
R. Coding Room/Gun Crew Shelter
S. CIC (Captain's Cabin Starboard)
T. Officers' Wardroom
U. Gun Plot (Ship's Office Starboard)
V. Peak Tank
W. Washroom (W.C. and Showers)

X. Officer Living
Y. Chief Petty Officer Living
Z. Storeroom
2. Mess Deck/Crew living
3. Cold Storage
P/S. Port and Starboard

framed canvas bunks stacked three high with barely enough clearance for their occupants to roll over. Personal lockers were small, with little room for anything besides uniforms. Privacy was nonexistent. Unlike sailors in a cruiser or battleship, destroyer crewmen knew all their shipmates by name.

The size and shape of destroyer hulls made them ride rough in even a moderate sea. In heavy weather destroyers could be downright miserable, with the main deck spending as much time under water as above it. Hatches and doors often leaked, making living and working spaces wet and uncomfortable. Destroyers moved less predictably than larger ships. Vertical motion was perhaps the most debilitating; the up-and-down pitch of the bow, or the vertical heave of the entire ship, made a simple matter such as eating a meal or staying seated on a commode a difficult task even for a seasoned sailor. Rolls were usually more predictable but could easily cause a loss of balance, and destroyer sailors heeded the old saying, "One hand for the man; one hand for the ship." Several days in moderately bad weather induced deep fatigue. Trying to sleep while wedged into a corner between a piece of machinery and a bulkhead or with legs and arms wrapped around a mattress while grasping a bunk frame was exhausting.

On top of the difficulty of eating, sleeping, and maintaining personal hygiene, each sailor had duties within the ship's routine of training, standing watch, maintenance, working parties, and drills. The crew normally would be organized into three watch sections, with each section standing a four-hour watch. The only exceptions were the two-hour "dog" watches from 1600 to 1800 (4 P.M. to 6 P.M.) and from 1800 to 2000 (6 P.M. to 8 P.M.). The dog watches precluded sections from

standing the midwatch (midnight to 4 A.M.) continually and facilitated
serving of the evening meal. The short duration of the dog watches
meant that the interval between watches was not always eight hours.
In shorthanded ships, a two-section watch rotation was necessary, with
each section standing watch for six hours on and six hours off. No matter which rotation was in place, the hours spent off watch were consumed by drills, meals, ship's work such as chipping rust or cleaning
boiler firesides, or underway replenishment of fuel, food, and ammunition. Six hours of uninterrupted sleep was a rare luxury; two to three
hours was the norm.

This busy and debilitating regimen was the peacetime routine. War
only made it worse. The murkiness of sunrise and dusk provided ideal
cover for attackers so that morning and evening general quarters,
(GQ)—that is, all hands manning their battle stations—were manda-
tory. Submarine and air alerts were obviously more frequent in the forward operating areas and, besides being nerve-wracking, also cut
heavily into off-watch time. Fatigue was a common companion, and
nerves already taut from the proximity of rapid, death-dealing attacks
were strained greatly.

Destroyers had no armor to protect themselves from enemy bombs
or shells, hence the nickname "tin cans." They had to rely on their
speed and guns for defense—a combination that had failed the mightier
British battle cruisers during the 1916 Battle of Jutland.[3] Battle cruisers
were capital ships; their construction and operation entailed the expen-
diture of a tremendous sum of state wealth (capital). Destroyers were
relatively cheap. In order of importance, destroyers ranked after aircraft
carriers, battleships, heavy cruisers, light cruisers, oilers, cargo ships,
and troop transports. Destroyers were currency to be spent to protect
more valuable units. As such, they were regularly sent in harm's way,
and fifty-two U.S. destroyers were sunk in the forty-four months of the
Pacific War.

This book is not a top-down naval history replete with maps with
sweeping arrows or neat battle diagrams drawn up after the fact by students of war sitting in quiet rooms. This book is, rather, a rare account
of a destroyer at war as given in the letters of an enlisted sailor, twenty-
six-year-old Yeoman 2/c James Orvill Raines, to his wife, Ray Ellen, in
Texas. During the war, diaries were forbidden, and all letters written by

---

3. For the problems with British battle cruisers, see Oscar Parkes, *British Battleships—Warrior to Vanguard: A History of Design, Construction and Armament* (London:
Seeley Service, 1957), chapters 111–112; and Sir Eustace Tennyson d'Eyncourt (the Admiralty's director of naval construction), "HMS *Hood*," *Transactions, [Royal] Institution of
Naval Architects* 62 (1920): 1–18.

officers and enlisted men on commissioned ships were censored by the ship's officers. As a result, most letters tended to be rather banal, with discussions of the war limited, by censorship, to wishes that it were over. Raines's vivid descriptions of his and his comrades' experiences in the Philippines, at Iwo Jima, and at Okinawa are what make this collection so unusual.[4]

Coming from a hardscrabble Oklahoma family, Orvill Raines had been a newspaper reporter for the *Dallas Morning News* before he enlisted in the Naval Reserve in November 1942. His letters provide a literate, unique insight into the grueling experience of destroyer sailors at war. His battle and watch stations were on *Howorth*'s bridge, affording him an excellent environment for observation. Raines's yeoman rating meant that he worked in the ship's office, where he had the opportunity to write almost every day; his letters often reached five or six single-spaced, typed pages. A liberal censor allowed his letters to pass with only two excisions: when he wrote the location of *Howorth* and when he mentioned the name of a sunken destroyer.[5] Since he was writing solely for his wife, Raines's letters, although personally biased, are sincere. They are not the admirals' hagiographies that fill much of naval history. His letters are those of a man who is trying to make the best of his status as a prisoner in an alien environment, a man whose future is captive to events beyond his control. His service provided him, as he put it, with the "feeling of doing my part" and helping "my country pull through a rugged time." He worried about his separation from his wife and, like the vast majority of the 16 million members of the U.S. armed forces during World War II, would rather have been at home. He was proud of Ray Ellen when she advanced to the position of office manager in a Dallas physicians' office, but he expected a return to a more traditional domestic arrangement after the war.

---

4. To my knowledge, the only other enlisted man's writing to come from the Pacific naval war is James J. Fahey, *Pacific War Diary: 1942–1945* (New York: Houghton Mifflin, 1963). An officer's recollection is Douglas Edward Leach, *Now Hear This: The Memoir of a Junior Naval Officer in the Great Pacific War* (Kent, OH: Kent State University Press, 1988). Perhaps the best-known portrayal of the Pacific naval war is Thomas Heggen, *Mister Roberts* (Boston: Houghton Mifflin, 1946). Another treatment is John T. Mason, ed., *The Pacific War Remembered: An Oral History Collection* (Annapolis: Naval Institute Press, 1986).

5. To ameliorate the chore of censorship, *Howorth*'s officers held "censorship parties" prior to arriving at a location accepting outgoing mail. Letters were piled on the wardroom table and then randomly read, stamped, and initialed by an officer. Raines apparently avoided this process by submitting his letters to his division officer, who supervised the ship's office, for clearance.

To sustain their marriage through their separation, Orvill and Ray Ellen agreed to continue to bid each other an "official" good night every evening on Dallas time.[6] Although *Howorth's* travels meant that Raines had to say his official good night in the middle of the preceding day, he faithfully did so. Through his letters, one comes to know Orvill Raines, to perceive the escalating stress he and his shipmates endured during their exacting year at war, and to understand better a seaman's view of the Pacific War.

Raines began his letter writing on the eve of *Howorth's* commissioning at Puget Sound Navy Yard. Describing his ship as "beautiful" and "big as a building lying down," he sought to reassure Ray Ellen of his safety once the ship would go to war: "I can see where my battle station is. Way up there where the torpedoes don't hurt, strafing is ignored, bombs don't hurt bad." But as spring turned to summer and *Howorth* made her way through various readiness checks and began the long journey westward toward the battle zone in August, Raines remarked on a change within the crew: "Everyone seems too withdrawn within themselves. ... Officers (new to this) and men alike are afraid."

His first introduction to the war occurred during a short trip ashore in the Admiralty Islands, where he observed a young soldier whose "left arm was torn up from wrist to shoulder" and whose "sobbing nearly tore my heart out." Despite all the propaganda that came out of Hollywood and the Office of War Information, the war was not an equally shared, demographically balanced experience.[7] The reality of the waste of war and the unequal distribution of its burden troubled Raines; he wrote Ray Ellen that he wished "the people of the United States and those union devils and high wage workers that I loathe so intently could see their boys coming back. The American people can't realize what they are into."

In describing his feelings toward the Japanese, Raines characterized the cooperative nature of naval warfare: "I get a joy out of being the man that holds a piece of iron in his hands that helps kill them. I don't shoot a gun, no one does the actual firing on here. We *all* do it." Raines's sentiment, fueled by the racism of the Pacific War, never waned, since war at sea provided little opportunity for the personal contact that British military historian Richard Holmes contended often mitigated the

---

6. Orvill and Ray Ellen often had difficulty ending their nighttime conversations. Their solution was to bid each other an "official" good night after which neither was allowed to speak.

7. For the cinematic, demographically correct fighting unit, see Jeanine Basinger, *The World War II Combat Film: Anatomy of a Genre* (New York: Columbia University Press, 1986), table I, 64–65 and 74.

"concept of a hateful and inhuman enemy." Although some diminution of hostility may have been fostered in other theaters of the war, Holmes's study of British veterans found few who had much postwar affection for the Japanese.[8] Nor would he have found such affection among most former inhabitants of the Japanese Greater East Asia Co-Prosperity Sphere.[9] From the 1937 Rape of Nanking to the end of hostilities in 1945, the Japanese army waged a war against the Chinese marked by a lack of distinction between soldiers and civilians, the use of chemical and biological weapons, slave labor, and organized drug trafficking.[10]

When war began against the Western powers, the Japanese Imperial Army High Command issued a supplement to 16th Army (Saigon) operations orders in January 1942 warning its troops not to treat Westerners "as if they were Chinese."[11] Yet Allied military personnel and civilians were almost as badly abused. The atrocities against prisoners from Singapore, Bataan, Wake Island, and elsewhere; the execution of Australian civilians at Buna on New Guinea; the vivisection of prisoners on Guadalcanal; and the impressment of slave labor throughout occupied Southeast Asia were part and parcel of the "longstanding regrettable practices" of the Japanese army.[12] The last orgy of violence against civilians within the Greater East Asia Co-Prosperity Sphere occurred in

---

8. See Richard Holmes, *Acts of War: The Behavior of Men in Battle* (New York: Free Press, 1985), 368, 374. For an excellent discussion of the racial component of the Pacific War, see John Dower, *War Without Mercy: Race and Power in the Pacific War* (New York: Pantheon Books, 1986). For the motion pictures' portrayal of the Japanese, see Clayton D. Koppes and Gregory D. Black, *Hollywood Goes to War: How Politics, Profits, and Propaganda Shaped World War II Movies* (New York: Free Press, 1987), chapter 9: "The Beast in the Jungle."

9. The Japanese presented their expansion into Southeast Asia as the beginning of a "Greater East Asia Co-Prosperity Sphere" in which Asians, freed from white colonialism, would work together to build a better economic future for the region. In reality, the peoples of Southeast Asia were cruelly exploited by their new Japanese masters.

10. See Meirion Harries and Susan Harries, *Soldiers of the Sun: The Rise and Fall of the Imperial Japanese Army* (New York: Random House, 1991), especially chapters 22, 24, and 35. For the research and development behind the biological weapons employed in China, see Peter Williams and David Wallace, *Unit 731: Japan's Secret Biological Warfare in World War II* (New York: Free Press, 1989).

11. An overview of Japanese army actions, including drug pushing and war crimes, can be found in Harries and Harries, *Soldiers of the Sun*, chapter 46: " 'Longstanding Regrettable Practices': Atrocities and Their Origins"; the supplemental order regarding treatment of Western enemies is quoted on p. 480.

12. See ibid., chapter 46. It is safe to say that some members of all armies have committed war crimes. What differentiates the Japanese was their lack of an "overriding moral authority" and remorse, outgrowths of the religious basis of the claimed superiority of the Yamato race, which "regarded *all* other races as inferior"; ibid., 478–480.

1945 when the 21,000 naval ground troops, under the command of Admiral Iwabuchi Sanji, were trapped in Manila, where they "plundered, raped, and murdered."[13] According to William Manchester, "In Manila ... hospital patients were strapped to their beds and set afire, babies' eyeballs were gouged out and smeared on walls like jelly."[14]

Marine veteran Eugene B. Sledge summarized the consuming enmity of the Pacific War:

> At the time of battle, Marines felt it [hatred] deeply, bitterly, and as certainly as danger itself. ... My experiences on Peleliu and Okinawa made me believe that the Japanese held mutual feelings for us. They were a fanatical enemy; that is to say, they believed in their cause with an intensity little understood by many postwar Americans—and possibly many Japanese as well. This collective attitude, Marine and Japanese, resulted in savage, ferocious fighting with no holds barred. This was not the dispassionate killing seen on other fronts or in other wars. This was a brutish, primitive hatred, as characteristic of the horror of war in the Pacific as the palm trees and the islands.[15]

The willingness of most Japanese soldiers to fight to the death was rooted in Emperor Meiji's 1885 Rescript to Soldiers and Sailors ("Duty is weightier than a mountain, while death is lighter than a feather") and encouraged by the imperial army's Field Service Code.[16] This resulted in bitter warfare in which the kamikaze was a natural development.

As *Howorth* escorted troopships to the invasion of Leyte Island in the Philippines in October 1944, Raines was depressed: "The men riding the ships I watch day after day are going to their death. ... The fact that we are taking so many men to a place where they are to be slaughtered worries me." Upon arriving in Leyte Gulf, Raines wrote Ray Ellen, "We have been going to G.Q. on an average of once every two hours. ... In the evenings it's more frequent than that. ... We get pretty tired of it and

13. Ibid., 436. I present Japanese names in the traditional style, family name first.

14. William Manchester, *Goodbye, Darkness: A Memoir of the Pacific War* (Boston: Little, Brown, 1979), 281. Although Manchester blamed the Japanese for the 100,000 civilian dead, the majority were killed as a result of the fighting between U.S. and Japanese troops. According to the evidence presented at the war crimes trial of Lieutenant General Yamashita Tomoyuki, the number of civilians killed in Manila and Batangas Province totaled just over 33,000; see the chart on p. 140 as well as chapter 1 in Richard L. Lael, *The Yamashita Precedent: War Crimes and Command Responsibility* (Wilmington, DE: Scholarly Resources, 1982).

15. Eugene B. Sledge, *With the Old Breed at Peleliu and Okinawa* (New York: Oxford University Press, 1989), 34.

16. Imperial rescript, quoted in Harries and Harries, *Soldiers of the Sun*, 25.

always in our mind is the fact that under our care is a large group of ships that ... make up the most precious cargo Uncle Sam has [invasion troops and materiel]. We cans are extremely expendable and ... must sacrifice all to save what is in our care."

Raines's first exposure to the quick and random nature of death in combat occurred the day *Howorth* reached Leyte Gulf. While observing air support for the ground operations on the northern beachhead on Leyte, Raines had a "sick feeling" in his stomach when he saw a U.S. aircraft "hit the ground going straight down at 500 miles per hour. ... One instant a beautiful plane with an educated man flying her and the next a mass of junk and a letter 'We regret to inform you. ...'" These first views of combat interrupted his letters, and Raines told Ray Ellen that he often heard the general quarters alarm when it was not sounding. He promised to "try and get a real good letter off as soon as I can. ... When we get out of this front area I'll be able to think better."

Three weeks later, ashore in the Admiralty Islands on ship's business, Raines saw a graveyard that underscored the personal cost of the war. He wrote Ray Ellen, "I think I said something like: 'Fellas, you got a raw deal and we might not say much about it but we have a spot in our hearts for you guys. You took it the hard way and a long way from home.'"

Six days later, while escorting Carrier Division 29 to Leyte Gulf, *Howorth* encountered a Japanese aircraft at dusk, and Raines and his shipmates came under fire for the first time: "The flashes of his guns and our guns lighted the bridge like some eerie hell." Within a week, the lethal potential of the new Japanese aerial suicide tactic was demonstrated by an attack on another destroyer. The location of the strike, on the bridge of the ship, the same location as Raines's battle station on *Howorth*, could not have escaped Ray Ellen, despite his emphasizing the chance occurrence of such an event. Raines's descriptions struck closer to home when a friend's ship went down and the crew had to be left to fend for themselves as "forty-millimeter and three-inch guns were firing on the survivors from the beach."

Reflecting his increasingly violent surroundings, Raines's letters included deadly images, such as a depiction of a destroyer whose "entire superstructure was a mangled mess of melted steel." Knowing the effect such news would have on Ray Ellen, Raines reminded her, "There is a war out here ... [but] overhead is God, looking down and guiding what perhaps He thinks is the best course. You and I firmly feel that He won't separate us. ... I realize that I am in the shadow but David's twenty-third psalm is printed in my mind and His rod and staff comfort me." In trusting in divine protection, Raines was employing what U.S. Army psychiatrists Roy Grinker and John Spiegel characterized as a common ego-protection method to minimize combat-induced anxiety.[17] In spite of his clear appreciation of the war aims of his country and his desire to defeat Japan—ideals that supposedly bolstered individual morale—Raines was succumbing to anxiety-induced stress.[18]

On December 15, 1944, it was *Howorth's* turn to face a suicide attack: Three kamikazes targeted the ship off Mindoro Island, where she had been deployed to destroy Japanese shore defenses in the vicinity of Mangarin Bay. Two of the attacking planes were shot down, but the third, coming in from astern, hit *Howorth's* mast and bounced off the forecastle into the sea, spewing gasoline over the forward third of the ship. Raines recounted the fear this attack caused in the bridge watch officers: "They stood almost frozen and when they turned and ran the few feet inside, they stared at every thing and saw nothing." Lieutenant Hamner, the twenty-two-year-old gunnery officer, made the following entry in his notebook: "Third [aircraft] flew over mast headed straight for [gun] director, just missed, glanced off bow into water—whew! Soaked with gas, scared to death, pieces of plane everywhere—living on borrowed time!"[19] The constant air attacks off Mindoro had been terrifying. Raines's only admission of his fright was his confession to Ray Ellen that he had "backslid on the Mindoro operation" and was again biting his fingernails as "an outlet of my fear."

After almost two months amid the chaos of the Leyte operation, Raines clung to his memories of Ray Ellen: "Everything blots out. I just see your face ... or you standing there in your red suit with a smile on your face. ... I can't see any of the terrible things in front of me. It is all you and the wonderful life we have led in the past." Given Raines's en-

---

17. See Lieutenant Colonel Roy R. Grinker, Medical Corps (MC), and Major John P. Spiegel, MC, *Men Under Stress* (Philadelphia: Blakiston, 1945), 130. These clinicians argued that at the beginning of combat tours, the majority of servicemen have a sense of invulnerability ("it can't happen to me") based upon their past "secure" existence. This protection from anxiety dissipates with the death or wounding of friends or close brushes with injury. A different method of coping featured a reliance on "faith in magical or supernatural power. Some men feel protected by God ('God is my Co-Pilot'), or have a fatalistic notion that their span of life is predetermined by Providence and that such incidentals as enemy activity can have no bearing on the outcome. From a psychodynamic view, such men have exchanged an uncertain dependence on the group for a dependence on a more reliable, supernatural power. The most outspoken example of this type of dependence in a soldier is found in the Psalms of David, where the Deity is ever being petitioned for more help, thanked for what aid has been given and soundly scolded for having been remiss"(ibid).

18. For a discussion of combatants' loyalties, see Holmes, *Acts of War*, 274–277, and Grinker and Spiegel, *Men Under Stress*, 37.

19. Lieutenant Hamner's brief notebook was provided by his sister, Joan Hamner Tuthill.

vironment, such visions were to be expected. Grinker and Spiegel concluded that combat service engendered an idealized image in which "the people at home become endowed with unrealistic attributes of beauty, kindness, generosity" and "as a haven from the dangers of combat ..., home assumes the characteristics of a magical fairyland."[20] Indeed Raines yearned for "the wonderful life we will lead in the future." His fondest vision was "the picture you will make at the station when you meet me and we run off to rest."

Raines and his shipmates spent Christmas 1944 at sea, escorting a convoy of Liberty ships from the Philippines to Humboldt Bay, New Guinea. In the tropical weather it was difficult to imagine Christmas. Raines wrote Ray Ellen, "Everyone tried. They said 'Merry Christmas!' but it was as flat as 'The Same to You.'" Red Cross "ditty bags" containing cigarettes, soap, candy, and other odds and ends were passed out in the crowded evening chow line Christmas night, but the usually noisy mess deck was, according to Raines, "quiet as a tomb," and he found himself having to "choke back a sob."

Howorth returned to Lingayen Gulf in the Philippines the first week of January and spent the next three weeks providing gunfire support for the troops ashore and submarine and air defense for the fleet. Raines's gravest impression of Lingayen Gulf was the Japanese "bodies, swollen and distorted, floating on the surface." While in the Sulu Sea en route to Lingayen, Raines expressed his loneliness and alienation: "We sure feel a long way from home. Guys that have been away from home for years are getting homesick for the folks. One guy, a Norwegian, who is a very rugged individual, confessed to me tonight that he got so homesick last night that he could hardly stand it. We haven't received any mail for almost a month now. It seems like six."

Raines and his shipmates were fearful that the Japanese navy would make every effort to interfere with U.S. operations in the Philippines as they had the previous October in the Battle for Leyte Gulf. The sighting of unidentified battleships was especially terrifying: "We would have had to stop them if it meant every life in the squadron. Our shipping was lying unprotected behind us." Returning to the relative safety of Leyte Gulf, Raines again expressed his homesickness and deep-seated fear: "Gosh, I just sit down sometimes and feel sorry for myself and pity me till I feel like crying. ... If the war were over, it would be different. We wouldn't be so afraid."

On February 1, 1945, *Howorth* departed for the fleet anchorage at Ulithi Atoll, where the invasion force for the Volcano Islands was as-

---

20. Grinker and Spiegel, *Men Under Stress,* 184–185.

sembling. Raines predicted that "this year will settle it." He fought in order to teach the Germans and the Japanese that they "can't run over the little people and kill them for selfish reasons," lessons that required ruthless killing, which was easier to call for from *Howorth*'s vantage point in what so far had been a relatively pristine naval war than from the infantry soldier's personal view of the war. "I pray to God that He will help the Russians and Americans, British, French and Canadians and Brazilians and Italians and Australians kill the Germans and Japanese," wrote Raines. "And last I pray that He will teach the Germans and Japanese peace. ... There can be no peace for the world as long as one kind of man has hatred or fear in his heart for another kind of man."

After arriving at Ulithi, *Howorth* was sent on to Saipan Island to escort troop transports. Just before midnight on February 18, *Howorth*, in the van of the formation, reported the initial radar contact with the Volcano Island group. At 9 A.M. the next day, the 4th and 5th Marine Divisions began their invasion. *Howorth* spent the next three and a half weeks alternating between radar picket duty and providing naval gunfire support for the marines ashore. Raines informed Ray Ellen that the continual shore bombardment had taken its toll on *Howorth*: "All the urinals in the heads have been bounced off the bulkheads onto the deck. ... We have 48 cups left of our 300 when we got out here. We are drinking coffee out of bowls. ... Boy, it's a mess."

By the time *Howorth* left for Saipan on March 14, the Japanese defenders on Iwo Jima had exacted 26,000 marine casualties. Raines sadly observed "two very neat grave yards on the island. ... They were still adding the little crosses when we left." He wrote Ray Ellen, "I will always remember Iwo Jima more vividly than any other place except perhaps Mindoro when I thought maybe I'd be holding up one of those crosses myself." Iwo Jima had been "the Devil's own creation."

After brief repairs and maintenance at the fleet base at Ulithi Atoll, *Howorth* left on March 27 to escort troop transports bound for the invasion of the Ryukyu Islands. Of this operation Raines admitted that his "belly isn't the only thing with the jitters this time. They effect my whole body. Okinawa. Just looking at it on the map breaks us out in a cold sweat. ... Okinawa spells Kamikaze Corps to us."

The invasion of Okinawa began on Easter Sunday, April 1, 1945. Five days later, the Japanese initiated a series of massed airborne suicide attacks termed *kikusui*, or Floating Chrysanthemum, as part of their Operation *Ten-Go* to repulse the Americans from Japanese home soil. Shortly before noon on April 6, Raines wrote Ray Ellen that "it's colder than a well digger's seat in Montana but everything is o.k. No sleep last night due to Bogies [unidentified aircraft] but things are squared away now. Bye darling. More later."

But there would be no "more later." Within five hours, the bulk of the first Floating Chrysanthemum of 355 kamikaze aircraft and 300 conventional bombers struck at the U.S. fleet around Okinawa. Two destroyers, one tank landing ship (LST), and two ammunition ships were sunk. Nine other destroyers, including *Howorth*, were hit. The attack killed 466 U.S. sailors and wounded 568 more.

Howorth's battle lasted seven minutes and forty seconds. Steaming alone to the aid of the destroyer *Hyman*, which was burning furiously on an adjacent antisubmarine station, *Howorth* was stalked by at least eight kamikazes and attacked by five. *Howorth*'s crew shot down three; the fourth crashed into the main gun battery director on top of the bridge. Raines and six other men were killed or mortally wounded and another sixteen were wounded and survived. As *Howorth*'s bridge burned, the fifth kamikaze was shot down astern.[21]

Before the Okinawa campaign officially ended on June 30, 1945, a total of twelve destroyers and destroyer escorts were sunk; eighty-eight destroyers, thirty destroyer escorts, thirteen aircraft carriers, ten battleships, and five cruisers suffered significant damage. The battle for Okinawa inflicted nearly 50,000 casualties on U.S. forces, including 4,907 sailors killed. Thanks to the need for stateside repairs and the Japanese acceptance of Allied terms for surrender in August 1945, *Howorth*'s war ended in April 1945. But for the families of those killed and wounded, the legacy of the war would last forever.

With the passing of the generation that lived through the Second World War, America's collective memory of total war is fading, and no subsequent experience can compare.[22] The United States' longest war, Viet Nam, was fought off center stage, and neither it nor the bloody struggle in Korea can match the level of U.S. involvement in the Second World War. For the entire generation that has come of age in post–Viet Nam America, military hostilities rarely last longer than a week, and U.S. casualties, in Grenada, Panama, and the Persian Gulf, have been "light" and limited to those who volunteered for military service.

Even the wartime experience within the U.S. military has changed since *Howorth* sailed to war. During World War II, servicemen had no fixed combat tours as in Viet Nam, save the mission limit for combat

---

21. The navy credited *Howorth* with seven aircraft destroyed during a sixty-eight-minute period on April 6.

22. For one retrospective tour of the Pacific War, see Manchester, *Goodbye, Darkness*. The reader should be aware that Manchester's is not a historical account; the author admitted that he "resorted to some legerdemain in the interests of re-creating, and clarifying the spirit of, the historical past" (p. 397). See World War II *Time* and *Life* war correspondent Robert Sherrod's review in *Sea Power* (November 1980): 29–30.

aircrew. In 1944 Orvill Raines and his shipmates went to war for the duration. The only way home was for the war to end, to be the recipient of a "million-dollar" wound that required evacuation to the United States, or for the ship to be sunk or so badly damaged that only a stateside facility could repair it.[23]

During his years in the navy, Orvill Raines wrote his wife several hundred times. In selecting letters for this volume, I omitted those irrelevant to *Howorth*. I shortened some of the letters by excising Raines's digressions regarding relatives and acquaintances as well as his most personal comments to his wife.[24] Where possible, I have identified the people Raines mentioned in his letters. Editorial comments are in brackets; with the exception of some minor corrections, the punctuation, spelling, terminology, and grammar are as Orvill Raines wrote them. The official framework of this book came from *Howorth's* declassified secret action reports and confidential *War Diary,* as well as the ship's confidential deck logs.[25] Not surprisingly, Raines the newspaperman recounted events more vividly than the sterile, official reports.

Studs Terkel titled his anthology of World War II oral histories *"The Good War"* to reflect the popular recollection of the war as one with fairly clear-cut moral distinctions separating the combatants. But Terkel's collection makes it apparent that the goodness of the "good

---

23. Rotation stateside for army personnel was initiated late in the war, but the number of men affected was small. See Samuel A. Stouffer, Arthur A. Lumsdaine, Marion Harper Lumsdaine, Robin M. Williams, Jr., M. Brewster Smith, Irving L. Janis, Shirley A. Star, and Leonard S. Cottrell, Jr., *The American Soldier: Combat and Its Aftermath,* vol. 2 (Princeton: Princeton University Press, 1949), 88–89 and chapter 10, "Problems of Rotation and Reconversion." The seeming endlessness of overseas and combat duty commonly engendered bitterness among those relegated to it. See the quotations from veterans of the Pacific Theater in Stouffer et al., *American Soldier,* 90. After forty to forty-five days of combat exposure, "emotional exhaustion" occurred, manifested by no "thought and hope of surviving combat...; one thing to them was certain, they would be killed"; p. 240 of Roy L. Swank, MD, and Walter E. Marchand, MD, "Combat Neuroses: Development of Combat Exhaustion," *Archives of Neurology and Psychiatry* 55 (1946): 236–247.

24. My deletions in Raines's letters are marked by ellipses using three or four periods that usually come at the ends of paragraphs. The reader should be aware that Raines used ellipses in his letters as well, although he generally employed five or more periods. In keeping with naval tradition, Raines typed his ship's name in upper-case letters. I have changed that, along with the underlined sections of his letters, to italics.

25. *Howorth's* action reports and *War Diary* are on microfilm Reel E-108, NPPSO–Naval District Washington Job No. AR-65-78, "*Howorth* (DD-592), Report File, War Diary," on file with the Naval Historical Center, Operational Archives Branch, Washington Navy Yard, Washington, D.C. The ship's deck logs are on file with the Modern Military Records Branch, National Archives, Washington, D.C.

war" varied widely for those Americans who lived through it. The *Howorth* story, as presented in the letters of Orvill Raines, personalizes the horrific experiences of one of hundreds of anonymous ships' crews who fought the "good war" five decades ago.[26]

In his book *Wartime*, Paul Fussell, who was wounded as an army platoon commander in Germany, made a forceful case that war—no matter why it is waged—is in its manifestation nothing more than a waste: a waste of treasure and a waste of people, an experience of "insensate violence and fear and agony."[27] Raines's letters reinforce Fussell's view and strip off some of the ex post facto orderliness, or just plain buffoonery, in American popular culture that overlays the true chaos and tragedy of the Second World War.[28] With regard to World War II, Fussell quoted Walt Whitman's observation on the Civil War that "the real war will never get in the books."[29] Although far from a definitive account, Orvill Raines's letters provide a glimpse into the fear, loneliness, boredom, and estrangement of the "real" naval war fought in the Pacific during 1944–1945.

---

26. Studs Terkel, *"The Good War"* (New York: Pantheon Books, 1984).

27. Paul Fussell, *Wartime: Understanding and Behavior in the Second World War* (New York: Oxford University Press, 1989), 4.

28. The visual media have been the worst offenders, with television leading the way. Probably the most egregiously false portrayal of the Pacific naval war was the 1960s television series "McHale's Navy."

29. Fussell, *Wartime*, 290.

PART ONE

TRAINING
&
TRANSIT

1

Commissioning and Stateside Training

April 2–July 21, 1944

James Orvill Raines was born on September 6, 1918, in Okmulgee, Oklahoma, the youngest of seven children. His father died when Raines was quite small, and his mother remarried when Raines was twelve or thirteen. He was the only child still at home when his mother and stepfather moved to a farm near the town of Dover, Arkansas. Raines was unhappy and went to Dallas, where he lived with one sister and then another while finishing high school. After his graduation, he set out to make a living during the Great Depression. He went to work doing odd jobs at a Dallas radio station, WFAA. He became interested in broadcasting and found some mentors on the broadcast staff. The management of WFAA also owned the *Dallas Morning News*, and when a position opened for an obituary writer, Raines, who had acquired a reputation as a bright, hard worker, was "transferred." His ambition and dedication caught the attention of the night city editor, Kenneth Foree, who took an interest in Raines, loaned him books, and tutored him in reporting. Before long, Raines was off the obituary column and working as a full-time reporter.

On April 20, 1939, Raines met Ray Ellen Gwin on a blind date, and they fell in love. When Raines received a pay raise from $18 to $23 a week in 1940, the couple concluded that they could finally support themselves. They married on June 1, 1940. Ray Ellen encouraged Orvill to continue to improve his writing skills, and by the time the Japanese attacked Pearl Harbor in December 1941, his byline was appearing regularly in the *Morning News*.

Taking the advice of roommates from his bachelor days, Raines followed them into the Naval Reserve in fall 1942. His newspaper background qualified him for an administrative rating, and he entered the navy as a yeoman 3/c. Raines was assigned to the censorship office at the naval district headquarters in New Orleans, remaining there over a year. He rented an apartment, and Ray Ellen was able to spend 1943 with him in New Orleans. But the expanding fleet needed sailors, and the newly formed female naval auxiliary service, the WAVES (Women Accepted for Voluntary Emergency Service), was designed to free men such as Raines from shore posts for sea duty. Raines was shipped out, destination unknown, at 8:30 P.M. on Christmas Day, 1943. He was sent to Norfolk, Virginia, where he was assigned to a personnel pool that supplied crews to destroyers. Ray Ellen joined him for several weeks in Virginia before he was ordered to the destroyer *Howorth* nearing completion at Puget Sound Navy Yard in Washington State. Because *Howorth*'s administrative unit was located at Treasure Island in San Francisco Bay, Orvill and Ray Ellen were able to stay together in San Francisco for almost three months while the ship was finished. At the end of March, Orvill and Ray Ellen were separated: She returned to Dallas; Orvill traveled north to Washington to join his ship.

When *Howorth* was completed and commissioned on April 3, 1944, her design embodied two years of war experience. Like all ships, though, *Howorth*'s true strength lay in her crew. The three and a half months following the ship's commissioning involved intensive hands-on training at sea in the Puget Sound area and farther south at San Diego to bring the ship to an acceptable level of combat readiness to operate with the fleet.

War at sea has always been a cooperative endeavor. But with the advent of steel battleships in the 1890s; their replacement by larger, dreadnought-style battleships after 1906; and the advent of even larger super-dreadnoughts on the eve of the First World War, the individual sailor was further subordinated to technology. Battleships whose crews numbered over 1,000 men had more in common with Henry Ford's automobile plants than with the wooden navies whose warrior-sailors, according to the popular idealized image, engaged in personal combat, cutlass in hand. Individual courage was of course present in sailors serving in the navies of the twentieth century. What was missing was the medieval legacy of war as a judicial process by which bravery and "goodness" are sustained. If the First World War demonstrated anything, it was that the soldier, despite all the rhetoric on courage and manliness, was no longer in control of his destiny on the battlefield.[1] Because of the nature of total war between industrial societies, the fate

---

1. Tim Travers, *The Killing Ground: The British Army, The Western Front, and the Emergence of Modern Warfare, 1900–1918* (London: Unwin Hyman, 1987), chapters 2–3.

of the World War II sailor such as Orvill Raines, whose individual exertions were part of a crew effort, was in the hands of superiors who dealt in accounting sheets that balanced friendly and enemy losses. "Personnel" was merely another category of resource, as reflected in Raines's observation to Ray Ellen just prior to *Howorth*'s departure from Pearl Harbor for the war zone: "Life is pretty cheap west of here." *Howorth*'s survival in the Western Pacific maelstrom would depend on the crew's training and luck.[2]

The period from April 3 to July 21, 1944, provided time for the basic training; luck would depend on the kindness of fate.

---

2 April 1944

Hello, My Darling Baby:

Well, I will try to give you an account of myself tonight. I am at the Bremerton Navy Yard and the ship is right out of my window. It is very impressive. I made a tour of it just a little while ago. I sure like it and my station on the bridge is very well protected. I was afraid I would be outside and on top but I will be inside behind plenty of steel plating and armor.[3]

I wish I could tell you about the other parts of the *Howorth* but I can't. The officers can bring their lady friends and acquaintances aboard and show them all over the damn thing but us enlisted men cannot do that. We can't even tell about what is aboard. Tomorrow is commissioning day and we will have everybody with gold braid in Seattle and Bremerton aboard for the ceremony. We also will have a christening ceremony. I can't figure why it wasn't christened when it was launched but nevertheless, it will be christened the U.S.S. *Howorth* tomorrow at 11:15 A.M.

---

2. Machine-age weapons, such as artillery, machine guns, and aircraft, minimized the relationship between professional skill and one's chance of survival on the battlefield; see Travers, *The Killing Ground*, chapter 3. For a World War II observation, see Bill Mauldin, *Up Front* (New York: Henry Holt, 1945), 94.

3. Raines was mistaken; although there had been design discussions regarding thicker steel for the bridge bulkheads to provide splinter protection, no armor plate, which is quite different from special-treatment steel (STS), was ever installed on *Fletcher*-class destroyers. See Norman Friedman, *U.S. Destroyers: An Illustrated Design History* (Annapolis: Naval Institute Press, 1982), 115.

There isn't much liberty up here. Besides, I am broke. [Signalman 1/c George] Lynch paid me the $10.00 he owed me and I have money but I don't want to take any too many liberties until I get caught up. I want to send you all the money I can and will do so payday. We won't be getting anything until about the middle of the month. We have a disbursing officer, "Pay," as Pop [Ray Ellen's father] calls them, and he told me yesterday that it would take that long to get things squared away. In going on liberty, we have to ride a ferry for an hour to get to Seattle and an hour back. Bremerton is just outside the gates and that, I guess, is good enough for me. I plan to get over to Seattle and try to find you a trinket before leaving. We may get up steam about the first of May and head out. We, of course, don't know yet where the shakedown will be. We expect to put into San Diego for a few days and then—. We have a paint job like no one has ever seen. A sister ship anchored out in the bay has the same type paint and she is parked not a quarter of a mile away and it takes some few minutes to make out where her bow starts and her stern ends. Actually, Baby, I couldn't make out if she was three, four or just one "Can." I really like the paint job, I guess you gathered that?

Our quarters in the barge aren't so hot. I sleep at the top of a ladder (stairway) and if I roll out of bed on the right side I fall about fifty feet to the bottom deck. Consequently, last night the left side of my sack broke loose with all my weight on it. Ha Ha. The chow is fair here. No complaints but it isn't as good as Treasure Island.

Well, Darling, I will try not to dwell on the subject of missing you. You know how I feel about that as I've told you so often. It still goes as sincerely as I can ever say and I am looking forward only to getting back to you as soon as possible.

I ran into the old bunch I met at Norfolk, of course, when I got here. They sure are a good bunch of fellows and I know I am going to enjoy the tour of duty more with them than anybody else. Since it has to be I am going to make the best of it.

Well, Darling Baby, it is time to go to the sack. I have worked from can til can't again today but will write again tomorrow. It will be another day just like this one but I'll have more to tell you. I'll try to remember all the details of commissioning so I can tell you about it. If things go as I plan, I will be able to write some of the other folks too. I know I am going to write Mother.

I sure hope you made the trip o.k. And am waiting patiently until I get your confirmation by letter. You can write me at:

James O. Raines, Y2c USNR
U.S.S. *Howorth* DD 592
Puget Sound Navy Yard
Bremerton, Washington.[4]

I am going now. Will write you tomorrow. I said good night officially forty-five minutes ago. It is now 9:15 P.M. (11:15 P.M. your
time). Good night my darling,

Your devoted husband,
Orvill

P.S. I LOVE YOU!!!

3 April 1944

Hello, Darling Baby:
    Well, we have that man looking over our shoulders up here and I'll
have to watch what I say. Censorship is what I have reference to.
Don't start worrying yet. It isn't that we are doing anything that
shouldn't be told the public. It's just that a Navy regulation calls for
censorship on a commissioned vessel.
    I won't dwell on telling you how much I love you. I think you know
all about that and I'll have to get over that feeling of "that so-and-so is
reading my mail." However, I've done enough censoring myself to justify someone reading mine for a change.
    We had our christening and commissioning ceremonies this morn-
ing. We stood at attention for more than two hours, someone told me
(I lost track of time). Either at attention or parade rest. I am still enthusiastic about the ship and crew. We have a very good bunch of enlisted men with a few exceptions that are expected. I think I'll feel
confident of being a fighting team with them. The officers seem to be
4.0 also with a few exceptions which I am withholding opinions.
    Under separate cover I mailed you an invitation to the ceremonies
this morning. Need I suggest that you not accept since it is so far up

4. Navy ships are assigned hull numbers (in *Howorth*'s case, DD 592) that include letters denoting the type of ship (DD for a destroyer, SS for a submarine, CL for a light
cruiser, etc.).

here and that we've already had them? By the way, the woman who sponsored the ship had to bang the fizz three times before spilling that precious stuff all over the bow. I didn't see her do the hitting (damn Marine guard was standing in front of me) but I heard the clangs.

Our skipper [Commander Edward S. Burns, USN] made full commander at the same time this morning. A Captain made the announcement at commissioning ceremonies, making both commissions arrive simultaneously. I was glad he made it (he broke out the new rags and scrambled eggs this afternoon) as he seems to be a nice guy. No funny stuff, as I've already learned. I made a slight error in letter writing form yesterday and he bawled out [Yeoman 1/c Edwin C.] McDonough for it. Now, don't get ideas. I couldn't help him getting tough with Mac. It wasn't much and it passed over neatly enough without my making an issue of it by admitting my own error.

Well, getting back to the commissioning. We had turkey dinner on the barge or houseboat on which we make our abode. A lot of the fellows had their wives, girl friends or members of their families aboard. Everyone was jolly and seemed to enjoy the whole thing. It reminded me of a picnic or church bazaar at Memorial Christian. (I'm such a sinner I can't spell Christian any more without blurbing.)

The executive officer [Lieutenant Commander E. B. Henry, U.S. Naval Reserve] is still stacking up as a very good fellow. All the men and officers are feeling quite good about it as I can gather. I can't judge the officers much but the men have a high morale. The exec as you know has more personal contact with the men than the Captain. Consequently, he is a very important man to us enlisted personnel. I've never seen fellows more enthused about going out. If nothing happens to that morale we'll make the Pacific (or wherever) a mighty hot spot for the Japs or Huns as the case may be.

Well, Darling Baby, I reckon I better go. I want to write Mother this evening and try to let her know how I am coming along. It is certainly a relief to know that she is recovering without undue difficulty. Remember that hard morning I told you good bye in the hotel? Well on top of all that she wrote me the following to conform with her letter and my card back to her: "Dear son, Am not o.k. Am cold, sick and hungry." Baby, I almost broke under that one. If there had been a hill nearby, I would have gone over it. One doesn't realize how important events at home are to a guy until he is out and has to think about them. I'm glad I didn't insist on any leave while at Frisco, however. Going over the job we have here has shown me what a big thing it is and it is better that I'm here no matter how bad I wanted to see Mother.

Well, good night officially Baby. Be a good girl and take care of yourself. Watch after yourself and be darn sure you start taking those pills again! I'm still worried about your getting home all right. Write me at the address below hereafter. The Fleet Post Office is a routing point and we are still at **[censored]**. When, how and where we shove off cannot be divulged. So, if the above comment gets past the censor this time, there must not be any further mention of it. So hereafter it is F.P.O. San Francisco and you can spend your quiet evenings guessing and plotting with Mr. Foree [Raines's former editor at the *Dallas Morning News*] where I am. That should take up a lot of your spare time. By the way, if you haven't done so already, call him up and tell him I am going to take an evening off soon and write him a line. Good night again officially, Baby, will write more tomorrow if I'm not too worked out.

Your devoted husband,
Orvill

P.S. I LOVE YOU!!!

---

13 April 1944

Hello, My Darling Baby:

Here it is a little after ten P.M. and I've just seen the movie "Lucky Legs." Remember how we tried to get together and see that thing in New Orleans? Well, I finally got around to it but it's some few miles from where you were when you saw it.

I will try to explain the conditions under which the guys of the *Howorth* see movies. The projection machine is set up in the mess-hall (on the barge where we are quartered) and we sit on the tables, benches, boxes and fl (excuse me) deck. The screen is a transparent cheese-cloth looking arrangement to allow the guys to sit both in front of it and behind. The mess-hall being long and narrow, this permits more of a public so to speak. Tonight I sat behind the screen and everything was backwards. Everybody was left-handed, etc. Quite an ovation arose when all the gals paraded on stage with gams gleaming. I might express disapproval at that type picture being shown to this particular audience but then I am the first to yell for legs. (Do I hear an echo?)

Honey, the meals here are edible but that's about all. Occasionally we have chow that would make a real meal but it's never cooked satisfactorily. We have had steaks a few times but they are too rare and underseasoned. Don't understand that I'm dissatisfied (Oh no!!) but it could be better. Overall I guess we have it pretty nice. Boy the Navy would be in a hell of a shape if it weren't for spuds. The tables we eat from reach arm-pit level almost and consuming the food is purely a matter of "scooping it in." Yes, I still get the grease and sloppy stuff all over my hands when I empty the tray. We dip our trays in a garbage can of very hot water to help rinse them off before washing. That's when I get it! I have to grab the top to hold it and now my dungarees are slightly used-looking. (I haven't had on blues since three days after getting here.) …

Anyway, Baby, be happy and have as enjoyable tour of "blankness" as you can and I'll be back some day. It hasn't even started yet, I can assure you, but then as I've said before it'll all come out in the wash. You know that. And when the right time comes we can pick up where we left off and go on with a very enjoyable business of being married to each other. The future is bound to look bright, Darling, because I thought I loved you about all a man could when we married. It's four years later now and I've noticed a definite improvement all the time. Therefore, it is bound to continue for the next fifty years—I will be about the happiest guy alive.

Well, good night my darling. I'll write more when I can make it. I'm buying a goodly supply of stamps tomorrow and will always have on hand airmails and special deliveries. When we shove off from here I will run for the nearest airplane and put a letter aboard telling you that I am well and that I'll always, *Always* be in love with you.

Your devoted husband,
Orvill

P.S. I LOVE YOU!!!

---

22 April 1944

Good morning, My Darling Little Baby:

Gosh, I'd like to see you. Well, it's about 7 A.M. and I'm up pretty early today. The *Howorth* is making her first trial run this morning.

I'm not going however, and am staying in the office ashore. The *Howorth* is just going to back out into the Sound and fiddle around a bit and loosen her muscles. She'll come in this afternoon about 4 P.M. I don't think I ever told you how we are situated up here.

The ship is tied up to a pier and they've been working on her like mad. Huge cranes four stories high have been putting the finishing touches on her. One crane, honey, is so big that her pilot house is three decks high. (They run on tracks like st-cars [streetcars] but about 30 ft apart.) (Not a full regular story but "decks.") It is supposed to be the biggest crane in the world and I believe it. It is built in the form of a "T" and on one end is the pilot house (control) and several hundred tons of concrete to counter-balance the lifting on the other end, the steel "arm" etc. Well, the pier I spoke of just now is right at the base of the building in which we have our office. I look out the window directly behind me and see the bow of the *Howorth*. Honey, she is a beautiful ship. Really beautiful and I'll bet she can fight to a fare you well. She is tied between two piers and has about six feet clearance on each side of her. I keep looking back to see when the Captain starts to cast off and move her out backwards without touching either side. I'll soon know if he knows his business (we all will of course). He is enough of a grouch and an old fire-eater, so if he can't get the *Howorth* out of her berth without trouble we won't be much proud of him. Except for myself, the most excited people about the trial are the boot [new] ensigns. They sure are excited. I get so tickled at them.

The *Howorth* is rolling just a little from the tide swells coming in from the Sound. The bow is rising and falling gently but with a good bit of motion. Only one line is holding her now. I hope you don't mind this blow by blow description of her maiden voyage. I think you'll enjoy reading about it; I know I get a big thrill out of telling you.

(Hey, before I forget it. Thanks for the lipstick impression. I can smell it today even and it sure pictures you for me. God, honey, I'd love to see you and hold you so close to me it'd hurt you and cross your bones.)

Well, Darling, there she is. She's just backed out into the Sound and is turning to go north a ways. She sure is beautiful. Big as a building lying down. I can see where my battle station is. Way up there where the torpedoes don't hurt, strafing is ignored, bombs don't hurt bad. Shelling plays hell with it though. Boy, she sure looks good. Slick as a whistle and boy she sure got underway in a hurry. Scatted off up the

Sound with a pick-up almost as good as that little green Pontiac. The men are standing on her bow like on the stationery you had. Remember when you asked me if it was a battleship? It looks just like that except it is smaller. It's about 300 feet I guess. Her guns look impressive as hell. The cans don't worry about airplanes in the Pacific anymore, you know. We've got too much fire power—they don't mess around at all. Submarines run like hell with they see a 2100 tonner [*Fletcher*-class destroyer] coming and all we have to worry about are other vessels shooting the "fish" [torpedoes] at us. But darned if I don't think she could outrun the fish the way she is cutting up the Sound. From the looks of her camouflage, you couldn't tell if she is a PT boat [motor torpedo boat] or a battleship. Well, maybe it isn't that good but almost.

Honey Doll, I wrote Mom last night and will mail it today. I hope it will do some good. Well, now that the *Howorth* is out of sight I guess I can close. I have a lot of work left behind and I've got to get at it. I take special pride in that ship. Me and every other rated man and officer aboard her did enough work in the last six weeks to put her in commission alone. There are a lot of the guys who feel by her just as I do. I hope we can take care of her out there and *certainly* hope vice versa.

Bye for now my darling baby. Be sweet as you always are and remember I love you with every particle of me.

> Your worshipping husband,
> Orvill

P.S. I LOVE YOU!!!

---

6 May 1944

Hello, Darling Baby:

… Well, this is one dreary Saturday night. We got paid yesterday but didn't get liberty. Tonight I have the duty and the other watch gets liberty. They all, of course, went into town to get soused. I'd hate to be the gangway watch because he probably will have to put them all in their sacks. The powers that rule discretely look the other way in cases of that kind. Hicky, Brooklyn and George [Lynch] are among those absent from the ship. I would like to "go over" too but there is so little to do. I enjoy the other fellows' company of course but drinking beer gets awfully tiresome, especially the beer they serve here. Whiskey can be purchased but I never took the trouble to apply for a ration book. It takes several days here. And too, I don't like to go in for drinking on such a scale. You have to hide the bottle and argue with the waitress before she'll bring soft drinks to the table for a mixer. That's too commercial for me. I like it the way we had it in the ice box with various mixers right alongside it in New Orleans. Ahhhh, what I wouldn't give to be relaxing on that couch right now with the various personalities with whom we associated down there. I can even feel the perspiration forming from the humidity. ...

Give my best to Johnnie and tell her God speed in going to New York. I haven't heard from Norv[5] so guess he has shoved off again.

Boy, what I wouldn't give for DE duty[6] like he has! Oh, well, a tin can isn't so bad. It's just that any day now, I expect the Devil to be in command. (No reflection on the skipper censor.)

Well, Darling, I guess that is all for tonight. I am getting a little more rest now. At least 5 hours nearly every night! The organization is shaping up nicely and a routine will soon be established. However, I mentioned the hours to the Chief today and he said I should have known that I gave up sleeping when I became a yeoman. But, like every other guy on the ship, I wouldn't have any other rate [rank]. (Except a higher one.)

Goodnight for now darling. Will be writing again soon. The memory of your sweetness is very dear to me. Remember that I love you and worship you with all my being.

> Your devoted husband,
> Orvill

P.S. I LOVE YOU!!!

---

5. Norval Schneringer was a reporter and announcer for WFAA in Dallas; he and Travis "Red" Arnold were Raines's prewar roommates. Johnnie was Norval's wife.

6. A DE was a destroyer escort, smaller than a destroyer such as *Howorth* and designed for antisubmarine warfare.

12 May 1944
(or is it the 15th of June?)

Hello, My Darling Sweet Baby:

How goes my Mommie today? Poppie ain't so hot. I'll try to write while I have a moment alone. So far I haven't lost my breakfast. Mainly, because I didn't eat breakfast. But I feel dinner coming up pretty soon. We had a very nice slice of roast beef. Of all days to serve a delicious meal (potatoes and ENGLISH peas too) is today when you can't find room on the leeward rail for a broomstraw. Everybody is sick but the *Howorth* is still steaming (rolling and pitching too). Only a very few men are still on their feet without pains. The tossing is effecting the veteran and newcomer alike. I heard scuttlebutt awhile ago that the CAPTAIN was rather puny [nauseous] himself.

However, anything can happen here I gather. (You gather, I presume, that we are at sea.) I can see where a larger ship wouldn't be so unstable in a sea of this kind. They call it "ground swells" and at times it looks just like that. I can make out valleys and hills, with little rolling knolls scattered about. Yes, darn it, even the hills have hills. (Maybe I'm sicker than I thought.)

Anyway, be proud of your poppie, Honey Baby. I ain't heaved as yet. My worries are just getting out of the way when somebody else wants the bucket. It is pretty dangerous in these waters here. You never can tell but at any time, you might step in some guy's bucket. Yes, extremely dangerous. Especially on that midnight till 4 A.M. watch I had this morning. We were issued foul weather jackets the other day and they certainly come in handy. I would have frozen without it. I had a good stiff argument with a quartermaster striker [apprentice] this morning over the bridge heater, too. He wanted all of it all the time and I didn't agree. Anyway I got so much of the heater for my pains that I almost blistered my seat. (Felt good too.)

Wait a minute until this typewriter comes down from the ceiling.

Now. That's much better. I can write when this thing is on the same ship with me but frequently it takes off across the Pacific with me hot after it. I just cut a [mimeograph] stencil though and made only, hmmmmm, let's see ..... three mistakes.

Honey, remember all the stories about some guy getting lost on the desert? There's a lot of them in Western Stories and etc. ..... Well, how about a date? I'd like to get lost with you on a desert somewhere. I don't think I'd get thirsty for weeks.

14 May 1944
(Is this Sunday or August?)

Hello, Baby Doll:

How goes it? Well, I haven't suffered too much on this trip. Never did get sick enough to lose any of my meals and today I got darn near half a chicken for dinner. Today is the first day I think the whole crew is able to keep their food down and they gave out with a pretty good dinner. I got white meat from the back to the pully bone, breast, etc. Oh yes, we had spuds too. I'll leave that off the menu throughout my Navy career: Breakfast, fried spuds; dinner, mashed spuds; supper, boiled spuds.

We pull into port this afternoon. I'm not sure when we will get liberty but I want to get in touch with Maud or Laura as soon as I go over. Has she returned home yet? Well, it will be too late I reckon by the time you get this to answer that so just let it go. I hope to see Maud anyway before leaving this sector.

Well, Darling, it is around noon and I've been up working or on watch a good many hours in the last seventy-two so I'm going to run and colapse collapse (choose the one spelled correctly). My efficiency has depreciated greatly in the last few weeks but more than likely will come back up as soon as I get accustomed to this routine. It isn't a hard life. Just tiring at first and I can tell that soon we'll all be broken in enough to take the load without too much trouble. I'll never get accustomed to being away from you though darling. I guess I've said plenty on that subject before, so will retire now. Bye my baby, and remember that I love you very dearly and will just about blow my top when I see you again.

Your devoted husband,
Orvill

P.S. I LOVE YOU!!!

P.P.S. Land sighted! Hope I have mail from you. Haven't heard in seven days. Bye again.

P.P.P.S. DITTO P.S.!!!

16 May 1944

Hello again, Baby Darling:

Well, today I received your box of cookies. Boy, they sure are going fast too. I got them today although they were brought aboard before we left port. Lynch and myself are in the office going to town on them. The First Lieutenant and another officer just left. They heard about the cookies and came storming into the office with "Hey, I heard Raines had some cookies." We all had a jolly time but now we two are writing letters and being interrupted from time to time by various and sundry characters and personalities who have received the "word" and come down for the eats. They are really appreciated by "all hands" because today we have had the three worst meals in the history of the USS *Howorth*. The coffee even had chlorine and salt in the water. The water supply has been cut off all day and was opened an hour and fifteen minutes. Of course, I had to go without washing all day and then had to be on watch during the time it was open.[7]

Honey, I've been looking into the Pacific all day today. (Not over the rail, either.) And the thing that impresses me so much is the blueness of the water. I know that it is as blue as your eyes. And almost as deep. I hope you don't mind, but I'm on the subject of your eyes and I want to talk about them a little. Always ever since I've known you, your eyes have played such a prominent part in our association. They were the first thing that impressed me the moment I saw you. (But heaven knows not the last.) Your eyes are great big and beautifully formed. They are set just right on each side of a perfect nose. Their largeness helps me to read the happiness and despair in your heart. They just sparkle when you are happy and when you kiss. They shine even more when those tears come into them. (An eternal simonize so to speak.) (Forgive me for that, I just had to kid a little.)

The Pacific resembles your eyes very much, in that it is a constant deep blue. Bluer than the sky even and it has an inspiring hue to it that fascinates one. Almost like high cliffs that make persons want to jump off, even though they know that death awaits them at the foot.

---

7. Turning on a ship's freshwater system for limited periods was common, as fresh water was distilled from seawater using temperamental steam evaporators. Even when the evaporators were functioning at capacity, fresh water was rationed, the ever-thirsty propulsion boilers having first priority. Under way, all hands were required to take "navy showers": wet down, turn the water off, soap up, then turn the water on for a quick rinse.

I'll never jump into the Pacific because of that but I am going to jump right in your arms one of these days and never let go. Then I'll kiss those beautiful eyes and lids until I fall asleep in your arms and cuddle up real close and just sigh and really live again. That's what I think of when I stand up on the wing of the bridge and look deep into the blue Pacific.

The sea was unusually rough today. We pulled out of port early and hit out for the deep blue. Then the ground swells started rolling in. We have been "heeling" very badly all day. "Heeling" if you remember is what the little "Kilocycle" did on White Rock Lake when we had a good wind.[8] Only this time we roll from side to side. Back and forth. We rolled twenty degrees to one side and forty degrees to the other a long time this morning. I was on the bridge and everybody almost fell all over everybody. The quartermaster skidded across the floor like Patsy does (the pooch) (when she tries to take a fast corner on linoleum at Mom's). Forty degrees lean is almost like climbing the wall. The deck is just a touch from being half-way straight up and down. Pop can give you an idea of how steep it is. We won't have many seas like this. Nearly everybody got sick again. I and Lynch have been about the only ones on board that stood up under it. (Darling, right now we are rolling so bad that every word or two I have to stop and pull my chair back up to the desk.) It makes me kinda exasperated too. I just start sliding backward across the deck and can't stop. (More in a minute gotta stop now and type up something.)

17 May 1944

Well, I stopped with the above last night and didn't get started again. Must run now my darling baby, be a sweet little good girl and love me as I love you if that's possible. God Bless You, you sweet precious Baby.

Your devoted husband,
Orvill

---

8. *Kilocycle* was a small sailboat Raines and his roommates in Dallas owned before the war.

I got your letter telling me about getting the money. Will mail this tonight. Yes, I am broke but I have enough for a movie tonight and we get paid Saturday. That's all I need, I spend all my time thinking of my Mommie.

     P.S. I LOVE YOU!!!

---

26 May 1944

Hello, My Darling Baby:

Well, I must hurry to get this off. I have to leave the ship in a few minutes if I'm to get over on the beach. ...

Honey, we have been firing lately. Firing everything on board. We are good, too. We will be traveling in fast company. That is about all I had better tell you. We were in rough seas yesterday and today. I withstood the pummeling very well and suffered not one iota of discomfort from the shaking up. My seasick worries were all in vain apparently.

My body is well Baby doll, but my heart is still bleeding. It will continue to bleed until I hold you again. That is the only thing wrong with me now. We will be in and out of Diego here for about three more weeks I think. I will inform you however of changes when they appear. ...

Good bye for now Darling and write poppy those sweet endearing letters that I adore so much. I love the very earth you trod my baby. Remember I worship you, every little corpuscle and cell is my god.

                              Your devoted husband,
                              Orvill

     P.S. I LOVE YOU!!!

---

1 June 1944

Hello, My Darling Baby:

Well, sweetheart, most wonderful girl in the world, here is another of those rare days. I began our fourth [wedding] anniversary on the bridge this morning and watched the second hand climb around to midnight. I had the midnight until 4 A.M. watch this morning and had to break out at 5:30 A.M. again to go to G.Q. I've just come down to the office. It's 6:15 now. We've been out three days now and I'm not supposed to have time to write you. I must squeeze this in before a certain officer catches me. I have a lot of work to do for him. He's a very nice guy and I like him about as well if not better than anyone on the ship, however he's forced to see that we get the job done. If you don't understand what I'm talking about just disregard it. I'm not thinking good lately. I've been on the bridge about thirty-five of the last forty-eight hours. I was feeling pretty bad when I got off at 4 this morning but the hour and a half sleep did wonders for me.

McDonough was promoted to Y1c [yeoman 1/c] today. I'm sure glad too since he is a swell guy and deserves it. I reckon I'll make it too in about three months. I have to wait until I've been second [class] nine months. Today is six months. I have a lot to learn about yeoman duties though but maybe can make it.

The weather has been very rough these three days. Everyone seemed to be over their seasickness but when we started out Tuesday morning we hit unusually rough seas and it came on all over again. I felt pretty bad myself but didn't get any worse than before.

I don't rate liberty tonight baby but somehow I'm going to get this letter off to you and get to a telephone. I must talk to you. I want you to tell me you love me lots again. It sure is important that you do. You'll never know how much these pictures have meant to me. I pull them out and look at them every time I get blue or worn out, which is quite often. I sure am crazy about you darling. Honey, maybe the *long* letter you deserve will be forthcoming tonight. If I finish that work I spoke of above, I'll write it. There are a lot of things I want to write you. I may be able to see LaVerne [Raines's niece] and her husband tomorrow night, if not I know we'll be in port Saturday. ...

Good bye for now Baby Doll. I'll write more tonight if at all possible. I love you with every part of my being baby. My chest swells almost to the bursting point with love and pride to be the one chosen to sign these letters.

Your devoted husband,
Orvill

P.S. I LOVE YOU!!!

3 June 1944

Hello, My Darling Baby:

Well, it's four years and about forty-eight hours since I took the step that made me the most fortunate man on earth. I still feel a nice warm glow in the chest from talking to you the other night.

Tonight is Saturday. Yes, like June 1, 1940. I have the duty. The men on board who could find a "standby" got forty-eights [forty-eight-hour liberty] this week-end. Of course McDonough and I couldn't decide who was to get the other to standby for him so we will split it up. Things are going along about the same as usual. Just getting along. The days are passing fast for me. I know they are slow for you but I'm doing nicely in that respect. We fired again today off the coast. A very beautiful small island about sixty miles from San Diego. San Clemente is its name. It's about half way between Diego and Los Angeles and out about thirty miles from the beach. Look it up on the map. It's simply beautiful, however, we tore up one side of it pretty badly. ...

Honey, you keep talking about rain in Dallas. I am beginning to gather that it is kinda wet down there. Well, I want to tell you about the rain we get here (at sea of course). We have had only one good rain out there and I went topside to go on watch one night and the rain hit me in the face. You have read books and stories where they referred to rain hitting like gravel. Well this was just like someone was standing in front of me and throwing rocks at me. Boy, it sure hurt and I got inside fast! If you just realize it, that is the way the rain hits our little windshield on that little green job. Think how well it protects us. You know. And when I think of that I like it even more and would *never* want you to sell it. ...

Hey, I miss my lipstick. Put some on every once in a while. It'll take too much for every letter but every three or four days drop those beautiful kissable lips on a letter for me. Please???? ...

Darling, don't ever think your letters are boring because they are of your doings and how much you love me. That is just exactly what I want to hear and read about. Nothing else matters but what you are doing.

Wait a minute. Must stop and type up something. Boy, they sure are nutty on this ship. It's ten minutes past 11 P.M. and an officer walks in with a three-page typing job. That's all right, though, he'll be on the gangway one of these times when I want off the ship. Bye for a minute. ...

Hey, did I tell you in last night's letter that I am sending Pop a Father's Day card? Well, I am. I sure am proud of myself too for thinking of it. Make him let you see it and tell me what you and he both think of it. Of course, don't let him know that I asked that. Ain't I a dickens though? Just too young I guess. ...

Well, Baby Doll, it's good night again for now. It's late (little after midnight) and I am going to bed. In the morning I will be able to sleep late. Even until 8 o'clock maybe if I'm lucky. I will be rested tomorrow and late in the afternoon I may go over into town. I will mail this then. Be a good little girl mommie and I'll try to get you a letter in the mail Monday.

God bless the most wonderful and beautiful creature on earth.

> Your devoted husband,
> Orvill

P.S. I LOVE YOU!!!

[15 June 1944]

Hello again, My Darling Child:

Well, here 'tis Thursday night. I was going to send a letter over by a friend tonight but I just couldn't bring myself to send the above over to represent a letter. I know that a little is better than nothing but I want to tell you I love you and I didn't get around to it above. Boy, have the last four days been dreary! No letter, no nuthing! I felt like a piece of machinery when we started in today. But here's a development that you might like to hear! The chief yeoman [George F. Sleeter] and I had it out the other day. After being up so much for the last month, I [was] almost played out and tried to get some sleep. Reveille was at 6 A.M. the other morning and I didn't get up until 6:15. At 6:45 I came staggering in the office and the chief said to me and the little striker [yeoman apprentice] (who came in on my heels): "Where the hell have you guys been?" I said: "I was in my sack, By God, trying to get some rest, etc. etc." I gave him a very good eating out and I guess he knew I'd get right in his eye had he said another word, regardless of the penalties. Anyway, he immediately started sympathizing with me and now we get along like friendly brothers. Ever since we left port last Monday, I have been taken off the watch. I work in the office only right now until we get caught up. Anyway, I come to work at a reasonable time after reveille (about 6:30 A.M.) and work on through until 8 P.M. about at night. Then I put on my hat and walk off and leave the office for bed. And not a word has been said. I figure that a good twelve hours a day is enough. Today I went out and watched the machine guns fire and depth charges dropped. He was out there too and we both enjoyed it. I feel better now than I have since leaving you. I am well rested with my eight hours sleep and do much better work than when I was so worn out. I have resolved to maintain my present degree of physical fitness throughout the remainder of my Naval career. Naturally there will be a few exceptions in the case of emergency but they will be few and I have developed an automatic blood-in-the-eye look that is neither pleasant nor unpleasant. Sort of determined you might say. Don't worry Baby Doll about my getting myself into it. I still realize the importance of keeping my rate. I also realize the importance of getting back to you as much of a man as possible.

Darling, I hope you will forgive me for not including my little P.S. on the last letter. I must have forgotten it thinking I would be writing more later. Anyway, I don't forget it often do I? ...

Oh yes, Baby, I want to tell you about the flying fishes we see out here. They actually fly it seems but they really swim real fast and then sail. I'm leaving room below to draw a picture. They only fly when something disturbs them and the ship cutting through the water scares them up. They almost come up on deck sometimes and I've seen some that weigh almost 2 pounds. (o.k. maybe 1 and 1/2 pounds, then. But their weight wasn't my estimation. One of the other guys said 2 pounds.) (He's probably as big a liar as I am though.) (About fish.) (When I get done with all these parenthesis's maybe I can get back to writing the letter.)

Well, Baby doll, it is midnight now and I must get to bed. We have our final San Diego inspection tomorrow and I want to look pretty. We leave for Bremerton about noon Saturday. Tomorrow night is our last night on leave here.

Bye for now my darling baby. Tell Nellie [Ray Ellen's aunt] hello for me and that I sure love her for being an aunt. Tell her someday I'm going to take a half-day off and tell her how swell and nice she is. Remember baby doll how much of my life you are. Remember that you are always in my thoughts and that my whole world revolves about you. Take care of yourself for me and I'll devote all my time here to taking care of me for you.

Your devoted husband,
"Poppie"

P.S. I LOVE YOU!!!

---

17 June 1944
8 P.M. Saturday
(almost official G-N time)

Hello, My Darling Baby:

Well, here's Poppie again, wishing I could do better toward you and feeling kinda bad about not getting the letter off yesterday. But I don't feel too bad about it cause I know you understand. You sure make things easy for me Darling, being such an understanding wife. Always making excuses for my shortcomings. ... Oh, yes, while I'm thinking about it. I had supper and spent the night at "Elsie's" last night with Nick. We had a wonderful time, I guess. Went over onto an island called Coronado Island and watched the sun set behind "Point Loma." It was truly beautiful baby and I wished and wished and wished for you to see it. I almost didn't enjoy it because you weren't there. But I did enjoy it because I knew I must so I can tell you about it when I get home. Ships were coming and going out of the haze miles out. An aircraft carrier stood out the size of a pin head ten miles away. A striking arrangement of clouds stood high over Point Loma and blazed away with a million colors with gold predominant. Point Loma is a peninsula extending southward from the north. 200 feet high and ends absolutely into the sea. It protects the San Diego Harbor from the sea. Atop it sets the Navy, watching. We stood behind the Coronado Hotel to watch the sunset, and Elsie cried. Nick and I almost did too but then she gave us some sort of religious medal that goes on our dog tag chain. It is Sterling and egg shaped about the size of a nickel. It has an impression of Mary on the front and a bunch of symbols on the back. I don't know what they mean on the back. On the front it says: "O, Mary, conceived without sin, pray for us who have recourse to thee." I was really impressed with Elsie. She is such a sweet woman (about 30 I guess). Nick and I sure liked the little gadgets and referring to the box and its contents, we threw the box into the sea and wished that "Never the twain shall meet." We wished it very hard because the medals were around our necks.

This morning we left the house and Mrs. Curtis (Nick calls her Mom) cried so pitiable for Nick and me. I sure felt like bawling myself. I don't know why they took so much interest in me, giving me that medal and being so nice to me. Elsie really bawled when we got out of her car and ran down the pier to catch the whale boat back to the ship. She is in love with Nick. That sure is a hard way to say good bye. ...

Hey, good night officially, darling baby. It's Saturday night and I'm stopping now to look at your picture and tell you good night officially at 8:30. Where are you? Wherever you are darling, be happy. Be happy for me and please keep that beautiful little chin up. Don't let anything make you unhappy. You are my dreams and my life. ...

Incidentally, have I mentioned that we are at sea enroute to Bremerton? Well we are and should be approaching a line somewhere just south of San Francisco but about 100 miles at sea. ...

Yep, the lipstick is fresh and good and delicious. George saw one of your letters a while back and very reverently requested that I just let him smell the odor of good fresh lipstick. He was quite impressed with it. His lipstick comes from Australia. By the way, did I ever tell you about that? He is going to marry a girl he knows in Australia. She writes him every day and has for the last year. He writes her constantly too. We are working on papers to get her admitted to the United States after the war. I hope he gets her. He is a real good boy.

Well, darling, it is 10 P.M. I have written two hours and will close. I must get to bed and get up early and start typing up leave papers for one third of the crew in the morning. I hope to get squared away and write more tomorrow night. I know I will but just in case:

P.S. I LOVE YOU!!!

18 June 1944

Hello, Darling Baby:

Well, here I'm is again. And I seen a whale! ! Honey, I actually did! And he wasn't thirty feet from me either! He swam right up beside the ship and came up and rolled a great big roll and went right down again! Boy, was I thrilled and would I have given anything for you to see it. Honey, it was almost the size of our car. I just saw his head and back. He rolled like a porpoise. Like those we saw at Galveston that May. He was swimming on a course to cross our bow. That's how come he came so close. (I'm plunging right into the narrative.) The water was stirring up over an area about the size of the top of our car and we watched the swirl coming closer. When he got right alongside the ship he came up and blew his bugle. I didn't see his eyes, but he headed downward then and his big old back just shined in the twilight. It was a very deep grey. (To me that is, I don't know what color he would be to you.) Anyway his back was as broad as the car. Some of the fellows said he was a small one and I guess so but boy, he looked plenty big to me. One of the Negro stewards said "Boy, if that's what they got out there, I'm staying on this boat even if she sinks!"

All I could do was wish for you. And I've been thinking. I had better stop wishing for you when things happen. Someday a shell is going to head for me and I'm gonna be thinking how pretty it is and wishing for you to be there and get it in the neck. And then it would be terrible if you were there wouldn't it? We'd both get it in the neck.

8:30 again tonight baby. God, how I wish you a pleasant good night officially. Be with you in a minute. Now. I just had a very pleasant dream about you darling. You were sitting in the chair at the apartment and also lying on the grass out at Neita's. I wonder where you are. I thought how pretty you look at both places mentioned above and dreamed a kiss off you. A very long one with 400 [Raines's quality rating of Ray Ellen's kisses] oozing out my ears. …

Hey, I haven't been seasick a little bit even on this trip. All day yesterday and today I've felt tip top. I'm sure getting the sleep now and the chief and I get along like we were crazy about each other. I think he likes me much better because I don't jump when everybody hollers. Least of all him. Knocking off for tonight honey baby. Got work to do. Will finish this tomorrow. We tie up day after tomorrow. I go on leave at 4 P.M. Wednesday. Just in case: P.S. I LOVE YOU!!!

Hello, Mommie, this is just a few minutes later than the above. I got through faster than I thought. I've been looking back through the letter and see that it is rapidly growing to enormous sizes, so added another airmail stamp. Do you want me to keep sending letters to your office[9] or do you want me to write more of them home? Let me know and I'll gladly comply. Whoops here's more work. Will have to knock off again baby. I'll finish this tomorrow. Good night my very own darling, remember if you can how very much I love you and worship you.

---

28 June 1944

Hello, My Darling:

As usual, when I want to write you, someone comes in and gives me a handful of work. Well, I'm not taking any chances, I'm going to write you first and then do the work. Because otherwise, I'd feel too tired to write when I got through with the work. Anyway, I'm not working too hard. I'm getting enough sleep. Food quality has dropped off considerably with other sections of the ship's personnel off on leave. The way that works, Honey, is that the ship's personnel is divided into three sections. I am in the first section and had leave first. When the first section came back the second shoved off. They will get back Friday morning and the third leaves then. ...

Darling, the lipstick is coming along fine. I just rubbed one of your kisses all over my mouth. It sure tastes feminine. Keep 'em coming. They also taste familiar. Guess I've had plenty of them in my time. The last three and half years. (More than that. Three and 3/4 years.) Gosh just think of it three and 3/4 years together and we're only starting. I just can never get enough of you. And never will I suppose. ...

Don't worry about my mailing these letters ashore, Honey. Have I told you how many guns and what kind we have? Have I told you about our [underwater] sounding gear and radar? True I told you where we are going but it is a well known fact here. The workmen here in Bremerton know more about where we are going than we do. They told us today that we will be out of repair on the fifth of July, leave the 6th with the [USS] *West Virginia* battleship and go to San Francisco. Then we will go in company with a convoy to Pearl Harbor. What

---

9. Ray Ellen's job as an office manager for a physician was not a marked departure from the normal employment for women in the prewar United States. For an overview of women's employment during the Second World War, see D'Ann Campbell, *Women at War with America: Private Lives in a Patriotic Era* (Cambridge: Harvard University Press, 1984), chapters 3–4. Also see Susan M. Hartmann, *The Home Front and Beyond: American Women in the 1940s* (Boston: Twayne, 1982), chapters 4 and 5.

good is security if riff-raff like they have working here in the yard know all about it. There are bums in large numbers working here and information wanted could be bought for a song. Yes, we are going to Frisco about the 6th and I don't mind telling you. I expect you to keep it under your hat though and I know you will, cause Poppie's ridin' this boat too! We will stay in Frisco about 5 days. Therefore, we will be shoving off from the States about the 15th and then Mommie, you mustn't know anything at all concerning my whereabouts. That is strictly secret stuff and we will all be safer without anyone knowing our whereabouts.

Honey, you sure would get a thrill out of seeing the *Howorth* now. We are in dry dock and completely out of the water. They are painting her and giving her a general working over. All alterations to suit the captain and different department heads and a lot of enlisted men. We have a fine bunch of men and officers aboard, although there are some I don't like. Which is expected, of course, there is bound to be a number that someone doesn't like. I guess they all aren't in love with me either. Honey, the first letter you get from me, say dated about the 23rd or 25th of July you will know that I'm on the pretty little island out in the Pacific. We may stay there a while for more exercises and then again we may not. Anyway, you just hang on for Poppie. Cause the war is gonna be over pretty soon, I betcha.

Hey, while I'm thinking about it. I found out today that I only get fifteen bucks payday. Maybe you better send me about ten dollars so I can get the pictures in San Francisco. Can you spare it? I want to have a little so I can get some chow and see a movie. We may not get paid before we get to Pearl and I'll need a fin [five dollars] or so out there. ...

I just had a good laugh. You mentioned taking your water to bed cause I wasn't there to get it for you. At first I hoped you would get in the habit but then I figure that is what I want to do. I always griped but did get a kick out of it because you always held your hand out for it so cute. And too (don't think this silly of me) I've always felt good when you held out your hand and I could put whatever you wanted into it. Remember the lights. Boy, what tussles we had! Remember the night we left it on half the night trying to argue the other into turning it out. I still feel the bitter pangs of defeat on that one. That's what made me laugh just now. Boy, memories are sure sweet, aren't they? Isn't it silly the way we could never be sure if we "pulled the thing out on the clock"? ...

Well, Baby, I'm mailing this tomorrow. I'll try to think of more to write tomorrow if I can. It's 11:45 now and I'd better get to work on that other stuff. I can sleep late in the morning though.

Poppie

Just in case: P.S. I LOVE YOU!!!

---

29 June 1944

Hello, My Darling Baby Doll:

No letter today. Boooo Hoooo! All tangled up again, I guess. No letters of yours to dig questions out of so will try to give you the low down on things. ...

Well, Baby, we came out of drydock today. The way they work that is thusly: We are tied up to a pier. A great big hole is setting over there about a block away. They fill up the big hole with water after setting numerous wooden props and stanchions in the right places. They open the "gate" or "lock" and in we go. They close the gate and pump the water out. The ship settles slowly onto the props and stanchions. With all the water gone we look upon the bottom of the ship, scrape its bottom (I said scrape, not scratch) and put on a new paint job. I saw her bottom (I blush) for the first time day before yesterday when we went in. Her screws (I blush again because her "screws" are her propellers) are huge things and really look efficient. I'd love to tell you her speed that we made on the trial run but it is important to keep that quiet. After working over all the miscellaneous gear that is secured to her bottom, the dry-docking process was reversed today and we pulled out. We are again tied up to a pier. Another can just exactly like ours pulled in after we left. I imagine that can will leave up here with us.

Honey, I hate to put into Frisco. I am bound to go by that hotel and remember things. I had rather have had a knife thrust into me than look back and see you standing in that doorway in your pajamas; the last time to see you for many months. I'll never get over that feeling. That's the first time you ever saw me cry isn't it? Baby, I really wept going down the elevator. I must get off that subject. I find myself stopping and thinking back. That is when that real hurt feeling gets me. Now I look forward to the fact that soon we will be together again. I know that we must because God can't keep us separated too long. The war is bound to be over within a few months and all these poor devils can go home again.

Honey, you know I told you in my letter last night that the food isn't so good? Well it still isn't but I'm not caring now. One of the negro cooks (they cook for officers only) came in for his leave the other day and didn't know what to do to get it. I fixed him up because I wasn't too busy and today I mentioned that I wanted a sandwich. It was right after lunch and he asked me didn't I like my dinner. I said "No, the food hasn't been fit to eat in several days." He said, "Well, you just let me know when you want good food. I'll fix you up. I got some ham in the ice box right now. Wait a minute." He came back in a few minutes with a ham sandwich with the ham a quarter of an inch thick. I almost hugged the black devil. He is a good negro, that is the reason I helped him with his leave, and he repeated that when I wanted good chow just let him know, that we'll eat officers' chow. It tickled me pink, cause they sure have beautiful food. ...

Well, Baby, I believe this is all for this time. Please know that poppie is hurrying home to you as soon as he can because these little scratches on my heart will eventually bleed me to death if you don't put your sweet little fingers over them and stop the blood soon. Bye for now and remember that your husband loves you so deeply that it hurts.

> Your deeply devoted husband,
> Orvill

P.S. I LOVE YOU!!!

> Sunday, 2 July 1944 noon

Hiya Mommie,

Here 'tis Sunday now and I've just finished eating dinner. Have you finished eating your picnic lunch yet? Bet not. Bet it's about 2 or 3 P.M. fore you get through. I have 1 P.M. liberty this afternoon but I'm not going over. I'm standing by for one of the quartermasters who has his wife on the beach. I kinda dropped off to sleep last night while writing the above. I leaned my head over on my typewriter to think and dream about the things we have done and I went to sleep. I woke up about 7:15 P.M. and at 7:30 they cut the light off in the forward part of the ship, where the office is located. That launches me into a typical night aboard ship with no liberty and nothing to do. I strolled down the starboard side of the ship's main deck. Hands in pockets and watching the sun glance off the cranes and ship's masts. I heard a hail and saw [Robert M.] Soyars, the first class boat'sun with a cup of joe in his hand. I went in and got a cup and sat around until 9 P.M. "shooting the bull" about our leaves. Soyars is quite a drinker and I couldn't get a word in edgewise. A little seaman came by about 8 P.M. and asked if we wanted anything from the canteen "Craven Center." We all ordered something (several others had gathered by that time). (All this takes place inside the "Boat'sun's Locker," a small compartment about five feet square containing rope lines, string, buckets, pulleys, belayin' pins, foul weather clothing, large sewing needles and other seaman paraphernalia.) I asked the kid to bring me some ice cream and a sandwich. (Couldn't locate my negro friend.) Soyars, a long tall good looking Virginia farming kid, said "Wait, you don't want any of those damn things they sell over there." He proceeded to pull an egg (quite stolen) from out behind some miscellaneous gear and dirty clothing. He broke it over a hot plate that appeared from beneath a large roll of line. Then he pulled out and unwrapped a loaf of bread. Cutting it on a small six-inch-square "table" that juts out from a ventilating pipe, he cut on through the bread onto the paint like cutting a table cloth the same way. He handed the two slices (cut with bowie knife) to another guy to hold. The egg was done by that time (fried in butter) and he flipped it over on its other side. A constant stream of conversation, cursing and lies is batting about the locker all the time. He flips the egg out onto the bread and hands it to me. By the time it gets to me it has been wiped over the deck and clothes, two pairs of dirty hands plus my own and I have to balance the sandwich on my filthy knee because the mud cup is hot. Boy, was that a good sandwich!! Honestly, it was one of the best sandwiches I've ever eaten. When the ice cream gets back we all sit around (shooting the bull 90 miles per hour) with the stuff dripping through our fingers from the leaky paper cartons. After finishing the ice cream it's time for the movie to commence on the foc'sle. Well, they are still working on the lights and can't get the projection machine rigged up. So we sit around until 10:30 P.M. waiting for it to start and I get disgusted and take my chair back down to the office while the rest wait for it to start. I do some work until midnight and that is about all. One of the quartermasters drops by and writes a letter. I pile up in the sack at about 12:15 A.M. and sleep until 8 this morning. They wake me up by trying to get two fellows out for muster. The two men are asleep (one's my negro friend) and are so drunk they can't wake them up. I felt sorry for them. They couldn't retain consciousness. They never bother to wake me. I'm the yeoman and don't have to muster. Even if they did, I get the reports and would just have to scratch my name off the list. I reckon that winds up the night.

Well, honey, Nick is going to Seattle to see our couple friends and is going to mail this for me. I'll go over tomorrow night and get you a letter off. Be a sweet girl My Darling, My very own God, and remember that I love you very very deeply, that my whole life revolves around you. My every action and thought reserves a spot in my mind for you. I never do anything without you being on my mind. I love you and worship you. The world is cloudy without you but beautiful and sunshiny with you. God bless you and keep you safe for your,

Devoted husband,
Orvill

P.S. I LOVE YOU!!!

---

4 July 1944 12:30 P.M.

Hello, My Baby Doll:

What are you doing today? Bet you have the day off, it being July 4th and all, and are having a big blowout either with the Gwin side of the family or Raines'. Anyway, I hope you have a grand time and my thoughts are with you. (I just added that last about two hours after writing the first three lines, Honey.)

I just finished going all over the ship from stem to stern, topmast to bilges, on Captain's inspection. He looks the thing over every once in a while and I go with him to take down the notes he gives out. I type up his list of criticism and give a copy to all officers then they see what can be done about fixing up the things that caused his complaints. I'm getting to know more about the ship than almost any other enlisted man on board. Officers too, I reckon except the Captain and Executive Officer.

Well, honey, the fourth isn't going to mean much to me this year except that I'm hoping that at least YOU can have a good time. If you do then that will be enough for me but there is a chance that you won't but I'm not thinking about that. Reckon I'll run over to Bremerton after a while and see what is going on. Drink a few beers and come back to the ship for a little sleep. ...

Well, Darling, they just announced liberty. It's 3 P.M. so guess I had better get going. I'll try and pick up some cafe chow. We had TURKEY! for dinner today. Dry as a clod of dirt but very good washing it down with water. Guess I'm going to get your habit of drinking water with my meals.

Goodbye for this time, Honey. Be a sweet girl like you always are and I'll love you forever and ever. I would anyway though and that's no joke. No matter what happened to us I'd love you till I drew my last breath. So long for now and Happy Fourth!

> Your devoted poppie,
> Poppie

P.S. I LOVE YOU!!!

---

7 July 1944

Hello, Darling Baby:

Well, Honey, I got a rumor today that this is "it." I don't believe them however but will give you the dope anyway. We are supposed to go to Frisco from here according to my information but a quartermaster a while ago said that he heard from an outside source that we are heading for Pearl from here. We are now a fighting unit. No longer in training, repair or maneuvering territory. We leave here for action. ...

Honey, I went over into town last night and got my pictures. They are terrible but the best I could do. I am getting them in the mail as soon as possible. They gave me an extra one so you can give it to someone else I reckon. I guess the pictures look like me but I also guess I kinda wanted to look better. I'm not so hot looking and I kinda hoped they'd improve on me. That's too much to expect of them I reckon.

By the way, I sent you three streetcar tokens last night. I thought about them after I'd finished the letter and didn't get to explain. However, they are self-explanatory. Tokens from San Diego, Seattle and

Bremerton. Anywhere else I visit without you I will send a token so someday we can come back to these towns and you get to drop the token in yourself. That is one way of insuring our coming back to these places. You know, I can't let a street car token go to waste don't you?

Seriously, Darling Baby, Poppie is going to be missing now for awhile. Don't worry about me too much. I have everything just fine now. One of the boys just brought me in an expensive pair of American Optical Company sun glasses (glasses that money can't buy now) and gave them to me for the SoPac (South Pacific). So you see, even little things like that are coming in my direction. I'm not having it hard. The worse thing hurting me is that you are there and I am here. I wish we were together. That's the only thing about this business that is really hurting me. I'll never get over being separated from you and my heart has turned black toward the enemy on that account. I guess I hate him for that worse than anything else. (My heart turning black is only figuratively speaking. It is still very red, bleeding badly and bursting with love for you.) I am such a fortunate boy to have a girl like you in love with me and as my wife. You are so sweet in every way a man could ask. There are no short comings in your makeup and my love for you frightens me sometimes. I am literally crazy about you my darling. And remember that you are going to be the most dreamed-of girl in the whole world. Do you remember how in the movies, some guy very deeply in love with a girl, and he looks into the sky, the sunset or something else and her face appears before him? I thought that was a lot of hokum but it isn't. I've dreamed of you so vividly that I could see your face on the bottom of the bunk of the man sleeping above me. I have seen your beautiful blue eyes in the deep blue sea. I see your beautiful face in the sunset and clouds and near the moon at night. I kiss the lipstick you put on your letters and see you looking up at me with your eyes shining and sparkling like stars and feel your heavenly body close to mine like in the hotel in Frisco that morning. Darling, if we are separated for ever and ever, I will always remember and love and worship you. It's so difficult to explain how much I love you. My only hope is that soon I can be in your presence and kiss the hem of your skirt on my knees. Darling, maybe it's wrong, but I have you on a pedestal of gold, studded with precious stones. You are untouchable to everything on earth but me. And by me only because of your consent. Thank you darling for being mine and such a wonderful person.

So long for this time. I will get you a letter the earliest possible moment. Don't think I will forget because I couldn't, you being on my mind constantly. God Bless you darling and try to imagine how much this mortal worships you as,

> Your devoted husband,
> Orvill

P.S. I LOVE YOU!!!

[10 July 1944]

Hello again, Baby:

This is Monday now. Not much to write about today except that when we arose this morning it was very cold. We even had to turn on the heat in the office. It has been cloudy all day and we can't go out on deck without foul-weather jackets.

Darling, you asked about Brooklyn, Hicky and Lynch. Yes they are still aboard and probably will be. The reason I don't mention them I guess is that Hicky and Brooklyn are "engineers"[10] and in another liberty section. A guy always makes friends in his own liberty section because they go "over" together. Nick of course is an engineer but we get liberty together. Lynch also is in the other liberty section but I see him pretty often on the bridge. We have organized co-laborately a club known as the "F.B.S.A." (Flag Bag Sitters Association). On the bridge, George's signal flags are in "Flag Bags," large metal racks with notches etc. and all the little gizmos necessary to hold them all. Across the front is an iron railing about four inches in diameter. The rail and flag bag are constructed so as to make a very comfortable seat with the right amount of distance between the railing and bag to permit a whistling of the wind across your posterior section. (Kinda like a country "smoke-house" in the winter.) There (these are some of the benefits derived from belonging to this association, which carries the staggering initiation fee and dues of 10¢ per three months) we get coffee (make it ourselves), the other guys have the pleasure of listening to

---

10. Engineers were crewmen who operated, maintained, and repaired the ship's propulsion system and auxiliary machinery.

Lynch and I use big words and carry on a conversation they can't grasp, peanut butter sometimes in the signalman's desk (crackers always), Esquire (to which Lynch subscribes), my Readers Digests, and all other various and sundry magazines with and without "cheese cake." We have oodles of fun up there and sometimes get to enjoy it for half an hour at a time without interruption. It is a very exclusive association. Only those given invitations are permitted to join. (There are still four guys on the ship that haven't been signed up.) No that was just a joke. There is about a dozen in the association and if I do say so, they are the cream of the crop of the crew. The Bo'sun from Virginia I told you about is one, a couple of torpedomen and one quartermaster and a quartermaster striker (Lance you know that came up to the hotel that night in Frisco). There are a few others that I can't think of right now.

Honey, don't think I'm still harping on selling the car. But why don't you ask Pop what he thinks. Ask him if he thinks it is time it was sold. Maybe it has reached that point where it will be more trouble and expense than it's worth. However, do just exactly what you want to do with it. Keep it forever if you want to. But ask Pop anyway for your own information.

Well, Baby doll, I'm about to the end of the page so will close for this time. I love you baby with all my strength and I'm going to apply all my strength to your waist when I see you again. Bye for now and remember I worship you very very dearly,

> Your devoted husband,
> Orvill

P.S. I LOVE YOU!!!

---

18 [–20] July 1944

Hello, My Darling Baby:

Looking at the letterhead up there I see "care of Fleet Post Office." It sounds kinda like "Somewhere in France," doesn't it? Well, it's the same thing of course but certainly seems remote from the letters posted "Somewhere in France" from the last war and Dad's letters home. I have only a few minutes to write before general quarters which is held at dark. Also at 4 A.M. now. I feel very badly tonight, not physically but like I had cheated you and myself out of something. Here's why.

We left Seattle Sunday at 10:30 A.M. We are steaming south and true to Navy fashion, failed to stop in Frisco. We are accompanying some other ships to San Pedro (their identity must remain secret until I see you after the war). The executive officer seems to think that we will just go as far as the sea wall and shove off for Pearl. If that is the case, then of course our telephone conversation is off. But my darling, I can assure you that if there is one iota of opportunity to call or wire you, I will seize it and get it on the way as soon as possible, day or night. I wrote Laura that I might see her and I know she'll be expecting just like you are. Nevertheless, that is immaterial and I want to express my sorrow, believe me darling baby, that I am sorry and disappointed. Maybe I'll have a chance to call you from Pearl.

Just in case I don't get to telephone or wire you, here are a few statistics on my health: I am very healthy, having gained several pounds making your Poppie now tip the scales at 168 pounds! I don't eat like a horse but then I never did eat much unless it was home cooking. My eyes aren't suffering from the strain either. My complexion is very clear for some reason (the soap I guess). I get plenty of sleep and am rested. There goes G.Q.!!

Hello, Darling Baby, well here it is 24 hours later and again I am in the little office writing you and waiting for G.Q. It may not come tonight as we are just outside San Pedro and will go in in the morning. The Executive Officer hasn't decided whether there will be any liberty or not. But I will be just off that point that we saw dimly in the afternoon sun that day you and I and Laura went down on the beach. Remember? It was off to the right and ships were coming and going out there. At least you have seen ONE place where I've been. I won't be there when this letter gets to you but you will know that I am just straight out to sea from there and over the horizon. Out of sight my darling but never out of your heart.

No matter what happens, ever, I will always be in your heart, my baby. And you in mine. Even if someday you decided that you couldn't love me anymore, I will remain in your heart because my love for you is so strong that nothing can remove its imprint from your heart. And if I ever decided I couldn't love you again (very very impossible) I never could get you out of my mind or heart. Isn't it funny how we both know that we will love each other forever? No matter what happened? I am convinced that God made us for each other and no other people will fit us. We don't fit with anyone else the way we fit together. I believe that ours is the most ideal marriage in the world and I know that I love my wife enough that I'd never do anything to hurt her if she knew. You are my life Ray Ellen and without you I can't live. It's as simple as that. Without you I can't live. I must get back to you as soon as possible. Oh, I can stand this war business and all that, knowing that you are waiting faithfully for me but any unnecessary delay would be murder. I lie and dream the most vivid dreams of you, Darling. ...

Darling, G.Q. didn't go off tonight but I have to go to the head. Will write tomorrow before mailing this. Bye for tonight. I love the hell out of you, believe me.

Well, Darling, here it is 6 A.M. Wednesday, July 20th. I've just come down from morning G.Q. True to Navy fashion, we got just close enough to San Pedro to see the lights and take our orders from the Admiral to proceed to San Diego. We get in there in about four hours. I still don't know if we will get any liberty or not but Nick sure is happy. He'll get to see Elsie again. He stopped me out on deck a minute ago and told me we'd go out if we got any liberty. So then I'll get her address for sure. I know I'll remember to get it if we go out. It sure would be nice to get another real home cooked meal. Which reminds me, breakfast is on and I gotta go eat. I ordered that it be sent up to my office but somehow they don't pay much attention to me that way. Bye for now darling. I hope this letter isn't too much for you. If it is, just laugh and say "What the hell, what a world with that husband of mine!" I'm a pretty good guy though, ain't I? Anyway, I love you like hell My Darling. It's so sweet just to sit here and think how much I love you, it's that wonderful pain in my chest, but then I get that "empty arms" feeling and I guess I'd better close. So long for now, Baby. Remember Darling I love and worship you with every bit of me and will forever.

Your deeply devoted husband,
Orvill

P.S. I LOVE YOU!!!

Darling last minute dope again. It's 10:30. Word just came that we are shoving off in eight hours. Bye again. Stand by my Baby. Will get you a letter as soon as possible.

21 July 1944

Hello, My Darling Baby:

Well, honey, there isn't much to tell now. We are shoving off in the morning. I do get liberty today and will go over on the beach. I must hurry if I expect to get over within hours because the liberty boat line gets so long. I am going to telephone you tonight and am looking forward to it very much.

I want to tell you now how very much I love you but I'm going to save it until tonight at which time I think I can do a much better job. Bye for now little baby darling. Please continue to love me because I worship you with everything I've got.

Will try to cable you from Pearl. So long for now and remember that I worship you and will forever.

> Your devoted husband,
> Orvill

P.S. I LOVE YOU!!!

The following afternoon, *Howorth* left San Diego for the Pacific Ocean War.

James Orvill Raines in late 1939 or early 1940.

*Ray Ellen Raines had this photo made in 1943
to send to Orvill overseas.*

A salary increase from $18 to $23 per week provided Orvill and Ray Ellen the means to marry on June 1, 1940.

A loving team. Ray Ellen and Orvill worked at home to improve his writing style. Their efforts paid off as Orvill's bylines began to appear regularly in the Dallas Morning News.

Orvill, Ray Ellen, and Orvill's co-worker Glenn Martin clown for the Dallas Morning News–WFAA–KGKO *employee newsletter shortly after Raines and Martin were called to active duty in the fall of 1942.*

Orvill was stationed initially in New Orleans. Here, he and Ray Ellen pose outside their apartment building.

Orvill (left) and Ray Ellen's cousin, Jimmy Bedwell, at home on leave in the spring of 1943.

Orvill with his brothers, R. C. (left) and Dick.

Yeoman 3/c James Orvill Raines, USNR.

Lieutenant Commander Edward S. Burns reads his orders to commission and assume command of Howorth. (U.S. Navy photo)

Her crew salutes as the national ensign is hoisted and Howorth is placed in commission on April 3, 1944, at Puget Sound Navy Yard. (U.S. Navy photo)

"A precision instrument of death. ..." With her 5-inch guns poised to deliver a five-gun salvo, Howorth's camouflage scheme—designed to confuse enemy pilots and gunners as to the ship's course, speed, and size—presented a menacing picture. (U.S. Navy photo)

Howorth one month after commissioning. The thin, "tin-can" hull plating of destroyers is apparent in the dimpling to the left of the anchor and above the "592." (U.S. Navy photo)

For almost half its length, the main deck was barely ten feet above the sea. (U.S. Navy photo)

(Left) Dungaree-clad shipmates pose in front of one of Howorth's *5-inch gun mounts. (Right)* Howorth *torpedomen maintaining one of the quintuple torpedo mounts. (USS* Howorth *Veterans Association)*

Alcoholic beverages were prohibited on board U.S. Navy ships. This rare beer party for Howorth *sailors was held on a Pacific island. (USS* Howorth *Veterans Association)*

Lieutenant Pete Hamner, posthumously awarded the Silver Star Medal for leading the gunnery team that shot down five kamikazes off Okinawa on April 6, 1945. At 23, he was Howorth's *senior officer after the captain and executive officer. He never saw his second child, Susan, born just before the Okinawa invasion. (USS* Howorth *Veterans Association)*

2

Fleet Training, Territory of Hawaii

At 5 P.M. on July 22, 1944, *Howorth* sailed from San Diego as part of a task group bound for Pearl Harbor, Hawaii. For the next month, the crew engaged in training exercises designed to integrate *Howorth* into fleet operations. Arriving at Hawaii, Raines was surprised by the bottleneck entrance to Pearl Harbor and found the concentration of naval power a grim contrast to the legendary beauty of Oahu. Battle practice off Hawaii included shore bombardment, screening of aircraft carriers engaged in flight operations, air defense firing, and surface engagements involving gunfire and torpedo attacks on simulated enemy shipping. The ultimate purpose of these exercises was underscored by an order to dye all white working hats blue as a camouflage measure.

Although the tempo of operations kept the crew fairly busy, there were times for liberty. Shore leave meant relief from the confined living and working spaces on board, but there was no escape from the wall-to-wall khaki and white uniforms of soldiers and sailors wandering the streets of Honolulu in search of any diversion, even something as simple as a meal of nondehydrated food. Raines's description of the Honolulu red-light district conveys the lowest common denominator reached by any military town—an artificial world highlighted by individual behavior that, for most, would have been unthinkable of back home.

But even with the distraction of training and the aimless and futile pursuit of something different and civilian ashore, the crew was fully aware that the ship would soon be heading westward toward the enemy and an uncertain future. A burial at sea Raines witnessed off Hawaii lent a foreboding quality to the routine of training.

At sea   24 July 1944

Hello, Baby Doll:

Well, Poppie has shoved off, Darling. I'm sorry I have to leave you but it must be done. The only thing we can plan on now is the future when I can go back to work whittling on that career we worked so hard on before this all started. I wish I could tell you where we are headed and a lot of the interesting things that have impressed me but as you know that will have to wait.

I dislike having to keep it all to myself since we have always been so close in telling each other everything that goes on. But remember darling, that everything I see that I feel is interesting or would be of interest to you, I am looking at twice as hard as I would ordinarily. So you just stand by for a great big long story when we do get back together.

Honey, the conversation the other night was marvelous. You talked so naturally that it was the best of all our telephone conversations. (And the longest!) You little dickens, so you want to own a gold mine too. Well, by golly you can have it. I am writing Art[1] very shortly and instructing him to standby for your check. I will tell him to write you the dope so you will be able to read his letter before mailing the money. That way you will be able in a minor way to judge him. I can sometimes form a fairly accurate opinion of a person by reading a letter. Don't pay too much attention to his grammar. He is a little short on that score (aren't we all darn it) but otherwise he is a prince. Won't it be fun telling our children how we got rooked out of a hundred bucks on a Canadian gold mine? Maybe we'll be telling them about a Canadian gold mine from behind a gold cigarette holder too, mightn't we? Honey, I guess if I asked you to spend our money on a slice of the moon you'd try to get it. Thanks a million for being a wonderful wife. You are THE best a man ever had. Why couldn't God provide every

---

1. Raines met Art Williams in Seattle and invested a small sum of money in gold mine stock through him.

man with a wife and mate like you? There'd be no dissention in the world today or ever. ...

Hello again baby doll. This is Wednesday, July—no it's Tuesday, July 24th. Wait a minute. Damn if I know when it is. Well, I checked and to the best knowledge of the ship today is Tuesday, July 26th, and I know darn well it's 1944. Whew, now where was I? Anyway, I wanted to tell you about getting five of your letters the same day we left the States. Almost didn't get them. It was a week since I had heard when I got them so was pretty darn glad to hear. ...

Now for the mail as time will allow: Oh, yes, you asked about the price of the pictures. They were not very costly: $5.65 to be exact. As I told you I was pretty low at that time and couldn't be too choosey about the picture as long as the price agreed with my billfold. Honey, you can have surgery applied to the extra one any way you please. And lots of luck to you! You'll need it! To make that thing look good.

Glad Mom and Pop got off on their trip o.k. I know they will enjoy their vacation. Well, Honey, I'm going to bed now. I have the mid watch which is the midnight until 4 A.M., meaning a lousy four hours for me tonight. It's all I can do to stay awake but I can find some coffee tonight. I think I could drink turpentine on that mid watch. Bye for now and I'll get a little sleep. You are my Baby, little one, and take care of yourself for me as I'm doing my damnedest to keep me safe for you.

Hello, Darling Baby:

Today is Thursday. We're still at sea so will try and knock out a few more words. Nothing has happened except that I've been put back on watch which makes it rather hard to keep going since I have to stand the watches and work in the office as well. It's not so hard as at San Diego however, and I get four, five and six hours sleep a day. Occasionally I get from one to two during the day but not often. I think we will be squared away soon in the office and we won't have so much work to do there except when we are in port. ...

Honey, I keep thinking about our last telephone conversation. It, without a question, was the best of them all and I'm going to try very hard to cable you when we reach a port, wherever that may be. Don't let the "Sans Origine" on the date line frighten you. It just means "Origin withheld" or "without origin." And is put on there for obvious reasons.

Darling, the sea is getting to be kind of beautiful to me. Its color is such a deep blue that I believe it is a large ink well. It is very impressive but never fear that I will learn to like it enough to stay in the Navy. Ye Gods, if it's that or death, hand me my gun, maw. I'll probably be so sick of it by the time I get back to the states that I'll never want to see an ocean again. By the way, honey, I ran into another Mason on the ship a few days ago. I had noticed his ring but didn't have much time for conversation with him. He has a little booklet that tells all about the business with symbols. You have to know a lot about it to be able to read the thing but I remember enough to work it out. We had quite a time worrying with it and he is in the same boat as I. He took his degrees very fast (in fact the first two the same night) and didn't have time to learn his work. I think I will be able to help him and myself too if we ever get enough time to work on it and find a place private enough to talk.

I hope references of that kind don't bore you darling, but those little things are becoming more important every day. I am actually enjoying the little things that I never felt existed before.[2] Someday soon, however, they will fade into oblivion again when the most important thing in my whole life takes shape again. By that, of course, I mean our reunion.

Well, Baby Doll, I don't know when we are getting into port and even if I did, I wouldn't be permitted to say. Anyway, I will close now and get this in the box for censoring so it will get off in the first mail when we DO hit port. I'm sorry, my baby, that I have to be away off like this but we both understand that it is only for an interval of time in which I am just existing and looking forward to the time when we will be together again. If it wasn't for my dreams of the future, I don't think I'd be able to bear the separation from you. I love you very dearly Ray Ellen and my heart aches to have you with me. You are my constant thought and I pray that God will speed the day when I can hold you in my arms and tell you never to be afraid again. I'll take care

---

2. Life at sea was (and is) monotonous; interesting conversational topics evaporated soon after a ship set sail and reading material was consumed quickly, with new books and magazines hard to obtain. Of the infantry in Europe, Mauldin reported that "soldiers at the front read K-ration labels when the contents are listed on the package, just to be reading something. God knows they are familiar enough with the contents—right down to the last dextrose tablet." *Up Front*, 25. For efforts to supply reading material to the American armed forces, see Fussell, *Wartime*, 239–242.

of all those many things that make you tired and worry you. I'm telling you good night officially in the afternoon now. As soon as I get accustomed to having someone read over my shoulder Darling, I'll try to write and tell you how much I love you, ... if that is possible. Bye for now and remain a sweet little girl like you always are.

> Your deeply devoted husband,
> Orvill

P.S. I LOVE YOU!!!

---

3 August 1944

Hello, Darling Baby Ray Ellen:

Well, Honey, it's Thursday night, 9 P.M., the sun just went down in a blaze of glory as publicized by this Pacific Island. It is 1:30 A.M. where you are though and I know that you are sleeping with your beautiful head comfortably nestled in your pillow with that gorgeous hair rumpled about in just a little disorder. (Either that or rolled up tightly so that it would scratch my arm were I there.) The sunsets are just as beautiful out here as they say darling. I watched it go down a while ago and a dozen colors seemed to mingle across the sky. In the background were the men-o-war. Very impressive as the enemy already knows. The moon came up just as the sun went down and shone just as magnificently as you could imagine.

Honey, I am disappointed in the harbor. Instead of embracing a large expanse of water with a vast and romantic beach, we have the thing almost enclosed by land. It is almost entirely surrounded by land with only a small bottle-neck for an entrance. I tell you that because the enemy was here so prominently one time and knows it as well as we do. The water is a sickly greenish color but just outside is a shoal; the water being foamy white for an area well over a mile square. I sure was surprised to see such a sight. It is shallow and beats back and forth across the coral causing the foam.

Oh, yes, I have some news. I saw Chief Decoteau this evening. I watched the sun set with him. Yes, his ship came out here and just arrived today. I told you in today's letter that Freddy Williams' ship was out here with us and after we tied up in the harbor, I was looking and watching for it to moor. Well, I couldn't find it because it had gone into a repair base and while looking I saw Deck's ship steaming slowly in. Boy, was I surprised. I then looked around for Sidney's and Dalton's ship but no soap. Deck's ship had their shakedown with Sidney's and they operated some on the East Coast together but Deck said they left it in Norfolk. (Their ship although a DD, is larger than the *Howorth.*)[3] While we were talking Freddy's ship tied up alongside Deck's but Freddy had been transferred. He is now on a DE like Norv's. That was really disappointing too because I anticipated a real reunion with Fred. George Lynch signaled Deck's ship for me before I went over just to check on his being aboard. When the signalman over there told him, Deck said he almost fell out of his chair because he didn't dream of my being here.

Well, now I guess I can tell you about my trip to the beach last Monday. Nick and I went over. We saw the main drag with fifty sailors to every woman. And the woman a Jap. The place is full of Japs, Honey. We saw only a few Jap men but the Japanese women just about make up the female population.[4] And some are pretty too. They are all just about the same size—Angel's. I sure got tired of looking down at them. They all look just alike and I had to look closely to tell about their ages. I saw only about three real Hawaiians, they being very dignified people although one was a woman barmaid.

We saw the Army & Navy YMCA, the largest and most popular I've seen, where they do everything from sell ice cream orders and exchanging "Mainland" money to local currency.

We went by the "Palace" where the ancient kings and queens held reign. Across the wide street from the palace is the statue of King Komehameha (Ko-ma-ah-ma-ah) who fought his famous hand-to-hand battle with a vicious savage on the edge of tall Diamond Head mountain nearby, to save his people. He was a kind and noble man, being so well loved that he became a legend to the natives.

Then we went out to Waikiki Beach and the Royal Hawaiian Hotel. The Navy has taken it over and sailors are everywhere. I saw only one

---

3. Probably a *Gearing* (DD 692) class.

4. In 1920 the total population of Hawaii was 255,912, of which 109,274 (42.7 percent) were of Japanese ancestry. The next year for which figures are available from the State of Hawaii is 1950, when there were 184,598 (36.9 percent) inhabitants of Japanese ancestry out of a total population of 499,769; *Historical Statistics of Hawaii, 1778–1962* (Honolulu: Department of Planning and Research, State of Hawaii, 1962), 8. Raines would have seen few young Hawaiian men of Japanese ancestry because so many were in the armed forces.

woman on the beach and she was brown as a native. Probably some government worker making all the men on the island who are away from home, Nick and I surmised. (Leave it to us to form such opinions.) The Beach at Waikiki was another disappointment, as well as Diamond Head. Neither stacks up to its reputation. On the other hand Honolulu is much more interesting than its publicity indicates. Always in the background are the towering Mountains with eternal clouds hovering above them. It is raining up there constantly, day in and day out. Several hundred inches of rain falls annually up there and it is uninhabitable. And oddly enough, on the other side it is almost uninhabited due to dryness. It is only on the mountain tops that the rainfall is so heavy. All the islands in this group are that way. We have operated all up and down the chain and they are the same. Volcanic, all of them. And by the way, volcanos aren't so hot. I wasn't impressed very much. But I maintained from the very start that you must see all of it out here. It sure is beautiful considering the influence of the war and all. Some interesting things occurred that will have to wait until after the war for telling. I am anxious to tell you all about it. (I bet you are anxious to hear it too, aren't you?)

After we had strolled over town a couple of hours (liberty is only during the daytime and everybody has to be off the streets at 10 P.M., sailors at 6:30 P.M.). (Started to write 1800.) Anyway, after we had strolled a while we went down into Chinatown to visit an eating place that Nick loved so well. I say "loved" in the past tense because it is only a beer parlor now (where we saw the native gal). I met the Chinese woman that owns the place with her Japanese husband.[5] Nick insisted that we wear leis and bought me one. He bought two, in order to give one to the lady but she had left. So we went up to the Franklin Young Hotel and had dinner (crab meat with eggs). Very good too. Then we went back down to the beer joint and gave the gal her lei (please notice the spelling). In the meantime, we had worn our leis up and down the streets and nobody else was wearing them. When one sailor reverently removed his hat as we passed, we readily withdrew them around our necks and carried them in our hands. I was going to send you one of the buds from mine but regulations forbid sending vegetation to the mainland.

---

5. It is interesting that Raines referred to this man as "Japanese" as opposed to "Jap." Perhaps he was making a distinction between Japanese-American ancestry and a Japanese citizen—a rare distinction for the time.

That's about all of Honolulu except the thing that impressed me most of all. The houses of prostitution are a thing promoted by the service and civilian alike. Across the street from each is a prophylactic station. I say across the street from EACH because of such a heavy volume of business that goes on in each one. I didn't believe what the other guys told me so Nick took me down in that section. You know those second-story hotels they have down on Akard in Dallas? Well, they are used by the women over here too. And believe me when I say the sailors were lined up down the stairway and out onto the sidewalk. Sometimes waiting an hour in line. I almost became ill when I saw the sight. Three dollars for three minutes is the byword. Sloppy sailors with filthy whites (yes whites of course now) came stomping down the stairway with the fronts of their trousers in terrible shape. Apparently they have no time to indulge in the pastime properly. Most of them drunk of course and those that aren't, pretend to be so in order to partly justify their being there for that purpose. It seems that in the Navy, when anyone wants an excuse for doing something wrong (of a minor or major degree) his statement is always "Boy, was I drunk." That is supposed to excuse him from all blame.[6]

That about covers that. We have dyed our working white hats blue. The better to camouflage ourselves. The heat is terrible and the only way we can live is to take the ends of our ventilator shafts off and let the raw wind blow directly on us. It isn't good with no strainer but then, being able to breathe the stuff is better than suffocating. In the office, the desks become hot to the touch. We haven't gotten to the worst part of the heat yet either. It will be a few weeks before we get really hot. I had my hair cut down to two and one-half inches so that no matter how it blows, it won't get in my eyes. I have very little time to comb it anyway (properly). When I put my shirt on to go up on the bridge on watch, it is hot to my skin. Like a suit of clothes hurriedly put on after leaving the steam press only a moment before.

I haven't lost any weight however and am still sticking to the food. We get the powdered milk now which is o.k. for cereal but definitely OFF for drinking. I wanted a drink of milk very badly the first morning

---

6. See Fussell's chapter 8 in *Wartime:* "Drinking Far Too Much, Copulating Too Little." On prostitution in wartime Honolulu, see William Bradford Huie, *The Revolt of Mamie Stover* (New York: Duell, Sloan and Pearce, 1951), chapters 3 and 6; and James Jones, *From Here to Eternity* (New York: Charles Scribner's Sons, 1951), book 3 (chapters 16–27), passim.

we had it and I turned up my bowl and took three swallows before I knew I was drinking the horrid stuff. Boy was I disappointed! However, I am doing very well and can't complain very much. The conveniences I miss of course but under the circumstances I am fortunate in being able to live without griping all the time like so many of us do.

Honey, keep me posted on what Art Williams does on that gold mine stock.

Incidentally, the enclosed are only temporary souvenirs. I will try and send a couple of more things I have in mind later.

I received two more letters today and the bedpan poem. Very good, Honey, I got quite a kick out of it. By the way, do you know that the letter you wrote the night of the 30th and mailed the 31st arrived today? Boy, that's fast service I tell you. I just hope it is as fast in the other direction. ...

Some of the pictures of other members of the family I think I will send home darling. No wait, on second thought, they won't take up much room. And they'll be nice to browse through once in a while. I'll just stick them back in my locker for future reference.

Well, Darling, I reckon this is all for this time. It's after eleven now (almost 4 A.M. your time) and I want to get to bed. I don't have [to] get up until 6 A.M. in the morning, isn't that wonderful? Ye Gods, what am I saying?! Six o'clock and I think it's late. Anyway, I'm taking advantage of it. So long for now Baby doll, and remember that this lonesome gob is sure in love with you. And has been since April 20th 1939. And will be until the world has turned to ashes and God has banked them up in formation of another world. Good night officially my precious darling. I worship you clear to my toes.

Your devoted husband,
Orvill

P.S. I LOVE YOU!!!

---

15 August 1944

Hello, My Darling Baby:

Well again it must be a short one. As time goes by darling, it seems that news gets scarcer and scarcer. But there is one item that might interest you.

I have been mistreated, imposed upon and usurped to an astounding degree! A guy cut my beautiful locks off. Not all of them, just in front. No, I didn't go over the "line" or equator. I was sitting in the radio shack tonight just minding my own business drinking their lemonade and eating their crackers. My hair kept falling down into my lemonade (I had had it cut some a few weeks back). Anyway, I held up a little handful to a friend who was playing with the scissors. I asked him to "cut this knot off." He first dived for my throat but I stopped him explaining that my head wasn't the knot I had reference to. Then, instead of cutting the tuft off in a gentlemanly manner up near my hand, he pressed the blades next to my pure white scalp and ground away. I was afraid to pull away fearing that he might slip in the excitement. Anyway my howls were heard down to the bowels of the ship. I have been saving the stuff for that day when I do cross the line. I decided that if they were to shear my locks, they wouldn't go to a lot of trouble thinking up something else to do me for. On the other hand, if I had robbed them of that pleasure, I dread to think what would be in store for me.

Speaking of lemonade, I think I shall try to explain a little about dehydrated foods carted aboard this iron jumping-jack. The lemonade comes in cans containing about the amount as a large can of cream. It is in powdered form and very powerful. I tasted a bit in the raw one night just for the sample. I could only whistle for a week. Persimmons? They don't even enter the question. Anyway, you make a paste of the stuff with sugar. Then pour the mixture in a container of water and stir like hell. (Nobody minds the noise.) A can makes about ten gallons of ade. There are two other ways of mixing the stuff and you get grapefruit taste and some other kind that I can't think of offhand. Isn't that something? I think I told you about the dehydrated potatoes being better than fresh ones if prepared correctly. The eggs are o.k. too, being a lot better than the stale henfruit they pass out when they can get it. I'll take the dehydrated stuff alla time.

Honey, I'm taking baths more frequently now that we are in warm weather. Sometimes twice a month. I don't always need one of course, but I figure if I stay clean my health will have a better chance.

Hey, we had chicken for dinner today. And pok' chops for supper. Rather an unusual day. Rawthur since I only had to stand six hours watch during the last twenty-four. That's the way the watches worked out today due to "dogging." (A little term that will stand explaining at a later date when I can gesture with my hands.)

Tonight I have the midnight till 4 A.M. When I get off watch in the morning my baby will be getting ready to go to the office. Don't work too hard honey at that job. I think I've said that though. I'm repeating also that I'm glad you like the position and it occupies your mind. I'll be doing a lot of thinking about you tonight. There isn't much doing during those wee hours and I can stand on the wing of the bridge and look down into the slightly roaring water being pushed aside to make way for "my ship."

The water is a fascinating thing to me (and your eyes). I've mentioned the similarity in the deep blueness but at night an additional thrill comes to me. I'm sure you're familiar with the phosphorous (hard one to spell) in the water. Well, when the bow rolls the salt water over, hundreds of phosphorescent balls are caused by the friction.

Balls as large as your hands and they sparkle and shine like the stars. Like the stars in your beautiful eyes when you are happy. And like the tears when you are sad. I only think of the happy stars though and can remember how beautiful you look. How very endearing to the eyes. I could watch it for hours except for the officer-of-the-deck yelling at me (the beast!).

Well, Darling Baby, this is all for now. I am quite healthy and am doing fine. My homesick troubles are the same as millions of other guys so can't complain. Goodnight for now and be a sweet girl as always and remember that I worship you very deeply and will forever.

> Your devoted husband,
> Orvill

P.S. I LOVE YOU!!!

[16 August 1944]

Hello again, Baby Darling:

It's Wednesday, August 16th, and I want to add a little more. I've answered everything in your letters I think. But I just want to say "I love you" again. I wonder how many times we've said that to each other. Have you ever stopped to consider? I know there hasn't been a day in the last five years and more that we haven't said it at least once. Has there ever been a day that we've been together that we haven't said I love you? Of course we can't remember exactly but I'm firmly convinced of the negative. I'm positive that we have always said it. I'll say it for a long time in the future too darling if you'll just let me. I want to very badly. I want to say it with your head on my shoulder and my arms about your waist. With your hair kinda in my face; your soft clean hair that feels so good against my cheek.

I spent a very enjoyable hour last evening listening to an electrician play his accordion. He knew Begin The Beguine but not all of it. I had him play it twice. Boy, it sure sounded good! I made everybody knock off their noise in the machine shop while we listened. Also he played that song of Russia "Tonight We Love." And a hundred others. He played by music at home and plays everything right. Not the sort of accordion player with "Coming around the Mountains" and other hill-billy stuff. I thought a lot of Frank [Raines's oldest brother] while he played. He reminded me of Frank with his dungarees, brogan shoes and being long and tall. Frank sure tried hard for years to play the accordion.

Honey, today I saw a man buried and his body committed to the deep. He wasn't on our ship but another nearby and I watched the ceremony through glasses from the bridge. I will tell you sometime who he was and how he died but can't now. I wish for you now Honey Doll. I realize that I shouldn't write things like that but I am aware that you know things like that happen and that I see them. I don't want to keep the things that impress me deeply from you. And that impressed me very deeply. George Lynch and I watched them and he had a man dip our colors when the mummy-like figure was slid into the sea. I wish for your arms Baby Darling and some of those sweet encouraging words you are so wonderful with. I'll be over it in the morning of course after I sleep a while. I suppose you know what a small kid I am really. I wouldn't admit it to anyone else but you know it anyway. Now honey don't think I am not doing all right. I have surprised myself at the way I am adapting myself to the conditions. I am a lot better off than 90% of the men because they are just as lonesome and homesick as I am. And think how much more I have to go home to.

Precious, you haven't mentioned Frank's condition lately. Think you might check up on it for me? I plan to write him soon.

Well, again I'll sign off. I like to write you Baby because, although it isn't comparable to letters from you, it is like a little visit and I can think about you without interruption. The men seem to respect the privacy of a man writing home out here.

I worship you darling. Be sweet as always and remember that that life, that human body that belongs entirely to you is,

> Your devoted husband,
> Orvill

P.S. I LOVE YOU!!!

> Sat. Aug. 19th.

Hitting port again. Darling, I love you, I implore you, please believe that I trust and adore you. That I worship you more than life itself.

> Your "Poppie"

Six days later, *Howorth* departed Pearl Harbor for Guadalcanal in the Solomon Islands.

3

Westward to the War Zone

Howorth left Pearl Harbor just after supper on August 25 under secret orders to escort USS *Sangay* to Guadalcanal in the Solomon Islands southeast of New Guinea. During the eleven-day voyage across the Pacific, Orvill Raines celebrated his twenty-sixth birthday. When *Howorth* crossed the equator at the 180th meridian, the largely pollywog crew (70 percent of whom had never been to sea before) were initiated into the realm of King Neptune with the traditional maritime festivities. After three days devoted to the tedious and backbreaking task of replenishing supplies and loading ammunition at Tulagi and Purvis Bay in the Solomons, *Howorth* was ordered northwestward to Manus Island in the Admiralty Islands.[1] Raines observed his shipmates become more withdrawn as the ship sailed closer to the combat zone. On Manus, Raines was affected deeply by his first sight of a wounded soldier.

The Admiralty Islands had come under German control in the late nineteenth century but were annexed by Australia as part of the forfeiture of Germany's Pacific territories after the First World War. Japan seized the Admiralties in 1942 as a defensive outpost of their Greater East Asia Co-Prosperity Sphere. The Japanese constructed airfields on Los Negros Island and in the vicinity of Seeadler Harbor on Manus. Southwest Pacific Area (SWPA, made up primarily of Australia, New Guinea, and the Philippines) commander General Douglas MacArthur's strategy was to advance northward from Australia and the Solomons to secure New Guinea, recapture the Philippines, and conquer or

---

1. Loading supplies and ammunition required an all-hands working party to manhandle supply cartons, canned goods, shells, and powder casings from a supply barge onto *Howorth* and then down into the various stowage areas within the ship. No part of the procedure was automated.

isolate Formosa in order to cut off the Japanese home islands from the Southeast Asian raw materials the Japanese empire desperately required. The U.S. 7th Fleet, which *Howorth* was joining, had supported the invasion of Los Negros Island and Manus Island between February 29 and March 3. Allied intelligence had been spotty, especially with regard to Los Negros, and the Japanese forces were larger than estimated. After stiff resistance, the Japanese were subdued, and Seeadler Harbor became a major port and base of operations for the 7th Fleet in their support of MacArthur's campaign against the Japanese on New Guinea. With the Admiralty Islands in Allied hands, the major Japanese fortress on the island of Truk in the Bismarck Archipelago, just to the east, was cut off from Japan and left to wither.[2]

Following a six-hour refueling from a tanker in Seeadler Harbor at Manus, *Howorth* escorted USS *Remus* to Humboldt Bay, New Guinea, arriving there on September 21. *Howorth* had sailed thousands of miles, and Raines wrote Ray Ellen that he was having difficulty recalling "remote" memories from his civilian life. After almost six months of training, Orvill Raines had finally arrived at the war on the far side of the world.

---

7 September 1944

Hello, My Darling Baby:

Well, today you have been celebrating my birthday. I am another year older and hope that when I get back I can double up my attention to you and make up for the time I've been away.

I'm very well, physically speaking, and getting along fine. I had a good steak tonight. Somehow the cook slipped up and left it over the fire too long and it turned out edible. It sure was nice to dig into it and clean it up.

There isn't much to write about except the very nice time I had last night and tonight. (Which will sort of give you an idea of what we consider entertainment.) We had a movie last night on the forecastle (you know, that's the bow. Way up forward under the stars). The breeze blew very gently and it was actually enjoyable sitting there, even waiting between reels.

---

2. For an overview of the Admiralty campaign, see Ronald Spector, *Eagle Against the Sun: The American War with Japan* (New York: Free Press, 1985), 280–285.

Yesterday afternoon I did some manual labor for a change and my back was sore this morning for my efforts. I went with a working party and helped load a barge with ammunition. And let me tell ya sister, I got tired. Today I went on another and helped handle pogey bait [candy] for our gedunk stand (ship's service) [store]. Why do I do such things?? Just wanted to get off the ship, I think.

This afternoon we had a swimming "party" off the fantail. The fantail is the aftermost portion of the ship and naturally sits lowest in the water. We jumped in and climbed out again and in again in the usual manner in which one goes swimming. The water was more salty than I've swum in before. It burned my eyes. I gather that it is caused by our swimming in a bay that apparently has no river or streams flowing into it. Tonight one of the boys (the one that plays the accordion) was on the forecastle playing and we sang while waiting for the picture to begin which was held up for the Captain who was in the ward room playing cards. We enjoyed it very much and the harmony was better than I expected. Last night we saw "They all Kissed the Bride" and tonight "Jamboree," the latter a corny git-fiddle affair that naturally appealed to me considerably.

Honey, have you seen "Four Jills in a Jeep" yet? I saw it the other day after being at sea a week or so and Alice Faye sang "You'll Never Know." I damn near cried. She really moaned it out. We have some recordings aboard of radio programs. You know, like the fifteen-minute jobs we had at WFAA? They are recordings of entire 15-minute programs and the radio shack plays them over our local crew's address system. In one an orchestra and chorus play and sing an arrangement of "Begin the Beguine." One of the radio operators is a bug on that song almost as bad as I am, therefore we hear "Begin the Beguine" quite frequently.

I received a birthday card from Laura and a little note. Also a letter from Harry Whistler. I know where he is now from his navy number. You remember how the fellows from CNO went to Panama and wrote back with "Navy 121" as their address. That's the way Harry's address is arranged. I looked it up in a book and know where he is. He gave me all the dope. (Dope that no one but Navy would use.) I hope to see him one of these days. He would be the first real friend I've seen since leaving home. I'm not anywhere near him now but think I might get up there in a few weeks or months.

Oh, yes, Darling, I got the five bucks o.k. I don't know how to tell you, but I sure got a laugh out of it. There isn't a darn thing I could use it for except for padding perhaps. There is no way of spending money out here except sometimes trinkets and gadgets can be bought from ship's service on other larger ships. I've tried a couple so far and had no luck. Cute about you stating not to open it until my birthday on the envelope. So I saved it until today. ...

I guess this is all Darling. There isn't much to write about except what I've covered. I'll go through your letters soon and answer any questions that might have come up. Please forgive me honey if I blow off about little incidental things. I love you so much that any infraction on your peace and normal living angers me considerably. I worship you my baby and someday I'll be able to whisper it into your cute little ear again. And on the dance floor at the Plantation too. Bye for tonight Darling and remember that I'll love you forever. Believe that.

> Your devoted husband,
> Orvill

P.S. I LOVE YOU!!!

---

12 September 1944

Hello, My Darling Baby:

We are at sea again. We expect to make port tomorrow so I am going to start this today in hopes that I can squeeze in enough words to justify your opening your mail to read it. It seems that every time we go to sea, I get hundreds or thousands more miles away from you. But my heart is still there Ray Ellen. My heart feels exactly the same way it did when I left you. The same way when I was made to come home to you and hold you and go into the dining room arm in arm to sit down to one of those wonderful meals you can cook so good. I still feel that my life would end if anything happened to the girl I love. No, not love, it's beyond that. Worship is the nearest word but it still fails to record the tremendous love I have for you Darling.

Every day I concentrate more and more on getting back to you. Lately we have passed over the scenes of many memorable sea battles.

Places named with Iron in them. Named so because of so many ships on the bottom. And, thank God, most of them are Japs.[3]

We get closer to battle each day. And as we approach, the men are withdrawing more to themselves. Conversation goes on as before but it is conversation between touchy men. Answers are short when rubbed the wrong way and that is frequent. Everyone seems too withdrawn within themselves. They are thinking too much about themselves. Officers (new to this) and men alike are afraid. If they thought more about the other fellow, they would be much happier. I wonder why so many people can't understand the happiness they can derive from making others comfortable or happy? If these men thought more of the other fellows (and not so much on the means of saving themselves alone) it would take their mind off themselves and the depression would lift somewhat.[4]

Somehow I'm not afraid as I gather the other men are. I won't say that I'm not getting all the details down that go toward survival in this damn realm of madness. I have just as much or more to go back to as any man on the ship. I feel it a great duty and responsibility to get back. God has given me the happiest life man could ask for and I'm going to give with everything I've got to get back to it. And I will in spite of the devil unless God sees fit that I've had my share of happiness. As I've said so often before, Darling Baby, the happiness I've had the five years I spent with you is more than many thousands of men and women have in a lifetime. You are a holy gift to me and I reverently thank God for giving this miserable mortal such a wonderful wife for my very own. The greatest gift to mankind is happiness and He gave to me from a cup that runneth over. I thank Him again for the appreciation with which I enjoy it so much. Thanks also go to you My Darling. But I plan a more appropriate way of doing it than on paper.

----

3. Raines was referring to Ironbottom Sound between Florida and Guadalcanal islands, the scene of four major battles between U.S. and Japanese naval forces during August to November 1942. Raines was mistaken in writing that "most of them are Japs"; one Australian, fifteen Japanese, and twenty-one U.S. ships went down in the sound, including the destroyer *DeHaven*, sunk by Japanese aircraft, and *Makikumo*, sunk by a mine on February 1, 1943.

4. A study of ground troops destined for the invasion of Normandy revealed an increase in "feelings of insecurity and irritability" during the period before combat; Swank and Marchand, "Combat Neuroses," 237.

Hello again, Darling:

I've got to finish up and get this in the mail. We're so damn far from civilization I'm afraid you'll never hear if I don't get this in the mail now.

The most important thing I want to say anyway is that I love you. I worship and adore you with all my heart. God Bless you Baby Darling. And until I can do better, please believe that this letter carries to you all the love any man can bestow on a woman.

Your devoted husband,
Orvill

P.S. I LOVE YOU!!!

---

16 September 1944

Hello, My Darling Baby:

Well, I think we will hit port about Monday so will try and get a letter off to you.

Darling, I'm sorry if I'm short on these letters but believe me, I'm trying awfully hard. And the most important thing I want you to believe is that I love you. I love you so much that I think of you constantly and worship the memory of having you as my pride and joy. Things aren't so nice over here now and sanity is pretty hard to keep.

A little thing that stays in my mind is a scene I saw on the beach the other day. They were bringing back the boys to a base near the line. The fellow that impressed me was a young fellow about twenty years old. A beautiful tan shone on his chest where his shirt was open. He was good looking, shorter than I and had a perfectly developed physique. His left arm was torn up from wrist to shoulder and he was half-walking and half-supported by two buddies. He had a stupid stare out of his eyes; a sort of madness and his sobbing nearly tore my heart out. They had just debarked from a small boat and they were staggering up the rusty steel pier. His companions didn't say a word to anybody, just looked straight ahead and carried him along with no choice of evading the man's crying.

That isn't much compared to the many much more serious cases, but the look in his eyes and his sobbing has worried me considerably. He presented a case of murdered young manhood of America. I wish the people of the United States and those union devils and high wage workers[5] that I loathe so intensely could see their boys coming back. The American people can't realize what they are into. I know, because I didn't either.[6]

Honey the enclosed letter was intended to be mailed to you last Tuesday but the facilities were inadequate. So I'm mailing it now. I am sorry I can't do better but when the day comes for me to actually show you how much I worship you, my darling baby will realize that she fills my heart so completely that there isn't room for anything else. You will realize how important you are to me. I am like a lost child without you Ray Ellen. Can you imagine a little two-year-old kid lost in the Christmas crowd, its momma running around trying to find it and the baby too bewildered even to cry? That's your full grown husband, Darling, feeling like a two-year-old urchin in a world that is going in circles. What chance have I, one who depends on you so much, to keep myself straight and on the path of sane thinking. Honey, things are so remote now that I can't get them organized. It's not that there's anything wrong with me or the war has affected my thinking. It's just that my memory can't connect these far-flung things with the past very well. Of course it will all come back to me immediately when I get back on good ole U.S. soil. Now I look at your picture to bring me back to the most real and wonderful thing that ever happened to me. Your face looking at me Darling does wonders for my morale. I get to thinking about the attacks against the Japs and how

---

5. Raines's bitterness toward high-paid defense workers parallels Mauldin's expression of soldiers' hostility toward civilians at home: "[The soldier] is naturally going to get sore when he thinks of selfishness at home. He got just as sore at the big company which was caught bribing inspectors and sending him faulty armor for his tanks as he did at the workers who held up production in vital factories. He doesn't have time to go into economics and labor-management problems. All he knows is that he is expected to make great sacrifices for little compensation and he must make these sacrifices whether he likes it or not. Don't expect him to weigh the complicated problem before he gets sore. He knows he delivered and somebody else didn't"; *Up Front,* 128. See the cartoon of Willie, with pick and shovel in hand, under military police guard, as a result of trying "one of them labor-management argyments wit' Lootenant Atkins"; ibid., 129. For a discussion of combat veterans' hostility to those who have not shared their plight, see Grinker and Spiegel, *Men Under Stress,* 186–188.

6. Americans' misconceptions were heightened by the presentation of the war in the movies, controlled by the government; see Fussell, *Wartime,* 190–192, as well as Basinger, *The World War II Combat Film,* and Koppes and Black, *Hollywood Goes to War.*

much longer the Germans will hold out. I just live and dream of the day I'll step off the train into your arms. Only I'm afraid darling that I'll be so happy that I'll be too weak to raise a hand. Just to look at your face again and I'd be the happiest man in the world. You can't realize how much I love you. Ray Ellen, you are wife, mother, God and life to me. I worship you till the "ends of the earth." You are the only woman in the world that is as pure and wonderful as you are.[7] There is, in my opinion, no one that can be as true as you are. Of course I know you aren't the only one that is faithful to her husband.[8] But that other thing I told you about that was so important to me. You know, the first thing a guy wants in a wife. That, coupled with all your wonderful characteristics, has made "a believer" out of me. I believe that I have the most wonderful wife in the world. She has done more for me by being a sweet believing person that believes in me and thinks I am going to amount to something someday. I will darling if you keep pouring those sweet endearing words at me that always did make me do a better job of reporting than I would have without them. I am making big plans Baby Doll. I am going to college, I am going to have an education and you are going to be proud of me. I am going to write like a demon and the right people will know me. (The ones that buy the stories.) I am going to be a red-hot reporter for about four more wonderful years with you and then I'm going to get into something else, I don't know what it'll be but it will be something that will buy my sweet little baby a house any size she wants (with a fish-wading pond), a big nice car of her very own (unless she demands to hold onto that little green job and then I'll get her a 100% perfect overhaul job), a diamond ring big enough that she'll have to wear a sling for her arm.[9] I want to see those lights dance in her eyes. I want to hold her in my arms while we dance together and she tells me how much she loves me. I just want you, that's all. Baby Darling, I wish I could see you.

---

7. See Grinker and Spiegel, note 18 in the Introduction. According to Holmes, "the process of basic training, and the subsequent welding of the individual into a unit, will have gone some way towards giving the soldier a military identity in which home and family are of diminished importance"; *Acts of War*, 79. This was less true of older, married servicemen like Raines. Also, Raines's newspaper background allowed him to enter the naval reserve as a petty officer and forgo basic training.

8. Swank and Marchand found that servicemen en route to combat increased their demands for love and fidelity; "Combat Neuroses," 237.

9. Another expression of an idealized postwar existence, see Grinker and Spiegel, note 20 in the Introduction.

Just to see you would be so wonderful. I know I will soon but that
(even an hour) is too long to wait. I want to touch you, maybe kiss
those beautiful slender fingers. They are so pretty and smooth and
shaped exactly perfectly. Every inch of you is perfect though and I love
every cell of your body. Every little atom is a sweet and precious thing
to me and I want you watched after down to the last tiny detail. You
are so precious and innocent I want you to stay in the soft cloud where
I have you. There, no rough edges will hurt you. You can lay back in
the soft mist and never get tired again. When the day comes that I can
provide you with all material things that I want, then you'll never be
without a thing you want. Every little wish will be carried out. (Except poking me in the ribs when I stretch.) Oh, Darling, I'm rattling on
like an insane man. But I AM insane when it comes to you. I always
have been and I know that as long as I live, I will love you so much
that I'll be insane the rest of my life. It is so wonderful to be crazy,
crazy in love with you. You return my love so completely that nothing
I ever did for you or to you would make any difference. That's the way
I feel toward you too. Nothing you could ever do could change my
love. I guess, Baby, you have me on your hands till that day when we
go beyond all these things to find our real rest. I just hope that I can be
as good as you are and not miss the train. I'm going to try very hard.
I've got to be with you.

17 Sept. (Sunday)
(Can't tell Sunday from July)

Good Morning, Sweet Baby:

Well, we have just secured from morning G.Q. or dawn alert. That's
when we get up about, well, sometime before daylight and keep a
sharp lookout for the enemy. We keep that watch until after sunup so
as to be ready during the danger period of the day.

It sure is hard to climb out of the sack too and climb four flights of
ladders. These damn ladders seem perpendicular at 5:30 in the morning.

Well, Baby Doll, here it is this afternoon now. Or rather evening. I
was interrupted again as usual but I am determined to get this letter
off when we tie up tomorrow. Don't know how long we'll be in but I
know for certain that the mail will get off.

Oh, Yes, Honey, don't worry about me anymore. I am fine. I guess
it's o.k. to tell you this. But I wasn't worried, scared or even bothered

by my first encounter with a fight. It was the coolest, calmest crew I ever saw in action. Orders of the Officers, petty officers and the action of everyone was superb. We all just took enough time to assure ourselves that our life jackets were where we put them. (It was too unexpected to have them on.) I stood at my post like a high-strung horse ready to take off (funny but that's exactly what I thought of at the time). Mind, body and soul of all those around me were consumed in the desire to do the job exactly right. And they did until it was over. There wasn't a hitch. And I'm proud to be one of them. I hope they continue to show the same caliber when we are really on the receiving end. This other was offensive with only a strong possibility of having been fired on. (Torpedo.)[10]

Well, to get on. Darling, that dictionary I mentioned for Christmas for me in the V-Mail[11] letter (mailing it at the same time) I want you to keep it home. I don't think I made it clear in that letter. I have completed the arrangements for your Christmas. Sure hope they go through. They are so uncertain out here. Anything can happen. But there's one gift I'm sending that I am especially proud of. I know you will be crazy about it. I will explain all about it with a letter in the same package. Now don't you open any of them until December 25th. That's an order. From the boss. I'm just bluffin'. ...... YOU is de boss! But I'm serious, no opening packages until you get 'em off the tree at Mom's. Incidentally, Honey, one package should come to you on Xmas day on Bishop. It will have to be gotten quick or it'll lose some of it's value. Maybe you ought to kinda drop by there during the morning. (I'm assuming of course that you'll spend the night at Mom's like always.) Maybe you can have a neighbor take it for you and call you on the telephone. Honey, I'm trying to make you a ring out of a half-dollar. It will be just plain silver. Do you think you could wear one like that? I'm sure it will turn out like the old fashioned wedding band but maybe you can wear it for something. I wanted to make it just to be working at something for you. I like to do that.

---

10. Raines was describing a submarine alert. There is no mention of this incident in *Howorth*'s confidential *War Diary*.

11. V-Mail was intended to reduce the bulk of mail to and from service members overseas. Letters written on V-mail forms were photographed and the film sent to distribution centers and reproduced. The copies were reduced in size, often making them difficult to read.

Honey, I hope the folks won't mind my sending you a Xmas present (they are plural though) and not sending anyone else anything. I'm sure they'll understand though. There was nothing to send them.

Oh, yes, the enclosed cards are self explanatory. We crossed long enough ago that their value isn't of much use now. No, I'm not going to send them. Will wait until later. I want to be sure it's all right.

Yes, you are right in assuming that I will be in on the Philippines. I guess everybody in the Pacific will be in on it. I'm not sure of course, no one is sure of anything, but New Guinea isn't so far so think maybe we'll be there too. It's a big fight out here now but Baby I mean the big boys are working on them now! We really have them on the run and their fight is a rapid losing one. This war will be over soon Darling and the *Howorth* gang will be the fightingest bunch in the PacFleet [Pacific Fleet] to get home. Yeoman Raines will be the fightingest sailor on the *Howorth* too! If you can hold on a little longer like I'm struggling to do, we will be happy again in another year. We still have a year and three and a half months left of my prediction. Hang on darling, I'll be back and devote all my energy to you.

As for being out here. Well, it was a hard go getting on to the ways and adjusted to being away from you. I'll never be adjusted to that nor get used to it. You will be the thing foremost in my mind forever. But I am getting a kind of enjoyment of being in on it. Freedom is a wonderful thing. And knowing when we whip these bastards all these boys will be going back to people like me going back to you. We won't have any fear of being treated like China is today. She has been raped and struggling with that Japanese demon for a decade now and soon will be free again.[12] Think how horrible it would be for that to happen to our people. We men folks couldn't bear for it to be done. We would all go mad and try to tear the entire world apart. And of course it would end in failure. I shudder to think of you being in the hands of one of them. And consequently, I get a joy out of being the man that holds a piece of iron in his hands that helps kill them. I don't shoot a gun, no one does the actual firing on here. We *all* do it. Everyone is directly concerned with getting the steel and explosives out. I get that feeling of doing my

---

12. Contrast this sympathy for China with the racist wartime song "The Japs Don't Have a Chinaman's Chance"; Fussell, *Wartime*, 185. See the motion pictures' false portrayal of a "modern" China (more consonant with U.S. ideals), featuring Caucasian actors (e.g., Walter Huston and Katharine Hepburn) with heavily made-up eyes, in Koppes and Black, *Hollywood Goes to War*, chapter 8.

part and when I get home I'll feel that I helped my country pull
through a rugged time. I'll feel that I helped protect my own home and
precious wife. Honey, I'd fight the entire Japanese Army and Navy
alone as long as I lasted for you. It's funny what a guy will do for a
woman. I love you so deeply and appreciate your love for me so much
that I'd do almost anything for you and to keep your love.[13] I hope I
never do the wrong thing and hurt someone else.

Well, I must close now. Ray Ellen, all my love is for you. I worship
you and adore you. It will truly be a wonderful day for me when I get
home to my waiting wife. Our lives will resume on their normal
course and I promise you a brighter future. One as bright as the four
and a half beautiful years we belonged to each other. And my damnedest efforts will be toward making them even brighter, if that is possible. Bye for now Baby Darling and remember that I love the hell out of
you and miss you like hell. I'll love you till I draw my last breath. I am
forever,

Your devoted husband,
Orvill

P.S. I LOVE YOU!!!

---

21 September 1944

Hello, My Darling Little Baby:

Tonight I am going to sit up until midnight if necessary to get a decent letter off to you. Although there is so little I can say. I am going to
go through your letters again and try to answer some of the questions
in case you asked any.

First off, I got a real bang out of that damn alarm clock business.
Honey, I'm going to buy a new one as soon as possible. If we don't,
we'll spend the next twenty years jumping in and out of bed to check
on that darn "thing," whether it's pulled out or not. Baby, that mention in your letter gave me my first real belly laugh in weeks. I can just

---

13. This corresponds to one of the common wartime fears Grinker and Spiegel identified: "loss of something that is loved, highly prized and held very dear"; *Men Under
Stress*, 120–121.

see you. Just wish I were there to argue with you to see who gets up to check.

Boy, is it hot here! I can almost throw a stone and hit the Equator. My fingers are slipping off the keys, the perspiration is flowing so freely. I guess I'll be able to tell you about the heat. I will enclose your "synthetic cards" this time. I reckon it's o.k. now. You couldn't tell where we are now from that. Anyway, I had my head shaved completely as a result of that initiation. I am a qualified shellback and to become one was one of the hardest beatings I ever got. I'll try to give you detailed dope one of these days. Anyway, I wear my hat at all times when on topside. They say if your head gets a bad sunburn, your hair won't come back in as thick as before. So you know I'm being careful! I've cut the tail out of my shirts so they won't be so hot and bundlesome stuffed down in my dungarees. The shirt is always wet with perspiration. I go up on the forecastle occasionally to let it dry. I stand in the shade of a gun and it's cool. I got my first sunburn through my shirt. My face was pretty bad after having to stand a watch on the bridge one afternoon but the pharmacist's mate kept it from blistering and peeling.

About the only recreation we get is an occasional swimming "Party" as I explained before. We "park" right around sunken Jap and American ships and we go over the side without giving it a thought. They are in deep water of course and it's sanitary.[14] Tomorrow, I get my feet on soil, terra firma, for the first time since the early part of August. That is unless we get orders tonight. We will go over and have two beers, the limit, and see and study the sand and trees and jungle. Quite interesting, I'm sure. Any, I'm looking forward to it. I will spend a total of 20¢ for a whole "liberty."

Darling, my mind keeps drifting to my favorite dream of you. (My favorite censurable dream that is.) You know what it is? Well, you know how we used to enjoy you laying your head on my shoulder just before going to sleep? That's the way I like best to pretend I have you with me. I lay down in my sack and start sweating, but I soon forget that because if I think about it real good, I can feel your head lying right on my left shoulder. If I am having difficulty getting to sleep, that helps me drop off. Your hair is so soft and sweet-smelling, your complexion just exactly right in smoothness and preciousness. If you

---

14. Raines was alluding to contamination from the entombed bodies.

could only realize how much the memory of your being so wonderful to me means to me now, maybe you could realize why I love you so much. It is almost a madness Darling. No, it isn't because we are separated and my imagination has made you more beautiful or anything to me. I have always loved you with a sort of insane ache in my chest. It aches now and every time I think of you, which is too often for me to have much peace.

I just looked over your birthday card to me (the one with "you" and "me" all over it). I am going to save it and the other one. They are really precious.

I got some magazines from you today. Four funny books and a "Gags" book. No, the Reader's Digest bunch didn't arrive yet. Boy, you should have seen me dig into those things after I read your letters. One of which was the local page of the News telling about the election job of the News-WFAA-KGKO. The cookies haven't arrived yet, either.

Honey, who is Eleanor at the office? I don't remember you mentioning her. I think she's, no, the school teacher is an old maid. Sorry, can't place her.

Yes, Darling, I still tell you good night officially. More often than you'd think. But it's 12:30 P.M. today when I tell you good night officially last night. Kinda confusin' but that's the way it is. I'm usually in the mess hall eating. I stop chewing long enough when the minute hand reaches that minute and talk a little bunch of sweet nothings to you. And sixty faces and jabbering tongues can't interfere with my thoughts of you lying in bed either. Nothing interferes with my thoughts of you, Darling.

Yes, I'll send your packages to the office hereafter, although the orders for your Xmas presents went off today to "our" home address on Bishop. Hope you don't have a lot of trouble getting them. I was disappointed in the turtle. It looks so cheap, especially with that (Egad) safety pin stuck on it. Anyway, it's the closest I could come to getting a "south sea" present. ...

I am proud of you honey. Haven't I always said you could do just about anything you set yourself to do? You have a good head on you. That's one of the reasons I fell so deeply in love with you. I had to have a mate of very very high intelligence to match my own!! WOW! Anyway, I couldn't have written a nicer letter myself, and coming from me, that's something, isn't it? Honey, the longer I live, the more I love you. You accomplish so many things the ordinary housewife doesn't dream of doing. How many school girl friends of yours could walk into that office and take over the way you have? You are bound to carry out my beliefs and confidence in you, or you wouldn't be happy there at all. That's the way to judge a person's efficiency. If they are happy at their job, it means they are successful at it. I am highly suspicious of people who don't like their work.

Incidentally, I have been writing Mother more often and have V-Mails out now to almost all the kids.

Honey Baby, how about some news of Mom? How is she getting along now? She must be improving since she is sewing for you. She sure is a swell egg. ...

Well, Baby Doll, I am going to close now. I am going to retire and get a little shut-eye. You are just rising for your breakfast and dash to the office. When I get up in the morning you will be just about getting off work or eating supper. Think of me often Ray Ellen Darling. I think of you all the time. Your memory will never desert me. My natural instinct of self-preservation becomes more prominent with the thought of you. I worship you Baby, my whole body and soul cry for you. There are tears mingling with the bleeding of my heart where your precious fingers scratched it that morning. God bless you Baby Darling and remember that the life of your worshipping husband depends on your loving me forever. My life will end when you stop loving me.

> Your devoted and adoring husband,
> Orvill

P.S. I LOVE YOU!!!

September 22, 1944

Good Morning, Sweet Baby:

I just heard "Begin the Beguine" on that record I told you about. That song is a paramount in music. And every time I hear it, I think of its running mate, the paramount in literature. I'm going to send it back to you now and send it straight from the heart Baby. Just like you sent it to me on April 20th. And with it goes all the appreciation I can muster in my chest that you should say such wonderful things to me.

I Love You

I love you not only for the things you are, but for what I am when I am with you.

I love you not only for what you have made of yourself, but for what you are making of me.

I love you for putting your hand into my heaped-up heart and passing over all the foolish and frivolous and weak things that you can't help dimly seeing there, and for drawing out into the light all the beautiful radiant belongings that no one else had looked quite far enough to find.

I love you for ignoring the possibilities of the fool and weakling in me, and for laying firm hold on the possibilities of the good in me.

I love you for closing your ears to the discords in me, and for adding to the music in me by worshipful listening.

I love you because you are helping me to make of the timber of my life not a tavern, but a temple, and of the words of my every day not a reproach, but a song.[15]

I wish I could have been the one to write this, if I had written it I could say I wrote it for you. Since I didn't—may I say—I mean every word— it's someone else's way of helping me tell you why I worship you so deeply.

> I love you,
> Orvill

(Could I ever be happy without you when I feel that way about you? Can this help you to understand how much I miss and want you? God allows certain things to happen to people during their lifetimes. You are that life He has given me. Without you my life would end, both figuratively and actually. God Bless you.)

---

15. Author not identified.

24 September 1944

Hello, Baby Darling:

Well, I have some news tonight. Not much to you of course but to me it's like a visit next door at home. I went over and saw Glenn Murray, torpedoman third class, on the [USS] *O'Bannon*. As for our location, we are operating somewhere out of the Fleet Post Office, San Francisco. Gosh, Honey, you always knew where I was before but now I can't tell you. But I'll sure tell you all about it when I see you.

Anyway, I had a good chat with Glenn. He seems to be a good kid and was happy to meet me. He is much quieter than I expected. He is kinda young but very settled and a cool thinker. He appears to be the best representation LaVerne had yet.

Here's the visit: I went over in our boat and went aboard the *O'Bannon*. I was asking the OOD [officer of the deck] permission to come aboard and see Glenn when a passing torpedoman said he would take me back. His ship is exactly like ours so I didn't feel very strange. He was the only one in the torpedo "shack" and the guy took me there. I stuck my head in and told him who I was and he grabbed my hand and wrung it soundly. He is well built, about my height, and tanned to a crisp. (I'm still white as a lilly yet.) He invited me in and started to pour me a cup of coffee. When about three drops came out of the pot I told him they had the same kind of pots we have. Always empty.

A first class came in then for the conversation and after introductions, the first class put on a pot of joe. Glenn and I talked a while about as fast as you and Mom when you get together. (We got a lot of dope from each other, didn't we? Ha. Sorry sweet little Mommie, I just couldn't resist it.) Anyway, the other guy kept cutting in so I gathered they were starved for a new voice and conversation. Another guy dropped around and in about twenty minutes I counted seven torpedomen and one yeoman (myself) in a space half or two-thirds the size of your bathroom. And we were "chipping our teeth" about as fast as we could. The coffee perked enough so we all poured out half-cups of boiling coffee in the cups and juggled the damn things around; trying very hard to drink it, talk, smoke cigarettes and keep from spilling it on each other and down our own belt-buckles. Boy, Honey, that place was really a riot. All their work was caught up and we just had a grand time. I haven't had so much fun since I left the States I don't think. Except maybe the "initiation" and that wasn't fun. When intro-

duced, all the guys said: "Is this LaVerne's uncle? Well, I'll be damn."
They all call her LaVerne like they had known her always and they
tried (jokingly) several times to get Glenn to reveal her address. Saying
they were getting transferred back to the states and wanted to keep
her happy. They made Glenn dig out his pictures (a very minor job as
he was anxious as they were) and we all passed them around. They lin-
gered extra long on the one of her in the bathing suit. As they did over
the one of your legs that Dick was messing around with. Yes, I pulled
out some pictures I had of LaVerne and they made me show those of
you (I reluctantly let them see them). A friend of Glenn's met Dick in
Long Beach it seems and also was nice enough to me to be a friend of
the family's. Considering the coffee, sweat, dirt and grease that covered most of their naked upper torsos, we had a very hot time keeping
the pictures clean but managed very well. Glenn and I finally wandered off to ourselves and talked a while. I think he's a sensible kid
and wants to get home very badly. He and his shipmates have been
through a lot together and they have lost their old skipper. The new
one isn't up to the same standard and they aren't as happy. However,
he likes all the guys in the "torpedo gang" and gets along fine. He is
kinda head strong and says he could have had a higher rating now if he
hadn't been the sort to not take "guff." (As you know "ear banging" or
"apple polishing" plays a major part in getting ahead in the Navy.) (We
call it ear banging in the Navy.) After a while, I saw my boat putt-putt-
ing around nearby and had to go over and wave them in to get me. He
said he would visit me whenever we got back into port together. I
don't think we will be here long enough for me to write you again this
time. So I'm saving your letters to answer until I get back. That way
I'll have something else to write about. I think I'll give Glenn some of
the pictures I have of LaVerne. (That is, if YOU aren't on the same
ones.) He, by the way, knew your name. Did you ever meet him? I
guess LaVerne wrote him about you so much he remembered. He said
she wrote him about yall going places, and things. He told me LaVerne
impressed on him to "keep a GOOD lookout for my ship" but he just
pulled in late yesterday afternoon and was busy with his fish [torpe-
does] today. He wanted to come over and see the *Howorth* tonight but
couldn't get a boat, I reckon. Well, Darling, I am going to sign off now.
Be a sweet girl. I hope I didn't bore Glenn with my conversation about
you tonight. I always talk my arm off about you. That's about the only
subject that I'll talk about though. And, BABY!! you are a subject?!!

WOW!!! ..... You cute little dickens. You're the sweetest little thing that ever lived Ray Ellen. I just love the hell out of you. God how I wish I had you in my lonesome empty arms now. I'd squeeze your breath out of you. Honey, if any man in the world loved a woman the way I loved you, he must be dead now from the strain. I love you so much the pain of being away from you almost crushes me. I'd better get off the subject now little Baby Doll or I'll be going to bed lonesome and blue. I'll be going now to think about you and kiss you good night. I love you darling and will until I draw my last breath. Bye for now, I pray every night for us both. I hope it isn't selfish. I love you with my whole soul and mean it from the bottom of my heart when I say I will be forever

> Your devoted husband,
> Orvill

P.S. I LOVE YOU!!!

PART TWO

"SOME EERIE HELL"

4

Invasion of Morotai Island, Moluccas Islands

While *Howorth* was steaming from Seeadler Harbor to Humboldt Bay, U.S. forces invaded Morotai Island. The Morotai operation was a compromise reached during a summer conference at Pearl Harbor among President Franklin Roosevelt, Pacific Ocean Areas (North, Central, and South Pacific) commander Admiral Chester W. Nimitz, and SWPA commander General Douglas MacArthur. As the war developed, Nimitz and Admiral Ernest J. King, commander in chief of the U.S. Fleet, wanted to bypass the Philippines and invade the island of Formosa off the Chinese mainland, using it as a stepping-stone for the establishment of bases either on mainland China or in the Ryukyu Archipelago just south of Japan in preparation for the final invasion of the Japanese home islands. This was in keeping with the navy's War Plan Orange, refined during the 1930s.[1]

MacArthur objected to the December 1943 decision by the British and American staffs to emphasize the Central Pacific advance over a SWPA-led thrust toward the Philippines. He decried any Philippine bypass as he fervently desired to fulfill the egotistical pledge he had made

---

1. For discussions of War Plan Orange, see Russell F. Weigley, *The American Way of War: A History of United States Military Strategy and Policy* (Bloomington: Indiana University Press, 1977), chapters 12 and 13; Edward S. Miller, *War Plan Orange: The U.S. Strategy to Defeat Japan, 1898–1945* (Annapolis: Naval Institute Press, 1991); John Major, "The Navy Plans for War, 1937–1941," in Kenneth J. Hagan, ed., *In Peace and War: Interpretations of American Naval History, 1775–1978* (Westport, CT: Greenwood Press, 1978), 237–262; and Spector, *Eagle Against the Sun*, chapter 3.

to the Filipino people: "I shall return."[2] The ouster of the Japanese from the Philippines would, according to MacArthur, redeem U.S. honor after the humiliating defeat there in 1942.[3] The Philippines would also provide a more suitable base of operations for the final subjugation of Japan. Appealing to Secretary of War Henry Stimson for overall control of the Pacific War, MacArthur claimed he could be in the Philippines in ten months. He chastised the navy-run Central Pacific strategy for its high losses, but as historian Michael Schaller observed, the Japanese defended the Central Pacific islands more vigorously than New Guinea since the islands could be used to launch air attacks on Japan.[4]

There had been considerable speculation over a 1944 MacArthur presidential candidacy. In early 1943 MacArthur told Lieutenant Colonel Gerald Wilkinson, Prime Minister Winston Churchill's liaison to SWPA, that he would "'respond to a nationwide appeal' from the American people to 'lead them as president in this time of trouble.'"[5] After MacArthur decided not to run in 1944, he told Roosevelt that if he wanted progress in the Pacific War before election day, island hopping to the Philippines via the southern route was the answer. MacArthur guaranteed that presidential support for his southern strategy, rather than the Central Pacific route favored by the navy, would have MacArthur landing in the Philippines "before November." If the president did

---

2. MacArthur had an effective, tightly controlled public relations organization that reinforced his high opinion of himself and successfully resisted any effort to recast his promise to the Filipino people as "We shall return." *Time* magazine correspondent Robert Sherrod characterized MacArthur as a "poser and an extreme egoist"; quoted in Michael Schaller, *Douglas MacArthur: The Far Eastern General* (New York: Oxford University Press, 1989), 65. MacArthur and his staff went to great efforts to control the outflow of information from the SWPA, ensuring that "no news left the theater unless, in the words of General Kenney, it 'painted the General with a halo and seated him on the highest pedestal in the universe'"; ibid., 72.

3. For some contemporary assessments of MacArthur vis-à-vis his command of the defense of the Philippines in 1941–1942, see Spector, *Eagle Against the Sun*, 117–119. Also see the condemnation of MacArthur in Dwight Eisenhower's diary, quoted in Schaller, *Douglas MacArthur*, 66. The commander of the forsaken 11th Division on Bataan, General William E. Brougher, expressed disgust at MacArthur's evacuation to Australia and abandonment of 20,000 Americans to "endless suffering, cruel handicap, death, or a hopeless future": "A foul trick of deception has been played on a large group of Americans by a commander in chief and small staff who are now eating steak and eggs in Australia. God damn them!"; quoted in Spector, *Eagle Against the Sun*, 119.

4. Schaller, *Douglas MacArthur*, 78–79.

5. Ibid., 77. For an assessment of the relationship among MacArthur's strategic plans, domestic politics in the election year of 1944, and the Philippine liberation plans, see ibid., chapters 6 and 7, especially 81–88.

not back him, MacArthur predicted, there would be a political backlash over failure to liberate the Philippines as soon as possible.[6]

His political aspirations and campaign for personal aggrandizement aside, MacArthur's plan to liberate the Philippines made more strategic sense. The King-Nimitz plan to invade Formosa would have involved a difficult amphibious objective (the island was ringed by steep cliffs, limiting the number of landing sites) and was close to major Japanese air bases on mainland China. Also, in September 1944 the Japanese *Ichi-Go* offensive in China overran U.S. airfields that would have supported the Formosa invasion.[7]

The September 1944 meeting of the Allied Combined Chiefs of Staff at Quebec resulted in authorization for MacArthur to invade Morotai Island in preparation for the invasion of Mindanao, the southernmost large island in the Philippines. A Morotai airfield would provide the U.S. 5th Army Air Force a stepping-stone to Mindanao and neutralize the major Japanese airfield on nearby Halmahera Island, a southern outpost of Japan's Philippine defense barrier. On September 15, 1944, the same day MacArthur's army troops and the 7th Fleet invaded Morotai, Nimitz sent the 1st Marine Division ashore at Peleliu in the Palau Islands, some 400 miles directly east of Mindanao.[8] After the Palaus were captured, Nimitz was to strike 200 miles east northeast in October and seize Yap Island and Ulithi Atoll in the Caroline Islands. The latter would serve as a major fleet anchorage. In November MacArthur and the 7th Fleet would invade the Philippines at Mindanao. In December

---

6. "The public, MacArthur told FDR, had 'forgiven' him for 'what took place on Bataan,' but would never reelect him if he approved a plan 'which leaves 18 million Christian American citizens to wither in the Philippines under the conqueror's heel'"; ibid., 87. For other historical treatments of MacArthur, see D. Clayton James, *The Years of MacArthur*, 2 vols. (New York: Houghton Mifflin, 1972, 1975); William Manchester, *American Caesar: Douglas MacArthur, 1880–1964* (Boston: Little, Brown, 1978); and Carol M. Petillo, *Douglas MacArthur: The Philippine Years* (Bloomington: Indiana University Press, 1981).

7. Schaller, *Douglas MacArthur*, 87.

8. The 7th Fleet commander, Admiral William F. Halsey, protested the invasion of the Palaus, arguing that they be bypassed. Nimitz ordered the invasion to proceed, as the invasion force was already at sea. Nimitz thought the Palaus would be needed as a staging point to get aircraft to Mindanao—poor reasoning in that Morotai served the same purpose and was closer. The resulting ground campaign for Peleliu was one of the worst in the Pacific. The 1st Marine Division suffered tremendous casualties (almost equal to the number of Americans killed on Omaha Beach during the Normandy Invasion). Perhaps the best personal account of the marine experience at Peleliu can be found in Sledge, *With the Old Breed*, chapters 1–6.

1944 Nimitz and MacArthur would then combine their efforts in an invasion of Leyte Island in the south central Philippines.

Howorth's first combat operation was to escort reinforcements to the Morotai beachhead.

Wednesday, 27 September 1944

Hello this evening, My Little Baby:

Well, Poppie is in "spitting" range of the Japs tonight. They are in front, on all sides and behind. But we've got the buffalo on them. No one is worried. (Forgot to mention, they're above and under us too.) ((A hellova lot of them are "under" us.))

I didn't know that I could get to thinking about you any more than I did before, but everything that happens I find you in the back of my mind. I guess it's so important that I get back to you. Honey, I've said this before, but I want to promise again: I'll do EVERYTHING possible to get back to you. I really love you and my life is there with you. Gosh, I worship you. I forgot to mention in my last letter about when I visited Glenn on the *O'Bannon*. He and his shipmates do not expect the war to be over out here in another year. I realize that they are in a better position to judge than I, but I still think it'll be over before January 1st, 1946. Honey, I'm putting a lot of stock in that prediction. I realize of course, that we shouldn't be too disappointed if it isn't. I mustn't allow myself too much hope in that date. The hardest part of the fight is yet to be fought. The sea is a lot safer now than it was but it's still a fight. Darling, the time for me to relieve the watch came sooner than I expected. I'll add more to this in the morning. I've got Jack Benny's show in the background, anyway, and it's really hard to concentrate on my grammar. (But not hard to concentrate on YOU.)

---

3 October 1944

Hello, My Darling Baby Girl:

Well we are all sitting around the office "shooting the bull" tonight and I'm going to try and write you a little letter. To add to the scrap of paper attached. That scribbling on the back is "pitch game" score; the "champions" (Raines and [Lyal G.] Bailey, Bosun's Mate 2/c) got de-feated twice in succession by a coxswain and first class gunners mate. Just before evening general quarters (we have dusk GQ now) we climbed up in No. 1 gun mount and started to play off a very heated argument. The argument consisted of loud take and gestures on the part of Bailey and myself trying to scare Brannon and [Raymond B.] Shepard out of playing us. Yes, honey, we do have a little fun together. I told you a long time ago that we have some good men on here. We kinda (assuming of course that I'm one of them) get together occasionally and have a card game. We laugh and carry on sometimes. We joke around about each other's rates and things like that. There isn't any happenings doing that we can chide each other about so we find the only thing left and work on that. I laugh quite a bit.

Darling, when I'm on watch at night, I can think of a million things to write. Watching the sea roll by in the wee hours of the morning. Nothing going on except to keep screening the convoy. I hang over the wing of the bridge and look straight down about forty feet into the water. The phosphorus water sparkling and all. I just stand there and dream of the wonderful girl you are. I think of the little nest egg we'll have to work on when I get home and pledge myself all the more to make up to us the maddening torture we are going through now. I know that I'll be the happiest man alive when I get you in my arms again. Please, Darling Little Baby, you are my sweet little baby girl and I pray every night that you can take it now and keep that sweet chin of yours up. That is the only thing that keeps me going at times. Knowing that you are at home waiting for me. When I see reports like in the press news the other morning about "authoritative sources" saying the war will be two or more years to finish I stomp and parade the deck like a madman. I can't think of what I'm doing and nearly run amuck. I mean that darling. Those pessimistic reports are bad for everybody on the ship. We will win soon though, I can already see that. We have been in and out of the immediate war zones a number of times without a contact of any kind. We can see fights and airplane raids on islands but we haven't fired a shot. We are walking away with it. Only the Philippines, Formosa, and Japan itself will be hard. Occasionally, like today, we get a blow but it is all minor compared to the past. A DE was sunk while convoying over a route we were on with a convoy three days ago. There were two DEs in the convoy and the other one picked up survivors and fought all day long but finally got the sub it believes. We didn't see any of it but did hear it over the radio system.[9] In the same vicinity day before yesterday we watched (3000 yards away) the Marines clean up a Jap Sampan beached near where we were patrolling. With glasses, we could see an occasional Jap jump and make a run for it and the Marines cut him down. I'm sorry I enjoy killing but I felt good to see the little insect fall.[10] As for Jap air power. The papers are not exaggerating when they say we have the air superiority. We patrolled all night a while back in a strait between a Jap island (large enough to have seven airfields) and an American held island. We were in firing range of both islands but not a Jap plane showed up except to conduct a nuisance raid over the American island. They never came within our range. They seem afraid to fire at us for fear it will reveal their guns' locations. We are in a position now to blow the hell out of them. Why we must fool around with islands that have no apparent bearing on the war I can't understand. Maybe if we take the jump into the Philippines soon we can eliminate taking all these small islands. According to the papers we are within striking distance now. And I verify that fact. We steam right into areas with Japs in front, behind and on all sides and are never bothered. (I mean major resistance.) Our planes are overhead looking after us and can take care of almost anything the enemy is able to send out. It's a little different on the beach of course, as they can hole up and fight like hell.

Well, Sweetheart, that is all for tonight I guess. Now comes the time to tell you I love you. If you notice the pattern of my letters, you will note that I save that part till last. If I get started on the subject of you, I never get any dope on paper. But Honey Baby, how can I tell you

9. Raines's chronology was off: The destroyer escort *Shelton* sank the day of this letter, not three days before. *Shelton* was hit in the stern by one Japanese torpedo off Morotai. Thirteen men were killed. *Shelton* capsized the night of October 3, 1944, while under tow by the destroyer *Lang; Lang* later sank *Shelton* by gunfire. See Theodore Roscoe, *United States Destroyer Operations in World War II* (Annapolis: United States Naval Institute, 1953), 413.

10. Raines's characterization of Japanese as insects was in keeping with American propaganda policy of portraying the Japanese as animals. Admiral Halsey referred to the Japanese as "bestial apes" and stated that "we are drowning them and burning [them] all over the Pacific, and it is as much pleasure to burn them as to drown them"; quoted in Fussell, *Wartime*, 116. See Fussell's section on "typecasting" the Japanese (pp. 116–119), including an account of the practice of collecting Japanese skulls, apparently common enough to elicit a prohibition from the commander in chief of the Pacific Fleet that "no part of the enemy's body may be used as a souvenir" (quoted on p. 117). For Western conceptions of the Japanese, see Dower, *War Without Mercy*, chapters 4–7 and the propaganda cartoons and posters on pp. 182–190.

how I love you? How can I ever realize why you were so sweet to me enough to marry me? You, of all the people in the world to choose me for your husband. I get such a stuffed head thinking about it. I know, you always say you aren't much. But you are in spite of what you think. I get a stuffed head because the woman I know to be the most wonderful girl in the world, chose me to be her husband. The privilege is something I endear more than my very life Ray Ellen. I worship every little atom of you and will do so until I die. You have captured me so completely that my very life depends on you. If anything should happen to it, my life would end. But I am happy and content my darling that nothing ever will. Keep yourself safe for me and don't take any chances that might cause you to get hurt in any way. By that I mean the pain would be more to me than to you. Be sweet my little baby and please be careful. Remember that this guy out here is still Orvill—your poppie and the same scared little guy that always worried about things and needed your help to keep going. Remember also that I will need your precious shoulder to lean on when I get back. I will have another fight on my hands to get going again and I need those wonderful words and your generous and kind confidence to make a success of it. I guess I'll sign off for tonight Baby. I'm getting "that" feeling again and it's so hard to bear that I get afraid. I'm a coward when I think of being away from you so I don't let myself think of it too much. I need you so terribly and love you so deeply. My strength will come back and I'll be able to whip anything when I get back to you though. I was never afraid to tackle anything when I was with you and I'll be the same again. Just to have you with me is enough to poke my chin out and take it like a man. It didn't hurt much either. I knew I had you to console me. Well, good night darling. I'll say so long now. Remember again that I worship you and all the good and fine things you stand for. I'll love you till death do us part Baby. Remember that always.

Your devoted husband,
Orvill

P.S. I LOVE YOU!!!

5 October 1944

Hello, Darling Baby:

Well, I have plenty of work to do tonight but we are getting into port tomorrow and I am knocking off to wind up your letter. I had to quit last night but my mind and heart is always with you so you know that I am going to write you often as possible.

Well ..... let me think back. Maybe there's something I've done to-day worth telling. Oh yes, pay day. That's not much, though. We had a fair dinner today. Fair enough (with mincemeat pie) that a machinist mate and I stole a whole pie. It reminded me of the Katzenjammer Kids [cartoon characters]. We ran off with that pie with almost every-body on the ship after us. I had it in one hand and was stiff-arming guys with the other. The MM held them off from the rear. I skidded up a wet ladder and darn near broke my neck. But the pie suffered not and I hid it before my friend Bailey (the bosun's mate I am "champ" pitch player with) found my hiding place. He is mess hall master-at-arms now and the "inner circle" gets away with murder. He just chased us to make it look good. I've still got half of it left and in about forty-five minutes am going down in the after engineroom and drink coffee with the MM and eat mincemeat pie. Ain't we the dickens though? Of course Bailey came around for HIS piece this afternoon. Some of our enjoyment though is making port tomorrow.

We are more or less back in civilization there and it is about the last geographical point where we can depend on getting mail. The whole crew is chattering like a bunch of kids. ... You know, Honey, mail is the only thing that can completely knock off work on this ship. But when the mail comes through, everything and I mean everything stops. Any motors running just have to run by themselves. The type-writers are quiet, no matter how hysteric the Exec is. Because he is hid out reading his own mail. You would think the ship had been gassed and was a derelict at sea to stroll around the decks and look at the guys. There is no movement hardly except a slight side-to-side move-ment of the head and the wind rustling the sheets of paper they occa-sionally turn over to read the next. The office is like a tomb. Then all of a sudden, everybody is almost through reading and everybody starts talking at once about what was in their letters. Of all the chatter, laughter, cursing, and other expressions of extremely mixed emotions, you never heard the like. That's the only time I ever get real mad at the kids. Right in the middle of reading your letters, they finish and start telling me all about what is in theirs. They've learned now to wait until I lay mine aside a moment before they start "chipping their teeth."

(Baby, looking back, I notice that the above is a rather lengthy paragraph. My english structure is suffering no doubt.)

I get to go over on the beach tomorrow afternoon for two more beers. YIPPEE!!! Good old dry, choking dust, stinking sweat and filthy bodies. I'm going over tomorrow though to try and buy some Jap or Dutch money for you. I'll try to get enough so you can give a piece or two to Dr. Scanland if she wants it. You see the Marines and Army at Hollandia use Dutch money. (The Jap stuff they "lift" from the "good" [dead] Japs.) We go over and they have a lot of the Dutch stuff and we buy a Dutch buck for 57 cents American. The Jap coins (no bills) are harder to get. There isn't much of it. We don't go into the town of Hollandia nearby. We'd never know a town was near. All we see is a dust bowl bull-dozed out of the jungle. I'll try to send it to you as soon as the censor allows. (I'm talking about the money now.) (Boy, do I ramble! Hope you can keep up, you always have.)

Oh, yes, I got another shot in the arm today. Literally too, and not figuratively either. But I don't mind talking about this one. It was for Cholera. That particular fever seems to have a habit of wiping out the use of a whole crew within a week so they shot the stuff to us. It didn't hurt a bit. ... Well Honey, I'm going to chop this off for now. I'll try to write a little tomorrow or the next day if possible. (It'll be a V-mail.) I love and worship you Baby Ray Ellen. I think the preceding page I wrote last night will explain why I will be forever,

> Your devoted husband,
> Orvill

P.S. I LOVE YOU!!!

5

Invasion of Leyte Island, Philippine Islands

October 9–31, 1944

Japanese defense of the Philippines was complicated by the islands' geographic expanse. They expected the Americans to strike first at the southern Philippine island of Mindanao, as it was closest to MacArthur's forces. But aircraft carrier raids carried out under Admiral Halsey's command in September 1944 exposed the relatively weak state of Japanese air power in the Philippines, and the Combined Chiefs of Staff ordered Mindanao bypassed and set the combined MacArthur-Nimitz invasion of the central Philippine island of Leyte for October 20, 1944.[1]

On October 17, minesweepers arrived at the east coast of Leyte Island and began clearing the Japanese minefields in the entrance to Leyte Gulf. That same morning, amphibious landings were made on Homonhon and Suluan islands on the eastern edge of Leyte Gulf and on larger Dinigat Island, which separated the southern end of the gulf from the Philippine Sea. These islands were captured by midday on October 18, and the naval bombardment force then entered the gulf and shelled the landing beaches.

The invasion of Leyte Island consisted of a two-pronged attack. The Northern Assault Force entered San Pedro Bay, which separated northeastern Leyte from adjacent Samar Island. The goal of the Northern Force was the seizure of the town of Tacloban and its nearby airfield for use by the U.S. 5th Army Air Force. The Southern Attack Force's objec-

---

1. I am drawing primarily on Morison's account; see Samuel Eliot Morison, *The Two-Ocean War: A Short History of the United States Navy in the Second World War* (Boston: Little, Brown, 1963), chapter 14. Also see Spector, *Eagle Against the Sun*, chapter 19.

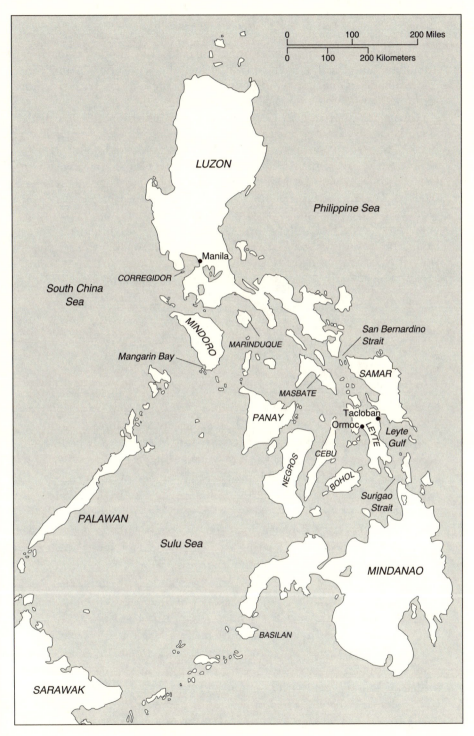

0   100   200 Miles

0   100   200 Kilometers

LUZON

Philippine Sea

● Manila

CORREGIDOR

South China Sea

MINDORO

MARINDUQUE

Mangarin Bay

San Bernardino Strait

SAMAR

MASBATE

Tacloban ●

PANAY

Ormoc ●

LEYTE

Leyte Gulf

CEBU

NEGROS

BOHOL

Surigao Strait

PALAWAN

Sulu Sea

MINDANAO

BASILAN

SARAWAK

THE PHILIPPINE ISLANDS

tive was the town and airfield of Dulag, located 20 miles south of Tacloban. Both the Tacloban and Dulag airfields were under Allied control when *Howorth* arrived in Leyte Gulf on October 22 with the first reinforcement convoy for the Northern Attack Force.

During the approach to Leyte, Raines and his shipmates had little sleep because of numerous air alerts and fears the ship would hit a mine. Those who could, slept on deck in order to avoid being trapped below. Although *Howorth*'s stay in Leyte Gulf was short, it was long enough for Raines to observe the death of one U.S. pilot and be mesmerized by the menacing beauty of antiaircraft fire from U.S. ships. *Howorth* left Leyte Gulf to escort empty transport ships back to the support base at Hollandia, New Guinea. From Hollandia, *Howorth* sailed to Kossol Roads in the Palaus and then on to Guam to shepherd the army's 77th Division to Leyte as reinforcements for what would prove to be a lengthy, and costly, campaign.

[Undated, written between October 17 and 19, 1944]

Hello, Baby Darling:

Well I can't think of anything to write you but I want to write you something. It makes me feel kinda close to you and that's where I'd sure like to be right about now. I thought of you a while ago up on the bridge. I mean I thought of now nice it would be if you were here. George and I were sitting on the flag-bag watching the sunset. Before it was gone, with the flaming flow still in the sky, the planet Venus came out and it is the brightest light I have ever seen in the sky. It brought to mind the way we move out here. Moving is a new revelation to me. You know how we drive like mad in order to cover ground in the car. Out here we are poking along at about ten knots and yet our destination draws nearer each hour. Our mileage meter can clock up to ten thousand miles and then it turns over and starts again. Last night on the midnight till 4 A.M. watch I watched it turn over for a new start, the fourth since we first left Bremerton last May. Where the planet Venus comes in, is night before last I watched her grow brighter at dusk. Our navigator (my favorite officer on board and my connection with whom is "navigator's yeoman") came out on the wing of the bridge and "shot" her [with a sextant]. Last night he did the same thing. It seemed that she had moved a few inches toward the beam. Tonight she seemed almost a beam of us when he came out to giver

[give her] the glass [sextant]. Our constant, never ending progress forward seems to cover the territory very efficiently. You see, no matter
what time you go outside, the water is going by day and night, day and
night, never stopping until we get where we are going. We eat, read,
work, sleep and watch movies. But the ship is moving on ahead without hesitation because all our needs are aboard. Except our hearts of
course and they can never be satisfied until the wounds in them are
healed by the gentle pressure of our loved ones against our chests.

It wasn't black dark tonight when I climbed down the ladder to the
radio-shack. I was impressed by the shadows and silhouettes that
make up our ship after dusk has settled. We are just a darker spot on a
dark ocean. We try to slip over the water as black and silently as possible. But try to imagine a large ship hiding on the surface of the ocean
with nothing to get behind. Imagine a giant shadow with many eyes
glued to binoculars looking out. Our chances are good. The radar is a
miraculous thing. It sees for us, tells us whether it is friend or foe.[2] But
the final test is the human eye that actually sees another black spot
doing the same hide-and-seek measures we are. Our cautious headway
reminds me of a comic cartoon in which a black-coated man darts
from tree to tree at midnight. Many of the trees having those funny
arms and hands and grotesque faces children imagine. Their eyes sine
[shine] across the picture and fearfully glance from side to side. That's
us now. But comes the dawn, nothing can hide from the enemy, nor he
from us. And I believe that with the coming of daylight, many factors
will be decided. Venus must move abaft of the beam before that daylight actually comes but we are now very cautious lest the false dawn
betray us: We are taking men to their doom. As sure as the screws are
churning us through the water, the men riding the ships I watch day
after day are going to their death. Not all of them of course. Many of
them are the shadows darting through the trees and with their brains,
hands, hearts and blood will light the dark forest so that no man need
ever slip from pillar to post and avoid the uncertain destruction that
haunts a man's mind as he progresses through the probing eyes of the
trees. The fact that we are taking many men to a place where they are
to be slaughtered worries me Baby Doll. I know there's no responsibil-

---

2. Raines was referring to the Mark III IFF (identification—friend or foe) interrogator
antenna located atop *Howorth*'s radar antenna. IFF could identify friendly aircraft by their
special coded transmissions.

ity attached to me but the idea is so depressing. Some of my shipmates may not get through the forest.[3] We are still what we consider to be on the lucky end. And we don't fear anything but the three days and nights we'll be at G.Q. Honey, this isn't a very good bed time story, is it? If you notice, I didn't date it and don't believe I can mail it even but I just had to kinda talk to you tonight. I'll try and see if it can be passed. Anyway, thanks for paying such nice attention to me. You always have been such a good listener and now I feel much better. Thank you Darling.

> Your devoted husband and
> worshipping sweetheart,
> Orvill

P.S. I LOVE YOU!!!

Evening, October 20th

Hello, Sweet Baby Doll:

Well, this evening we are playing tag. The strange part of it is, we don't know yet who is "it." A Jap sub has picked up our convoy and annoyed it since noon. The news is wonderful from the beach ahead of us. "Everything according to plan." Yet we've got this little thing worrying us all. Tonight may reveal many things to us. We been steaming along peacefully but today a Coast Guard Frigate[4] made contact. He dropped a pattern of depth charges, sending huge mushrooms into the air that were much higher than the mast tops of the Frigate. His efforts failed it seems and the Captain was ordered to continue his search for the sub "indefinitely." In other words, the convoy commander wants all efforts expended to prevent the sub from getting in our midst tonight and playing hell with the ships. He can shoot in any direction and hit something. And it is more practical to pick off the escorting vessels first. And he has been playing around about ten miles

---

3. This was typical of Swank and Marchand's findings with regard to the soldiers earmarked for the Normandy invasion: "The soldier frequently expressed by word or in letters, that, although his comrades might become casualties, he would come through alive"; Swank and Marchand, "Combat Neuroses," 237.

4. During the war the coast guard was absorbed into the navy, coast guard ships operating with the navy in both the Atlantic and Pacific.

off on our side of the convoy. I'm not worried about it much but tonight will sleep with my clothes on and with the fireproof mattress
cover intact. The fireproof cover must cover the mattress at all times
and it will take about ten seconds to cover it if I take it off and that is
too long. Many of the men seem to have strained expressions but
nothing like the movies would portray them to be. You see, the sub
being here reveals our location and destination to the Japs ahead. They
know we are here now in addition to the ones that hit Leyte this
morning. They don't want the reinforcements we are bringing to arrive. They don't have many planes it seems but their sub, PT boat and
mine warfare is pretty effective. We can expect all of the above mentioned attacks. But Honey Baby, none of it is worrying me! I can't figure myself out except that my always boastful way of saying I'm not
afraid of anything is true. And if it is true, it is as much of a surprise to
me as anyone else. Our chances are no better than the other fellow's of
course but somehow I believe we will have no trouble. At least I sure
hope so. I also hope we can get a little of our heavy ammunition cargo
over the side too. About as fast as the guns can poke them out. Well,
Darling Baby, this is all for this evening. We must go to general quarters soon and watch the sun go down. Don't worry about me Baby
Doll. We'll see if the pigboat [submarine] boy is scared tonight or if he
will give us a pyrotechnic display with American bodies framing the
picture. Good night officially, now Baby. I love and worship you. My
dreams and memories of you do wonders for me. Thanks for being
you.

Your devoted husband,
Orvill

P.S. I LOVE YOU!!!

---

22 October 1944

Hello again, Baby Darling:
    The sub shoved off last night.
    I'd kinda like to talk to you again tonight. It's 2:30 A.M. Sunday, and
I'm sitting in the office and doing a lot of thinking about you. I haven't
been asleep yet and don't expect to get any tonight. We are progressing
slowly through very dangerous waters. We have an enemy held island

on our starboard and an enemy held island on our port. It is the only way in here and the Marines landed some hours ago to prevent our being subject to bombardment by shore batteries. It is pitch dark outside. I've been watching the ships all around us. A moment ago we almost rammed a huge troop transport in the darkness. When we began signalling, their light seemed almost in our faces. Fortunately, a collision was avoided by swift communication and skillful maneuvering.

Our greatest danger is from untethered mines. As I said we enter between two islands. Mine sweepers came in ahead of us and swept out the channel. They couldn't get all of them of course and a few are floating about with a small part of them exposed above the surface and no line holding them steady. They are floating with the current, back and forth. The Captain has been working himself to distraction tonight. He nor the Navigator will get any rest until we have safety assured. As for the Japs; they have had the hell beat out of them again. Our air support bombs, kills and destroys constantly. They have no opposition in the air. All the Japs can do is retreat and die. They are doing an encouraging amount of both. Down below in the mess hall, some of the men are still playing cards. They may as well. At 8 P.M. last night, I went down to go to bed and to sleep. My mind wasn't bothered about the mines; feeling that one place is as good as another. I passed by Bosun friend with whom I play pitch and he asked me to help take on two other fellows. I told him I was going to bed and the bunch was very surprised. They talked to me and were so damned frightened they couldn't go to bed, that soon I began to worry. I began thinking how close my bunk is to the hull. (I sleep with my head less than twelve inches from the water and two feet below the waterline.) (Just the exact position for a mine knob to scrape along and go off.) Soooo. ... the Bosun and I beat our opponents eight games out of ten. I hesitate to think what would have happened had a log or box scraped along our side during the game. (You can hear them bump and scrape.)

I got up once to go to the toilet and had to pass through two sleeping compartments. Everyone had his mattress cover and all his clothes on. I walked quietly naturally, until I heard low buzzing bits of conversation. Upon closer investigation, I found not one man asleep. A while ago I went up on the bridge and tried to sleep on the flag-bag. (George was on one and I on the other.) It began raining and George disappeared, so did I. After soaking the bag, it quit raining and I came down to talk with some of the boys on "mine lookout" near one of our guns.

Barely discernable up on the very tip of our bow, stood the most frightened man on the ship. He is the foc'sle lookout and is looking so hard his eyeballs are almost poking completely through the binoculars. (And not that I blame him.) It was then that I got my first real scare. I was talking with the boys and suddenly, a very strong, bright and quick flash lighted up the entire ship. Our guns hadn't fired and I instinctively ducked. Light is bad for night steaming. I felt that a bomb had hit somewhere and I hadn't been able to hear it. It seemed to come from right between the guy I was talking to and me. I thought perhaps my hearing had been shattered because I heard nothing. I only ducked for a quick instant and learned my mistake just as rapidly. At any rate, when I arose to a standing position I was alone. No less than eight men had completely vanished without a sound! Then I saw them straggling back very cautiously and the first one said "God Damn, what was that?!!" It was decided that our tension with the help of a quick-flash of lightning had scared the hell out of us.

Now Darling, I think I'll go to sleep up here on the desk. I have quick access to the outside in case of a hit but am one deck below this if I go to my rack. So good night officially now Sweet Baby and thanks for listening again. It does my mind a world of good to talk to you kinda. I do feel close to you when I write and close to you is where I'd rather be than anywhere in the world. I love and worship you Baby Darling, remember that forever because that is how long it will last. Bye sweetheart.

Your devoted husband,
Orvill

P.S. I LOVE YOU!!!

---

23 October 1944

Hello, My Little Baby Doll:

Well, it's all over but the shouting. And we didn't fire a shot. As a matter of fact, we haven't fired a shot since getting out of here except in practice. Wupp! No more tonight, Baby. Write tomorrow.

"Poppie"

24 October 1944

Good morning, Precious Baby:

We get into port this afternoon so will try and finish this up this morning. I haven't eaten breakfast yet and the office is kinda deserted so think maybe I can. I was about to tell you regarding the above. Before the sun rose that morning we were all on the bridge (I having slept on the desk top for three hours about). As the sun lighted our surroundings, I could see the other ships and the two islands that we had had to hang around all night, not being able to go on "in" until daylight. Everything was under control. (I'm having to omit a lot of the interesting details baby but will fill them in later.) Uncle Sam's forces seemed to have nothing to worry about. Except a few that MacArthur himself hasn't announced yet so can't do so myself. A can that came out about the time we did took two of those mines I told you about but didn't sink. She looks good as new already.[5] We saw a lot of friends when the sun did come up. By friends I mean other ships that we had operated with before. We went on in and routine took up most of the day.

About the middle of the morning, I and two other fellows got glasses up on the bridge (George too) and watched the air action over the island. It was down pretty close to the beach and we got a good view. George and I were watching together and saw them drop pamphlets. Every other plane dropped pamphlets and every other dropped bombs.[6] We decided that one plane dropped pamphlets telling the Japs they should surrender because they had no chance of survival. The other plane dropped a bomb to add the exclamation point and prove it wasn't a lie. I got a sick feeling in my stomach though when I saw one plane. It commenced its dive very high in the sky and I remarked to George how fast it was dropping. We agreed it was going straight down at about 500 miles per hour. I said "Boy, this bomb is going to hit

---

5. This was the *Fletcher*-class destroyer USS *Ross*. *Ross* hit a mine at 1:33 A.M. on October 19 and a second twenty-two minutes later. Although Raines described her as "good as new," *Ross* had to be towed back to Pearl Harbor and then to Mare Island Navy Yard in California for almost six months of major repairs. See Roscoe, *Destroyer Operations*, 435.

6. It is doubtful that leaflets were comingled with bombs. Mauldin described a 105mm howitzer outfit that expended all their leaflet shells, waited five minutes for the Germans to exit their positions for the customary leaflet/toilet break, then poured in high-explosive shells: "Psychological Warfare probably got as sore about that as the surviving Germans"; *Up Front*, 97.

hard." I watched the plane reach the point where they all "pulled out." Except he kept going. No smoke, no debris, or anything, came from the plane. He kept diving. He hit the ground going straight down at 500 miles per hour. My stomach did funny tricks and I almost dropped the glasses. One instant a beautiful plane with an educated man flying her and the next a mass of junk and a letter "We regret to inform you. ....."

Later in the afternoon, we gathered around the speakers that had been tuned to the air frequency. The planes received their instructions and carried out their missions. For instance: "Go down that road until you get to the river, by the bridge you'll see a white truck. Work that damn thing over and return to your present assignment." The next moment the guy in the plane was shooting and had his radio on at the same time. (Incidentally, the shooting sounds exactly as they record it in the movies.) The pilot reported that the truck had been "neutralized" and [he] was returning to his former mission. All very interesting inasmuch as they continually hunted the enemy down and shot him to pieces. A party climbing a ridge was wiped out by a fighter squadron that was directed to the spot by ground informants. Added to the interest was a play by play of a rescue of a pilot in the water. His plane had been shot down but he was rescued.

Just before dusk a cruiser alongside us about 1000 yards set up a bombardment of a hill, dimly seen in the distance with mist putting it in the "secondary vision" range. Another hill was between the cruiser and its target but we were in a position to see, being off to one side. She blasted away for an hour and after the first few salvos the hill was one mound of smoke and dust. We could see the cruiser firing and then changed our glasses to the hill in time to see them hit. (Again, it looked just like the movies. So you can see some of what Poppie sees, can't you Baby?) The Captain had requested earlier in the morning that we be permitted to carry out a bombardment assignment but apparently no missions within our scale came to the commander's attention. We could have used the practice nicely. It would have added interest for the crew, although it was all very interesting.

Tokyo Rose (I'll write later and explain about her in case you haven't heard of her)[7] promptly came out with the propaganda of how

---

7. Tokyo Rose broadcast propaganda to U.S. forces in the Pacific; for an account, see Masayo Umezawa Duus, *Tokyo Rose: Orphan of the Pacific* (New York: Harper & Row, 1979).

many ships the Nips had sunk of ours. We got a laugh because we
could go out on deck and see the very ships she claimed had been
sunk. At one time we heard the word that WE had been sunk. They
seem to know a lot about us but it is always bum dope. I'm writing
this because we are no longer there and our present position would be
even a mystery to them. Just don't worry about their claims. The little
bastards are being beaten to death on all sides. I've watched it with my
own eyes.

Late that evening, I got my first view of concentrated anti-aircraft
fire. It was the most beautiful pyrotechnic display I'd ever seen. And
since it was for keeps, it held a menacing sort of beauty. (Like when
you're mad at Poppie. Just teasin'.) It was especially menacing when
we couldn't tell exactly whether any of them were coming at us in the
late tricky dusk. Our lookouts again poked their eyes through the
glasses. Never once did I see them take their eyes from their glasses as
seems to be the habit when the officers aren't watching them. They
dropped a few bombs on the beach but weren't around but a very few
minutes. The fire was so heavy they couldn't get through effectively.
I'll try to explain it further when I have more time baby.

Incidentally, while I'm thinking about it. Never, since I've been
away from you, have any of your letters been censored. So don't worry
about telling Poppie all about everything. They do *not* censor mail
coming this way. They just don't want *us* having free rein on mail
going that way. We've still got a long way to go before winning this
war. But looking back to a year ago, we have come a long way. Maybe
in that next year and two months I have left to get back to you by Jan.
1, 1946 will tell the proper tale. I'm afraid now that unless more encouraging things happen in Europe that Japan will be whipped by the
time the boys over there get through. I hope they don't send them
home for leave when they finish. We need them too badly out here,
even as much as I'd like to see them get leave. They've been away better than two years now, haven't they? Joe and Russell would enjoy it
for instance. Although in their cases, I don't know what they will be
greeted with when they do return. Boy, is this war messing up a lot of
lives. But I know two that it isn't messing up. And if it lasts ten years,
I will be as sure then as I am now that My Baby and wife will be faithful to me and will stand by until I get there. We've got a lot of living to
do together and our love for each other will hold water until the
proper time for me to take you in my arms and tell you that it is all
over. The wash is done and it came out all right. It is a grand washing

but think how wonderful the payment will be when it is over. The payment is well worth it. God gave me life once, but you will give it to me again and will keep it going in happiness until we succumb to His wishes. Well, Baby Darling, I must go now. Eat breakfast and get to work keeping up my end of the washing. Be a sweet girl and don't worry about me. In spite of the danger on the surface, it isn't as bad as it appears. I love and worship you baby and soon will sit down and take about six pages to try and tell you how much. Good bye for now, God Bless You and keep you safe because you are my life.

> Your worshipping husband,
> Orvill

P.S. I LOVE AND ADORE YOU!!!

---

30 October 1944

Well, Baby, Hello:

It's been two weeks now since getting a letter from you. We left port October 16th and haven't been back to one since. I got a letter off to you a few days ago when we hit a point that would take mail out but didn't bring any in. It seems that another two weeks or more will pass before we get any mail. They didn't have any at Palau for us but we kinda expect to get some at Guam. We won't be based at Hollandia any more. I was talking to a guy in the post office in the Philippines. They haven't set up any post office there yet though. Of course I'm pacing the deck wanting mail from you but if I can get a letter off to you every week or so, I'll be satisfied.

Well, the big fight for the Navy is practically over with out here. In spite of Jap claims, their fleet is on the run and is like a dog with a can to its tail: Every jump they take the American Navy is banging away at them. The straight dope is that they're whipped. But good. And you should hear "Radio Tokyo" dish out the propaganda! Everyday our "losses" mount up. The latest from there yesterday was that we had lost nineteen carriers in five days fighting. If what Tokyo said is true, the "mighty" *Howorth* would have to win the war alone. But actually, we have plenty of company and aren't worried at all. We didn't get off without a scratch of course, according to the paper, but our losses were minor and far beneath our fondest expectations. Those slant-eyed devils just can't get any strategy through their thick skulls. Our

Navy was waiting for them and hoping they'd attack our fleet. The fleet *Howorth* is in was bait for the trap. They hoped to wipe out our force but casualties were minor. As they came after the "gravy" our boys with Halsey beat the hell out of them and they turned and ran without ceremony.[8] All this time, of course the damn *Howorth* would have to be to hell and gone from there. We didn't even get a smell. But looking over one of the cans that limped into the last port where we were, it might be a good thing. They had five inch shells all through her. All torpedoes had been fired at one Jap wagon seven had hit. A fourteen inch shell had hit her spud locker and exploded inside. That can had mashed potatoes all over the ship. It was comical but tragic too. But only a few men were lost, her bridge unscathed.

Darling, this must be all for now. I've lost so much sleep and the ship is pitching terribly. We just missed a storm yesterday and the sea is very heavy. I'm getting dizzy and "urpy" rocking back and forth in this chair, so please may I be excused now? I am going to sleep somewhere. I know this is a poor letter Baby Doll, but you understand. My health is the same; the ship is o.k. and hasn't fired a shot at the enemy yet. And it looks as if we won't. The only thing unchanged about me is my complete devotion to you Ray Ellen. Please remember that no matter how tired I am or how sick I always love you and will forever. I still think of you night and day. I love you baby darling, God, how I love you. Please don't think I'm forgetting because of a short letter. I worship you and will forever. Be sweet darling and always love me very much cause my life depends on it. Bye for now sweet Baby,

Your devoted husband.

P.S. I LOVE YOU!!!

P.P.S. Honey, today I signed the voucher for reimbursement of your travel from New Orleans to Bremerton. Wow! That damn supply department finally got that squared away. Now all you'll have to do is wait another three months and they will mail the check to you. Let me know how much it is for, please ma'am. Bye now darling. Sweet Baby, I worship you!!!!!

P.P.P.S. I LOVE YOU!!!

---

8. Raines was presenting an understandably skewed interpretation of the Battle for Leyte Gulf.

6

Supporting the Leyte Campaign

Howorth's late October escort duties to Hollandia, Kossol Roads, and Guam removed her crew from what historian Samuel Eliot Morison characterized as the "greatest naval battle of all time."[1] Despite their setbacks at Midway (June 1942) and in the Philippine Sea (June 1944), the leaders of the Imperial Japanese Navy believed that a decisive naval victory could still be won and that the concentration of the U.S. 3rd and 7th fleets' efforts at Leyte provided an opportunity to smash the U.S. invasion force and inflict a signal defeat on the U.S. Navy.

When U.S. forces arrived off Leyte Gulf on October 17, 1944, the commander of the Japanese Combined Fleet, Admiral Toyoda Soemu, ordered Plan *Sho-1* into execution. This plan called for a four-pronged advance: A decoy force, which included aircraft carriers, would serve as bait to draw Halsey's 3rd Fleet northward, leaving the Leyte invasion force lightly defended; an attack force, commanded by Vice Admiral Kurita Takeo, would sail from Malaya to Brunei, North Borneo, where Kurita detached Vice Admiral Nishimura Shoji, commanding the older battleships *Fuso* and *Yamashiro*, a heavy cruiser, and four destroyers. Kurita's force would steam to the Philippines then proceed eastward through the San Bernadino Strait to Leyte Gulf. Nishimura was to rendezvous with a cruiser-destroyer force from Japan commanded by Vice Admiral Shima Kiyohide and approach the U.S. amphibious forces in

---

1. Morison, *The Two-Ocean War*, 436, note 2. For an interesting analysis of the magnitude of the Battle for Leyte Gulf, see C. Vann Woodward, *The Battle for Leyte Gulf* (New York: Macmillan, 1947), 1–6.

Leyte Gulf from the south through Surigao Strait. Fortunately for the Americans, the Japanese operation exceeded their command and control capabilities and *Sho-1* failed.[2]

In countering *Sho-1*, U.S. destroyers were involved in several engagements with Japanese surface forces. The most disastrous battle occurred northeast of Leyte Gulf off the east coast of Samar Island shortly after dawn on October 25, 1944. Kurita's strong battleship and cruiser group successfully passed through San Bernadino Strait and steamed southward toward the lightly defended Leyte Gulf invasion fleet. The Japanese ran into six small escort aircraft carriers, three destroyers, and four destroyer escorts. In the running gun battle that followed, the U.S. force retired eastward into the wind to launch its aircraft while desperately calling for help. Intermittent rain squalls and smoke screens limited visibility, and the Japanese misidentified the small U.S. escort carriers as larger fleet carriers and the three destroyers as cruisers. Fearing that he had blundered into Halsey's 3rd Fleet—which, unknown to him, had already been suckered north—Kurita ordered a "general attack," a combination of "fire at will" and "every man for himself," which provided his ship captains too much latitude and resulted in limited tactical, but no strategic, success.[3]

During the melee, the expendable American tin cans paid a dear price for launching torpedo attacks on the Japanese battleships and cruisers in order to cover the escort carriers' retreat.[4] Kurita blamed the U.S. destroyers' torpedo attacks for separating his major units, further contributing to confusion on the Japanese side.[5] By the time Kurita broke off his attack at around 9 A.M., one U.S. escort carrier (*Gambier Bay*), two destroyers (*Johnston* and *Hoel*), and one destroyer escort (*Samuel B. Roberts*) had been sunk by Japanese gunfire. A second escort carrier, *St. Lo*, was hit by a kamikaze and sank at 11:25 A.M. Total U.S. casualties numbered 1,130 dead and 913 wounded. When unidentified battleships later appeared near a convoy *Howorth* was protecting, Raines's fear was stimulated by the battle off Samar and its demonstration of the precarious nature of destroyer service.

With the Americans committed to the land campaign on Leyte Island and naval plan *Sho-1* a failure, the Japanese concentrated their Philippine air forces in southern Luzon Island to strike the U.S. armada in Leyte Gulf. The Japanese also began to shuttle troops from other Philip-

---

2. See the account in Spector, *Eagle Against the Sun*, 429–436 and Woodward, *Battle for Leyte Gulf*, chapters 1–4.

3. For an overview, see Morison, *The Two-Ocean War*, 437–438. For Kurita's decision to break off the engagement, see Woodward, *Battle for Leyte Gulf*, 200–205.

4. See Woodward, *Battle for Leyte Gulf*, chapter 5.

5. Ibid., 183.

pine islands to Ormoc Bay on Leyte's western shore. In the last two weeks of October, the U.S. command estimated that the Japanese brought in 45,000 fresh troops and 10,000 tons of supplies.[6]

While the Battle for Leyte Gulf was going on, Raines and his shipmates were escorting transports from island to island. They went for a month without mail. On Guam Raines hunted for souvenirs amid the flotsam of the recent invasion and unwittingly stepped on the corpse of a Japanese soldier in a pillbox. At one end of the island, Japanese holdouts were still being killed.

Howorth left Guam on November 3 as part of the convoy bringing the 77th Division to Leyte. During the twelve-day voyage to Seeadler Harbor, the lack of mail and isolation from home caused Raines to wonder if his absence from Ray Ellen would transform him into little more than a memory. After a day at Seeadler for refueling, the convoy sailed on to Leyte, and *Howorth* came under air attack for the first time, a scene Raines vividly recounted to his wife. The next day, November 23, *Howorth*'s convoy anchored in Leyte Gulf, which was being subjected to regular Japanese air attacks, including kamikazes. *Howorth* spent ten days as part of the air defense umbrella in Leyte Gulf. The continual threat of air attack was enervating, and Raines became more depressed when the Japanese sank a friend's destroyer off the west coast of Leyte. In writing to Ray Ellen about this loss, he described his own plans to avoid being killed by strafing planes or hostile shore guns if he ever had to abandon ship. In doing so, Raines typified the second of Fussell's stages of rationalization and perception for World War II infantrymen regarding wounds or death: "1. It *can't* happen to me. ... 2. It *can* happen to me and I'd better be more careful. ... 3. It *is going to* happen to me. ..."[7] Raines optimistically (and naively) believed that combat

---

6. Morison, *The Two-Ocean War,* 471. For the battle for Ormoc, see Spector, *Eagle Against the Sun,* 511–517.

7. See Fussell, *Wartime,* 282. The sense of the inevitability of wounding or death is common among the men of "C" Company on Guadalcanal in James Jones, *The Thin Red Line* (New York: Charles Scribner's Sons, 1962). A classic but dated study of wartime fear is Lord Moran, *The Anatomy of Courage* (Garden City Park, NY: Avery, 1987), based upon Moran's experience as a medical officer with the British Expeditionary Force in France during the First World War. His equation of courage with morality and concern about the bravery of "town" (lower-class urban) recruits is typical of the Edwardian army; see Travers, *The Killing Ground,* chapter 2. Moran's emphasis on race as a determinant of courage (Anglo-Saxons fare better in adversity than do other ethnic groups, such as Italians, who were so afraid "they jumped overboard rather than fire a gun" during the World War II naval action off Matapan) is disappointingly Anglocentric. For Moran's brief treatment of the behavior of British sailors at war, see chapter 9. A more useful study of the effect of combat on Americans is Stouffer et al., *The American Soldier,* vol. 2, especially chapter 4.

would provide him a situation over which he would have some degree of control.

---

2 November 1944

Hello, Darling Baby:

Well, I'm sure glad I can write you 'cause it's been so damn long since I've heard from you that I'd be afraid you'd forget me if I couldn't let you know I still am here and lovin' you with all my heart alla time! Gosh, we haven't gotten any mail in three weeks now and from all indications it will be three more before we hear, cause from where we are going there will be no mail service for some time. We know that we've got bags on one of these islands but don't know which one; the hell of it is, nobody on these islands knows where we will be at any given time. Therefore, hit or miss is the watch-word.

Speaking of islands, I will try to transfer to you some of the more interesting things I've seen of late. We are in a port now just off a very famous island, Guam. Yesterday, I went ashore with a bunch of the boys for a beer party. (We hit the beach as soon as we can whenever we hit a port cause we are almost always on one-half to two hours' notice to get underway.) I was too dirty and tired last night to write but kinda knew we'd be in today; so is it o.k. that I write me mommie now?? Anyway, we have a radio station here and is in constant competition with "Radio Tokyo." They call it the Pacific American Expeditionary Forces Station, "On the Road to Tokyo." It plays a lotta music and gives us the dope on the war.

Well, I started to tell you about the trip to the beach yesterday. (Always running off my course Baby like I always have. Guess I'm too enthusiastic over this little "visit" with you.) We hit the beach early in the afternoon and saw Marines and Soldiers in their typical encampments. Not many are engaged in fighting on this island now. Only about 1500 Japs cornered on one end and have been starving about six weeks now. They are at the stage right now to start running amuck and our boys are cutting them down like rabbits. All their supplies are gone and the soldiers are sitting back waiting for them to go nuts. I like it that way. Starve them to death, let them rot in their own stinking barbarism, the filthy scum! (I'm tough Mommie!) Anyway, they have a beach with about 300 yards of sand all cleared away for "recreation." We took our beer down from the ship and it was good beer this time. We got it in Seattle last July and have kept it in our hold ever since. We gave away a few bottles and the soldiers really went wild over it. They have forgotten what ICE is apparently. Well, to get on, a friend and I began wandering around looking for souvenirs and ran across a Jap pillbox (one of many that covered the beach. The same beach being the strip of sand our boys crossed when they landed). Inside were a pile of human bones. No skulls but other bones. Apparently the flesh had been burned off with flame throwers. Further down the beach we came across a large number of spent and unspent shells. All Jap, and we hunted around and located the pillbox back on the shore; nestled and almost impregnable back in the coral. Coral on the beach means very jagged and sharp stones. You have seen coral. This is the same only it is in huge chunks and it being so jagged it cuts and tears clothing and flesh almost at the touch. Back around a bend we found blankets (torn and burned) and many small caliber shells. Detonating charges, bulk gun powder and evidence of grief for the Jap boy. I picked up a fairly well preserved 20 millimeter shell and brought it back to the ship. I took it apart and found that all the detonating charges [were] intact. Immediately, I turned the job over to a gunner's mate friend who finished the task.

Poking around like true rubberneckers and souvenir hunters, [Forrest E.] Shrider (my hunting mate) and I found other bones. Treading cautiously lest I step on some booby trap overlooked by the clean-up squad, I stepped upon some broken planks about two feet long with stones intermingled with them and felt a give under my feet. Shifting my weight from one foot to the other, I realized a sense of rubber underfoot. I reached down and tossed aside a few planks and rocks and noted evidence of my worst expectations. I was standing on a Jap body hastily covered in the march onward. I wasn't scared but two seconds later, 500 yards down the beach, I remarked to Shrider how careless it was of them not to tear the Jap to small bits so we wouldn't worry about it bursting under my weight.[8]

We then climbed a hill overlooking the harbor (which I regrettably cannot describe) and looked over the airfield. As far as the eye could

---

8. Raines, who had not seen death firsthand, seemed not to be shocked by what must have been a ghastly sight and fright. Contrast his reaction to battlefield dead with those chronicled by Holmes in chapter 5, "Pale Battalions," in *Acts of War*.

see, ringing the field were wrecks of Jap Zeros [single-engine fighter aircraft] and "Bettys" (Bettys are two-engine medium bombers). They were wrecks of twisted aluminum and steel. They had the appearance of piled junk. My opinion after observing a while was that SeaBees,[9] coming in to clear up the field, had taken their bulldozers and put them in "high gear," rammed into the wreckage on the field (over a hundred planes must have been shot down) and scooped them right off the field. Dirt was piled up with the wreckage which gave me the idea of bulldozers having done the job. We went up to a "Zeke" (Zero) and looked it over. Going from one to the other, I finally found a souvenir worth keeping (they had been picked clean by the Army). Sooooo, I now have the firing key from a Jap Zero. I also have a little piece of rubber I'm going to send Pop and tell him it is the reason his tires aren't so hot; the Japs having gotten all our rubber.[10] Getting kinda late now, Shrider and I strolled back toward the landing. ...

Honey, I think once I told you I'd tell you about Tokyo Rose. Well Rose is a kinda gal that everybody wants to feed some Spanish Fly [aphrodisiac], go outside and lock the door so nobody can get in to her. (That's pretty horrible language but it's the correct interpretation of what these vulgar men propose.) Tokyo Rose has an interesting voice because it is so much like American. It is a pleasant voice and her conversation is interesting. Everyone hates her of course and here's my idea about her: Judging from her voice and listening closely, I believe she is American about 90% and Oriental 10%. (That makes 100% doesn't it? Yep.) Her Oriental blood could have come from Japan, China, India, or Siberia; any of these Asiatic countries could have been hers. Only a person who has studied enunciation and pronunciation like I have can tell the slight deviations in her voice. You know the most American-educated Oriental still has a marked accent. She doesn't have and it's really hard to detect it. Damn it, Honey, I've got to close now. We are getting underway very early in the morning and it will probably be sometime before you hear from me again. Be a sweet girl and remember that I worship you. I have to close now because the mail clerk is leaving as soon as the Captain and Exec get back to the ship and they are due now. I was just reminded of it when

---

9. The popular derivative from the acronym *CB* for construction battalion.

10. An Allied rubber shortage was one of the by-products of the Japanese conquest of Malaya.

the mail clerk walked in with the bag over his shoulder. I've got to route this thing and get it in his bag before he shoves off. I believe you had rather get the letter as is than not any at all. So Darling Baby, be sweet, I love and worship you like no man has any woman. I honestly believe that because everything I do and everything I think of is about you. So long now Darling.

Your devoted husband,
Orvill

P.S. I LOVE YOU!!!

By the way: We are going out on another of those "Trips" again soon but don't worry about me. We have a very good "go" of it and are about the safest bunch in the Navy.

---

6 November 1944

Hello, Darling Baby Girl:

Well, tomorrow is my second anniversary with the Navy. Just two years ago I got on that train in Dallas and the whirlwind began. I pray to Holy God it won't be another two years before it ends. I'm writing tonight but won't be able to mail it until we get to New Caledonia several days from now. (I hope to see B. C. Pearson and maybe Hewitt. Remember Hewitt, the red-haired kid you kissed on Canal Street New Year's Eve 1943?) He's down there with a base of some kind. I am now near another buddy but won't get to see him. Harry Whistler. He's at Eniwetok, Marshall Islands, and we are passing nearby but won't stop for hell or high water. We are on an important mission now. I was wrong on that other dope. About the "trip" I mean. We headed south in the other direction but are going east first and then cut south. It's almost a 4,000 mile trip and we are already getting tired since we have been underway for so many days lately anyway. George and I hope he gets to see his girl friend in Sydney. His reasons are obvious of course, but mine are to see the town and Australia. I would like to see it before going back to the States but if it meant missing Australia I'd pull out for the states *right now*. Honey, when I ever do hit the states, no matter what part, you are going to be there. Even if it's Seattle. We have enough money now so you can come to me when I am there and no more will we have to separate just because we don't have the money. I have vowed to myself that I would never be broke again and I mean it. Never again will I be away from you because I don't have the money to bring you along. Those days are over forever and if I have to cheat and "deal" never will I be that broke again.

Darling, will you send me the measure of your waist? I need it for one of the boys to make you a belt. He is going ..... never mind. Just going to make you a belt. I want it to be a surprise so won't tell you about it. Anyway, you will learn about it Christmas because I sent you a package and letter that will explain it all. You just have to wait until Christmas, that's all.

Oh, yes, Baby Doll, do you think you could find a map (two of them) kinda large say, about 18 by 24 inches, or thereabouts for George Lynch and I? We want to keep an account of where we have been. We can trace the lines on it and keep track of our past movements. We have been getting around the Central, South Southwest and West Pacific so much that we want to keep it. George said a few nights back that we have covered more territory in the few months we have been here than most cans cover in a year. I want it so I can show you all the places "Far over the world" when I get back. And you know, the guys in the Torpedo Shack have the nicest map. It is small but shows the whole United States and Pacific Ocean clear over to India. And the nice thing about it is: It has DALLAS set right down there in Texas where it oughta be. It's really silly I know, but I can look at that map and see Dallas there. Then I visualize the city itself and you darling. I say to myself that you are right there. Not so far away and there's no reason for me to be so worried about you. You are right there on the other side of the map from me. I can reach over where I am and then right over to where you are. Well, that's all for that. Maybe you can't understand but get you a map and see if it doesn't help.

Honey, the days are creeping up toward a month now since I got a letter from you. I counted up today and the last letter I got was on October 11th. We got mail up to the 13th but I didn't get any those two days. Hardly anybody did and we think it's because they had started sending it elsewhere. We sure can't figure where, though. We are hoping against hope that we will get it where we are going. It's pretty slim though because it was a surprise to our Captain even to get orders for New Caledonia. It's so far down there too. But I'm still hoping. I read back through some of your best love letters awhile ago and still get that wonderful thrill to read your "I love you." Darling, no matter what form it is in, I still love that phrase from you. I love you too Baby Darling and will forever. I feel awfully close to you now. I can almost smell the perfume and powder. And your freshness. You know, you never did present any picture but that of freshness as long as I've known and worshipped you. Tired at times of course but always your kisses had a spark that regenerated me and told me what a lucky fellow I was. Never in the world is there anyone that can kiss like you can. Darling, I don't even let myself think of those 400s. They are too good to imagine. I almost go crazy thinking of the hopelessness of the situation now and if I think too much about you and the way you can love, I can't stand it.

Darling, I'm going to close now for tonight. I'll write more tomorrow or the next day. But let me say now; in case you are worried about me. Don't worry so much. Only every once in a while am I in any danger. It isn't all the time like so many people think. We just go into a danger zone, stay a while, looking around, and then come out again. We have been doing a lot of convoy work and when the landing is made in China, (speculated to be within the next very very few months) about all the Asiatic Navy will be doing is convoy work. Maybe even back to the states. If that comes about, this ship will go nuts. We are dying for a Coca Cola or some ice cream. When you go down to the drug store today how about drinking a Coke for me and maybe eat a little ice cream? Don't tell anybody you are doing it for me (except maybe Roy [a woman nurse who worked with Ray Ellen]) but just take a sip through those precious and delicious lips of yours and say to yourself, "This one is for you My Darling." I'll add to the billion other reasons why I love you so much and drink your Coke for you sometime. (Joke.) I'd have a heck of a time taking it away from you first, wouldn't I?

Well, Baby Doll, be sweet and love this guy like you always have. Save your precious energy for me when I get back because you are going to need it. I pledge to you and mostly to me that I'll not turn loose of you for weeks. You are going to be kissed, hugged and loved so damn much you'll need vitamin pills to keep you on your feet. Good night now darling. (Or I should say good morning. You are about leaving for work now.) I'm going down and get some sleep. You are going to work this morning and I am going to bed tomorrow, boy that's screwy isn't it? But then I'm going to bed tonight and you are going to work yesterday; all at the same time. Oh, well, no matter what the time, the difference in the time, where I am from you; the story will always remain the same in my heart. Love and worship Darling forever and ever, until death do us part and death will have his hands full when he makes a grab for me. I've got so damn much, I say so *damn* much to get home for. Bye for now My Darling little Baby, God bless you.

Your devoted husband,
Orvill

P.S. I LOVE YOU!!!

---

9 November 1944

Hello, Darling Baby:

Well, two more days and it will be a month since hearing from you. I have been all over the Pacific and the memory of getting letters is becoming more vague all the time. I feel so neglected. Of course, I'm not because almost every sailor or soldier out here has had the same experience. But it does seem like such a long time, the States so far away and you wondering where I am and what I am doing. Well, I can answer the latter. I am getting up in the morning; eating breakfast after an hour at G.Q.; stand watches day or night; work in the office; hit the sack. Same thing over and over every day except that sometimes I am on watch when everybody gets up. The days pass swiftly but as far as memory goes, they might as well pass very slowly. The last month has seemed like several. Even my visit to Guam seems like it was weeks ago. ...

Honey Baby, you pretty little doll, let me thank you again for sending me your pictures. I have it propped up before me now and it sure has helped the last two weeks. Did you notice you have a mischievous look on your face in the one on the right? Just like when you are about to punch me in the stomach when I am stretching. I look at it and in kinda baby-talk like we always do I say something like: "Hello, dere, you little dickens. Hi, you pretty little devil, you precious imp. Wish I could take you in my arms and squeeze the heck outta you." Silly, maybe, but not to me.

Then I look over at the other one. There sits a beautiful girl with a faint trace of a smile on her face. I get very serious and say: "Hello, Baby Darling. Gosh, you're beautiful! I love you so much. Why do I worship you so much and have to be away from you like this?" That goes on for quite a while and I kinda choke up and decide it's best to fold it up and get my mind on something else.

Baby Girl, is there ANY way I can get over to you how much you mean to me. I've tried very hard to think of some way to tell you but it never is quite up to what I want to say. I guess the nearest way of describing it is that if anything happened to you or to us, my insides from my heart up and down would just drop out. I think that would be the feeling I'd get. I would feel numb and like a shell.

Maybe you can't understand it all Darling. I can't think tonight. Just awhile ago I watched the most beautiful sunset I have ever seen. It put me in another world entirely. I felt spiritually removed from all the past except my conception of your face. It is with me always. Even when I saw the sun reflecting off the clouds I ached to turn to you and remark about it. I imagined the expression you would have on your face looking at it. The water was "smooth as glass," actually so, and the reflection of the blazing sky was even more beautiful as it multiplied. Baby, I'm going to close now. We still don't know if we will actually pull into New Caledonia. We may get within sight and get orders to turn around and come back. In that event, we will not get mail, nor get any off. If you receive a V-Mail dated a day after my last "addition" to this letter, you will know that we entered Noumea and are staying a few days. I'll write V-Mails from there if we are in more than two or three days.

I am enclosing a hurried account of our Shellback initiation. I tried several times before to write it but got started on it only today and wound it up. I hope you can visualize things more vividly than I described them. I didn't mention that everybody (the shellbacks) was clad in pirate clothes except those that I described otherwise. Maybe I should keep it and re-work it but I'm afraid it'll be another two months before getting around to it. So hope you enjoy it.

Good night for now Ray Ellen sweetheart. Remember that I love you constantly and forever, Baby. You are all that I have now holding me together and I want you to realize every minute of the day that I am worshipping you. Wherever you go, wherever you are, I worship

you constantly. I dream of you and the day I'll see you on that plat-
form at the depot. I know you will be the same sweet little girl I left
and that gives me a wonderful glow in the chest. If it'll give you a glow
..... I'm still the stupid absent-minded guy that loves you so much he
cried when he left you. So long for now, Baby Doll, I worship you.

> Your devoted husband,
> Orvill

P.S. There are no women (white) in New Caledonia except nurses
and officers. There are so many men that the women can't be seen
even. The native girls look like hell!

P.P.S. I LOVE AND WORSHIP YOU!!!

"Crossing the Line"[11]

"All hands, ATTENTION!" blared the loud speaker. "This is Davy
Jones, just came aboard from Davy Jones' Locker. I bring you a message from His Majesty, His Highly Exalted Royalness King Neptunus
Rex! His Majesty is greatly displeased with the scummy crew and
lowly pollywogs aboard this vessel. Captain Burns, His Majesty directed me to ask you WHY you DARED bring such a scurvy lot of
crewmen into his kingdom."

The entire crew dropped his work, pollywogs spilled paint and gun
oil. Straightening up, they all faced the nearest loud speaker, be they
on deck cleaning guns, below watching gauges, lying in their bunks
reading or drinking coffee on the boat deck. Some snickered; others
like myself were too interested to note intruding sounds. What sort of
game is this? The Chief Bosun's Mate (even though authorized to impersonate Davy Jones) Talking to the "Old Man" like that! We all
waited for the Captain's answer. This was August 30th and his Royal
Highness wasn't to come aboard until the next day.

"Davy Jones," the Captain began, "it's been two years since I've
talked with you. Each meeting has been a pleasant one except the

---

11. Maritime tradition calls for the initiation of "pollywogs," those who have never
crossed the equator, in order to transform them into "shellbacks," suitable subjects of
King Neptune.

FIRST one. (Banging ears, you see.) Please take my apologies to King Neptune. I regret that I must invade His Highness' kingdom in such a degrading manner, but I have orders that I am sure His Greatness will honor."

"Have these slimy worms been informed that they are to meet the vengeful treatment bestowed on all impostors who dare enter the lower world. And WITHOUT INVITATION!?!?!!?" Davy Jones is getting tough now.

The Captain stammered, "Yes, they have been informed. And may I add: The ship is yours. We are at your command. We place our LIVES in your hands."

"Have the Bosun's Mate set the watch. Lookouts on the fantail and foc'sle. Have the scurvy ship's yeoman be prepared to keep accurate account and reports of the coming dire events. Bring forth the chariot and chariot-bearers. I will have a turn about the decks to see that the ship is fit for His Royal Highness' presence."

The sea was beautiful. There was no roll and the sun was about to sink in a manner known only to those who visit the South Seas and breathe the pure air that has been untouched by human lungs. The sea was a deep deep blue.

Davy Jones climbed down from the bridge, attired in shorts (his skinny legs looked like Australian boomerangs), a red sash and a black head scarf with skull and cross-bones painted thereon. In his right hand he wielded a hefty shillelagh (Irish club). He climbed into a decorated first-aid emergency stretcher and the four Negro mess attendants picked it up. They started carrying their holy cargo around the main deck of the ship. Preceded by a band; composed of: Trumpet, clarinet, trombone, accordion, dishpan, and large telephone talker's helmet.

Stringing out behind were miscellaneous "watch standers." We had been yanked below and Raines' clothing consisted of: Shorts, mattress cover, blue wool watch cap, (that "sock-cap" of mine), shoes and boot leggings. (My skinny legs looked better than Davy Jones'.)

On the second turn, we dropped off at our respective stations. The lookouts (with binoculars constructed of coke bottles and fire hose nozzles) took their stations on fantail and foc'sle. With the warning from Davy Jones: "If His Highness comes aboard here without your knowing his approach, your filthy bodies will stuff the bellies of the sharks!"

Came chow time. I am in the office awaiting some dreaded summons; and it comes! I am led down into the mess hall. The Chief Master-at-Arms has dragged me before all the world to see and hear. I say hear, because I am told to sing! "And SING, you disgraceful wretch!"

"What shall I sing, Most Abhorrent Detective?"

"Sing 'Yes Sir, That's My Baby' and pat your foot!" (He didn't get my "Abhorrent".)

I sang. LOUD.

The Shellbacks threw me out.

At sundown we were relieved and allowed to retire. But not after having to eat at one table over in a corner. There being almost three hundred pollywogs to about fifty shellbacks, it took a long time for us all to eat at that table. Any table at which sat a shellback, the lowly pollywog was shooed away. (Our curses and vows for the morrow were censurable to a very high degree.) It grew very tiresome, holding a tray of food about twenty minutes. We made the guys ahead of us choke it down. The guys behind us made us choke it down!

Sunrise! "All lowly pollywogs lay up to the foc'sle. The first one who peeks aft of the weatherdeck hatchway feels the swift slice of the sharpened scythe. His guts go to the gulls, his remaining body and head to the royal sharks of His Majesty's Kingdom."

Our spine is creeping up so that our tail-bone is embracing our clavicle. We begin romancing the idea of revolt. Mutiny! Take their clubs and sticks and grease away from them. They are outnumbered five to one. Nope. Never do; they got electric torches back there.

From here on, everything must bear an exclamation point after it. The shouting, excitement must be maintained to keep the confused pollywog confused.

The hatch opens! "You first five bastards step through here and fall to your knees!"

I am in the fourth batch, just time enough for the massacre to get into full swing. I say "swing" because that is all I ever saw any of them doing. E-Gad! My turn came; I fell on my knees on the hard deck. (I had laid my shoes up on the boat deck to save throwing them away.) No sooner had I hit the deck when a strong fire hose shooting salt water at the pressure of 100 lbs. per square inch, hit me full in the face. I played hide-and-seek behind the rump of the guy ahead of me and managed to get a breath of real air every two minutes. That guy with the hose could make that stream curve, I could swear!

All this time, a guy behind me with an automatic spring in his right arm kept banging away with his shillelagh. Of all times for a bottle-neck to materialize, this was it. We were to crawl a ladder of eight steps on our knees. Someone was holding up the works at the head of the ladder. And I was at the tail of the line. The guy with the hydraulic arm had no one else to pound on; my rump being the most conve-nient. He was rather cruel with it and two days later got a shellacking on the fantail from one of the boys more short tempered than I.

Finally (after four days) we hop up the ladder. I was ready to quit be-fore we got started. (Hereafter I will recount in script fashion.)

DIMATTIO:	On your knees, you slimy bastard. What are you?
RAINES:	A lowly pollywog!
DIMATTIO:	Not loud enough!
RAINES:	A LOWLY POLLYWOG!
BANKS:	Get up off your knees, who told you to get down there?
RAINES:	He did, Ba___
DIMATTIO:	SHUT UP! GET ON YOUR KNEES!
BANKS:	GET UP FROM THERE! WHAT DO YOU THINK THIS IS? DON'T YOU KNOW THIS IS A HOLY COURT?
DIMATTIO:	(Very menacingly) Get on those knees, pollywog, or I'll cut your heart out.
RAINES:	Yes, sir, but he sai___
G. LYNCH:	NEXT MAN! COME OVER HERE, YOU ___!
MR. HENRY:	(The Exec) Wait a minute! Son, I'm the Chaplain (I noted that he carried a huge dagger in his belt). What have they got you up for?
RAINES:	Parson, I don't know. All I was doing was standing there and they yanked me up here.
MR. HENRY:	Sounds like a frame-up to me. Here, you take this sympathy chit. Show it to the judge. This is a frame-up. Tell the judge he can't do this to you.
RAINES:	(meekly) Yes, sir.

I walked (or rather slink) over to where Lynch was waiting. He was court bailiff. McDonough was sitting at a box made to vaguely resemble a desk. The judge (Chief Commissary Steward) sat behind a like box. To the right, backs against the forward smokestack, sat the king. To his left, a boy waved a sheet of sheet-metal, fanning him. In his hand (he was Chief Torpedoman) he had a brass pitchfork—charged with electricity. On his right sat Chief Sleeter (Yeoman) who was Queen of the Realm. She was enticing with voluptuous breasts except for a very heavy growth of black hair that grew well up on her chest. At the queen's feet sat the Royal Baby. Our fattest seaman (five feet six, two-twenty pounds) with his body bared to the waist and pants rolled up to the knees. In his hand he held a baby bottle filled with bitter milk. Around his naval was thick gun grease an inch thick and smeared all over his belly. To the right of all, sat the jury on ready service ammunition boxes. Now to get on.

LYNCH: STRAIGHTEN UP YOU! CHIN IN, CHEST OUT, BELLY IN, RUMP IN.

MCDONOUGH: GET THAT CHIN OUT, CHEST IN, BELLY OUT. WHAT'S THE MATTER WITH YOU?

LYNCH: YOU'RE DISOBEYING ORDERS! STICK THAT CHEST OUT, HOLD YOUR BELLY IN.

RAINES: (meekly) Yes, sir. Yes, sir. Yes, sir. Yes, sir.

LYNCH: Just a moment, Your Honor. (Pulling a pair of fingernail clippers from his pocket. Lynch proceeds to trim my "insipid" mustache that he had threatened several times before. He could have done a better job with a pair of pliers.) (By the way, it's gone now never to return.)

JUDGE: WHAT IS THIS SON-OF-A-BITCH CHARGED WITH?

MCDONOUGH: WHY HE, ETC., ETC. (On my Subpoena.)

JUDGE: WHAT!!!? HE DID THAT??

VOICE FROM
THE JURY: TO HELL WITH THE JUDGE!!

LYNCH: WHO SAID THAT??

VOICE: HE DID! (pointing at me)

RAINES: But I didn't say anyth___

MCDONOUGH: SHUT UP! GET ON WITH THE TRIAL.

VOICE: THE JUDGE IS A SON-OF-A-BITCH!!

LYNCH: WHO SAID THAT??

VOICE: RAINES DID. I HEARD HIM!

RAINES: LOOK FELLAS _____

LYNCH: SHUT UP! GET THAT RUMP IN! (Banging the right place for emphasis)

JUDGE: WHAT HAVE YOU GOT THERE? A SYMPATHY CHIT?

RAINES: Yes, sir. (And remembering the kind (?) words of the chaplain, shouted) THIS IS A FRAME-UP! YOU CAN'T DO THIS TO ME! I AIN'T DONE NUTHIN'!

VOICE: KILL HIM!!! THAT'S MUTINY AND A CURSE AGAINST THE ROYAL KINGDOM!!

RAINES: (looking at the Chaplain; who's dying of laughter; "Dutch" hitting me with both hands on his shillelagh) Things don't look so good.....

LYNCH: GET OVER THERE AND DRINK FROM THE ROYAL BABY'S BOTTLE.

RAINES: (I drink. My mouth on the same nipple as the whole crew. I wonder, of all times to think of such a thing, if that is the way it feels when a man buys a prostitute. With that thought I lose control and squirt the distasteful milk into the belly of the Royal Baby. The insults, shouts and beating shillelaghs are too numerous to recount. My memory failed.)

LYNCH: KISS THE ROYAL BABY'S BELLY.

RAINES: (Realizing the futility of struggle, I do so. The sweet royal baby, gentlest of all babies, places his hand firmly behind my head and vigorously rolls my squinting puss around in the gushy grease. I know I got most of it because he had to re-grease himself when my face came away. I forgot to mention, all this time King Neptune was flicking me with his electrically charged pitchfork and while on my knees before the baby, a plate also charged kept hitting me. I was kneeling on it.)

RAINES: (some more) I turned to the chaplain. He is too laughter-stricken to talk so I move on. Groping my way because I had to look slightly to port to see around the grease. Back down on the main deck, Skabik the Coxswain, my friend in ALL times of need, gently wipes away the grease from my eyes—and rubs it in my hair. (He also prods me down the deck with a swab handle that has more electricity in its point.)

CARTER: WAIT A MINUTE HERE, MY SORRY FRIEND! I'M THE BARBER. LET'S LOOK AT YOUR TEETH.

RAINES: (groan) Yes, sir.

CARTER: H-m-m-m-m ..... what do you think doctor? (Turning to a co-pirate) Yep, I think so too ..... let me drill a little ..... say ..... that's worse than I thought ..... now ..... give me some filling ..... hold it ..... right there ..... is that enough ..... no ..... again ..... now ..... wait a minute ..... gotta shoot some pain killer in there.

RAINES: Gurgle ..... choke ..... God Damn ..... Jesus that stuff's terrible ..... what did you "fill" it with? Ye gods! DECK SOAP.....

CARTER: No charge, my friend ..... recommend me to your neighbors, that's all I ask.

FAEHNER: Are you through, Doctor?

CARTER: Yes, doctor ..... you want him now?

FAEHNER: Yes, Doctor ..... I'll take him now ..... lay down here my ..... you look very sick.

RAINES: No, Doctor, on the contrary, I feel fin——

FAEHNER: NO YOU DON'T. YOU FEEL LIKE HELL AND I KNOW IT!! Lay down there!!

RAINES: Yes, sir.

FAEHNER: Let's see your tonsils. Open wide. That's bad ..... nurse, hand me the purgative (poking a rubber glove down my throat forced me to swallow about three drops. It was enough. I knocked him aside and ran to the side of the ship. I heaved my breakfast, stale by now. I could tell then that the coating (blue and acid-like) was going to stay with me several days. It stayed three weeks!! And that's no joke!)

GRAHAM: HERE WE ARE, POLLYWOG! COME ON DOWN. I'M THE DENTIST. LET'S LOOK AT YOUR HAIR.

RAINES: My hair's fine, sir, Michalec cut it yesterd——

GRAHAM: ARE YOU GOING TO ARGUE? ME, THE BEST DENTIST IN THE NAVY?? I CAN CUT YOUR HAIR SO YOU'LL NEVER KNOW IT.

RAINES: That's what scares me.

GRAHAM: SIT DOWN THERE AND SHUT UP!!

RAINES: (Sits down. Steel chair. More electricity. Three guys cutting my hair. Grease and hair falling in my lap and over my face.)

GRAHAM: DON'T YOU LIKE THE WAY I'M CUTTING YOUR HAIR? ISN'T IT PRETTY??

RAINES: I WOULDN'T RECOMMEND YOU TO MY TEAM OF MULES BACK HOME.

GRAHAM: WH-A-T-T!!!? GIVE HIM MORE BOYS. THE WHOLE WORKS.

RAINES: (They were going to anyway.) (Got a clean shave up there that evening. They cut down to the scalp in three places.)

PINARD: RAINES! RIGHT THIS WAY. BEND OVER.

RAINES: (Numb by this time and given up hope of living another two hours) Yes, sir.

PINARD: Put your wrists through there ..... your head through there ..... (I realized that I was being securely fastened into a stockade affair with my rump prominently exposed for all to see and take an unobstructed swing at with their shillelaghs.)

SMILINICH: He's a good guy ..... just dry out his pants ..... WHAM ..... WHAM ..... WHAM ..... (I tied myself in a knot. It hurt so bad I tried to turn over so my rump would be on the deck. I almost succeeded. I felt like killing them and would have if they had turned me loose.) (After being released, I felt back there, very tenderly, and sure enough—it was damn near dry. I later sneaked back for a look at the other guys and honey, the water sprayed in an actual fog when they hit those fellows. It atomized the moisture and one guy cried.)

LT. CONYERS: HEY YOU, YOU NEED A BATH, SIT UP THERE. (I sit up there and they shove me backwards into a tank of salt water. It was supposed to be punishment but it felt so good, I stayed in longer than they wanted me to.)

LT. CONYERS: NOW, WHAT ARE YOU???

RAINES: A LOWLY POLLYWOG!!

LT. CONYERS: PUSH HIM UNDER AGAIN ..... NOW, WHAT ARE YOU???

RAINES: AN HONORABLE SHELLBACK!! (It worked.) (They turned me loose.) (Only one more obstacle now. Crawling through a canvas affair twenty feet long, laid horizontally on the deck and raised at the ends so it would hold water, oil, garbage and someone later told me it contained "excreta." I have yet to find the man who put *that* in the bag and will vow that if it is thirty years from now that I find him, I will give him the beating of his life. The initiation was complete without that heathenism.)

NICK: HEY, BUD! C'MERE ..... STICK YOUR HEAD IN THERE ..... KEEP IT DOWN SO WE WON'T HIT THE WRONG HUMP AND CRAWL LIKE HELL TO THE OTHER END.

RAINES: Yes, sir. (I crawled like hell and reached the other end. A guy was there with a "punishing" salt water hose wetting me down thoroughly. I enjoyed it immensely.)

THE INITIATION IS OVER!!!! I go back to put on my shoes and they have been stolen. I stagger into the after head. In the middle of the deck are two buckets of diesel oil, with which to wash the oil off. I duck into it and it runs into my eyes, ears, nose and all over my chest. I climb into a shower after rubbing in diesel oil twenty minutes. I take three showers, one after the other. I go out into the sun ..... diesel oil still on me ..... the sun causing it to run down my forehead ..... I go in ..... take two more showers this time note what is around me. Lining the bulkheads and crowding the head are former pollywogs with hind ends bare.

Darling, I felt ashamed to be a part of anything so vulgar. Those men's seats were blue from halfway to the knees to the small of their back. I mean really ..... caused by bursting veins I suppose. I looked at my own and saw it was the same way. I didn't mind the initiation. I enjoyed it throughout except when they got cruel. It seemed they tried to put us all in bed ..... they succeeded with two boys. But the only thing I really can't understand is that business in the bag I told you about. Nick was posted there and doesn't know. He said he would have thrown him over the side. He knows it was there because he saw evidence. Perhaps it is best I can't find out, because there are severe punishments for murder.

Well, Baby Doll, I think this is all. May God have mercy on my soul and never allow me to go through it again.

Your devoted husband,
Orvill

P.S. I LOVE YOU!!!

---

12 November 1944

Hello, Baby Darling:

Well, here's Poppie again, this evening. I worked awful hard all day today to get caught up with my work and be able to write you without any "unexpected" interruptions. The "unexpected" always happens though. I also wanted to get the office "squared away" for Mac. He starts his week's turn to down here tomorrow. I go back on watch at 3:30 A.M. in the morning. You see, the way we work it, we started out both being on watch and working in the office too. That was too rugged as there is so much paper work to be done. We argued that one of us should be taken off watch and won. Now we work it this way: Mac stands seven days' watch duty and I do ALL the work in the office. He doesn't have to do anything but stand watches. The next seven days I stand watch and he does all the office work. I usually drop around occasionally but I practically haven't seen Mac this past week. We've been going pretty hard and he's had a rough go of it. By the way, ole Mac is about the best guy I ever worked with. When he has something to do, he'd rather kill himself than have me do it while I'm on the watch. It works both ways and we've never had any kind of argument or misunderstanding or bad feeling since we began working together. Just a little irritable during shake-down and early days out here. But we've never said a cross word to each other. (Hope my saying that doesn't wreck the harmony.)

Yes, Honey, as I (and Mac) feared, we changed course a couple of days ago (the morning after I wrote the above letter) and headed due west. We won't get to New Caledonia but expect to hit port at Manus Island again. That is o.k. because we think most of our mail is there. Boy, sure hope so. We don't know where we'll go from there. The Philippine situation looks like it is going to require our services. We have been changed to another destroyer squadron, Honey Baby. The famous "Squadron Twenty-One" is not doing its hell-bent-for-Tokyo work anymore (we suspect the Navy Department is giving them their much deserved rest with convoy work) and since we are new, we are being transferred to another squadron. We have its number and all but don't know what fleet it's in nor where it is operating. We may be joining it in the next few weeks. I can't tell you its number but it is a high one and we think (always looking for the worst) that our next assignment will be right in the middle of the new "Torpedo Junction" between the Philippines and China. The Japs are running in too many troops in too many ships still floating and apparently we will have to thin them out like Dad does his cotton. I'll give you more dope later as the law allows. ...

I lay there and thought back over the years that you have been my inspiration. It was an hour before I could calm down and sleep but I really enjoyed thinking back. I mean thinking back in an organized manner. I thought mostly of the two years at Mrs. Parker's. We thought we were having a rough time of it but we had it rather nice didn't we? All we needed (and will ever need) to straighten us up was a slight pressure in each other's arms. Boy, $22.50 wasn't much to live on was it? Especially with $2.25 going to the church every week. Remember how we'd sit up in bed and study my English lessons? Honey, the wonderful way you always kept behind me and right up with me was something that so few men get. With that inspiration, how could I have done otherwise than work like the devil? And I did, even to causing you unhappiness in staying out all night on my night off. I still have to finish that argument with you about that. I still think it was best and if I remember correctly, you conceded it later didn't you? And I explained how you had more or less "raised" me from a poor ignorant country boy that wore putrid green suits and decked me out in real impressive business-like clothes. I know it was bragging (I explained to the kid that I was but that I always did where you are concerned, I can't help it Darling); I can't help but remember what a poor dupe I was when I met you. Fresh from the sticks and corn all over me. You are always such a nice impressive person with what is known as "class." That's what I told Dan and Mark that night. You stole my heart the moment I laid eyes on you Baby Darling and you have kept it ever since. The one I have now is just being used by me to keep me alive. My real heart is right where you are Baby. It's lying there next to yours. It has been there five and a half years now and has grown its lining to the lining of your heart. Please don't ever tear it away Darling. If you do, it'll be torn and broken so badly that it will die. It would be the slowest death by torture, a punishment greater than any ever achieved by any Oriental madman who specializes in human pain. I know you won't though Darling. I firmly believe that I placed it in the gentlest hands in the world. You have nourished it so competently since I gave it to you. And it certainly hasn't suffered. I plead with you to believe me that my heart has felt so good since you took it over that there is no other way in the world that it can be satisfied. Baby, I'm trying to make love to you. I can't do it like we did when we settled in each other's arms and I put my face in your hair and my chest swelled to the bursting point. All I can do now is give you my solemn but miserable promise that when I return, you will never lack the encirclement of my arms as long as you want them. They and everything about me belongs to you completely until the day you decide you don't want them. They will do everything in their power to make you happy. All energy is going to expend itself to making you happy, Darling. I worship you Ray Ellen, and nobody, divine or otherwise can cause me to love it like I do you. And I will feel that way forever. ...

You have always maintained that I did it myself, but we both know better. You have always kept after me in a way that I like rather than dislike and you almost succeeded in making a gentleman and businessman out of me. Just give you a little more time when I get back and all the big shots had better back off because I'm coming into the picture.

Our progress at The News was pretty fast wasn't it? Have you ever stopped to realize exactly what we did accomplish? Think back like I'm doing and remember that book "News Gathering and News Writing" I bought with our last two dollars and seventy-five cents. Our work at home with that and the English book and my study at the office made me one of The News' outstanding reporters, didn't it? (I'm saying outstanding on the strength of writing the front pages of the last several Monday morning papers while I was there and Ted Barrett's remarks the day I left.) Of course, I'm not really outstanding but I believe we'll succeed in making me so with a little more work don't you think? I'm sure going to try hard when I get back. Well, Darling, I must go for tonight. God Bless You and remember that I love and worship you with every atom in my body.

> Your devoted husband,
> Orvill

George just came in the office; said tell you "HELLO!!! Hope you're feeling fine and wish I could see pretty you."
P.S. I LOVE YOU!!!

---

13 November 1944

Hello, Baby Darling:

Well, there isn't much to write tonight. We enter port the evening of November 15th and that means I'll be pretty busy tomorrow and the next day. We are always busiest just before entering port and during the first few days. We don't expect to get much time there but anything will be o.k. if we just get some mail. It seems I am further and further from home all the time and it gets worse when I don't get to read your letters.

Darling, will you bear with me a moment? Will you remember what I said long ago about guys being away from home so long and so damn far away that their minds start playing tricks on them? It is true that we feel so forlorn and helpless out here. We let our minds take over for flashing moments and we can't help it, no matter how unjust the thoughts may be. I want now to sort of get on my knees before you. I want to beg you, Darling Baby, please don't let me slip into the

back of your mind. Don't misunderstand; I'm *not* meaning to imply
that I'm afraid you'll ever do the wrong thing with me; the knowledge
of the contrary is what makes it possible for me to be away and for me
to be confident and happier than many many boys out here. I'm meaning only that in my absence I might become to you just something to
remember. All our wonderful Memories may not form a picture for
you for the present and future. I expect to be away from you another
whole long year. That's twice again as long as I've been gone already.
And it's quite possible that I'll be away much longer than that. I'm on
my knees before you Ray Ellen: you are such a wonderful person and I
am so thankful for having you that I can't live without you. You have
become so important to me and so much a part of me that if you are
taken away from me, I couldn't bear it. You see why I tried to apologize before I started this? It is ridiculous, I know, but I love you so
much Baby Darling, I pray that you will remember that the boy who's
writing you these letters all the time is the same boy that worshipped
you a year ago; the same one that you were so happy with. Remember
we laughed and cried together. Like that time in New Orleans we
rented the back room to that guy and his wife. One minute we were in
the depths of trouble and in the depth of debts. The next moment we
had money and our future for another month was secured. Remember
how we danced and sang and laughed and then ran down on Canal
Street and saw a movie? It was Saturday night. I'm the same guy, Ray
Ellen, and I have My Body sitting here writing you in the dim light of a
desk lamp just like we used to sit together in the apartment with the
floor lamp on. It's me, Baby, Orvill. ... I love you and worship you.
Like I always have and will until God takes me away. I'll love and
worship and adore you even after you've gone to Him, if I outlive you.
But that can't happen for long. I adore you so much Darling that if you
go first, you will have me with you in only a few days.

   My writing like this Baby Darling is stupid I know. But it will do
me good and set my mind at ease. You see, it's just a little talk with
you; I want you to know forever that I'm completely yours and that I
am feeling much better now because I've asked you to keep me right
up front in your mind. That's where you are constantly and always. I
know that my asking you that is the same as making it so. In spite of
the way my writing is appearing, Baby, I know that you love me. I'm
crazy happy about it too and wouldn't ever let myself think otherwise
even if I had reason (which I *do not*).

Well, Baby, good night, now. I've got to get to sleep. I have the midnight till 4 A.M. watch tonight and want to get in a little sleep. I know you'll understand what I mean by writing like this. You always did have me figured out before I knew what I was going to do anyway. I gave you that job four and a half years ago and by golly you gotta answer to me in keeping it the rest of our lives. Good night again Darling Baby. I worship and adore you Ray Ellen. I love you so much that I just sit and worship these pictures I have of you. They are so wonderful for me. Can't you send me some more? I've noticed that I haven't gotten any snapshots in months. Bye for now Baby, I'll try to finish this page tomorrow or the next day before mailing. God Bless You Darling and remember that every moment I live I am

> Your devoted husband,
> Orvill

P.S. I LOVE YOU!!!

---

14 November 1944

Hello, Darling Baby Girl:

Well, this will be the last addition to this "volume." We arrive in port tomorrow. Today was payday, poker games and dice games all over the ship. For the first time I'm free of obligations. I've paid off all my debts (the whole sum of $25). See what tremendous sums you cost me? Oh, yes, your ring is coming along. So fine in fact that a half-dollar is too much silver and I'm making it into one for me so we'll have one alike. I'm going to start on a quarter for you. Your stinkin' little ole fingers are so slender they're just two-bit size. Just kiddin' honey, they're million-dollar size and I was telling [probably Stanley B.] Johnson (the metalsmith) about how pretty they were. He didn't believe me until I showed him your picture. Glad your hands are in it, they are so pretty and I like to remember the way they touch me; cook my meals and scrub my back in the shower. I have been doing the work on the ring in Johnson's shop. He has all the tools needed for such work.

Well, Darling, I've gotta get this on its way. We are all excited about hitting port even if it is just a dot of an island in a million miles of ocean. We've been out so long. Hope we get a few days rest. We've been at it too much lately for some of the boys. Bye for now Darling. If I'm in port any length of time, I'll write you some V-Mails. Sure hope I have about a hundred and fifty letters at Manus. Bye for now Darling. Write you soon. Bless you Darling. Please stand by Poppie, I'm doing the best I can under the circumstances. And sure do love you for being the wonderful person you are. Believe that,

Your devoted husband,
Orvill

p.s. I do love you Darling and will forever!

---

16 November 1944

Hello, Darling Baby:

Well, we got in port last night and got three letters from you. There is more tonight and mail clerk tells me but I know not enough. We expect to be underway soon and this may be my last letter for a while. We go on two hours' notice at midnight tomorrow and I want this to get off the ship tomorrow. I know I must have a pile of mail somewhere. You write me so often I know I'll have a field day when it does arrive. Darling, you are the sweetest kid in the world to write me so faithfully. You'll never know how much it means to me to know that if ANYBODY gets mail I'll get at least one. And you've never failed me. There is always at least one letter in all piles unless we catch up all the way like at Hollandia and you miss a day. That's o.k. too, because an occasional day missed will be all right. You know, I never could leave you alone when I was with you; I was always kissing you or hugging you or something so much you couldn't do anything hardly; well it's the same way now. I need your letters to keep me satisfied like kissing you. That is the closest I can come to it and it is a poor substitute but couldn't get along without them. (See what I mean???)

Baby, I went over on the beach today and saw a graveyard. The white crosses were spotless and shone in sparkling rows. Beneath each one lay a man; a man like the kid I told you about that I saw (it was here) that was crying. It was my first battlefield graveyard to see. Six or seven men were working keeping the grass cut and the trash out of it. It was so pretty. I had to stop and look at it. Perhaps two hundred graves there and you know me, I had to say a little word and let the goose-pimples creep all over me. I think I said something like: "Fellas, you got a raw deal and we might not say much about it but we have a spot in our hearts for you guys. You took it the hard way and a long way from home."

That was my only experience since writing you Baby. But it was pretty important to me. I know how they must have felt if they didn't go too quick. They must have felt pretty bad to know they wouldn't get back home to their Baby.

Well, we'll be following Admiral Halsey and his Third Fleet hereafter, I suppose. Plenty fast but the Japs are still running and will continue to do so in view of the power we have out here. We expect to get underway for the Philippines very shortly so don't look for too many letters hereafter. Honey Darling, have I been doing all right with the mail? I've told you all about when I'm at sea and when I'm in port. Maybe you think I should write more. Maybe also you *won't* think so after getting my *fourteen* page letter this time. Boy, that was a piperoo. Did you enjoy reading it? The initiation?

Darling, there isn't anything else to write about now. I'll write you another good one when we are underway this time and answer the questions in these letters I got from beautiful, wonderful you. I'll try to make it as long as the last one, huh??? Darling, sweet baby, good bye for this time a while. Don't, please don't worry about me. I have a good go of it and am pretty lucky. I can't explain just how that is so but don't worry about me sweetheart. Just keep your heart so full of love for me it hurts and I'll be repaid for all the love I give you constantly.

Your devoted husband,
Orvill

P.S. I LOVE YOU!!!

---

24 November 1944

Baby Darling:

This will be just a short one Darling. I wrote one the other evening but G.Q. sounded and I had to wad it all up and stuff it in my pocket.

This morning it was too wrinkled to finish. So I'm starting this one and hope to get a little said.

First, we can "see the white of their eyes" anytime we look around for a while. For instance, it was night before last that I wrote the other letter. We had been given the "once over" by a snooping Jap plane that afternoon. Well general quarters sounded and we have been going to G.Q. on an average of once every two hours since. In the evenings it's more frequent than that. About two hours before sundown, a "bogie" comes over; we go to battle stations for about half an hour; secure and start down the ladder to the main deck. By the time I reach it, the beep ..... beep ..... beep ..... beep goes again. We get pretty tired of it and always in our mind is the fact that under our care is a large group of ships that are, and what they contain, make up the most precious cargo Uncle Sam has. We cans are extremely expendable and realize the importance of being so. Someday I'll be able to tell you why. Anyway we must sacrifice all to save what is in our care. We will be relieved of that obligation this afternoon and we all breathe a sigh of relief.

The same evening I broke off my letter to you, we (in the vulgar language of the sailor) lost our "cherry." In other words we are no longer virgins on the field of battle. I'll tell you what I can about it. It was a lone "Kate" (torpedo plane) that came in over our formation and it being very dark we were late in picking him up with our guns. The darkness is what saved us however, as he came in at an angle when he thought he was coming in straight. I have never in my life seen such a vicious scene as a wicked monster driving a plane straight at me at 200 miles an hour with six wing guns going full blast. It looked as if he was after me personally.[12] But strangely enough, I wasn't scared; just worried. I thought: "That son-of-a-bitch is going to hurt some of the

---

12. Although identified as a Nakajima B5N2 "Kate" torpedo bomber in *Howorth's* action report, this aircraft could not have been a Kate, if Raines was correct, as Kates only carried two forward-firing 7.7mm machine guns (mounted in the nose cowling), not the six Raines claimed; *Jane's Fighting Aircraft of World War II* (1945–1946; reprint, New York: Military Press, 1989), 191. The aircraft could have been any one of the A6M Zero series, which mounted six forward-firing machine guns and cannons, but spread between the wings and fuselage. In any case, the action was quick, and the plane was Japanese. See the secret "Special Action Report (Anti-Aircraft Action by a Surface Ship)" for the November 24, 1944, attack on microfilm Reel E-108, NPPSO–Naval District Washington Job No. AR-65-78, "*Howorth* (DD-592), Report File, War Diary"; note 25, Introduction above.

boys and it's too late for us to get him." The flashes of his guns and
our guns lighted the bridge like some eerie hell. But I was wrong, he
wasn't coming straight at me because I wasn't hit. Neither was anyone
else, nor the ship even. He had been fooled by the darkness and all his
slugs went well over the ship. His fish went across our bow and passed
astern of another can and went through without hitting anything.

Well, Darling, that was all of that. We don't know where we go from
here. At any rate, don't worry about me because all the Japs can throw
at us are those "lone" planes. They don't have much to work with and
I know they must be crying because of the further fight they must
continue to carry on, just like we cried three years ago.

Honey, my hair is growing back. I can just barely comb it and tell it
but it *is* coming back and will be o.k. by the time you see me (Thank
God). I am healthy, not overworked and feel better (much better) than
when on shakedown. I have lost my trace of "businessman pouch."
My shorts almost slide down over my hips. My weight has gone down
only about 12 pounds instead of the 20 I thought at first. I am getting
plenty of food to keep me going but still don't like it. We have it so
much better than the Army or Marines on these blasted islands. My
bed is clean and most important of all, I *have* a bed instead of the
ground. I can "come in" out of the rain and a lot of other conveniences
are to be had by us on ships. I don't sweat in bed like I did. I tied a pair
of pants on a ventilator and trailed the wind-filled legs to the head of
my bunk. The air (fresh ocean breezes) blow from my head to feet. You
should see me in my telephones, huge helmet and "Kapok" life jacket.
I look just like those real handsome men you see in "buy war bonds"
posters. (The *more really handsome* men.)

Darling, I know this isn't much of a letter but you will understand.
So many times I thank God for giving me such a wonderful wife.
There is no way to describe the feeling I get in my chest for having you
Ray Ellen. I can't imagine what I ever did to deserve you. I don't really
deserve you. But since I have you, nothing will ever make me let you
go. I must have you for the rest of my life Darling. I *worship* you.

I will mail this today. Whether you will get it I don't exactly know.
We are transferring some mail to another ship that is "supposed" to go
back to a port with a post office. If they don't, they will pass it on to
another ship, to another ship, to somebody else, etc. So it's indefinite,
Darling. But I will try and get a real good letter off as soon as I can. It's
hard to concentrate now kinda. When we get out of this front area I'll
be able to think better. I annoy myself an awful lot hearing the beep

..... beep ..... beep ..... when it isn't really going.
So long for now darling, I'll write when I can.

Your devoted husband,
Orvill

P.S. I LOVE YOU!!!

P.P.S. Just a little addition in my personal handwriting: I love &
worship & adore you Ray Ellen. Always stay as close & in my heart as
you are now. I can't get any closer to yours. I'm so close now I'll never
be able to leave. God Bless you Darling.

P.P.P.S. I LOVE YOU!!!

---

25 November 1944

Hello, Baby Darling:

Well, sweet Baby, as I explained in the letter just preceding this one
about the letter I wadded up and put in my pocket to go fight the Jap, I
will rehash as much of it as possible. I have about an hour to spare at
the moment and may not be disturbed for another five minutes anyway. We were followed in here by Jap plane "snoopers" and have been
under constant observation and intermittent attack ever since. They
wanted our very valuable cargo to go to the bottom but have not succeeded in doing anything but knock loose a few rivets.

I won't try to organize this into dates; I'll write it as it occurs to me
and try to keep the continuity straight for you. Anyway, the most important of all is that I saw two Japs die the most beautiful death yesterday that I've ever seen. Setting quietly, minding our own business, us
and our convoy was alarmed to general quarters just at dinner time
yesterday. (We've been going almost constantly the last three days
anyway.) But seldom do we actually see the planes. They are either
shot down or run off before we get a crack at them. Anyway, this one
got through yesterday. He made a dive on one of our prize "super cargo" vessels but missed.[13] His bomb shot water high in the air. We were

---

13. Aerial bombing studies performed by the navy after World War I indicated that
bomb detonations in the water adjacent to a ship's hull often resulted in significantly
more damage and subsequent flooding than a direct hit. See McBride, "Challenging a
Strategic Paradigm," 79. Not that the pilot in this case was aiming for the water. For the
myth of precision bombing, see Fussell, *Wartime*, chapter 2.

very close by and felt the concussion. He circled and came in for another run. P-38s had been notified however, and saw the water from the first bomb.[14] It was more thrilling and beautiful than anything the movies can capture. Two P-38s dropped out of a cloud at over 300 miles per hour; they tagged onto the tail of the Jap dive-bomber and all three went "in for the run" so to speak; one after the other. The gap between Jap and P-38 was closing so rapidly that the Nip pulled out just a moment too soon and didn't get to drop his bomb. It was super-tremendous and heart-swelling to see and hear those P-38s tear him to pieces. (The shooting sounds like the movies.) As the Jap came out of his dive the P-38s opened up. The P-38s were going so fast they had to "peel off" to miss crashing into him and let him flounder till he hit the water. He floundered a while but suddenly pulled into a steep bank and aimed himself at one of our ships. We held our breaths because he still had that bomb he failed to drop on the other ship. He sailed down and it looked like a hit dead center; but it wasn't. He hit the water just at the waterline of the ship; causing two men on that ship to jump over the side. He blew up and smoke moved skyward. It drifted away however and the only damage was a few rivets loosened or ripped out. An hour later another one came in, a torpedo-plane. He was a long way off and it was all I could do to see him. We began firing at him while he tried to run away. We received the word to cease firing as P-38s had gotten the word to "get him." They got him all right. And so fast that our last bursts caused him to turn right into the beautiful guns of a P-38. The splash way out in the ocean was really pretty. Baby, those Nips must give their hearts and souls to the "Imperial bastard" or something when they come in like that. They have no possible way of getting out alive. They invade our captured territory but never go back. At least that is the case of all I've known. We went to G.Q. once but the raiders were intercepted too far away to see. We heard the radio ask the P-38s if they had found any "bogies." The P-38s answered (forgive the language but I like to give it to you as accurate as censorship allows): "Hell, yes, a piss-pot full of 'em." Somebody said later that several "scrambles" (dog-fights) were taking place in that vicinity. Later the P-38s commander said: "The pot's empty, resuming normal patrol." So you see Honey, it isn't so bad. We have a

---

14. The P-38 Lightning was a single-seat, land-based, twin-engined fighter with distinctive twin-boom tails, flown by the army air force.

lot of coverage protection. We aren't tied up with a bunch that does sea battles so we needn't worry about that. It is pretty hot in that little slot between Samar and Leyte though because we are so far back up in between them that we can see Samar on the right, Leyte on the left and the little stream separating the two islands. They must figure they have us boxed in there but no, we are tempting bait luring them to hell. We don't spend all of our time in there, sort of in and out. That's about all of that I reckon.

Darling, I saw my first waterspout the 22nd, just before we came in here. A water spout as you know are those long twisting things that reach way up high, like a cyclone you've seen in pictures. Well, this was about five miles off our port beam and seemed about thirty feet in diameter. It reached way up in the sky. At the water's surface there was tremendous splashing and spray covering an area of about 100 yards. It appeared to be mist and spray for about a quarter of a mile up, but the half-mile that reached up into a very black cloud seemed to be a solid tube of water. The cylinder was perfectly shaped. It had a bend near it's middle yet retained a perfectly rounded form. I watched it move toward us for about ten minutes then clouds all around the spout began pouring rain. The spout was consumed by a tremendous deluge of falling water and soon disappeared.

I want to tell you about the whales the other night. Can I? (Fat chance you have of saying "No" isn't there?) Anyway. The Captain and I were looking over the windbreak on the port side of the bridge. Sort of day-dreaming in the late twilight. Suddenly the Captain shouted "What's that over there, Raines?" He startled me and I had to focus my brain as well as my eyes. "It looks like a log, Captain," I answered. "HARD LEFT RUDDER!" he shouted. The [bridge] wing was crowded by then. The "Old Man" said it looked like a submarine conning-tower to him and so we proceeded over to shake it down. Just before we hit, we saw it was a whale; he was blowing and steaming contentedly. We startled him though and he lazily turned over and started for the briny deep. He was too late however and we felt him rolling and bumping along the bottom then a rip sort of (more imagined, I believe) when the screws chewed into him. We looked back and a large patch of water was reddish-yellowish. We turned to go back and see for sure and saw him blowing again. The Captain aimed to miss him by a good margin, not caring to chance banging up the "tin can" side of our home. As we came closer I thought, "good gravy, did we cut him into that big a piece?"; but no, there were five of them altogether. The injured one lay between two others (all weighing about 4,000 pounds according to the Captain). The ones on the outside were blowing but the one in the middle had its head well down, probably cut to pieces. Just as we got the bridge alongside, they all turned leisurely over and pointed head down except the middle one. It just lay there bleeding. The others' tails pointed up deck-high to attain depth in their dives but after we passed, we saw them coming back to sympathize with the wounded member. Then I got mad as hell at myself. I got chicken-hearted and worried all evening about "hurting a poor innocent whale not doing anything but eating his supper or something." It makes me so damn mad to be so soft-hearted about anything like that. Honey, what the hell is a whale to me anyhow!?[15]

Hey, surprise! I split a "coke" with you the other night. Remember me (see how the pitching causes my typewriter carriage to stay up when I put up the "Caps"?) Remember me asking you to take a sip for me? Well, I returned the favor the other night when they managed to get us some aboard. (Before we left the last port.) I liked sipping for you and pretending so much that I played I was taking a sip for me and then one for you. I've done that two times since and sure like the game. I pretend (imagining of course) that I can steal a kiss too, hope you don't mind. By the way, wonder why there are no coke bottles in the states? Well, I got a good idea. We never save the bottles. It is too much trouble to transport them back to the states so we have to throw them over the side. They come packed in pretty white-pine wooden boxes. The wood is so pretty I hate to see it go over the side. And every time I see anyone break a bottle on the side I think of our struggles to keep the cokes and bottles even up while back there. You have enough cokes now? Maybe you are wondering why we break the bottles on the side. Well, it has become a habit never to throw anything over the side that will float ... all bottles are thrown away by dashing them solidly against the side of the ship so the shattered glass will sink. Anything floating back will give the enemy (if there is one) a trail to follow us by. All cans are punctured in the bottom as well as the top to insure rapid sinking. All garbage and trash is thrown over just after dark so we'll be a long way from it next morning. Wood waste is also thrown over at night.

---

15. Compare Raines's attitude regarding the inadvertent death of this whale and his joy and amazement at seeing his first whale in his letter of June 18, 1944, in Chapter 1.

Darling, I explained to you in a recent letter about my being rated yeoman first. Well, damn it, I was straightened out a couple of weeks back and was told I'd be rated the first of December but just twelve days [later] (Nov. 18th) we received a letter from the Bureau of Personnel that all yeoman second and first rates were "closed." Now that takes in ALL rates of the navy now. They closed most of them about four months ago and we expected yeoman to be next on the list. They were and I was twelve days too late to make it. My only chance now is for McDonough or Chief Sleeter to be transferred. And Sleeter is to be transferred soon so my case isn't hopeless. It will just set me back another three months. Sleeter received an appointment as "Ship's clerk" which is a warrant officer's rank. (Just short of Ensign.) He will be transferred and I can make first class. I hope Mac will make chief soon if things work out all right. I was kinda hoping on sending you some extra money from time to time for spending money but guess it'll have to wait. Thought I'd send enough for a tire one time, maybe a housecoat or something another time, etc. Oh, well, I must be wicked. They say there's no peace for the wicked. And my ambition won't let me have any peace while I'm in the navy.

Yes, Darling, I finally got Mom's [Ray Ellen's mother] card to me. Boy, I sure was confused! She wrote it on September 5th, my birthday was the next day and she mailed it on October 28th. I sure couldn't figure it out. The only thing I could figure was that Pop had stuck it in his pocket or among some papers at the office and forgotten about it.

You asked about my complexion. Well it is much better. An occasional hickey comes out but not many. Overall the sun has tanned it considerably and it has cleared up very nice. I even like it kinda myself. As for tanning. I have a good one on my arms and face. The rest of me has been covered up. I keep my shirt on because white makes a good strafing target. Planes come in so fast you don't have time to put on your shirt and run for your battle station too. Some of the guys got good tans on the way out but I was too busy. I notice that George keeps his shirt on too. So I guess I'm not alone. It is a good idea to have a tan though in case of being shipwrecked and have to float in the sun a long time. I explained about my hair in another letter. Guess I'll start putting vaseline hair tonic on it soon to sort of train it. Honey, I must have missed the letter telling me about your pen. The first dope I heard you were writing about "getting it back in a few days." Of course, you told me about it in previous letters but there always is a gap between them when we miss several days. We get the last ones first and later get the first ones. Do I make myself clear? Guess not. Anyway we ran off from Manus and left 27 bags of our mail on the beach. We left in such a hurry that we couldn't get a boat over for it. We got scuttlebutt today that some arrangements have been made to get our air-mail letters up here by "skytrain" plane. (That's a C-47, I think.) We now have a post office up here on the beach so expect to get some before many more weeks have gone by. Boy, is that stuff precious to us now! It's as rare as automobiles too. You can't buy either one. By the way, how is the little green baby coming along? I think the little girl is the only thing I've ever been permitted to call Baby besides you. But those cooing words and sweet urgings sure got us where we wanted to go and when, didn't they? No, Darling, I won't ask you to sell her, no matter how much trouble you have, until you say so yourself. I hate to think that when we reach old age, the General Motors museum will come around trying to buy it from you. I bet the answer will be the same. But that's all right, if you want to keep her that long, by golly, you can. I know that I bought the car and told everybody it was "mine." You also told them it was "ours." Then called it "mine" and so it has been ever since. But the way you get things out of me will work for ever darling. Just kiss me once and you have me where you want me. What I wouldn't give for one of your kisses now! It's been so long darling. Please hang on for me. I worship you darling and my life depends on you. It's an awful lot to ask a beautiful girl like you to do while you are so youthful and precious. I may not be so beautiful but I am youthful too and precious, I hope, and I'm doing it for you. It's different, though, since I couldn't even if I wanted to. We had a boatload of Filipinos come alongside the other day and there were three pretty girls in it. I sure laughed when everybody ganged up on the fantail and started shouting insults at the sentry when he made them scram. Boy, they sure raved but I could understand their desire to break regulations. They don't have any reason not to. Baby, whenever I talk like the above and ask you such ridiculous things as to "behave," please don't misunderstand me. I trust you to the ends of the earth. If I didn't I would go crazy and certainly lose my mind. It is simply that I want you to understand how much depends on it. I wish I wouldn't do it. I'm afraid you will get the wrong impression. Please don't; I beg you. I thought at first I was going a little "cagey" being out here and so far from you but I remember that night in New Orleans, we lay in each other's arms and we talked about it and I begged you then to please, please keep faith with me. I am sticking to it if it kills me. I've not had any trouble, it isn't so bad. In fact I get a satisfaction out of doing something that so few men can do and in keeping my word. I still have that conviction of a man retaining his self-respect by keeping his "word." And I've got to maintain my self-respect if I am ever to look you in the eye and hope to have respect; about the most important thing in the world to me. It has so much to do with my keeping your love. Guess I'll get off that now. I guess I'm still a scared little guy that needs your so nice shoulder to lay my head on occasionally to get my bearings. ...

Well, Darling, one of the strikers has come in to go to sleep. Poor kid has to sleep in the office on the deck because he hasn't got a bunk. We are so full up (too well-staffed war complement) that several men have to sleep in hammocks and on the deck and "live out of seabags." (They don't have lockers.) I must run now so he can get to bed. He sleeps on life jackets and will have to get up at 3:30 A.M. in the morning. Good night for now, Baby Darling. I worship and adore. Please believe that I adore you. Every atom of you.

Your devoted husband,
Orvill

P.S. I LOVE YOU!!!

---

26 November 1944

Hello again, Baby Darling:

Hi there you sweet little dickens! Boy, wish I could grab you around the waist and hug you real tight up to me! Funny, my most pleasant thoughts and most enjoyable times I ever have are when I think of things like holding you and kissing you, and then I have to stop because I can't bear it. Sometimes I just let my imagination run wild and remember all the delicious associations we've had and it's just about proven too much for me. ...

Honey, NEWS, my fingernails are still long. Today I had to file a whole lot of them off (all ten fingers and thumbs too)! I almost back slid when we were in the fighting a few days ago but managed to get by. I *did* bite them all off the first time we went in with the initial landing. I think they were shorter then than they ever were before. Boy, what a night! But now I look at them and they are so pretty (to me after so many years of ugliness) that I want to eat them all the more. I think I will manage to break the habit entirely now. ...

Honey, I hope I DON'T run into Jimmy Woodall. He is on a submarine and we don't take time to ask who they are. We sink 'em and then ask questions.[16] We aren't supposed to know where they are based either so can't look him up. Maybe I'll run into him one of these times but hope not while aboard ship. Boy, I wish something could be done about our mail! I bet I have just piles of it from you and when I DO get it, I am going to withdraw and read them real slow and thoroughly; like I sipped that first coke I had the other day. I just hope you don't stop writing because I'm not getting them. Keep it up darling unless you are tired of evenings because I MUST know that you are writing. Some nights when you are too tired, please don't write. Just go right to bed and say that extra hour is "on Poppie." (The sleep.) And don't ever say again that your letters are inadequate. I know the feeling you have by having to make "I love you" sound convincing on paper; I have the same trouble. But remember that your letters and mine to you are about all we have now and you must think how important mine are to you. Yours are all the world to me. It ties me up with you, our lives and everything back home. They are very important, Baby Darling and when you write "I love you" on paper, I'll know you mean it because I believed you when I was with you and you MUST know that I love you. "You'll never know if you don't know now. ..."

Darling, I'm going to close now and go to supper. Still tell me g-n officially? I do you; right when I'm eating noon chow! My eyes kinda glaze over I'm afraid but no one has ever said anything to me about it. Nighty night for now. I'm gonna see a movie in the mess hall this evening. (Boy, is it hot and sweaty down there with a hundred other guys rubbing their naked chests up against mine, sweat running down; but

16. A sad example was the sinking of the submarine *Seawolf* by the destroyer escort USS *Rowell* in a submarine "safety lane" off Morotai. Safety lanes were areas in which U.S. submarines were authorized to operate and were supposedly safe from U.S. attack. See Roscoe, *Destroyer Operations,* 413–414.

we just gotta have our "recreation." Below is a picture of how much of the screen I can see. The pole in the middle holds up the "overhead" (ceiling to you). If I ever sit on a cushion again, see the entire screen and without the interruption of changing reels, I'm gonna faint happy.

> Your devoted and adoring husband,
> Orvill

Darling, P.S. I LOVE YOU!!!

---

30 November 1944

Hello, Darling Baby:

Well, Honey, I finally hit the jack pot on the mail situation. I got just oodles of mail and have enjoyed it for two days. I couldn't get you this letter off before this because we've been so busy. Believe it or not, I haven't even had time to address the envelope and get it off. (Of course, I stole enough time to read your mail.) Except this morning I got about fifteen from you and haven't gotten to them yet. I am sitting here typing and the sweat has come through all my clothes. My shirt is wringing wet, it's running off my forehead and I wipe it off and it gets all over me and my fingers slip on the keys. I'm going to mutiny though in a few minutes and read them. I got several packages including the Christmas cards. Will send them out soon. Got both of the packages from Dick and Nannelle. Tell her for me will you, I will write her as soon as I can get around to it. Also get Dick's address for me.

Honey, I can't tell much more than has already gone down before. We are still blazing away at them but they are getting so weak it's pitiable. It's just certain death for them when they attack. Last night however, one of our sister ships (one our "balance crew" trained on while we were in Frisco) got a bomb hit and the same Jap pilot was knocked down and he suicide dived on the bridge of the destroyer. He missed but tore the hell out of the after end of it. It was just lucky that he hit them at all of course.

Darling, here is an order. When you hear of some big battle going on out here, don't you dare worry about it. I am as safe as can be under the circumstances and I don't want you worrying about me. I know,

Darling, you can't help worrying about me; I can't help but worry about your safety sometimes; but we must watch ourselves and govern our thoughts. It is so important to me that you keep well and happy. Please don't worry darling. I'll tell you why soon when I get time to write you a decent letter.

About the most outstanding thing of interest happening to me lately is yesterday. It was humorous and I was careless. I volunteered for an ammunition handling party. I didn't have to go but did to help out. I was sent down into the bowels of a huge ammunition ship that we were tied up alongside of. (About four stories down compared to a building.) We were throwing highly explosive powder around when the anti-aircraft fire began. Both ships sounded general quarters. The five of us down there amid all that explosive hell were topside in "nothing flat." We jumped down onto our ship (superdeck, the main deck too far down) just as the *Howorth* was getting underway and pulling out. I laughed because we had no reason to be afraid. We always sound G.Q. ten minutes before the enemy is sighted.

Darling, real news, you know the gold mine stock? Well it has gone up to 25¢ per share. That makes our $100 investment worth $250 now. Good huh? Tell you more about it later. Well, so long Darling precious. The enclosed is Jap money they printed for the Philippines. The big one "Ten Pesos" is yours; the "Ten Centavos" is Dr. Scanland's in case she wants it and the "One Centavo" is your mailman's "In payment for all he's done in the past." Tell him it's worth about 1/3 cent American money and consider himself indebted to me for about 1/6 of a cent. (He can work it out with future efficient deliveries.) Bye for now Baby Doll. God bless you and keep you safe. I pray that almost every night, My Baby. Please remember that my whole life and being belongs to you. My every thought in fact is in your possession because my every thought is of you.

> Your devoted husband,
> Orvill

P.S. I LOVE YOU!!!

---

3 December 1944

Hello, Darling Baby Girl:

My precious little baby darling. Gosh, honey, I love you. How it hurts me to think about it; you'll never know how I feel about getting back to you. Darling, we are sitting here in the bay and I lean over the rail with a cup of "joe" in my hand thinking about you and home; how far we all are from our homes; the boys on the beach slugging through the mud and rain and foggy mists that rise every morning over the low hills that stretch almost down to the water's edge. On one side is the swampy land, the mist clings until almost noon every day. Then we start the smoke screen. We keep the screen on always in case of air attack. We are doing all we can for the boys on the beach, us and the air corps. We keep them hidden and the fliers keep the flies away. We saved their life a few weeks ago by beating the hell out of the Jap fleet.[17] That was a very marked improvement on our situation out here. The Navy came through again on that and it was a battle that should hold the highest honors in its traditional boasts. And it is no bologna. The Japs took a licking they'll never forget. Their navy is practically out of the fight now. Just a little more and it will be completely finished. I am proud of the fleet to which I am attached. It did a grand job.

Darling, I was just interrupted. I have some bad news. The Executive Officer called me into his room and it was an hour before I started to continue writing. Anyway before I could start, Chief Sleeter came in with the news. A couple of days ago the Captain wanted to go around on the other side of Leyte and help chase off the Jap reinforcements. His superiors refused him. Tonight we got the word. Our group intercepted the convoy. They were sunk or driven off but a submarine sent a torpedo into Sidney Benn's[18] ship. I didn't even know he was over here. Sidney's ship broke in two and the air attacks were so heavy and the threat of submarines so strong that they had to shove off without picking up survivors. This happened about 9:30 P.M. and air attacks began and continued until daylight. The last anyone saw of the

17. Raines is referring to the Battle for Leyte Gulf.
18. Benn was a friend Raines made while assigned to the destroyer pool at Norfolk.

[censored] was its bridge awash.[19] Forty-millimeter and three-inch guns were firing on the survivors from the beach. God, maybe I shouldn't write you this! But maybe if we had been over there we could have helped. Of course, I'm not sure Sidney was killed. He may have made the beach and been captured or even hiding out. He may have been transferred to another ship sometime ago but the chances of his being alive are too slim to count on. I'm going to wait until later to write more. I feel just like you do and it's difficult to pound these keys hard enough to type. Good night Darling Baby.

4 December 1944

Good evening, Baby Darling:

Well, the news is better tonight. Lynch and I were on the bridge today and saw one of the ships that was with Sidney's come in the bay. Lynch signaled by flag over to get the "dope" on the sinking and we learned that the first reports, as usual, were exaggerated. Half (almost) were saved. Another group came by the scene to assist in the fight after it had moved to another locale and they picked up what men they could find. From all reports some others made it to the beach, being only 12 miles offshore. Nope, they weren't that far, only 300 yards (I was thinking about 3,000 yards). That's a pretty short swim. Lynch just came in the office with another straight (?) report; another ship's signalman said the men were *not* picked up and the few that might have reached shore were probably prisoners now. Well, if he is among those, it won't be so terribly long before he is set free. At Ormoc, they are still on their last pins and it may be over any day. They are still encircled and it's a mighty tough fight but they will have to give way soon. They will be chased off the island altogether and more than likely they won't have time to take prisoners. They will either be left alive or ??????

... Darling, you mentioned maybe I'll change due to being out here. Well, I haven't been able to figure it out yet. Maybe I will change on the surface a little but everyone has to form a little "crust" on their surface in order to maintain their rights. Everyone seems to think he is supposed to be tough and finagle the little things out of others. You

---

19. This destroyer was USS *Cooper*; see the account of her loss in Roscoe, *Destroyer Operations*, 444.

have to be a little tough to keep them from running over you. If I do change on the surface (there is no question of my changing inside. I'll always be the same there because I have you there and I must keep it just like you want it). If I do change on the surface, only a little time with you and the folks, the guys at The News, and I'll be the same again. You see, I try to figure things out that will strengthen my chances of getting back home. A couple of instances in which I am trying to outsmart the enemy: One: in case I'm in the water, our ship sinking and planes come over strafing, I have a twelve foot small line tied to my life jacket along with my whistle. If they come over I slip out of the jacket, expel the air from my lungs and sink, holding onto the end of the line. When I reach the end of the line (I hope to have started sinking in time to reach the end when he comes over) I will be well protected by the water from the shells. As you know, water stops a .50 caliber bullet in three and one-half feet. Even a 20 millimeter cannot penetrate more than six or seven. It will just slowly sink after that. Then ..... I can come to the surface for air and a quick search for other strafing planes. That may not be a masterpiece of an idea but I believe it will help. At any rate, it will beat remaining on the surface at their mercy, a thing which they do not have. Another idea: like Sid's ship night before last, they jump over the side next to the beach. Sinking men always do that. Consequently, the strafers and beach firers know where to shoot. I can go over the side opposite and may make my way to a friendly beach. You see, a single man is a very small and very difficult object to see in the water from the air or the beach. The chances are much better for his getting by undetected. And in case a friendly ship comes by to pick up survivors, he isn't so far away that he can't swim back and get aboard. Darling, these are two of the many reasons I spend a lot of my thinking time with ways of killing in order to stay alive and making plans to help me stay alive. Those things may be needless but I want to be prepared. Like our torpedomen.....there have been ships out here since the beginning of the war and have yet to fire their fish. Nevertheless, the torpedomen constantly keep those torpedoes in tiptop shape for action in a split second. I have always prided myself in being able to "think," when it comes time to think. I believe I can do that. Perhaps we won't see any action at all that will endanger the whole ship. More than likely we won't be assigned any tasks like Sid's ship. (We being in another fleet.) Anyway, I want to be ready.

But underneath, Ray Ellen Darling, you can always depend on my being the same guy that left you with a prayer and begging God to return me to you. God knows very well how important it is for me to get back to you. I don't believe He will allow anything to come between us. It will be a long time yet the end *is* approaching. Always remember that Baby Darling, the end is coming; we don't know yet when it will be but it *will* end. We must keep our chins up; I depend a lot on your love for me to keep mine up. ... As I told you so many times, you have grown to be so important to me Ray Ellen, that I must always be careful not to do anything that would bring contamination to you. For instance: I could not undergo an affair with a woman without soiling you. And you never with a man. It, to me and the way I look upon you, would be like throwing the filth of the people upon a spotless white statue. Never could I look upon you again as the idol untouched by "unclean" hands. Therefore, it must never be; on either side.[20]

My Darling, I rattled on up there, just writing what I thought and let myself think; getting as close to feeling you near me as possible. I hope you can understand what I mean. It is exactly the way I feel about you. You are the closest thing to God that I know and have. Now, I'll change the subject. Sometime ago I looked over the bow of our ship at Peleliu Island in the Palau Islands. It was the first one taken by the Marines.[21] It was early morning and the sun shined down beautifully on a smooth sea with a few ripples a slight breeze blew up. From where we lay anchored we could see both ends of the island. The beach was very close in front of us and I took the binoculars and scanned the beach closely. At the water's edge it rose in a bank about three feet. It was the most torn up piece of ground I have ever seen. A farmer's plow couldn't have done a more complete job of tearing it up. Our Navy apparently had stood off about a mile and pounded it unmercifully. That is as it should be, to decrease the number of boys lost even though it was a very wicked fight that followed.[22] The palm trees were a mass of broken sticks. The only hill on the island, about 500

---

20. Refer to note 8, Chapter 3 above.

21. Raines has forgotten earlier amphibious assaults such as those in the Gilbert, Marshall, and Marianas islands. For an overview of the Pacific amphibious war, see Allan R. Millett, *Semper Fidelis: The History of the United States Marine Corps* (New York: Free Press, 1991), chapter 14.

22. See Sledge, *With the Old Breed*, chapters 1–6.

feet high, rose about two miles inland and was a chalky white with black earth occasionally turning it grey. It was a miniature Gibraltar; rising with a gentle slope to the right and reaching its peak that dropped quite suddenly on the left. This hill also was torn up by shell fire. It was so close to the sea that even destroyers shelled it continually. The enemy's guns atop the hill (known appropriately as Bloody Nose Ridge) could not be brought to bear without being knocked-out. All their guns were quiet then but it must have been a hell during the fight. The whole scene was so peaceful that I actually felt good, looking on one of nature's most beautiful scenes. But then there was the aspect and evidence of war off to the left that couldn't be ignored. I'll be able to tell you what it was sometime later. But the most impressing thing about the entire island and the hill was a white cross. At the utmost top of Bloody Nose Ridge stood a shining white cross. It shone so brightly that I didn't need any glasses to see it. I looked it over good and a damn good size lump came in my throat. It was, in my humble estimation, exactly the size cross on which Jesus Christ was hanged at Calvary. It stood alone and certainly symbolized something to me. It could be seen from any point of the island; perhaps the Marine graveyard is atop the hill but their crosses were not visible. I believe the large white cross will stay there a long time.[23] The winning of that island means a lot to our freedom and liberty. And perhaps they'll never know it, but again I gave the boys my personal thanks and gratitude "Some must die, so that others might live." ...

Well, Baby, standing by the rail looking over to the land, one can see the island of Samar on the right and Leyte on the left ... approximately five miles to each. We have such a force firmly established here now that the Japs have not been able to get in sight for the last week. Why we are sitting here, no one knows. But early in the morning, at dawn alert, I can look over the wing of the bridge and see the foggy mist hanging over the swamps and the bottoms of the hills. It cuts the island into two pieces horizontally; we being able to see the very bottom and the very top. Toward noon it goes away and our small ships

---

23. In 1978 the U.S. Army monument, placed on Bloody Nose Ridge by the 321st Infantry Regiment that augmented the marines on Peleliu ten days after the invasion, was decrepit, the inscription "Lest We Forget" missing whole letters; Manchester, *Goodbye, Darkness,* 322. A part of this long-term neglect by the U.S. government has been remedied by the 1st Marine Division Association, which, with help from the navy, installed a marine monument on Bloody Nose Ridge in 1984.

pull in close to shore and commence the smoke screen. It is maintained until darkness falls again. The water in the bay is a sickly green; filthy with the toilet wash of many many ships. ...[24]

Well, Darling, the description of the islands isn't so good this time. Maybe you'll kinda gather that Poppie ain't so hot after all. Anyway, maybe I can do better later on. I keep thinking of Sidney and how he came out that I'm not much good any more. But one thing Baby Darling that you CAN depend on is that I love you. I worship you very deeply and will forever. Remember that will you darling? I actually adore and worship you. You are a very important, in fact, THE important, factor that keeps me going. I think of you constantly and all I do is with the ultimate goal of getting back to you. Gosh, Baby, it's so wonderful to be with you. To hold you and kiss you. I'm afraid you will have a rough time getting rid of me when I get back. Well, Darling, good night now. I will close for this time. Will go through the rest of your letters later. So long. Give the kids a piece or two of this money. Tell Chick he can put a Ten-Peso bill up in his store and tell his customers that "My little bud killed a Jap and took this away from him." Bye for now Darling, I worship you and will until God sees fit for our separation.

Your *devoted* husband,
Orvill

P.S. I LOVE YOU!!!

---

24. Ecological considerations were not a part of 1940s warship design. Saltwater flushing systems carried sewage from commodes to the sea. Leaky pump gaskets in the steam end of pumps and leaking packing glands in the fluid end produced oily bilge water that was also pumped overboard.

King Neptune presided over the festivities as Howorth *crossed the equator en route to the war zone. (all initiation photos courtesy of the USS* Howorth *Veterans Association)*

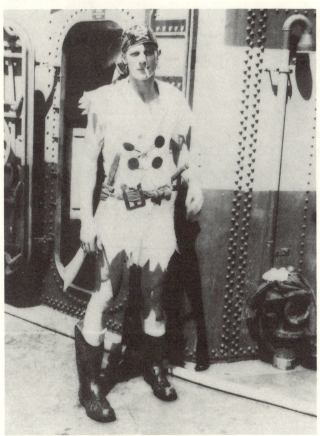

One of King Neptune's piratical retainers.

The Royal Baby—typically the youngest, fattest crewman. Pollywogs were compelled to kiss his greased belly ...

... and drink the odious contents of his bottle.

The bar of "justice" where pollywogs faced the charges preferred by shellbacks.

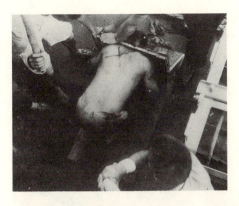

Neptune's justice: A pollywog miscreant in a jury-rigged stock.

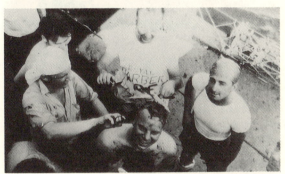

A pollywog, Ensign Jack M. Bishop, the assistant first lieutenant, has his hair cut by shellbacks.

The trough—the pollywogs' final torment.

Five new shellbacks.

Japanese naval pilots, such as this lieutenant departing on a suicide flight, flew the well-organized attack on Howorth *in which Orvill Raines was killed. (U.S. Naval Institute photo)*

A Mitsubishi A6M series Zero fighter (termed "Zeke" by U.S. forces) takes off on a kamikaze mission. This type of aircraft was used in the coordinated suicide attack on Howorth *off Mindoro in the Philippines and in the deadly attack off Okinawa. (U.S. Naval Institute photo)*

Surviving kamikaze attacks was often a matter of inches. Here an Aichi D3A "Val" dive bomber attempts to crash on a U.S. cruiser. A Val was the first plane to attack Howorth at Okinawa, rolling between the funnels and ripping out the ship's radio antennas before crashing into the sea. (U.S. Naval Institute photo)

 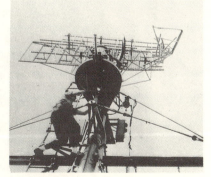

(Left) Howorth crewmen hold a piece of the kamikaze that damaged the ship off Mindoro in the Philippines. (Right) Howorth's radar antenna bent by the third Mindoro kamikaze. (USS Howorth Veterans Association)

A view from Howorth's *fantail as she comes alongside a small escort carrier (CVE) to receive supplies. (USS* Howorth *Veterans Association)*

One of Howorth's *5-inch shells explodes atop Mount Suribachi on Iwo Jima in February 1945. (USS* Howorth *Veterans Association)*

7

Invasion of Ormoc, Leyte Island, and Mindoro Island

December 9–21, 1944

On the morning of December 9, 1944, U.S. forces landed at the port of Ormoc on western Leyte Island to prevent the continuing disembarkation of Japanese reinforcements there. *Howorth* arrived at Ormoc Bay at 4:30 A.M. and covered the landing craft as they approached the beachhead. Air attack was a major concern, as Japanese kamikazes had sunk the destroyer *Mahan* and destroyer minesweeper *Ward* in the same location two days earlier.[1] *Howorth*'s stay at Ormoc was brief, just four hours, before she escorted empty transports back to Leyte Gulf. *Howorth* remained in Leyte Gulf for two days, then rejoined the invasion force for the central Philippine island of Mindoro, located approximately 200 miles northwest of Leyte Island. Mindoro would provide a useful air base for U.S. 5th Army Air Force operations in support of the forthcoming Lingayen Bay invasion to reclaim the island of Luzon and the Philippine capital of Manila.

Japanese resistance on Leyte was more stubborn than expected, and the originally scheduled landing at Lingayen Bay was delayed from December 20, 1944, to January 9, 1945. During the voyage to Mindoro, Raines observed the tremendous conflagration from a devastating kamikaze hit that killed over 130 men and wounded another 190 on the cruiser *Nashville*.

---

1. See Roscoe, *Destroyer Operations*, 443–446. Admiral Thomas C. Kinkaid, the 7th Fleet commander, was concerned about the threat of Japanese suicide attacks in the restricted waters of Ormoc Bay, and *Howorth*'s brief stay reflected that uneasiness; Spector, *Eagle Against the Sun*, 515.

The landings on Mindoro were made in Mangarin Bay on the southwest coast.[2] The initial goal of the ground troops was the seizure of the town of San Jose and the construction of an airfield. While the landing forces made their way ashore a little after 7 A.M., *Howorth* was sent to the restricted waters near Caminawit Point to destroy Japanese gun emplacements and troops. *Howorth* bombarded the beach for eighty minutes before sighting and firing upon several Japanese "Zekes," the code name for what was more commonly referred to as the Zero fighter aircraft. Thirty seconds after this first group was taken under fire, three additional Zekes popped up over adjacent Ilin Island and streaked toward *Howorth* at 300 knots, flying just 500 feet above the water. One plane was hit and fell away smoking. The other two continued to close in a suicide attack, with the second slamming into the water within feet of *Howorth*'s hull. The third plane hit *Howorth*'s radar antenna atop the mainmast and bounced off the bow before hitting the sea. *Howorth* had been lucky. Two tank landing ships (LSTs) were not. Suicide hits turned them into burning hulks sunk later that day by U.S. destroyers.

Shortly after 7 P.M., *Howorth* began a return voyage to Leyte Gulf, arriving in San Pedro Bay on the afternoon of December 18. But even while the ship was anchored in the relative safety of the bay, *Howorth*'s crew had no reprieve from Japanese air attacks and fired on two planes on the evening of December 20.

Raines and his shipmates had witnessed the kamikaze terror tactics firsthand at Mindoro Island. They knew that the upcoming invasion of Luzon Island would provide more of the same.

---

9 December 1944 (16 days til Xmas)

Hello, My Darling Baby Girl:

How you feelin' this evening? Sure hope you are in good shape cause I'm feeling pretty good myself. Been kinda busy the last three days though and will tell you about it some time. Been doing a lot of thinking about you. The crowds downtown Christmas shopping; all the preparations and things. Sure hope the folks at home have a good time this Christmas. And don't think we guys out here won't be enjoying it with you. Of course we'll be wishing with everything we've

---

2. For the Mindoro invasion, see Spector, *Eagle Against the Sun*, 517–518.

got that we could be there with you but it does our heart good to know
that the ones we love are happy and having fun. It probably will be
Xmas and past by the time you get this baby but nevertheless, the feeling is the same. Look back and know that on December 26th out here
I will be spending Xmas day with you out at Mom's and Pop's. I'll be
doing everything with you, Baby. Getting up early and running into
the living room. Squealing and hollering and everything. (I'll even
have an "extra" Pink Lady with Pop in the afternoon.)

Well, Darling, maybe I can give you a little picture of the Philippines. Yesterday and today we saw a lot more of them. There are 7,083
islands, 2,441 of them large enough to bear official names. We are on
the main highway to Japan now and today made an invasion landing
in the very teeth of the Jap resistance at Ormoc. I stood on deck and
said a good sized prayer that Sidney got away while our ship stood
over the spot where his went down four nights ago. We were lucky, we
didn't have to fire a shot. A lot of shore bombardment went on and a
half-mile stretch of beach was a gray cloud of dust, smoke and flying
dirt. We had reports of resistance but that failed to materialize. Our
boys landed the "hard way" to knock out their elongation of resistance on Leyte Island.

Darling, the "West Side" [of Leyte] is beautiful. We weave through
the numerous small islands, continually changing course. Always uncertain what lies beyond the next point. It reminds me of when I used
to play "rubber-guns" with J. E. We'd hide from each other and then
sneak around trying to find ourselves, always expecting a quick slap
and sting in the face or back. Mostly the land comes down to the water in steep slopes. The hills rise to between 300 and 500 feet. Eternal
very low clouds hang over their tops all day (at least they did today
and this is such a seasonal section). It is very rugged and uneven on
the west side. The hills reminded me of the jagged back of a horned
toad with a clayish tint. Tiny islands dot the intervals between sizable
islands. They may not be more than ten feet across and twenty feet
high. Just rocks; but vegetation grows on them. Some are ten feet in
diameter at the water line and may be thirty feet in diameter at the
top. The water having washed away the rock through the centuries.
Almost like ice cream cones. In the battle areas where the Navy has
expended its ammunition to churn up the slimy bastards lying behind
machineguns waiting for our army and marines, the beach is beaten to
a pulp. One hill (you remember me telling you the first time we came

in here about the pilot who plummeted out of the sky at five hundred miles per hour to crash on the hillside). This same hill now looks like a plucked chicken. A few scraggly bent trees remind me of the sparse sprigs of hair on the head of a bald man. (Honey, forgive me of all these things that remind me of such ridiculous things. The tiny islands I mentioned above remind me of moles on the otherwise beautiful face of nature. Some description, huh?)

Well, honey, we shoved off the other day from port and left our mailman. He has been there three days now (on the beach) hope he has some mail for us. Boy, I bet he is mad. He hates the beach. It is filthy muddy, crawling with vermin and insects. The women are filthy horrible and venereal disease runs very high. (Even back in the "bush" venereal disease is prominent. Must have been brought down here by the slave traders out of China many centuries ago.) Surprised that I know such things? Well the Philippines is the melting pot of the orient. Pirates and slave traders quartered here. They captured pretty women from raided villages and took them to China for the houses of prostitution. They visited the houses themselves and brought the diseases back here and infected women by rape who were not pretty enough to sell on the block. It was near the island of Leyte that Magellan, the first man to encircle the globe, was slain by the spear of an angry Moro. (Probably trying to date up the guy's wife.)

The reason why we left the port so hurriedly the other day is that we "rushed to the rescue" of a convoy under heavy air attack. It was a good fight but as always the mighty *Howorth* arrived too late. (I think the sight of us coming into the fray is too much for the enemy; he pulls freight.)

The next day we patrolled all day and night in the most dangerous stretch of water here. Did anything turn up? NO! We sleep all night. Several ships shot up the bombs on others and we don't even break out our guns. Well, I'm satisfied if that's the way they want to do it. But it stands to reason; we can't let the other fellow do all the fighting; we must help if we expect to end the war sooner. The more rounds fired the sooner we clean 'em up and come home.

Did I ever tell you what heavy antiaircraft fire looks like? Well take a fork and dip it deep into a large platter of spaghetti and lift straight up. If it had golden sequins strung along the spaghetti, then you'd know exactly what antiaircraft fire looks like about dark. It's beautiful. When the shells hit a bright flash glows for an instant and you shout "Plane hit on the port quarter" or wherever it might be. It isn't a large flash but the splash usually is pretty large especially if it is a big bomber trying to skip bomb. And did you know that antiaircraft fire would bounce or richette richiette richechette (some filthy devil stole our dictionary) (ricochet) off smooth water? The fire was so thick the other night that some ships fired into others and the bouncing projectiles glanced off the water into the sides of some. We were off to one side jumping up and down, gleefully shouting "Kill the bastards," "Come on you guys, hit 'em." All the Japs got out of it was a lot of "pyrotechnics" (your word) and death. Several [downed] planes bring the bottom of the bay closer to the top now.

Well, Darling, we get in in a few hours. We pay no attention to the sun any more. Except when it rises and sets. And when an attack is on. We look into it with special "Polaroid" glasses that you know about. You might use your own judgement in passing this information along: I got "scuttlebutt" that Glenn's ship got hit the other night. If it did, it couldn't be bad because it is alongside us now steaming without strain. Will check up on the gossip tomorrow if I get a chance.

Bye, tonight baby darling. I worship you and wish I could write better letters. Do I have to tell you again that I love you to make you believe it? No, I am sure you know that I love and adore you. You'll never know if you don't know now will you? Bye darling. My heart, soul and body are yours to command in any direction you desire forever and ever. God bless you, wonderful baby girl.

> Your devoted husband,
> Orvill

P.S. I LOVE YOU!

---

10 December 1944

Hello, My Baby Darling:

Well, tonight, we are sitting in a bay again. The enemy is only giving us enough trouble to make us go to general quarters about every three or four hours. We don't mind it so much except that we never know exactly when he is coming "in." About four-fifths of the time, he just fools around out of range until our planes go up after him and then he tears out for tall timber. One-fifth of the time he tears in hell-bent-for-hades from over the hills and swoops down very fast and makes a run for safety. So far since we've been here only one has made it back over the hill. All the others either fall to our guns or the boys up in the sky knock him over before he can get back in the foggy mist just at hilltop height. A really thrilling sight is watching our planes take off to intercept them. They take off; fly as fast as the machines will go for about two miles, and just before hitting the side of a hill turn their noses straight up in the sky; the engines shatter the stillness that usually prevails in the tropical twilight. The noise seems to take your head between its hands and shake it vigorously. And it must be said, Uncle Sam trains his men wisely. It is truly a wonderful and sigh-heaving sight to see our boys "tag" the devils without strain and shoot the hell out of him. He falls flaming but a mushrooming splash quenches the fire soon after. I'd like to picture the fighting we do out here Darling but I'm afraid I can't do it on paper. For instance, when our interceptors start climbing straight up in the sky, I can't convey to you the feeling I get when they keep going that way. For a long time after all reasonable judging and when I think they must stop or lose flying speed, they continue roaring upward ..... higher and higher and then when I'm dying for a breath of air that I discover I've been holding for full minutes, they straighten out and level off for horizontal flying. But then on the other hand. ..... the other morning at 2:30 A.M. I was sitting in the chart house with the phones on. It was drizzling rain outside and I was sitting on some foul weather clothing, huddled up half asleep. A shadow slowly moved past our starboard side and our inter-communication set up a constant chatter. The shadow was a destroyer, just in from a terrible fight. Bombs and shells and even a suicide Jap plane had plowed into her. Her entire superstructure was a mangled mess of melted steel except for bridge and radio shack. (Radio shack directly underneath.) She was crying and bleeding like a dog set upon by a pack of wolves. She needed blood ..... her men were burned, shot, cut, torn and shocked. She was asking us all for plasma. To me, sitting there so apart from everything but my imagination, she took on human nature and we all felt like everyone in the bay. She was a good ship. She was hurt badly and was ashamed but yet proud that she had stood up under all the beating they had given her. We could tell that in the firmness and confidence of the man on her speaker. He was proud because she had done more than her share to win the war. But now she needed help and her comrades came to her aid on the run. All the pretended competition between ships was forgotten ..... everyone was her buddy ..... our boats shoved off with help and doctors volunteered. Half her dead was buried at sea, the others taken to the beach to lie beside the Army and Marines.

Darling Baby Girl, it may be unwise for me to write such things. Perhaps I should try to cover up those details. But in my mind I retain the memory of how parallel our thoughts run their course. You know as well as I that some men die and others live. Perhaps, though, you don't know that where one ship suffers like that, there are six or seven hundred others here that are uninjured ..... go through hell fire and all they can throw at us and never get a scratch. But all this is in my mind and I want you to know and feel exactly as I do about it. Our love has been so successfully based on truth and frankness to each other. There is a war out here. Many many men are set against each other to destroy what the other owns and operates. And to destroy the man himself. Overhead is God, looking down and guiding what perhaps He thinks is the best course. You and I firmly feel that He won't separate us. As long as we cling to that belief, we are protected from the worry and strain of the unknown. I realize that I am in the shadow but David's twenty-third psalm is printed in my mind and His rod and staff comfort me. I often speak to God, just to renew my reminder that we feel the way we do and ask Him to see to it that we are not disappointed. I'm not trying to dim your picture of my situation with false statement and untruthful letters. Always we have seen our way so closely together that I can't bring myself to lie to you. I fear always that I might worry you but in my mind I know that you see as I do and I pray that you will continue to do so, no matter how trying it may be.

You see, Ray Ellen Darling, I worship you very deeply. I have nothing else to hold in my breast and cherish. I have many other things I could hold there but with you occupying my heart, I do not wish anything else to intrude. Forever, when a man is in trouble, He must have something to which he can cling for the future. It is when a man has nothing to inspire him when in trouble that he is lost. With you and your goddesslike image engraved in my heart along with your tiny scratches and the impression you made there during our sacred years together, I am one of the most fortunate men out here. I look at the dreary beach and the depression of my predicament weights heavily on my heart and shoulders ... but I bring your memory to mind, always ready at will, to soothe the ache in my body and mind. What you are doing for me is the most any woman can do for a man. You are keeping my body and soul together, my mind sane, for the day when I can return to a sane world and take up again the normal course God intended His children to pursue. Perhaps He too, owes you a bit of thanks. However valueless He may consider *my* humble faith, He would not even have that if it were not for you. There are many times when I have been on the verge of doubting Him. There have been times when I've stood at the rail watching black shadows carrying thousands of men to a hell and I've suddenly had an insane desire to raise my face and curse Him. What a terrible thing! But it's true. I feel perhaps that He could stop it. Why do I blame Him? He is trying to give man his freedom and if He steps in, He will rob them of the freedom of thought. I forget that in those moments but something I cannot forget is the way you would feel toward me if I actually did raise my voice against Him. You would be horrified and perhaps I would then become distasteful to you. And, My Darling, the worst of all punishments would be for you to dislike me for anything I've done. I wish I were there with you so you could help me a little. You always see things so clearly when I'm all jumbled up. That's just another of the many reasons I need you. And don't think, Darling, that I'm twisting up inside. It's just that I'm very bitter but believe me, my first look at you and the first feel of you in my arms will cause all that to disappear. Don't fear for my cracking up Baby Doll; I have looked at it from all sides (as impartial as possible) and feel that I am one of the sanest men aboard. It is just when I get in a depressing mood that I think those terrible things. I never unload them except on you and that has been your job to "take it" since our marriage. (A reason for my believing in God; no one but He could have given such a wonderful creature to me.) And I do thank Him deeply.

Ray Ellen, I adore you. You are so sweet to me and thoughtful always. I can never do enough to repay you the happiness you have brought me. But some day this will be over and I will commence doing everything in my power to try. I just want to shout "Eureka" or something when I think I have the rest of my life to spend with you. What a phenomenal future. Darling, I must stop now. I plan to go to bed and think about you. (Yes, I'm naughty but you can't stop me from dreaming.) I will write more tomorrow night and get this off the ship as soon as possible. Good night Darling. It's midnight and I must arise early. God Bless you.

Your devoted husband,
Orvill

P.S. I LOVE YOU!!!

---

11 December 1944

Hello, Darling Baby:

Well, this one will be short. As always, our orders come suddenly and I never get to finish completely anything I start. I wanted to add about four or six more pages to your letter tonight and finished up my work so I could do it. But we are ordered somewhere and I have many special reports to get out before we sail. I have an idea that we will be gone some time and you won't hear from me for about two weeks or more. Now be a brave little girl Darling and remember that your little boy is looking out for himself as best as can be done and God is doing the rest. By the time you get this, I suppose you will have read about it in the papers, but I have an idea that this will be another hot time. I think we have just about bled the Japs to death in the Philippines; anything they have anywhere else is to be considered trivial. (At least I hope.)

Good night now Darling Baby. I love you Baby Doll. Please always remember that. You know, I did a very stupid thing the other night. After writing to Norfolk, Va., for a street car token to complete your collection, I left it in my dungarees when they went to the laundry and one of the guys found it and when I asked him about it he had lost it himself. (Whew, what a sentence!) He may be able to find it sometime and if he does I will send it on to you. Baby your silver ring is almost ready. I told you I had to use a quarter; well it's in pretty good shape now and I will start drilling a hole in it. Hope it fits. I'm just guessing at the size but I bet I can guess pretty close. What you think, huh? Oh, yes, I mailed out all my Christmas cards you sent. Thanks a million again Baby Doll. You do the sweetest things and always are so thoughtful. I was the envy of the ship. No one else on here had a single card to send except me. The officer censors said if they had known I had them they would have tied me up and sent them themselves before I had written all over them. Some of them may be a little late except these I sent airmail. (You, Mom, Nell, Mother, Foree and Al Barnes.) By the way, I have a Filipino "Fifty Centavos" silver coin I'll send you soon. I want to shine it up a bit. I received it from the sticky, grimy fingers of a Filipino youth a few days ago. (He had his money tied up in a filthy handkerchief and was trading it off at two-to-one in favor of U.S. coin.)

Well, Baby, good night officially now. I still tell you that real often at 12:30 P.M., do you remember to at 10:30 P.M.? Nighty Darling. I adore and worship you. Don't worry about poppie, Baby, I'm o.k. and will make out fine. God bless you.

> Your devoted husband,
> Handsome

P.S. I LOVE YOU!!!

---

16 December 1944

Hello, Baby Darling:

Well I should be sleeping but then I know you will have been worrying about me a couple of weeks when you get this so I am starting it on to you now. Everything is fine. Our first "red hot" action came yesterday and today we are a proud bunch of guys. Proud because our fighting ability is all that saved our lives. The best place to start I suppose is at the starting, eh? Well, we got underway a few days ago and steamed right into their teeth. Past Jap airfields within visual range by using "long glasses" (telescopes). We fought them for three days before the landing and yesterday morning bright and early we started punching them toward the beach. But first, on the way around and up here, we were under intermittent airplane attack. It was a hard fight and were at G.Q. most of the time. At night however, it was all right inasmuch as we had chosen a time when the moon was not operating. It was very dark and they couldn't work on us much then.

We were not attacked individually on the way up but about the middle of one afternoon, a dive-bomber came in over a hill of a small island, roared over a three-mile stretch of water, circled and suicide-dived on a cruiser in company with us. I couldn't see him hit, all I saw was him coming over the water at about 250 miles per hour, as I was on the helm and was too busy spinning the wheel from "hard left" to "hard right" and vice versa. Two other planes were with him and we were dodging those. They didn't come in close though and were used for diversion. Our attention was on them while the other hit the cruiser. It was such a loud blast that those men who hadn't seen the plane, thought a fish had hit the cruiser. I was relieved on the wheel shortly after and saw him burning. It was a very furious and hot fire but soon came under control.

Later that evening, a destroyer got hit. We went to general quarters and stayed almost all the time until we hit the beach thirty-six hours later. Just as it was getting light enough to see (the island looked like a shadow lying down) we steamed in close and commenced pumping in the shells on houses, villages we knew were occupied by Japs and railroads. Honey, it felt good in my insides to see our shells blowing up the houses. It was a complete surprise to the Japs (they thought we were going to hit elsewhere) and I knew they were being blown skyhigh although I couldn't actually see them.

We were given the most difficult job of going in between the main island and a small island with a narrow channel. We couldn't maneuver very much. We had finished our job and were just starting out when three planes came in over the small island. They thought they had us cornered, and they did! They came in on our port bow and flew aft a ways about four miles out. They then turned directly in toward our stern. Flying about 250 miles per hour. Our gunners and boys feeding the shells did an admirable job. They sent out more than twenty shots from one of our bigger guns in less than a minute. (That is really punching.) They came in close enough now for the machine guns to open up. We had a direct bead on them. All three were smoking half a mile from us. Two came in directly at us and we knew then they were going to dive. The other turned off astern. Our machine gunners kept shooting at the two coming in. Honey, they turned right at us and to every man on the ship, it looked like they were after them personally. The feeling of chance and uncertainty was almost unbearable. Right in their faces the boys kept firing. They were hitting them all over. I can't imagine what held them together. They were Zeros but didn't explode like they are "supposed" to.[3]

The first came in like a hornet. The Captain was shouting "hard left rudder!", thirty seconds later, then "hard right rudder!", we were fish-tailing as fast as we could at high speed. That's all that saved us. The first barely missed our after smoke-stack and landed in the water. We rose with a pitch to port when she landed on the starboard side. I was in the pilot house and looking out those ports I told you about a long time ago. I saw the Jap's seat cushion (half of it I should say) come fly-ing by. Parts of wing and fuselage. Mighty waves carried them by and they all sank immediately. She had carried no bomb, thank goodness!

Slightly less than a minute the other came in. Seeing the first had missed, he was more determined than ever to hit us. The officer-of-the-deck and junior-officer-of-the-deck stepped to the port hatch and placed one foot outside and one inside. They stood behind each other ready for a quick mad dash for cover (scant as it was). They looked up (I couldn't see him for getting in their way and I wasn't anxious to be trampled on when they ran) and watch the second one come in. I watched their faces as they gave us the range and probable direction of the hit. As he flew closer and closer, bearing down right at them, I never saw such fear on anyone's face. They stood almost frozen and when they turned and ran the few feet inside, they stared at every thing and saw nothing. They were scared stark out of their wits. I eas-ily understand it because the three seconds between the time they shouted "duck" and when he actually hit, I have never felt so far from you Darling and yet so close. I still maintain that I wasn't scared. At least like the rest of them. I didn't duck. I felt a tug overhead and in-stantly a crash forward of the bridge. I looked forward and barrels of water and gasoline hit the ports a foot in front of my face. I thought "That bastard has knocked our foc'sle off." I couldn't see anything for the filth on the glass and the ship gave a mighty heave and groan, twisting and staggering like a bull clouted with a hammer. Then I real-ized that I had heard no explosion. The plane had not carried a bomb either. I reached up and turned on a port wiper and saw our forward guns still there. Also our anchoring equipment. Everything was intact. I looked down at my feet and two feet to the left was a small torn

---

3. The Japanese Zero's light frame and lack of self-sealing gas tanks resulted in an air-craft that was relatively flammable when hit by antiaircraft projectiles.

twisted piece of aluminum plating painted a machinery grey. It had bounced inside through the port hatch. Gasoline was all over the ship. As the last plane passed over, one of our guns had opened her gas tank, spraying the entire ship top to bottom, bow to stern. The planes had carried "gasoline bombs" which were supposed to ignite and burn upon hitting. They didn't because so much water had been mixed with it when they hit. The plane hitting forward had glanced off the port side of the foc'sle. (Just went to G.Q. They didn't come in.) (Back to the story.) Wreckage was scattered all over the ship, including a piece of sweater sleeve or neck the size of a cigarette package and a piece of the Jap's cheekbone picked up by the medical officer.

We were saved from serious damage by the Captain who, contrary to my former and fortunately incorrect opinion, is a real fighter. He always got excited when he was in operation with superior officers but when it comes to Japs he just shouts very loud so he can be heard and his spinning the wheel at the proper time kept the second Jap from landing right on the bridge. I think very much of him now and feel confident that our chances are improved even more than my former optimistic views. We have a good ship, proven by our men who did not run when it was time and excusable to run. We got an assist on the third plane because although we shot it down, the pilot managed to crash into a small ship and burn it up. It and another small ship was the only damage we suffered (except to us and I can't tell you all the damage although it was slight). The two small craft burned all day and far into the night until one of our destroyers sank them with shellfire.

Now, to explain why I wasn't particularly scared. You see, standing where I was, the planes approaching from the direction they were coming from, could not hit me without going through our mast, fire control director which is a very heavy and solidly mounted affair, and down through the heavy beams of the reinforced pilot house. I was standing on the far side and in back of other solidly mounted gear that I can't write about now. Zeros being as light as they are could not penetrate that much barrier. I knew I was safe even with a direct hit. And I think I explained to you that being on the bridge is the direct center of a target. And also how hard it is to ever hit the direct center of a target. Only a miracle and spinning the wheel saved the boys outside on the open guns. They can thank the Captain for their lives.

I will admit that after it was over, little Orvill was nervous as hell, because even feeling the way I do about being in the "center of a target" I know those devils were aiming at me personally. (I got kinda mad about it but when that cheekbone showed up I figured he had been amply repaid for his foolish mistake.) Had his gasoline bomb mission been properly accomplished, it might have been rather hot in the pilot house as it ran back and forth across the deck with the roll of the ship. But I had my phones unhooked from around my neck (sometimes I think of them, and the line being my "hangman's knot and rope"). I could have ran if running is dignified. Of course it isn't, but neither were the looks on those guy's faces. By the way, McDonough (also a talker on the bridge) didn't duck either. He explained that he was petrified and although he tried with everything he had he couldn't bring himself to move even.[4] There are many humorous sidelights that I don't have time to tell you about now, Darling. But someday I'll get around to telling you all about the "fights I had the last war." (Probably many many times more than you'll care to hear.)[5]

Well, Darling, that is about all I reckon. After that scorcher yesterday, the G.Q.s and other fighting is relatively insignificant. We are still kept topside, ready for battle stations and probably won't get any real sleep for two more days. I want to get this off now so you'll know that the landing, as far as I am concerned, on Mindoro was handled safely. There was not much opposition for the boys on the beach either.

So long for now darling. I may get to add more below and on the back before we get in but I doubt it. Be sweet and brave, Darling, and remember that Poppie is o.k. and safe as long as you love me and the memory of you is in my mind the way it is constantly. The thought that God intends to spare me for you and myself helped a lot yesterday. Many thoughts pass through a mind during the two minutes that you start and cease firing. Bye darling baby girl and remember that I worship you and sometimes wish that we could get a good hit so we could get back to the States for repairs and leave. If it wasn't for the fact that somebody has to die in order to get hurt that bad, I would

---

4. An inability to move is a manifestation of an anxiety-induced psychological breakdown, which in more serious cases may extend into a memory lapse or sustained amnesia, all designed to banish fear (in this case, of the attacking kamikazes) from the mind. See p. 472 of S. Kirson Weinberg, "The Combat Neuroses," *American Journal of Sociology* 51 (1946): 465–478.

5. Robert Lyons (see Preface) told me of the exuberance he and his young shipmates displayed in the wake of this near miss. Their celebration was cut short by an older gunner's mate who reminded them that they were not playing a game and pointed out just how close they all had come to being killed.

wish it. God Bless you Baby Girl and kinda pray a little, huh? We can always use it, all of us. I love you Darling.

> Your devoted husband,
> Orvill

P.S. I LOVE YOU!
No Baby I don't mind you letting other people read my letters occasionally. Thanks for the compliment. I hope your friends aren't bored by them.

> Sunday, 17 December 1944

Hello, Baby Darling:

Well, I do get to write a little today. First of all, I want to apologize for not telling you earlier in the letter—Sidney is o.k. I got a letter from him written the 10th of December and his ship went down about five days before that. He said that he could see me from where he was quartered. They won't tell us of course where they are because they want to keep things as secret as possible. I have written Neva (he enclosed her address) and gave her as much information as I could and tried to set her mind at ease. I interpreted Sid's letter as asking me to do that. I'll send it to you soon. Also, he said for you to try and write her. ... Oh, yes, Sid made chief yeoman. He may get a trip back to the states and a new ship out of this. (Being routed the same way around through Norfolk, etc.)

Boy, sure hope we get some mail when we get back to the other side. I am about to lose my mind, not getting your mail properly. When I do, it's all SNAFU as to continuity of dating.

We have all day today to run the gauntlet between the islands. We have been going to G.Q. for half an hour to an hour on an average of eight to ten times a day. We are still under intermittent attack by planes but none have gotten within machine-gun range. They come in singly and in twos and our bigger guns drive them off or shoot them down. We can't claim any of them as all ships fire at the same time. We keep a rather good barrage up and they usually get clipped before getting in too close. Those that get away are downed by our air coverage about 95% of the time. That is good, because when the devils leave their airfields and don't show up again, it is good for decreasing morale. (Of the Japs.) Honey, we have them whipped. It's only a matter of saving our boys from the fanatical suicides they are taking in order to escape the consequences. They are firmly convinced that we plan to pull their toenails and hair out by the roots and slice them to pieces a little at a time. That's humorous but tragic too. Perhaps they would quit if they realized we aren't atrocious as they are.[6] The bastards are a beautiful picture falling with a trail of smoke though. We have found no surface opposition anywhere in the islands. Only a tanker and troop transport early one morning about four days ago. It was on the other side from us and the other ships had the pleasure of sinking them. I'll get a lot of fun telling you about a sea battle. It is very impressive. We were supposed to go after a Jap destroyer day before yesterday but our Admiral wouldn't let us because of the minor damage done to us by the planes. The damage was minor but to a very valuable piece of equipment [IFF interrogator]. The Captain and all of us were plenty mad. The other can gunned it up on the beach and left it burning furiously. Survivors to be knocked off by our soldier friends. The army can't kick about the way we set them ashore up here. There wasn't a shot fired on the beach, no mines or barbed wire. Very neat and efficient.

Well Darling, I'm going to close now. I wanted to tell you about Sid. I sure am glad he is alive. He's a pretty old guy but I like him a lot. (Old in actions I mean.) So long darling, I'll write you a more "personal" letter when I can get those planes off my mind. Honey, I dreamed about you last night. I came home on leave and met you at the office. You were closing the door and had a great big frown on your face. I grabbed you and you started sobbing and crying. I asked you what was the matter and you answered "not now, I'll tell you later." Darling, is something the matter? Are you having trouble or something? I've never had such a dream before and I don't want you to be frowning. Please write and tell me how things are, huh? Bye for now Baby Doll, I love and worship you, please believe that. God bless you Darling and remember that I am your worshipful slave forever.

> Your devoted husband,
> Orvill

P.S. I LOVE YOU!!!

---

6. But the Japanese government had its own effective and pervasive propaganda effort to encourage hate for their enemies. See Dower, *War Without Mercy*, chapter 9: "The Demonic Other."

19 December 1944 (Six days til Christmas)

Hello, Baby Darling:

Last night I got a whole handful of mail and I worked until about ten P.M. and then read letters until midnight. I was sleepy this morning but happy as a lark. I sure felt nice and still do. I have your letters here now and will attempt to answer them tonight. I've worked pretty hard today as we are transferring about fifteen men back to the states. McDonough and I don't ever hope though because when the Chief gets his Warrant commission, we will be here forever of the duration. You see, we are allotted so many yeomen and when he leaves we will be under complement two yeomen and it's a cinch they will transfer no one when we have fewer than we are supposed to have.

Today I had a visit from a very nice guy. Glenn Murray came over. First he sent me a "PVT" message via flag signals to Lynch on the Bridge. A "PVT" message being "private" and unauthorized. They are illegal and not to be sent but for good friends the signalmen break out the flags and send silently. I am enclosing the message he sent just for the originality and uniqueness of the thing. By the way the "AAA" means just plain "period." (PVT MSG TO ORVILL RAINES Y 2/c AAA I am trying to get over today but don't think I can make it AAA If you can try to come over here AAA Signed G R Murray TM [torpedoman's mate] 3/c.) He made me break out my pictures and show them all and asked me to give him one of you and I together. I showed him the one we had hugging each other on the lawn at Lula's in the spring of '43 and LaVerne and already sent him one like it. He took a few I had of LaVerne (I figured he welcomed all he could get of her) and some of us and the family. I had a couple of all of us and he took one of them. LaVerne had sent him a bunch like the last bunch I got last night. (The ones taken at Neita's of yall) I took him back to the torpedo shack and introduced him to Smitty [Warren H. Smyth], TM 1/c, a good buddy of mine, and they had a very nice chat. He thought we had a nice clean ship and actually expressed a desire to be transferred over here. It would be nice but on the other hand I feel kinda like the Navy on "all the chickens in the same coop."

He said he prayed for us the other day when the planes came in. They looked to him like they would hit direct on the bridge. (He wasn't sure I was up there though.) His ship was the closest one to us but out of range and couldn't help us fire on the three planes. We got credit for all three planes and the Captain complimented the crew

highly in his report to the Commander-in-Chief. We also shot one up
on the beach that was parked and got credit for that too. So we have
four [Japanese] flags [painted] on the bridge now and one palm tree for
the bombardment and two skulls and cross-bones for suicide divers. It
was the first time (we believe) that two planes had crashed on a destroyer. Destroyers being as small as they are, they try to waste only
one plane on them. A cruiser however is different. They are larger and
better "meat." By the way, the plane that crashed into a ship I told you
about in my last letter killed 125 men and 18 officers and wounded 50
others because it landed smack in the middle of the chow line before
the guys could run. I heard about two weeks ago that Glenn's ship had
been hit but he told me differently today. I think I wrote you about it.
Anyway, they weren't and he is o.k. He looked better today than before. He had cleaned up. Boy, I sure get a kick out of this "cleaning-up"
business. We really go to town with shave, shower, clean socks and all
the other trim and then don DUNGAREES! Reminds me of Arkansas
when we used to dress up in overalls to go to church Sunday morning
and night. Oh, yes, probably the way the story got started about
Glenn's ship being hit is that they spent three days and nights on the
"suicide patrol" outside Leyte Gulf and were attacked by nine Jap
planes. They downed one and scared the others off. They dropped their
bombs in the water a safe distance out and ran off. We had one day and
night on the suicide patrol the second day after his ship came back in.
We think we will leave soon for a base farther back from the fighting
zone in a couple of days to get our repairs effected. They don't have
the facilities here to do the job. I expect a little beer out of it and an afternoon on the beach. I've been on this baby now without getting off
since the 3rd of November if I remember correctly.

We could all stand a little rest. We don't have to go to G.Q. in the
morning early and don't have our hearts jumping into our throats five
or six times a day when the beep ..... beep ..... goes for an air raid. I
folded up my last letter to you the other night and we had a real bad
scare about five minutes later. A two-engine bomber (Jap of course)
came in riding a rain squall. We couldn't see it very well as it was late
dusk. It couldn't see us either very well and was making a stab at any
target of "opportunity." He started diving on another ship ahead of us
and then our forward stack began smoking. I have the circuit to the
engine rooms (telephone circuit) and started chewing. In the midst of

the smoking, he spotted us and turned into our port side about a mile out. We began shooting with everything we had and drove him off. It was really too much fire power for him. Then I went out on the wing of the bridge and sat down (after my nerves steadied somewhat) and I pressed the button of my phone down and started chewing. For five minutes without a let up I cursed and explained the reason he came in on us. We were the only ones he could get a good "spot" on because of the smoke. I told them to knock it off and cursed every machinist's mate and water tender down in the engineering spaces. It is the worst chewing I ever gave anyone and nobody else on the line said a word. Just kept their mouth shut and when I finished I was sweating profusely and the engineers really started apologizing and explaining how hard it was to keep down the smoke. It is hard but very important as exemplified by that bit of dodging. After G.Q. secured I swaggered down the decks ready to clout anybody that gave me any "guff" but I was slightly mistaken, everybody concerned agreed with me 100%, even the guys I had cussed out; they understood; and those not concerned were glad because they were looking at that plane come in. Another time we had a bad fright because we couldn't see the plane at all. The other ships were firing but we couldn't even see the devil. That shook us up because that is worse than watching him come in. We could tell somewhat his course by looking at tracers. He passed close aboard to port but was hit by another ship and our "air coverage" went in for the kill twelve miles away where they caught him and he hit the water before they had to fire. So the other ship chalked up another one. That was a hard haul, Honey, but well worth the effort.

I am anxiously awaiting the time when we will go into Manila Bay. Today will be a mighty rough fight and worse than anything we've seen yet but the "big boys" will be in there to push back the surface enemy with their long range guns. We will have a better time of it there than here but the wagons [battleships] and cruisers will fight a hard battle. When that one is done, I expect it in a couple of months, the fight out here will practically be over I believe. Of course, China will take a lot of time but that won't be our fight I don't think. And another angle, the Japs may cover up their heads and really quit when we start hitting their home shores with our main Navy; which will be done when we take all the Philippines.

So much for war, Baby Darling. I hope I don't worry you with it. But

I maintain that I should give you all the facts that I can. If you don't want me to write about them, please say so immediately and I will stop it. I won't mind at all. I really want your opinion and wishes expressed. O.K.? Just place your beautiful hand in God's and carry on; keep that lovely chin up and those wonderful eyes as dry as possible. I'll kiss the tears away when I meet you at the station; I'll hold that chin in my hand and kiss those precious lips; I'll kiss those smooth white flawless fingers and hands and worship and adore you forever and keep you close in my arms for as long as you live if you so desire.

While I'm on the subject of informing you of my activities, let me say that I don't mind your showing my letters to other people. I was kinda worried about your showing that letter to Foree because I just sat down and wrote it without putting in any real editorial effort. I was just kinda writing and talking to you and I don't pay too much attention to grammar and such when I have a conversation with you. And another thing, if you ever show any more to him, explain that it isn't to be printed; if the Navy got hold of it it would lead to serious trouble for me. Everything is to be reviewed and released by Naval authorities when they are published for public consumption. I appreciate yours and his thoughtfulness and think it was nice of him to print a little of it but sometimes the Navy might see it and drop a line out this way. Of course, the chances are miniature but then you never can tell. And too, I don't like very much publicity; even if it is just a four-inch story. I think a reporter's publicity should be limited to a by-line; otherwise people begin to think his work is "authoritative" and he gets dinda [sic] gradually and unconsciously puts in some of his own personal views on things, etc. and that is for men who are a little older than I and have more experience in judging things. In time, I will accept such things when I feel I am capable. (Please don't think that I now consider myself a national "commentator" or "analyst" due to a four-inch story!) Ha.

An incident occurred today that might interest you. Ever since we got out here, Lynch (who has a very fertile mind) has talked up the "good-luck" properties of dropping coins in his "flag-bag." In fact the Flag Bag Sitters Association figures largely in this little "business." Anyway, just before going into a place where we feel we might see some action, a large number of solicited guys come around and drop coins in his flag bags for good luck. We now have a fairly sizable sum in the bottom of the bag. A "guard" is placed over it when his strikers go down to clean it out. Today, he was airing his flags, i.e., all the signal flags strung up on the lanyards to flap in the breeze. The Captain and I, discussing some letters, stopped by there and he looked down. "Good God!" he exclaimed. "What is all this?" "LYNCH! What's going on here?" Lynch explained what it was, adding that the FBSA (Flag Bag Sitters Association) planned to pitch a good one when we got back to the states on the proceeds from the wishing bag. "O.k. but what do you do for insurance when a guy like Raines climbs down there to sleep?" Lynch explained that no one slept "in" the bag but on "top" of it. The Old Man said, "Well, I'll tolerate this underhanded racketeering if you cut me in on half of it so I can pitch one too!"...

By the way, did I tell you about George and I collaborating on attempting to write some short stories? We are but haven't gotten very far as yet. It will take us some time to get going as it is new to us and our ideas are slow in coming. And Honey, I think I've got my idea for the book. "The" book! There are several angles to work out yet of course and I plan to toy with it for a couple of years before writing it. But anyway, I "think" I have the basic idea. I'll review it for you sometime when I have the time and am in good physical shape. I really think you will like it. Mostly, our work now is sorta to prepare us for our civilian jobs and I want to keep as much at a typewriter as possible. (I mean with creative work.) I think maybe if I look into our library and study a little I can keep active enough not to be "ignorant" when I go back to The News. George plans to go into a book store business with his brother and sister when he gets out. He is a well read young man, more on the "far-fetched" side perhaps, but acquainted with all the better authors. (Raines in particular!)

Baby Girl, I didn't get far with answering your letters tonight. I wrote about the things I remembered and there are still some others yet but I am so tired I'm going to bed now. I will mail this "Special" [delivery] to make up for it. Night now, I will think about you a long time tonight. I can always tell when I have you on my mind so much I'll think about you. I plan to find out exactly what time it was in Dallas when the planes came in on us the other day and maybe you can remember what you were doing. I doubt it seriously but maybe something will recall you to the time. The whole thing, from sighting them to picking them out of our hair, took only two minutes! Night darling. I literally worship you.

Wednesday Night, 20 December 1944

Hello, Baby Darling:

I just came down from the bridge at general quarters. Leyte Gulf is fairly secure now inasmuch as action is concerned. It was our first general quarters all day today. We didn't even have dawn alert this morning and I slept until 8:30. Tonight though, two "Nells" came in (two-engine land-based bombers) right at dark when they are always so hard to see. They passed over the whole harbor at about a mile altitude. All of us opened fire and they started diving lower (don't think they intended suicide though) and heading in our direction. One came in directly but our fire hit him slightly and he turned away—right into the fire of about four other ships. The other plane was mobbed then with all guns of all ships. It actually lifted a hundred pound weight off my chest to see him turn away very slowly and very very slowly fall off and smoke pour out of him. He hit hard and made a big splash. Glenn's ship was anchored right next to us and was firing to beat hell too. It seems his ship is always nearby. Almost every move we've made, he has been right with us. They were the ship nearest us when we had the trouble the other day. But, I didn't get to go over and see him today as I had hoped. He told me to try and make it this afternoon but it is a pretty hard job to get away out here. We are so advanced that we have to stay close to our "guns" so to speak.

Well, I'll try to answer some of your questions, Honey. I got three more letters from you tonight and one from Neita. One of yours inquired about Vaughan Hubert. Well, he is still on here and is fine. He was about three feet in front of me the other day during the action. He was on the wheel. He was the man doing the "spinning" of the wheel like I was a few days before. That is his regular G.Q. station and is a good man although his senior quartermaster is much better yet. He was a very scared boy too, I looked at him and he was white as a sheet. When the officer-of-the-deck shouted "Duck!" I thought he was going to run. He started and then thought better of it. I can't blame the kid at all. I saw him night before last long enough to talk to and his folks had written him about his aunt meeting Mom and Pop and talking about it. We had a great big laugh. Really, when you look at the situation it's funny. Of all the destroyers in the Pacific Ocean . . . . . they had to get together and have kids on the same tincan. Boy, that beats me. We had a big laugh about it. I told him they hadn't heard from him in a long time but he didn't say anything. I didn't say anything. I didn't

advise him to write, though, that is his business. You see he hasn t
spoken to his father in over six years. Can you top that? They had
trouble and stopped speaking completely. He only speaks to his
mother when he visits. His mother, I think, is an invalid or semi-
invalid. I can't figure the guy not writing though Everyone else has
time and he has more time off than I do. So much for that. (No, he
didn't have his tonsils out, he's o.k. no complaints.) ...

Darling, I understand about your waiting and looking for the mail
and worrying about me. It's all right ..... if you didn't worry I guess I'd
not like it. The can you said the radio revealed about the time you
wrote that letter mentioning it was Sid's that went down. A few
others have been officially announced too since then. But I'll always
tell you that "I've lost your picture" if we get it. You will have to not
tell your friends because it is important that those things be kept
quiet. Important to me and the whole Pacific Navy.

Honey, I SWEAR you are wonderful. Even standing up and writing to
me on a filing cabinet. There's no doubt that I'm right in saying you are
the most faithful and devoted wife a guy can have. And don't think it
isn't both ways Darling. I'll always worship you for it. It means so very
much in my heart to know you are the kind of girl you are. Honey, I got
a letter from Frank the other day too. All he could write about was you
mostly. I'm proud that my folks can recognize what a rare prize I got.
He said "Boy, you sure have a wonderful girl in Ray Ellen. And I mean
she is ALL YOURS." "That's about the most important thing of all, I
guess." Wasn't that nice? He couldn't say anything else though. Baby,
you know, in addition to being what you are to me, you have given my
family something they never had before. You have brought jolliness and
real friendship among a group of people who have almost always argued
among themselves a little at times. At first they were kinda afraid of
you because they were and are the kind of depressed people who look
upon those with a "brick home" as being in a class beyond their reach.
(Can you get what I mean?) Semi-poverty I mean, has almost always
been their lot. And you coming from a "brick home" and "refined parents with active brains and practical education" to accept them and enjoy their company with true sincere friendship. That's one of the reasons they love you. The other is that people just can't help loving you.
You are so good. You always take things on the chin and never lash out
with a bitter tongue when things don't go to please you exactly. It's
your refined principles that cause you to reserve bitter feeling on an
issue that might hurt another. I get a "gloating" feeling inside me to know

that they can't criticize you. It is quite the contrary and you are the first to establish that record. Gosh, Baby, I could go on all night singing your good points. And I mean "singing" because that's what my heart does when I think of you.

Honey, you're getting around quite a lot lately and I'm glad. Don't tire yourself out, though. Get plenty of sleep and don't age worrying over me like you say. Let me do all of that. After the raid tonight I said over the phones "Boy, I'll be as old as Mathusla (spelling?) if this keeps up much longer. I age five years everytime those babies come in." The First Lieutenant was on the phone and said "You're right, Raines. Mathusla seems kinda young to me and our experiences already." We all got a laugh and our nerves settled a little.

Gosh, Honey, every time I get a letter or group of letters from home somebody mentions sending me something. No wonder the mail situation is as it is. My packages are clogging up the transportation system. Darling, you folks don't have to put out so much for me. It's really nice but heck, I want yall to take it easy and not worry about me. I know how YOU feel honey. Anyway if you feel the way I do about sending you things. You know a person doesn't realize that giving is more pleasure than receiving until they get grown. When I was a kid I sure couldn't understand that principle. Now I do, I wish I could give you the whole world. (Is that what makes men like Hitler?) Maybe some woman IS behind him. She certainly isn't like you if there is. I have done some more work on your ring and will have it completed soon. I carry it in my pocket all the time and work on it when I can sit down and piddle with it. By the way, you will have gotten your purse by the time you get this letter. Boy, I sure hope you like it. I'm nuts about it myself. (Remember those pillow slips of flour sacks Mother sent us for a wedding present? Well, I'm afraid that I, in my masculine taste, might be sending you a purse you wouldn't step out of the house with and I think is real snazzy. Sure hope not.)[7] Honey, little Skabik (I wrote you about) is being transferred back to the states. He was one of the lucky ones. Sure happy for him too but I'll miss him. His wife had an 8-pound boy for him. He is about to run wild knowing that and that he will be sent to Frisco probably or maybe San Diego which is better.

---

7. Raines had prevailed upon a boatswain's mate to manufacture a small purse out of small stuff (twine), using various knots known collectively as fancywork, for Ray Ellen. The purse has been donated to the Louisiana Naval War Memorial's ex-USS *Kidd* (DD 661), permanently berthed in Baton Rouge.

Darling, speaking of babies, I must confess something to you. All these years you have been wanting a baby, I wanted one too but I didn't realize how the feeling really effected you. Until the other day I was reading through of all things a comic book and saw a little golden hair girl about five years old and I got such a terrible craving feeling in my chest for one. I truly know now how you felt about it and believe me the minute I get home I am going to take definite steps to alter the situation favorably. (You probably never thought a comic book would do me any "good" did you?)

Glad you folks are getting to see Mother. Neita tells me she is breaking fast. Sure hope she can hold out until I get back. I still entertain optimistic hopes on the war situation out here and can't help but believe that it is better than most people think.

Guess the five packages did give you a "bad time" as they say in the Navy. But heck, you could have opened at least one anyway. Boy, I bet you could clout me for saying that NOW instead of before Christmas, couldn't you? Guess I'm getting in the dog house more and more on that Christmas deal. The selections were pretty poor but it was the best I could do, Darling. Anyway the most important of all is that my heart is there in each box you open and it is all *yours*. I am your husband, lover and sweetheart *always*. And *yours alone*. ...

Say, You, what's the idea you sitting up and tearing your stockings shooting dice with my in-laws, etc.? And poker! In the living room! And on Sunday morning! Boy, I'd better hurry back and straighten you out. I got a kick out of that though. I bet you guys do have fun. You always do though, you little louse. If it isn't legal you tickle somebody's ribs at least.

I got the letter Johnnie wrote you and the picture of the baby. Boy, she and Norv are just like all the rest of the parents and the way we'll probably be. "Hercules," the "biggest and strongest baby I ever saw," and the "handsomest kid in the world," etc. All that stuff, I've heard all my life. It'll be lots of fun kidding them about it. I will send the picture back after I've looked at it a while. I'll drop them a line soon.

Bet yall have fun (or rather *had*) at the Xmas tree at the apartment. And the neighbors had misery. Oh, yes, I wanted to tell you. Did you know we can't have any Xmas music out here? They don't send us any records with Xmas carols on them, no "White Christmas" or anything like that. It is too home-sickening for the boys and we get hot-stuff, blues songs and all the other. And no "My gal's gone and left me" stuff either. I've noticed that ever since we left the States. It does make things easier. As a matter of fact, Christmas will be just another day to us. If I wasn't a yeoman I would never know what day it was. The guys always have to ask me. Sunday may be Thursday to them. Christmas will be the same way except that the Pharmacist's Mate friend of mine has a pint stowed away and will "break it out" Xmas Eve. (That will be the night before for you.) Just a round apiece will be all I guess. Just enough to mix a good drink in some stolen pineapple juice or orange juice we got from the commissary department.

A very beautiful song is coming over the set in our office right now. It is the best of them all we have aboard except "The Song." It's "I'll Walk Alone." Its message is sure a wonderful thing. It sorta generates peace when a guy imagines his love is singing it. The human mind will forever mystify me with its operating qualities. Here I am, I can walk out on deck and see death and destruction, deadly ships lying in shadows ready to fire guns that will brighten the pitch blackness to the visibility of the day, and I can stand there and let my mind go back. Everything blots out. I just see your face ... or you standing there in your red suit with a smile on your face. I can actually recall the sweetness of you close to me. The exact texture of your hair when I brush my lips into it. Your cute little ear and the perfume behind it. Your slender soft hands touching my face. I can feel your shoulder snuggle under my arm as you wiggle closer to me. I can't see any of the terrible things in front of me. It is all you and the wonderful life we have led in the past. Or maybe it's the wonderful life we will lead in the future. My plans will visualize before me. And the most prominent is the picture you will make at the station when you meet me and we run off to rest. Rest ..... it will be a Godsend. And with you it will be even more holy and wonderful. I look forward to it with every cell in me. ...

Yes, Honey, I was for Roosevelt too. He is the only guy for the office right now. Later after the war I hope for a change. My reasons are that he is too extravagant (but is necessary to win the war now) and too he is getting too much power. If it isn't cancelled shortly after the war is over, then I'm going to do some howling. You understand that he is now in possession of emergency war powers that gives him more authority than any president the United States has ever had. He very nearly approaches a dictator but it is necessary at the moment. But if they show hesitation in revoking it once the emergency is over then it is time to do something quickly. He is a very intelligent man and a wizard at politics. I might even say a genius at politics. He is too smart to let go too long.

You wondered what kind of shows we see. Well, I saw *Three Jills in a Jeep*; a whole lot of third grade pictures and once in a while some pretty good ones. I can't remember any names now because they weren't much good. Entertaining though inasmuch as they are different from the regular routine. We haven't had movies in a long time now. It is unsafe to have so many men crowded in the messhall when G.Q. or something is likely to come at any moment. And too in case of bomb or torpedo, too many in one spot. Like the boys in the chow line I mentioned earlier in the letter [of December 16]. ...

Baby, I got the letter you said to not open until Dec. 25th. I have it in my pocket and will save it unless we go into some more hot action. I will read it under those conditions because you never can tell. However, it is only five more days and we still haven't gotten any information on repairs yet and it will take almost five days for them to be effected. So you can depend on it being opened on Dec. 25th.

Well, Darling, this is all for now. I didn't get to get that time "of the attack" for you and it's too late now and I want to get this in the mail tomorrow because we may get underway in the afternoon. We never know exactly what is going to take place. Even the Captain doesn't always know. I just hope they don't send us out on any more of those runs for a while.

Good night Baby Darling, and try not to worry about me any more than you can help. I know you worry a little but try and not let it get the better of you. Always remember that I am in here pitching with all I've got to get back to you and anytime a fire or anything starts on the bridge, I will be the first one in the water after George. He (due to his experience before) is a very scary guy now. He puts on his life jacket and helmet at the slightest excuse and I follow his example. I notice that all the guys who have had to swim for it before don theirs too. So I feel that I am taking sound silent advice. I'll never beat George over the side but I'll sure be second. Bye for now darling, I probably won't even be going over the side, we have it pretty good all around. Be a sweet girl like I know you always are and never forget for a moment and I will be

Your devoted husband forever,
Orvill

P.S. I LOVE YOU!!! I WORSHIP YOU!!!

8

Lingayen Gulf and the Luzon Island Invasion

On December 22, 1944, *Howorth* led a convoy of twenty-one transport ships from Leyte Gulf to Hollandia, New Guinea. Six days and a depressing Christmas at sea later, *Howorth* entered Humboldt Bay, where the radar antenna, bent by the kamikaze at Mindoro, was repaired. On January 3 *Howorth* began a ten-day voyage escorting the second supply group for the January 9 invasion of Luzon at Lingayen Gulf. The convoy came under suicide attack on January 12, one day prior to arriving at Lingayen.

On the evening of January 14, *Howorth* provided fire support for U.S. troops ashore on Luzon, firing fifteen five-gun salvos into a "designated Japanese-held ridge."[1] Regular shore fire missions in support of ground troops followed. Interspersed with gunfire support was tedious duty in the naval picket lines guarding the approach to Lingayen Gulf. Finally, on January 26, *Howorth*'s time at Lingayen Gulf ended, and she led a convoy of fifteen Liberty ships back to the relative safety of Leyte Gulf, arriving there on January 31.

For Orvill Raines, *Howorth*'s lengthy and arduous duty at Lingayen was marked by a lack of mail, fatigue from hours spent at battle stations, periodic moments of stark fright, floating Japanese corpses, anger at the constant motion of the ship, anger at home-front commentators who predicted that combat veterans would return home different from when they went to war, and a dream that the Japanese had suddenly surrendered and the war was over.

---

1. See the secret "Special Action Report (Shore Bombardment)" for the January 14, 1945, mission on microfilm Reel E-108, NPPSO–Naval District Washington Job No. AR-65-78, "*Howorth* (DD-592), Report File, War Diary"; note 25, Introduction above.

27 December 1944

Good evening, Little Baby Girl:

Well, Darling, I guess the only thing I've got to talk about this time is Christmas. It is over and done with. Christmas morning I stood the midnight till 4 A.M. watch on the bridge. We were underway and the moon and stars were treacherously shining brightly. The water was a beautiful blue as I hung over the wing of the bridge. The phosphorous shined too and I thought of it as the imitation snow on Christmas trees back home. The foam was the snow. I had an enjoyable time but had difficulty imagining it Christmas with the weather so warm and the atmosphere so balmy. (We crossed the Equator the seventh time this morning.)

Everyone tried. They said "Merry Christmas!" but it was as flat as "The Same to You." The evening before, my friend the ship's cook asked what watch I had that night and when I told him, he said to drop around to the galley about 4 A.M. and he'd have me a "buzzard sandwich" ready. We were having turkey for Christmas dinner so thought I'd have a bite of chow before retiring for an hour's sleep. Well, I went in the galley and for the first time that day (or night) heard a real merry "Merry Christmas!" The lights came on (they go out automatically when we open a hatch for blackout purposes) and I saw to my surprise an all night crew of rugged individuals I call my best friends. It was a collection of bosun's mates, machinists mates, cooks, radiomen, strikers for almost all the rates, and water tenders. On the galley range sat a bucket, a large aluminum affair with the top closed air tight. Out of this came a copper tubing that took several twists, the bottoms of which were submerged in a bucket of cold water, thence down onto the deck into a gallon jug. Out of the tube slowly dripped pure perfect distilled alcohol. This impressed me very favorably and I looked around at my friends. We were a jolly bunch and I saw only one inebriated shipmate (my bosun mate friend). The rest were just jolly tight. A bowl of alcohol mixed with grapefruit juice was thrust into my willing hand and I drank deeply. I drank that one and another mixed with orange juice. It was plenty and I felt a glow although not enough to misjudge my bearing while walking around on the slippery deck.

We had a guitar and [Dean B.] Kelly, the machinist mate, played and we sang. We sang so lustily that the noise went up the ventilator shaft and aroused the Officer-of-the-Deck. He couldn't leave the bridge so sent the Junior O.O.D. down to investigate. The latter practically forced his way in (we all had gained admittance by name only) but the first we "carolers" knew of his presence was the slate-gray of his pants leg as he thrust it over the hatch bottom. I give us lots of credit for our quick wit. Instantly, from a lusty and hearty bellow of "Down by the Railroad, the baggy old Whore, etc." to a very soft and harmonious and melodious rendition of "Silent Night . . . . . Holy Night . . . . . etc." Our expressions were very serious and the JOOD was convinced of our "chastity" before we were forced to struggle through the second verse which none of us knew. Reveille and G.Q. finally sounded and broke up the party. I went to sleep out on the deck that morning but arranged for a friend to "give me a growl" at 9:30 A.M. He did and then I opened your card that you had written "Don't open till Dec. 25." I read it then because it was 7:30 P.M. Christmas Eve in Dallas and the kids were just about arriving at the apartment and a lot of shouting and stuff was going on. I went back to sleep more or less contented and awakened at 11:30 to eat and go back on watch. At twelve, it was 10 P.M. there and I knew the party was in full swing. From then until 2:30 (12:30 there) I had a very enjoyable Christmas Eve party interrupted only by the infrequent requests of the OOD for telephone information. Everyone was in a sort of preoccupied mood and my drifting thoughts went unnoticed. I put you to bed at 1 A.M. (3 P.M. here) but decided if you went out to Mom and Pop's it would be 1:30.

About the dinner. We had turkey, dressing, English peas, carrots, cranberry sauce, rolls, fruit cake, pie (Mince), sweet spuds, candy and other things I guess. They passed out Red Cross ditty bags (like those Lula sewed. I fancied that she might have sewed one of them for us) containing soap, shoeshine rag, candy, nuts, a book, cigarettes and oodles of items like that. As I entered the mess hall with my tray full, a cook was sitting on the end of the table passing out little bags of candy. He looked at me and in a painful voice (we all felt silly saying it) said "Merry Christmas, Raines." "Merry Christmas, Worley," I answered. Usually, at a big dinner like that the mess hall is buzzing with din. But it was almost quiet as a tomb. And damn it I had to choke back a sob, as others did I guess when Worley gave me that stupid "Merry Christmas." I went over and sat down by McDonough. He said nothing and neither did I. We usually have lots to talk about but nothing on this occasion. When he left first, neither still said anything. It was pretty morbid but I hope the others had in their heart the peace and contentment I had. I knew that at that moment My Baby, even

though she missed me terribly, was having a good time and was not in
fear of mistreatment. I knew that my brothers and sisters were talking
loud and having fun. The men folks probably slipping back in Nell's
room to sneak a drink. I believe they all missed me but were carrying
on just the same. The others must have felt somewhat the same because none moped. They were just quiet and thinking all day long. I finally tucked you in bed and at 4 P.M. went down and slept on the deck
again. I ate supper at 5:15 P.M. and you were still sleeping in a nice
cozy bed. I slept some more and at 7:45 went back on watch until midnight. I got you out of bed at 9:30 P.M. (7:30 your time A.M.) and you
ran into the living room and had one of those wild squealing times
you always have when you open packages. Well, yall finally wound
that up (you got the purse and read the letter) and when I finally got off
watch for the day, I went below and drifted off to sleep with you helping Mom (or Bessie) with dinner or arguing with Pop. Nell telling a
smutty joke and Pop trying to slip another "Pink Lady" and Mom trying generally to keep order throughout the household. When I got up
for G.Q. and had breakfast and then went on watch for the 8 A.M. till
12 noon, I couldn't figure where the hell you were. You could have
been anywhere for Christmas Day night.

So ..... transpired Christmas, 1944. And the one bit of philosophy
that came out of it was from a chief machinist mate friend I had
wished an enjoyable season. He said "The same to you Raines and
many more of them." And again we had withdrawn from the hot and
furious front battle line just in time. Today a Jap force steamed into
Mindoro and landed troops on the beach and bombarded our boys
there in exactly the same spot we had shelled 12 days before. I can't
believe that Halsey is stupid enough to let that happen unless he has
another trap set. We will know in a couple of days. I believe he has it
under control but can't help worry some. We are in a peaceful and
quiet zone now and tomorrow I rate going over on the beach at Hollandia and drinking a couple of beers. It will be my first [time] to set
foot on dirt since November 4th. Lynch is going to try and go with me.
He hasn't been off the ship since we left Pearl Harbor. He told me he
didn't care to go over with anyone but me and we are in different liberty sections. I am arranging the correction to that (being a yeoman,
ahem!) end. We arrive in port at 6 A.M.

Darling, Your ring is ready. I just want to put the finishing touches
on it before sending it. And I made it all myself!! It turns pretty badly
out here in the salt water (I've worn it and slept in it two nights now

to kinda break it in) but think you can keep it in better shape there. Maybe you'll have to polish it a little before you wear it each time. I don't want it to take the place of your real wedding ring but it will serve as a novelty.

Boy it is certainly hot. You know the phones I wear? Well the ear pieces are of a fine grain spongy stuff and black. Since we have been out here, those things have actually melted on our ears. I'm not exaggerating, Honey, those things are half melted away. We get so hot and sweaty that we can squeeze water out of them. We wear one over an ear and the other one pushed back on our head so as to hear orders better. They get to hurt after a while and our ears are sore as boils (completely well though an hour after pulling them off). We switch ear pieces and when we put the other down over the ear we can hear it squish and feel the rubber stick to the sideburn part of our cheek. I'm gaining my weight back though because I have air to my sack. I sleep comfortably and rest well. Hard work will wear well if you get proper rest.

Well, Darling Baby, I feel very humble being away from you this Christmas. It is so important to us. This, if possible, may serve to make it even more important to us. At any rate, I'd like to take this opportunity to renew my pledge that because of hundreds of little things like our conduct at Christmas time and anniversaries and others make me love and cherish the life we lead together. My happiness is absolutely complete with you. I am becoming more tolerant of my absence because I have forced it on myself. Otherwise, I might be a mental case. I live solely for the time when I can resume our wonderful existence together because Baby Darling, my whole life depends on you and your love. Someday I'll be able to tell you in person and God knows, because He is told almost every night, that He will win my undying gratitude if he returns me to you well and healthy. I adore and worship you Ray Ellen. Always keep that spot in your heart for me, because if you don't mine will cease to beat. It is as simple as that, mine would cease to beat. God bless and keep you Darling. I Promise You that forever and ever I'll be,

> Your devoted husband,
> Orvill

P.S. I LOVE YOU!!!

---

29 December 1944

Hello, My Darling Baby Girl:

"Merry Christmas and Happy New Year." I don't know where I'll be New Year's so will say that now. I've already told you Merry Christmas once but wish it bad enough to do it again. (Please excuse those erasures. I'm not as good a typist as you are now.)

Well, I went over on the beach today and walked two miles up to a hospital and had my eyes examined for glasses. I explained to the doctor that my eyes were giving me trouble and etc. etc. Well, he was a grand guy, an elderly Lieut-Commander with grey hair and a real kind face. He told me my eyes were as good or better than any one else's so not to wear glasses. Therefore, I walked four miles on a dusty, dirty, truck-churned up road on New Guinea for nothing. They have it pretty nice here, though. As I got back down to the boat landing, I saw a canteen (Navy) passing out free lemonade. Only it looked kinda like orangeade and tasted like limeade. (They just make sour water and sweeten it and we drink it like good ole Coca-Cola.) Army and Navy, Marines and SeaBees alike were in line and it moved fast enough to enjoy. We could "Drink all you want boys. We got barrels of it." I had seven cups. Right across the "street" (a path really) was a Red Cross tent. And Honey, I saw THREE WOMEN! Real live WHITE women. Livin' and breathin' in plain sight. The first white women I've seen since leaving Pearl Harbor last August. They were pretty dirty and shoddily clad but don't think I censure them for that. It struck me funny though that they all had "typewriter" seats. Actually big flat bottoms. I commented on it to a soldier nearby and he said all the girls here had big bottoms. He went on to give me the "dope" on the WAC and other female situation here. They have a "date" bureau here. (Strictly unofficial but nobody seems to do anything about it.) The soldiers get a little slip of paper entitling them to a date from the WAC [Women's Army Corps] Bureau; they call at a tent set up for handling the traffic; they get their girl and with the gal and the slip of paper, call on the jeep pool and are provided with a jeep and a .45 pistol. Two couples must use the jeep and they high-tail it off toward the jungle (which is completely free of Japs now) and the soldiers can depend on a "sure _____ ." I got kinda sick listening to it. On the way back in the boat I looked up as we passed a huge troop transport and saw a girl sitting way-up on a super-deck (super-decks and super-structure is that part of the ship built above the main deck). Anyway she was sitting there surrounded by soldiers and sailors. Her dress was half way up to her hips as she sun-bathed. She saw us guys in the boat looking at her so she waved very "prettily." I guess it's o.k. but damn if I'm not going to be prejudiced and probably blame some innocent girls, but hereafter, when I hear someone say they were in the WACs or WAVEs or any such organization I'm certainly not going to care much for their character.[2]

Baby, George is sitting at the desk next to me writing with your green "high school" pen to Phyll, his Australian fiance. We are spending more time together as time goes on and apparently our friendship is developing into one of those "buddy" types that will probably prove lasting. He is a grand guy. The only thing is, he still owes me 50¢ for a carton of cigarettes I bought him last week.

Honey, I'm not going to write much tonight. Mainly because there isn't much to write about. Oh, yes, George and I went over on the beach yesterday and drank our three cans of beer. It was very very very very very very good!! Afterward, we walked up the road a piece and ran into our boys engaged in a death struggle of soft ball with another ship. George took over the umpire's box and I took first base. We trounced them soundly. (We had to beat the hoard off George twice but he lived.)

Darling, I don't know when we are getting underway. When we do it will be quite some time before I can get a letter off to you. Our movements are secret as are all advancements. I know what's coming but can't tell you. That is best though, the letter might fall into the wrong hands even if the censor allowed it. Our repairs aren't completed and probably won't be before we leave here but they are so minor that [in] operation with a few other ships we won't even feel the damage. Even so, there is a tightness inside that prompts me to get closer to God like always when trouble faces us. But my attitude has narrowed down (at the moment) to full steam ahead policy. Sort of

---

2. For a recent account of U.S. servicewomen during World War II, see Hartmann, *The Home Front and Beyond,* chapter 3, and Campbell, *Women at War with America,* chapter 1. According to Campbell, a "nationwide underground slander campaign painting all women soldiers as sexually promiscuous began in 1943, at about the time of increased government publicity emphasizing how badly women were needed to release men for combat" (p. 37). The soldier's comments to Raines may have been along the same line or may have reflected the true situation. Raines was released for destroyer duty when his administrative shore duty billet was reclassified as one to be filled by WAVES. There is no mention in Raines's letters of 1943 and 1944 of bitterness or resentment at being replaced by a woman and sent on combat duty.

"Damn the torpedoes. Full Speed to Tokyo." And that won't be so long either I believe. The British fleet is on its way out to help now and I think China and Britain will furnish the ground forces to retake China, that is if Germany folds soon. We don't get much news anymore. Our radio gang is beaten to their knees practically with watches. Day before yesterday is the first time they have gotten off "four on and eight off" since we left Pearl. This is the first time they've been able to sleep all night long. And they all go to bed rather than go up to the movies on the foc'sle. By the way, last night I saw "Till we Meet Again" and "On a Wing and a Prayer." Two very good pictures. The only thing, cans were tied along port and starboard and they had their own movies. Boy was it hard to keep organized. Noise and talking from all sides. We would be looking at Ray Milland holding that gorgeous creature tenderly in his arms and saying "Say yore prayers, hombre, I'ma gonna let light through yore gizzard!"

Well Precious Baby Girl, I want to get a night's sleep tonight. It's 9:30 now and I arise at 5:45 so if I hurry, I can get 8 hours. Be a sweet kid Baby and try to realize how hard this mug loves you. I'm just one guy in 11 million in this war but I love you as much as the other 10,999,999 guys love their wives and sweethearts put together. I love you passionately and with every atom in me. I want the war to end soon. I pray often that God will do something about it. I don't necessarily want to kill ALL the Japs, just enough to make them see that they can't win. So we can all go home. Damit, darling, we are losing a lot of good time and I want to get started again. Well, so much of that. It isn't necessary to load you down with that as you already know how I feel. Be sweet darling and remember that I worship and adore you like mad. God bless you Darling Baby. Keep your chin up and "stand by."

> Your devoted husband,
> Orvill

P.S. I LOVE YOU!!!

Oh, yes, I've made progress. The Chief turned the office over to me. Apparently, not exactly satisfied with Mac's running it. He told me to take over and get it squared away. I am now in charge but can't make first class until he (chief) leaves.

P.P.S. DITTO P.S.!!!

31 December 1944

Good morning, Baby Darling:

Here it is before breakfast and I want to drop you a line. I got some mail last night and your long letter of Dec. 17th. It was a sweet letter and I sure thank you for it. You were apologizing for writing notes beforehand but I haven't received the notes as yet. You see we had 35 bags of mail here just before we got here. They sent it on up to Leyte (Tacloban) about the time we started down this way. That's the way it goes. Anyway, I also got the matches with my JOR on them. Baby that was really sweet. The best Christmas present I could hope for. In addition to being pretty and thoughtful of you, they are quite practical. You see, I forgot to tell you my lighter isn't working because we can't buy lighter fluid. We can't stock it on the ship because of its inflammable nature. If we got a hit nearby, a large stock would practically burn the whole ship. And the match situation is pretty bad. We can always get them but they are the penny box kind, wooden. Unhandy. And I give you the book you kept. You little dickens, you are always dipping your finger into something that belongs to me.

I also got the box of candy Bud and Velma sent. It is that good "Texas Pecandy" like Neita sent and the best stuff I ever ate. I had to fight Mac and George off of it to keep them from "making themselves sick." Really, I wanted to save a little. I'm stingy I guess. But I didn't even give them a single book of matches. They're all mine.

Oh, yes, honey, I want to explain a little more about my eyes. I think I said just enough in my last letter to worry you. Anyway, they aren't in any bad way. I was just working on a very difficult job the other day and decided I ought to be wearing glasses again. The doctor said I had a slight inflammation in my lower lids due to strain and to apply cold compresses four times a day. Well, all I do is go down to the scuttlebutt and wet my towel real well with cold water and lay down and doze about fifteen or twenty minutes. I had a headache yesterday morning and that made it go away. Last night I was thinking too much about you and I knew I would lie there hours thinking of you and feeling like hell being away. But I put the thing on my head and very shortly after went right to sleep. This morning water was all over my pillow, the towel, and another towel I had laid underneath me. I slept all night without waking. Eight hours too! My eyes don't bother me much anymore. In another week I guess they will be in good shape. And too, the worst job I have on the ship I am splitting up with the two strikers. One is taking half and the other the other half. (This is due to Raines being BOSS now.) I have struggled through these months with the worst job I ever had and am now getting rid of it. That is the job that's caused my eyes to tire so. But now that's over. I'm going to have more time to write you and the folks too. The duty won't be so hard from here on out, Raines feels that he has done enough to keep this ship going and the other boys are going to get their "chance."

Darling, please don't be disappointed in this short letter. I am going down now and eat breakfast. I figure you had rather get this than nothing. Have I told you I love you yet? How stupid of me not to! I take it for granted so that you know that my entire world is wrapped around you that I forget to mention it for ten minutes at a time sometimes. I sure hope you had a nice Christmas Baby Darling. Mine turned out to be pretty good after all. Funny, I never thought a box of matches would make me so happy. (It's that "personal" touch you put to everything.) God bless you Darling. My whole being belongs to you, will you remember that always? I love you and worship you till I draw my last breath. God, how I love you, Ray Ellen!

> Your devoted husband,
> Orvill

P.S. I LOVE YOU!!

P.P.S. Those Kleenex you used to pack the box of matches, recalled very fond memories. I suppose a box lasts you a lot longer now, damn it!

---

2 January 1945

Hello, Baby Darling:

Surprise! Forty bucks! Well, I didn't have anything particular to do with it so thought you might be able to use it. No, no poker game. I have quit poker and this is just an accumulation of the last few paydays. I have nothing to spend it on but you and I get more fun out of giving you things than all other enjoyments together. Do with it whatever you please baby. I thought it might kinda help out with the car acting up and etc.

I've wanted to drop you a line before now. I'd like very much to write you every day when in port but we are busier then than at any

other time. And when I'm at sea everything is in such turmoil with
G.Q.s and things. I guess maybe I ain't such a hot husband after all.
But I do know this; I am the most faithful writer on this particular
ship. (I mean to the same girl.)

There really isn't much to tell. I've not gotten any more letters from
you since writing the other day. Yesterday, George and I went over on
the beach. (I had to leave work piled waist high to do it, as Mac did today.) We drank our two beers and started exploring. We walked about
two miles over mountainous roads. Not really mountains but the
roads looked like those in the states. Red dirt. We were picked up by a
truck and rode about six miles more and got off in Hollandia proper. I
didn't know it, but the day I went to see the doctor I was in Hollandia.
It was exactly nothing except the fleet post office and red cross tent. ...

Oh, Yes, last night we had a USO show. Some small-time night-club
entertainers that were really welcomed by the boys. Very nice entertainment considering the location and all. They wouldn't have rated a
decent first look in the states but we appreciated them out here. They
were strictly third rate but gave with all they had and we thought it
damn nice of them and all had a grand time. They put it on on the ship
tied alongside us. We climbed up on the boat deck, gun mounts and
machine-gun mounts and applauded loud and long. Oh, I was going to
tell you but almost forgot. George and I by our circu[it]ous route, got
to ride out to the ships in the same boat with them. There were four
women and six men. ...

Oh, yes, Darling Baby. We get underway at 0530 in the morning.
Underway for some more fighting. That's all I can say now but when
we finish this operation the war will be closer to its conclusion. By the
time you get this, you will know where I am. All our minor repairs are
completed and we are in good shape for a fight. Our experience will
make it easier for us this time. We have lost only one man due to
nerves. He has a wife and three kids. He got weak the other day and
had to go to bed. A few hours later (he had already heard "scuttlebutt")
he got worse and tried to kill himself. A good friend of mine, a pharmacist's mate, said he had been watching him closely for several
weeks and saw it coming on.[3] He knew it was genuine therefore was

---

3. Such breakdowns are more documented with regard to army and army air force personnel (as noted in Grinker and Spiegel, *Men Under Stress,* and Swank and Marchand,
"Combat Neuroses") but did occur among sailors at sea. See Fussell, *Wartime,* 273, regarding the necessity for handcuffing "stark raving mad" sailors to their bunks during
depth-charge attacks.

ready for such radical action and saved the man's life. I asked my PhM friend how I was doing. He replied that he had been watching everyone for signs of it, as it is the worst ailment of all since it involves a man's mind, and that I was in about as good or better shape than anyone else on the ship. He had observed me when the suicide planes came in he said, and added that I showed less fright or panic than anyone.[4] I feel I must compliment him too because if he was doing his job well enough to observe the others that closely, he deserves a "well done" in doing his duty. I felt rather proud when he told me that because I want very much to stand up under the hammering and the less I suffer that way (mentally) the more readily will I revert to normal living when I get back home. I'm not going to return to normal living exactly though. I am going to go mad and run wild trying my best to keep my darling Baby, the girl I simply adore, happy. I really understand now more thoroughly than ever, the wisdom I employed when I decided to make my most important ambition one to make a good husband. Lots of times, Baby, when I am on watch and doing nothing I think of ways I can make you happy when we are together again. I am going to beat you at least once a week so you will appreciate me the rest of the time. Won't that be sweet of me? And isn't it a brilliant idea?! (You can lay in the sun and tan the *rest* of your body.) (After these cracks I'm making tonight, bet I'm closer to divorce than I've ever been.) But really, Baby, I have been thinking a lot about the ways and means of making a better husband. There is plenty of room for improvement. I realize that I'll never be as wonderful a husband as you are a wife but I am going to approach it as closely as my humble attempts will allow. If I can make you half as happy as you have made me then my ambition will have been accomplished. My heart just sings when I think of you belonging to me. My happiness is so great that a person with just half that much happiness should be content with his lot. As for my own I sometimes marvel at my good fortune. Oh, Baby, it's so hard to try and give you the real way I feel. I must hold you close to me and press a little and kiss your ear. Kinda run my face through your hair and feel you pressed against me. The way it is, my chest just aches when I think how much I love you. And how feeble are my attempts to tell you by letter. God knows I worship you

---

4. Moran classified soldiers into four groups with regard to fear: "men who did not feel fear; men who felt fear but did not show it; men who felt fear and showed it but did their job; men who felt fear, showed it and shirked"; *Anatomy of Courage*, 3.

and my whole being is a slave to you. I just pray that He can communicate to you the feeling I have. Please, Darling, even though I can't give you much happiness now, remember that when this is over and just a memory, that you will possess body and soul a man who has pledged to God and all mankind and to you that his every effort will be to make you happy. I promise you that with every ounce of my reasoning and strength, I love you and will devote my life to making yours the most happy on earth. Just to be allowed to do that for you is all I ask of God or life hereafter. Just let me give my life to you. You, a girl who has never done a wrong intentionally and who sincerely frowns on the unpleasant side of deceit and spite. Darling, I have you on a pedestal and worship you on my knees. I will forever I guess. I just can't find anything wrong with you. Else I wouldn't have been so mad about kissing you and making love to you after four years of constant loving and devotion. You must believe me because so many others get tired of continuous loving and petting after a few years but I have never tired. Each kiss is [a] renewed caress of that first date. Each time I can look up and honestly smack my lips and give the "O.K." to whoever may have observed. I pledge to you that forever I will remain the same. You are so wonderful to me that I couldn't be otherwise. Pray for me and us darling. I will do everything I can to do a good job of getting back. God Bless You.ps.ily!!!

> Yr dev hus.
> Orvill

[margin note] Darling, you won't hear for quite a while now but you just stand by. Poppie will get you a letter as soon as possible. I love you.

---

8 January 1945 (four months and 2 days since my 26th birthday)

Hello, Baby Darling:

I'll attempt to write again this evening. I don't think we are going to get mail off tomorrow but I will write anyway. First, I'll tell you about my dream I had last night. It's been on my mind all day naturally. I dreamed that the Japs suddenly gave up and the boys in Europe had walked clear across Germany and into Berlin. I cannot describe the feeling I had. It was so wonderful. You will know the feeling when the real thing comes but everything was so nice. I woke up while we were steaming back to the States east of Pearl, San Diego was just a few days ahead. I felt terrible when I awoke but I know that someday it will be over in reality and we will steam back to the good ole U.S.A. My dream was a sort of a prevue of things to come. I hope it's an omen or something indicating a near victory. I still can't see the war lasting more than a year honey. It may be spring '46 before I get home but the war will be over I'm sure. Lots of guys are still hollering two and three more years but others are hollering six months so really, don't any of us know for certain. Nimitz and MacArthur have a good idea of course but I can't get them to talk.

Boy, it sure is rough today. I've had to type with the ship rolling sompin' fierce. Just to give you an idea, I won't try to keep my lines. Damn it to hell! I am sitting in a straight chair and the ship is rolling so badly I heel back and lean on the bulk head and forward till the desk cuts my stomach. I sure get tired of working like this. When we first started I got so sick when we rolled but now I just get mad. I opened the cabinets today (supply cabinets) and the whole contents spilled down in my face. One of the strikers put it back again and I did the same thing again an hour later. I had to put it back myself because the striker ran, the cowardly dog. He volunteered the first time but I had to pull a knife on him.

Tuesday, 9 January 1945

Hello, Baby Darling:

Well, I suppose you are wondering what's going on. I just had to leave the machine last night. It was so rough that honestly, I couldn't stay in my chair. I went down and "hit the rack." The only way I could lay in it was on my back. You can take a pretty steep roll that way. I had to grab onto something to keep from falling out of bed when I lay on my side. I went to bed at 8 P.M. and got out of it at 7 A.M. this morning. Eleven hours in the rack! And I barely got eight hours fitful sleep. I would wake up in the night laying on my side and have to grab quick. I darn near fell out several times. I sure got tired sleeping on my back. (I got an idea how you will feel the first few weeks when I get back.) Oh, yes, I've been wanting to tell you. I am the only man on the ship besides the Captain who rates a personal call for breakfast. I told you I'd moved my bunk out of the messhall, I have one of the very few best ones on the ship now. The Master-at-arms of the mess hall, a bosun mate, is a good friend of mine and he calls me every morning just in time for me to go wash, brush my teeth and get in the chow line without waiting. We sure clicked it off the last three weeks too. We get a lot of fun out of joking about personal calls. We joke about the most trifle things out here.

Honey, we are back in the danger zone again. Tonight we went to general quarters twice within five minutes. The first time it was cancelled before we manned our stations (plane proved to be friendly) and the second time I was in the shower soaped all down good. Boy, I never got out of a shower so fast in my life. The first time it went I was shaving but it was cancelled before too much damage had been done. I had rinsed off the soap and one side was clean shaven and the other had four days' growth of beard on it. (Honey, did you know your Poppie could grow a beard? Well, by golly I can because the other day the Captain looked at my hairy face and said "Raines, are you growing a beard?" I said "No, sir. It would be too much trouble to keep.") Some of the boys have grown them but they have rates that do not require too much work when they are off watch. I don't like them anyway. They look too nasty and only lazy men grow them. They do it so they won't have to shave but the Captain makes them keep them in good shape and they put in as much time on them as they would shaving. (Boy, what a sentence!)

We put our fire-proof mattress covers on today. From now on it will be G.Q. all day long from well before daylight until well after dark. Glenn's ship is still with us. We haven't been discovered by the enemy yet. This will be his first Pacific action I'm pretty sure. He will find it quite different from the Atlantic melee I bet. (I sound like a veteran don't I, well, I feel like one.) We are now entering a "slot" that puts the old Slot of Bouganville and Guadalcanal to shame. It is so much worse because it is 800 miles long between island after island in Jap hands. But don't worry about it honey baby. We have the material on our side now. We have so much more than they. The Americans still do the incredible by matching destroyers against cruisers and sinking the hell out of them. The Japs definitely cannot fight (on the sea and in the air).[5] It is only occasionally they get in a blow but it is almost negligible. It is a case of hoping our ship isn't the unlucky one. We are still a pretty proud bunch of guys on here. We still haven't found another "can" that escaped two suicide divers. Incidentally, that now is the only thing that we fear them for. The Japs are using it as a last resort and are obtaining some results. They are still losing in the long run but it is the best they can do. It is causing a lot of talk naturally and the Navy is (or has) taken steps to combat the menace. We believe that the suicides will increase appreciably the closer we get to Tokyo. We understand today that our boys are having a tough time of it today. Although Radio Tokyo's claims are immensely exaggerated as usual. It's a slugging match and I hope it's over before we get there. We were slated to be in that bunch but our repairs caused us to be left out. I'm not sorry now.

Oh, yes, I wanted to tell you. Today I received my efficiency marks for the last six months. The last time I got them I had a 3.8 all way through (you understand the method of 4.0 the Navy used). Well, today I got a straight 4.0 all the way across the board. Efficiency in rating, conduct and ability as a leader of men. Poor Mac got a 3.8.

His last time were 3.9. He dropped and I picked up. I feel pretty proud although they don't mean a thing in particular. It's just an idea of what your superior officers think of you. (I should have told them last summer they were rating the wrong man. I should have been the first, shouldn't I?) Seriously, though Mac is pretty old and it would hurt him pretty badly to take orders from me. Say, I wanted to tell you that the letter I sent with the 40 bucks was supposed to have been registered. I left it at the post office with a note and the mail clerk said he didn't see any note and sent it regular. I hope it arrives o.k. Honey, I'm making you a bracelet out of a piece of the Jap Zero that hit us a while back. I am trying to find a Filipino half-dollar to solder on it. It is too

---

5. At this point the Japanese were fighting with fewer veteran personnel and less materiel than in the first year of the Pacific War. Their naval night-fighting ability repeatedly surprised the Americans in the 1942–1943 campaign for the Solomons. See Spector, *Eagle Against the Sun*, chapters 9 and 10; also see chapters 6–8. In addition to having qualitative problems in personnel, the Japanese were victims of a fragmented research and development program and a technical community and industrial infrastructure unable to develop new military technologies or even copy captured Allied equipment. See Harries and Harries, *Soldiers of the Sun*, chapter 35.

plain without something and that is all I can find to stick on it. I have a fifty-centavo piece but it is too worn. If I can't find a better one I'll go ahead and put it on. I'm telling you this so you can tell me in a letter whether you want it or not. It isn't much but sort of a souvenir to keep in a box at home. I'll send it on if I get it finished before you have time to answer. Well, Baby Darling, I'm going to close for tonight. I go on watch in the morning and Mack comes down here. I get up at 3:30 A.M. and will be on the bridge until about 8 P.M. tomorrow night. Hope to get a little sleep tonight. (It is calm now, so many islands to keep the swells out.) I love you precious. God bless you. God, how I love you!!

Your devoted husband,
Orvill

P.S. I LOVE YOU!!!

---

10 January 1945

Hello, Baby Doll:

Well, it's late evening. We've secured from dusk alert and it is dark as a coal-digger's armpit outside. The Japs couldn't find us if they hunted all night. I guess you are getting the reports at home now and feel kinda worried about me. I sure wish this wouldn't be so long in getting to you. I'm kinda worried myself. We know we are having lots of trouble ahead. We expected it of course but still hoped that we would steal a march on them. We are having to land (already announced) in one of only about four places an army could land on Luzon. It is the same place the Japs went in in December 1941. So they know where we would have to land. Our wagons, cruisers and cans blasted the place three days and took a lot of fire in return. We heard that we knocked down 79 planes the first day. We know how they were knocked down though ..... hit 'em and then they dive on you. I know we suffered a lot. We have all kinds of hard-hitting planes in the air but they can't stop them all. Some get through when our fliers can't see them. They will be pretty well cleaned out when we get there though. I hope we even have an airfield secured but that's too much to hope for so soon I'm afraid. We have some good strips developed on Mindoro though and that is less than an hour's flying from the fight. Our very latest type fighter plane has made its appearance in this operation.[6] It is a beautiful wicked thing and we just love 'em. They tear across the sky like a bullet. You can't imagine the speed until you see them. The Japs have seen it and know what it means. It means they must suicide even more to compensate for their short end. Today Mr. Henry passed the word over the speaker, telling the boys all about what is going on. He said that we were having a rugged time of it but that things are coming along according to schedule. He added at the end: "We can be sure of one thing. The Japs won't take this lying down . . . . . but we can be sure of another thing too. . . . . he's sure as Hell *gonna* take it . . . . . right in the teeth."

We have had a couple of G.Q.s but no contact with the enemy yet. I don't think he is aware of our presence yet. Glenn's ship is still way back there, just a dot in the distance. They have the job of rounding up stragglers and seeing that they keep up with the rest of us. Those DEs are a fine little ship. Fight like hell. Just little tin-cans and catch the rotten duty like we do. For several weeks now we have been leading the boys in. We were the front can in the Mindoro operation, in charge of the entire convoy down to Hollandia, and now right in the vanguard of this one. We're kinda proud of our assignment but we have to be especially alert and start shooting first to "show them the way." We didn't stand G.Q. all day today. We probably will start it tomorrow. Then we will be at it for I don't know how long. We have no idea how long we will have to hang around. The Japs naturally will try to reinforce the island and we probably will be assigned to hang around and help intercept them. We were told yesterday to conserve our torpedoes for future emergencies. (We sometimes expend them to sink badly damaged ships of our own but in case of that now we will shell them under.) That's one reason why I don't have any idea when this will get off. If it is real long and I write a lot of pages I won't enclose the two enclosures I told you about in the first part of the letter.

Honey, I feel like I think the rest of the boys do; we sure feel a long way from home. Guys that have been away from home for years are getting homesick for the folks. One guy, a Norwegian, who is a very rugged individual, confessed to me tonight that he got so homesick last night that he could hardly stand it. We haven't received any mail for almost a month now. It seems like six. We got a few letters in Hol-

---

6. The P-51 Mustang.

landia but only a few and I've not heard yet about your Christmas. It will be Thanksgiving I guess before I get the "real dope." Maybe I put too much of my time and thoughts to my former happy life. But it is all I've got to go on. Things you do are so important to me. I love you so deeply. Darling, I must confess it's hard to concentrate on a lot of things. I can't remember very well how to go about reporting. It's been over two years now and before I get back it will be better than three. Maybe almost four. God only knows! Anyway, I will be pretty well left out of things as far as newspapering is concerned. I lay down this afternoon for a short nap and got to thinking. I am going to have to practically start all over again. I may have to start working on my nights off at the beginning Baby. If I do, you will understand why I do it won't you Darling? I have got to put my entire body and soul into "getting on the ball," and cutting my own groove again. This time will be a little different though. My contacts will still be waiting. Foree will see that I am given better opportunities and better stories to cover. If he doesn't, and Barrett is slow responding, well ..... I'm just gonna have to do the little stories so damn well that he will *have* to put me on the good runs. I am going to school and study like mad. I know how to study now, learning to be a Yeoman taught me things about studying I never knew before. And I will have inspiration. You know without my telling you that you are the inspiration for me. I promise you right now that when I walk into the city room at The News, the copy boys and reporters will turn to visitors and newcomers and say "That's Raines, the red-hottest reporter on the staff." "You know him, you read his by-line stories all the time." Also I'm going to present you with the best grades out of SMU [Southern Methodist University]. If we decide that you will continue working after I get back then I will compensate for your efforts by showing you that I will study like hell and you will know that its smartest student sleeps with you every night. (E-gad, what a way to put it.)

15 January 1945

Hello again, Baby Doll:

This is Monday, January 15th, it's been five days since my last addition to the letter. I had to finish up the last paragraph just now because I was called away by general quarters the other night to stand by while we investigated what we thought were Jap torpedo boats. There were none. Ever since then we have been at G.Q. almost constantly and when I get off watch I just die in the rack. You see, I'm standing the watches now and when I get off G.Q. I have to stand a four-hour watch at night too. So ..... in addition to G.Q. from 6:30 A.M. until 8 P.M ..... the four-hour watch about does me. Tomorrow is my last day though and Mac starts getting the hard end of the deal. He had the watch when we came up to Mindoro and I spelled him a little. He hasn't offered to help me this trip so I'll just take it easy and have a "happy" life for the next week. Well, honey, Baby, we didn't have much trouble on the way up. We were taken under attack by suicide planes only twice. They were after big meat though and dived on the Liberty ships in company. Glenn's ship had moved up and was steaming right along-side us when we were brought under attack. Another ship had occupied that position the night before and probably some egg-head is captain of it. Anyway, about 2 A.M. we changed course to the left and he thought it was to the right (he was on our left). He very narrowly missed ramming us and we had to take violent maneuvers to avoid him. Our captain got on the radio and chewed him out good and the next morning he and Glenn's ship changed places. It was shortly after noon when the first attack came. Two planes [flew] very fast over the convoy and one dived straight down. He hit a liberty ship and exploded. There were no casualties, which is miraculous. The other plane ran. Two hours later four planes came in. Three dived on the liberties. One came straight down like a duck diving on an insect in the water. He was falling about 550 or 600 miles per hour. About 1000 feet from the water the pilot must have been killed; he turned sharply to the right and narrowly missed. The second came in on a steep glide, straight as an arrow and didn't die. That is, until he hit. This is the kind of hole he made. The explosion was as big as the ship itself and attached itself to the side of the ship. Several men were injured and others knocked overboard. (Lots burned and shocked.)

The third pilot was killed and he missed by a wide margin. Our guns really put the stuff in the air. We figure the more flack and ack-ack in his way, the better chance the enemy has of getting himself killed. Then he can't aim his plane so well. We steamed in here (Linga-yen Gulf) two days ago. I had the midnight until 4 A.M. watch the next morning and the shooting on the beach went on all night. Giant flashes and rumbles went up all over the beach. The fighting was well back on the mainland. Last night we were assigned a shore bombardment mission and contacted the Army on the beach. We were firing

on batteries shooting at our boys. When we started firing the man on
the beach told us on the radio that "we are under heavy shelling attack." That was the last we heard from him. We picked up and fired
our quota of shells over. We were unable to tell if we did any damage.
This morning we were assigned to do a much heavier shelling job and
did so, causing the dust and smoke to roll skyward over an area of several miles. We were too far away to tell much about the effects but
when we finished we got a "well done on a fine job" and the Army
pushed ahead some more. I enjoyed watching the shells last night. You
know, they seem to travel very slowly when you watch them. They
seem to float across the sky like slowly falling stars. We were shooting
seven miles and between were layers of clouds and smoke. I stood on
the wing of the bridge and watched the red balls disappear and reap-
pear in and out of the layers. It was so far away, I could see only a very
few tiny red flashes when they hit. I couldn't see the shells this morning but did watch the smoke very very slowly rise from the beach.
When it was over the visibility on the beach was zero. We really
messed it up.

There has not been a single Jap plane come over since we got in
here. We are at G.Q. just in case. This morning we secured after firing
and will be free all day except for watches. The fight has taken a turn
in tactics although the base is still the same. Suicide Japs. They are
like fanatical animals. Their method here is suicide boats. Small boats
with large cargos of TNT or dynamite. Or maybe a torpedo. When it is
dark they leave the beach and aim themselves for a ship. They ride it
on in until they crash unless taken under fire and destroyed or turned
away. Another method is swimmers. Naturally, there is a lot of debris
and junk in the water after a big fight like they had here. Many broken
empty boxes are floating on the surface. The Jap takes an armload of
dynamite under one arm and sticks his head under a box and swims
out to a ship. If he can attach the explosive to the side he does so and
swims away before the fuse goes off. If not he stays there and holds it
against the hull so the explosion will blow a hole in the side about six
feet below the surface. Since my new bunk is about that far beneath
the surface, I naturally sleep topside at night. We posted a heavy guard
about the ship and no one has had any trouble the last two nights.
(This is 17 January.) (You can see I'm trying, can't you Darling Baby.)
Well, to sum it up, my gravest impression of the bay here is the bodies,
swollen and distorted, floating on the surface. Of course they aren't

American. The first thing they do with the bodies of our men is give them a decent burial on the beach. It would be bad for morale to let them float in sight of other men. The Jap body though is a different story. They bury them when they find time. Some small scow will come along in a few days and clean out the bay and burn all the debris.

Well, Baby Darling, I guess I can tell you about the chow. It's bad, going from dead bodies to food but we've changed routine lately and I'll tell you about it. We eat an early breakfast, consisting of coffee and a roll, about thirty minutes before G.Q. in the morning; then at 9:45 A.M. we have sandwiches, and coffee; at 3:30 we have a hot meal; and then at 8 P.M. an hour after sundown and dark, we have sandwiches and coffee again. It's pretty hard eating because the sandwiches stick in my throat. I am not suffering from malnutrition, however, as I have me an ok friend who provides me with suitable food. I now at this moment have almost a full apricot pie hidden. If I get hungry, I go to the galley and my friend gives me a cup of coffee and I come back and have pie and coffee. Some people would call me a diplomat, earbanger or just downright racketeer. *You'd* probably call me a rat. But nevertheless, I eat and am in good health. I got a full night's sleep last night (10 hours) and felt pretty good all day. I will get eight hours tonight and that will fix me up fine. I have to get lots of rest when I'm not on watch so I won't have a lot of trouble when I'm losing sleep.

Well, Baby Darling, I'm sure sorry I can't get this letter off the ship. We are patrolling now, looking for Japs and can't find them. (Fortunately.) We haven't had a man on the beach since leaving down yonder. We don't expect to go back to Leyte so there's no telling when we'll get our mail from home. I know how you feel Darling; it's different when you don't get mail. You read all the terrible things that's happening over here and you don't know what the heck I'm doing nor where I am. Naturally you figure I'm right in the midst of everything that goes on. That is far from true because when we contact the enemy, it is a part of us at one time and another part at another time. Even if we are just fifty miles away, we won't get in it. Right now we are patrolling but our chances of contact are very small. There are task groups between us and the enemy and the only way we could ever get in a fight is for one or two to sneak through and that is very hard to do. In fact, the Jap is so busy in his own back yard he can't spend any time defending what he has across the sea. We are still walking away [with] the Philippines. The fight is hard but we are steadily winning. No credit to MacArthur, though, in my opinion. That filthy glory hunter is still a lousy general in my opinion. The Navy is winning his war for him. The Navy and General [Henry H. "Hap"] Arnold's Air Force.[7] That's no discredit to the boys fighting on the beach. They are doing their job and then some but the brains behind it is what has my attention.

We lost Glenn's ship the day we pulled in here. We all broke up and separated and I haven't seen it since. I guess he turned around and went back with the convoy. Honey, I have been intending telling you about my fingernails. I have backslid. I backslid on the Mindoro operation when the planes kept hounding us. I let them grow back after I got over being nervous but this afternoon I bit off another. We were called to G.Q. because on the horizon we could see two battleships and four tincans. They looked Jap in the far distance. We were badly outnumbered inasmuch as there are only cans in our crowd. It would have been a tough fight if we hadn't identified them and they us. They were friendly and sure looked good when we got close. There wasn't any question but that we would fight; even had there been a dozen battle-wagons. That's the way we do things. We would have gone in at very high speed; pray with everything we had and launched our fish and scrammed if we were still afloat. I know I shouldn't bite my fingernails, even under such circumstances; it is purely habit and not a nervous condition. I believe now that it is an outlet of my fear. Of course I was scared when I saw those wagons and thought they were Jap. We would have had to stop them if it meant every life in the squadron. Our shipping was lying unprotected behind us. It means more to our effort than this little group of cans. (I believe we could have gotten them too if they had been Japs.) Darling, I'm going to continue trying to stop biting them. I believe I will have it bested before I get back (I'll probably have plenty of time to do it). Well, Darling, I'm

---

7. According to Schaller, MacArthur's SWPA publicity organization "convinced most of the American public that not only was MacArthur's theater doing most of the fighting against Japan, but that he singlehandedly 'was the one who was licking the Japs.' Years later, most Americans still credit Douglas MacArthur with Pacific victories won not only by his forces, but by the navy and marines"; *Douglas MacArthur*, 73. General Robert Eichelberger, whom MacArthur ordered to "Take Buna [New Guinea] or not come back alive," thought MacArthur delayed the award of a medal for doing just that in order that MacArthur's rather than Eichelberger's name be associated with the first Allied victory in New Guinea; ibid., 71.

going to bed now. I'll say a little prayer for you. It'll be a little one but I'll sure mean a lot in it. Take care of yourself Baby girl, this guy sure loves you and if anything happened to you it would surely kill me. Sure enough, Ray Ellen, I definitely could not live without you. You are everything in the world to me and I live only to get back to you and take up again where we left off in November 1942. I worship you and always will I guess. When I dream of anything it is always of you. I never picture anything or any of the folks or crowds back home that you aren't dominating the picture. (You come in such a nice frame I guess.) Good night officially Baby Darling, I worship and adore you. Always be the sweet girl I remember and trust and love so very deeply.

> Your devoted husband,
> Orvill

P.S. I LOVE YOU!!!

---

18 January 1945

Hello, Baby Darling:

Well, here 'tis Thursday night, January 18th, and I'm writin' just a leetle more. There isn't much to say. I just came down from watching the dark sea go by and I was humming the tune "I'll Walk Alone" and these words struck me: "Please walk alone. With my love and my kisses to guide you. Until I'm walking beside you. Please walk alone." Think I'm sentimental? Well, I sure am where you are concerned. I feel pretty good tonight. I haven't worked very hard today. It's been pretty easy and the chief and I get along pretty well now. Yesterday when he came down to the office I was taking over for my first day of the week. The "Action" basket was jammed full. This morning after G.Q. he dropped by and it was slick empty. He looked and got a big grin on his face and said it was sure nice and unusual to see that basket so completely empty.

Hey, I bet you don't remember giving me a little bottle one time marked "Empirin Compound" on it. Well, for about the last month now I've been carrying some headache tablets in it and keep it in my pocket all the time. I seldom need any but sometimes when I'm on watch and have been smoking too many cigarettes I get a little headache, so I just keep them in my pocket in case.

It looks like we will stay in Lingayen Gulf from now on. We thought we would go back to Leyte for mail but I don't think so now. We are no longer operating with convoys. We are operating with other fighting ships. Honey, it is really beautiful to watch a line of real fast fighting babies steaming along in formation. These little cans pack a powerful wallop and can get it around to so many places in such a short time too. We aren't slowed down by a convoy. We can put on the steam pressure and really turn the screws. The only thing, we will drop the hook less often. (The anchor, little baby, in case you wonder what the "hook" is.)

Darling, I hate to harp on this but gosh, it sure seems a long time since I got a letter from you. As I said last night it is different with you. You have to worry a lot but I don't, thank God!! It is just lonesome for me and makes me feel so damn far from home. There are no prospects of our getting any in the near future either. Boy, when I do I hope it's a whole bag full. And I ain't particularly interested in anybody's but yours either. You maybe hadn't better mention that to anybody but that's fact and I can't help it if everything I think and do is with you in mind.

Well, we think we've got the Jap suicides licked. They are getting such small percentages out of it. I read in the paper yesterday where they had announced the attack on our convoy. It stated four planes shot down and a little damage to the ships. Only one got hit (two altogether, one in the former raid). One hit out of four planes is pretty bad average considering the necessity of conserving their planes. And when I say we've about got them licked, I mean that our planes are knocking them out of the sky so fast they can't do much about it. We really have the air power over here. They can take care of anything they bring over. (That is if they are warned in time to intercept them.)

Honey, when are you going to get a raise? (Leave it to me to change subjects so radically.) Anyway, you have been there quite a while now and $150.00 a month isn't enough for your services. I demand that they give you a raise or you quit! Seriously, though, I'm wondering if they have given you a raise. I don't want you holding out on me and spending the difference on beer and candy. Hell, you might have had two raises without my hearing. I still have some of November's mail to receive yet. I won't hold it against you if you haven't gotten one. I haven't been making much headway myself. But that's just another of those reasons I often wonder what divine guidance showed Providence the way of giving me you. You know, honey Baby, feeling so far away (far enough now to rate the Far East campaign ribbon) (that makes four if MacArthur gets out a ribbon for the Philippines and I know he will, and four [battle] stars if they award all that I think they will).[8] As I was saying, feeling so far away gives a guy an uneasiness of being insignificant. We are just a part of a machine and personalities are so remote. We realize that we are as important to the folks at home as they are to us. But we get kinda afraid something will happen to it. I know that what I have will always remain the same even if it takes me two or five years to get back to it. I "have no worries" as Dick put it in his letter to me. But I can easily see where the other boys do. I'm speaking now of jobs and the future. I know what I'm going to do. Many of them have asked me what could they do when they get out. I try my best to give them sound advice but you know how that is, every man must speak with himself and give himself honest answers. He must wipe away the beautiful pink clouds and dreams and hold a practical discussion concerning his own merits. I know what I'm going to do. I told you earlier in the letter. I know I am going to do that because I have it in my heart and mind to do it. Those aren't dreams. Those are hard hours and days ahead of me but I'm going to do it. I'm going to devote my life to making a home for my wife and some children. Children which we are going to start working on the minute I get home. (Maybe it'll take only half a minute.) Children are what you want Baby Darling and now I see the light as plainly as you do. Perhaps marrying, buying a home, owning a car and a lot of stuff, such as nice furniture and pretty clothes, raising a family and wiping their little noses; maybe that isn't the ideal life many men and women want. But are they happy? If those things are what you want and will make you happy then that's what I'm going to work toward. Also toward our spending time together and being happy with each other's company. I want to earn enough to lay it back for the years when we are older and

---

8. *Howorth*'s crew was awarded five battle stars for their Asiatic-Pacific Campaign Medal: one for the Morotai landing west of New Guinea, one for the landings on Leyte, one for the Lingayen Gulf operation, one for the invasion of Iwo Jima, and one for Okinawa Gunto. As Mauldin put it, "Civilians may think it's a little juvenile to worry about ribbons, but a civilian has a house and a bankroll to show what he's done for the past few years"; *Up Front*, 133–134.

can retire into just a happy existence with each other. If that is what you want, that will make me happy to provide them. You see, Ray Ellen, I am making love to you; I'm romancing you. At the moment, my offerings are very humble. All I have to offer is myself. I give me to you and I will do everything I can to make you happy. (With an occasional argument to make the peace more blissful.) My happiness will come from being with you and being allowed to give you the things you want. I look at your picture on the desk before me and I don't see the girl at home. I see part of my life, probably what God intended for me. Perhaps He made me expressly for the purpose of providing for you. If He did, I'm glad. I try so hard to make the model husband but when I feel I have almost accomplished it, you do some little thing for me that I never thought of having done, and then I realize that always my goal is ahead of me. The many wonderful things you have done for me make me realize that perhaps He made you, too, for the purpose of making me happy. My Darling, you have certainly done that. As I've said before, if we were separated now forever, I'd still have more happiness and a more complete life than the majority of men. The four years we had together were more complete than many men and women have during an entire lifetime. Just our being together has made us happy. I know I've harped on this before Baby Doll and I wish I could think of a better way of saying it but it is just that way. Always, we had fun together. We could do almost everything or any little old thing and have fun at it. Even to just driving in the rain or snow. Seeing a part of little ole Dallas County we'd never seen before. Shooting the rifle in the snow out behind Trinity Heights. If everything else failed to entertain us, we'd just jump into each other's arms and hug and kiss a while. That'd make everything swell. Baby, I'm sure anxious to do that over again. If God will just let me come back to you then I'll look out for everything else. I'll handle the other end of things. Just He return me to you and by the sweat and blood of my brow I'll make Him a good man.

Darling, I'll close for tonight. I hope you understand how I feel. That I want very badly to get a letter mailed but we can't. We are in the middle of the sea and even if we were to land, there would be no place to mail this. We tried to mail some official mail three days ago and were refused. I'll send this the fastest way though Darling. Just keep that beautiful chin of yours up and remember that every thought I have is of you. I belong to you completely and "You is de Boss!!"

24 January 1945

Hello, Baby Darling:

How goes it tonight? Huh? Poppie is o.k. Things are certainly dull though. ... We've been out on patrol across the entrance to Lingayen Gulf for the last TEN days. It is monotonous as the devil but pretty safe. Although the moon has been a bright full traitor the last week. Tonight it is really big and bright. I am going to sleep on the flag bag with George tonight. We now have a worry. A big one. We have received a report of six Jap subs headed this way from Tokyo. All ships are on the lookout; more than likely they are headed for here. And of course we all feel we know their intent. We think they are headed this way to attempt to get through our patrol and probably suicide into our ships in the harbor. We are really alert and on the job. We received a report three days ago that a plane had sighted a sub inside the gulf and boy, that is like a bull in a china shop sure enough. He can just launch his fish in any direction and hit the jack pot. Have you ever slept on a mattress with thousands of points making a huge pin-cushion of it? Well, that is how we felt. Many of the boys didn't even sleep.

Last night something just short of a miracle happened. Bogies (Unidentified planes) came in about an hour after dark. Two planes. They came in and went out several times. We never fired nor did they attempt to attack us. We actually saw one of them just once. The way they went about their movements indicated that they were looking for us. We had been here more than a week and they probably wanted to get rid of us. Even so, we would be replaced immediately if we were sunk. (There are other cans with us but I can't divulge the number of course.) Well we secured and an hour later one came in and attempted to hit one of the other cans. He missed and pancaked into the gulf. We understand he was alive when the can picked him up and is still alive. Earlier in the invasion a ship picked up one that was whole (pilot). Dead of course but unusual in the fact that he wore a very black flying suit of silken material with black helmet and glasses and a bright golden dragon was embroidered on the back of his tunic. (Or whatever that blouse affair is called.) It is my opinion (and probable fantastic guess) that they probably hold a big ceremony at the airfield for those guys when they take off. (Our radio is on now and tuned to a Stateside station; just now a Jap station cut in and some gal is singing in Jap. It is a pretty high pitched voice she has and makes me think of a very small woman with a stiletto in her elongated silk hose.)

Last night at general quarters, just as it was getting dark, we noticed small fires on the beach. They kept getting bigger and bigger and half an hour later the whole beach looked like it was blazing. It was the town of San Fernando going up in smoke. Probably our boys took it today so the Japs burned it last night. They burned some town named something like "Tarlac," a town of approximately 50,000 people, a few days ago. You probably have gotten all that news. Anyway, we are wondering what Manila will be like when we get there. Between the B-29 bombing (which undoubtedly will take place as soon as we get Clark Field operating) and the Jap scorched-earth policy, Manila will probably be a bowl of ashes when we move in. I hope we get to visit the city after we take it. I'd like to buy some souvenir gifts for you and the folks. I speculate, however, that we will get no such liberties because of the pace of the war. Roosevelt is carrying out his policy of "pressing the enemy, keep pressing him without letup" and we will be too busy to stop for such recreation. Personally, I am willing to forego the pleasure if it will hasten the completion of the war. Right now, though, I'm too worried about those six subs headed this way.

Honey, I want to straighten out something. I read in the September (I think) issue of Reader's Digest an article by Miss Dorothy Parker, the bitch in Washington that writes editorials and articles "analyzing" the world situations and social relations, etc., etc. This particular article was entitled something like "What will they Be Like when They Get Home?" It dealt with service men coming home after the war and being "strangers" to their wives. She made such remarks as "the men will have faced death, starved, eaten scant rations, co-operated and saved each other's lives, slept with other men in the very reach of death, etc." that "They will be strangers to their wives. They will miss those friends they made and long again for their companionship." Just let me set you straight in case you ever feel the feeling that such a thing may be true. That woman has always been an idiot. My feeling for her is in the same league as the hate I feel for Mrs. Roosevelt and Madame Perkins, Secretary of Labor. Miss Parker is wrong. Dead wrong. In the first place she isn't even married. I won't say she has never had marriage relations because undoubtedly she has. Let me say that people like that are causing a lot of rotten, unbased uneasiness among the people at home. It is wrong. Not only myself, but every man I know on this ship, other ships I've visited (a lot too), soldiers, marines and seabees I've talked to on the beaches throughout the

Western and Southwestern Pacific, long only for the home they had before this started. They make friends, yes, but for God's sake they aren't the kind of friends that take the place of the feeling they have for home. Why such stupid people write those articles I can't understand.[9] George and I are so mad about it we are going to "attempt" to write an article and send it in. It probably won't be published but then we'll feel like we've had our "bitch." Don't you ever dream or imagine my feeling in such a way, no matter what you read. I've seen numerous articles about "How the 'Boys' feel," by people that have never been outside the District of Columbia or New York State. They don't know a damn thing about it and I want to say "They are strictly full of S___ ." That word is so repulsive to you but it's the only descriptive way I have of telling you strongly enough how we really feel out here.[10] (That Nip gal is now singing "Jingle Bells" in English. She probably knows we weren't allowed to hear Xmas music last month so they are belatedly trying to get us to cry in our beer now.) (Pretty though.) (They waste a lot of money and time really entertaining us

---

9. Dorothy Parker's article ("Who Is That Man?") was condensed from *Vogue* and appeared in the September 1944 issue of *Reader's Digest*, 79–80. Parker was clearly identified as the wife of "Lieutenant Alan Campbell of the U.S. Army Air Forces in England," so Raines's attack on her for writing about marriage as an unmarried woman is puzzling. Raines also ignored the six rebuttals that immediately followed Parker's article; they were written by General John J. Pershing, an educator, a Catholic spokesman, a Protestant spokesman, Bonnie Gay (a columnist for the Baltimore *Sun*), and a neuropsychiatrist.

10. Parker's prediction was borne out by the alienation combat veterans felt after returning to society. See, for example, Holmes, *Acts of War*, 400–403. Raines's irritation with home-front commentators was an understandable reaction from an inhabitant of a war zone. Although Raines may have talked with a "lot" of soldiers and marines, he probably did not come in contact with many combat veterans. One should not make too much of his castigation of Parker together with Eleanor Roosevelt and Secretary of Labor Frances Perkins. Both male and female commentators were writing on the subject Parker addressed, but Raines, one must remember, had *extremely* limited access to newspapers and periodicals. His dislike for Secretary Perkins may have been either gender based or political. He was not alone among Pacific-area servicemen in disliking Mrs. Roosevelt. The rumor that she advocated that those who had venereal disease be quarantined on an offshore island before their return to the United States brought out bitter feelings among those serving in the Pacific Theater; see Fussell, *Wartime*, 38. In a similar vein, recounted William Manchester, a "prominent New York clubwoman suggested that we [marines] be sent to a reorientation camp outside the States (she suggested the Panama Canal Zone) and that when we were released there, we be required to wear an identification patch warning of our lethal instincts, sort of like a yellow star"; Manchester, *Goodbye, Darkness*, 273.

guys and for nothing to their ends.) Getting back to the article, I just want to add darling that all I want to do when this is over, is to hurry back to you as fast as I can. If it is possible I love you more every day and you know it was a hell of a lot to begin with. (It'll soon be our fifth wedding anniversary.) The only friend I've made out here to amount to anything is George. And the way I feel about him doesn't even approach the friendship I have for Norv and Red. And you know very well, the friendship I've had with those guys never hindered our happiness. And I vouch I won't be a stranger, darling. I may be a little bashful but it won't take me long to pick right up. Guys may be strangers with their wives who married just before leaving, but not people like you and I who are too much in love and have had years of wonderful relationship and living and struggling together. Heaven knows, that is the ONLY life for me. If I don't get you and that life back, I won't want any other. I mean that too Baby Doll. I love you, worship you and adore you. You are so beautiful to me and so smart. To me Baby Girl, you are the nearest thing to perfection on this earth. And I know you will always be that to me too. Well, Baby sweet the bottom of the page. I'll try to write another tomorrow night. Bye for now. I LOVE YOU.

Your devoted husband,
Poppie

P.S. I WORSHIP YOU!!!

---

27 January 1945

Hello, Baby Darling:

I didn't get to write the next evening like I thought but can get around to it now. Nothing is going on to amount to anything. Right now Manila is about forty-five miles to the east of us but today we Yanks took Clark Field. It probably will be in use soon and very much to our advantage. Much to our relief since we are in such easy attack range of the field. And at night too. The moon is great big and bright as hell tonight. Night before last the boys on the fantail were reading magazines on the midnight till 4 A.M. watch. Now, I know that's hard to believe but they actually were looking at pictures and reading the cut-lines below them. I went back to the head and looked myself.

Those moonlight nights you hear about in the SouthWestPacific are not exaggerated. They are simply beautiful baby. The moon seems just a few miles overhead and is like a ball of silver fire. We stopped patrolling yesterday and the captain is the boss on this job. I'll tell you where we are going after we get there. Something may happen (it can at any time) and this letter fall into the wrong hands. So just before we get in I'll tell you the destination. The subs are still a big worry. Our detecting gear is really working vigilantly. And the boys working it are reminded at least three times every day by every man on the ship to keep on the ball. With the moon shining so brightly all night long, they can see us for miles. We are even highly vulnerable to night air attack. I'll be glad when we get where we are going. I'll be able to sleep without my clothes on. Something I haven't been able to do for the last month.

I'm going to try and remember to send this letter special Baby. I realize that this is the second letter in over a month that you have gotten from me. I'm sorry again I can't do any better. It is all I can do though Darling. But even if I don't write; don't think for a moment I'm not thinking of you. I do that all the time. Honey, this is all tonight. I've been pretty busy and really need some sleep. I'll write more before we get in. Bye for now. God Bless you Baby Darling. I sure do love you.

30 January 1945

Hi ya 'gain, Little Baby Girl:

Here 'tis Tuesday night, Jan. 30th and we get into Leyte tomorrow sometime. The big thing at the moment is "Will we get our mail here?" It has been so long since we got mail. One complete month without *anything* and two and a half since we got a lot. By that I mean since we caught up with our mail and got all of it that is out here. We know we must have more than a hundred sacks wherever it is. This has been a hard trip down. The Captain has been in charge and boy we've really had a time keeping everything together.

We had an unusual thing happen today. One of the ships in company recovered a body from one of its flooded compartments and conducted a funeral. All ships were notified and everyone of us lowered our flags to half-mast and no official orders were issued until it was over. The only thing we can think of as causing the guy to be in a flooded compartment is the suicide Jap swimmers of Lingayen Gulf. One probably swam up to the side, held a bomb close by and caught the unfortunate guy inside. What impressed me though is the way the entire group of ships showed their reverent respect for the man killed in action.

Well, to change the subject a little; my little friend up in the radio shack caught a broadcast from the states the other night and heard the "Hit Parade." He wrote down the names of the songs for the week and we passed it over the ship. No one had heard a single one of them except an old one, "Always." Probably brought back by sentiment of the war and Bing Crosby. Boy, will people look at me in a peculiar way when I go down the street singing "Marizy Doats" and "Jingle Jangle Jingle."

Honey, the scuttlebutt is going about that we are changing fleets. If so the new fleet we will be in will curtail my letter writing considerably. It won't be the front line fleet; it is the fleet hundreds of miles AHEAD of the front line fleet. We are in the front line fleet now and [have] our five hashmarks for planes (we got credit for one we didn't expect) and three hashmarks for shore bombardment. Therefore, they probably consider us capable of being "rookies" in the real "fast fleet." But don't worry, Darling, it will be just as safe as the bunch we are with now (safer in my own opinion) because we will move much faster. Everytime we go anywhere it will be "full speed ahead" and none of this dilly-dallying with slow fat bellied ships we have to give everything to protect. Naturally, from the nature of the action I won't be able to give you the dope on where we have been even after it's all over because that will be important to keep quiet. However, I will give you as much information as I can spare.

Baby, the radio is on again. I just listened to a news broadcast in English and thought it was from the states. After the program's conclusion however, the radio started singing in Russian. And it is revealed that the program and newscast is from Russia itself. Gad, I never thought I'd be as close to Russia as this.

Well, Little Baby Girl, one of these days I'll figure out something interesting on this ship to write about. I hope these miserable four pages are enough for you this time. I can't write about so many things. And I'll only be repeating myself if I tell you what is in my heart. You know very well what is there. Baby, honey, I miss you so much and need you so badly. Gosh, I just sit down sometimes and feel sorry for myself and pity me till I feel like crying. The news is good now and the Russians are rolling but Damn! you never know what to expect.

That is what is so hard out here. We don't have any exact idea when we will be home. If the war were over, it would be different. We wouldn't be so afraid. We don't particularly mind dying so much; it's the fact that we won't get back home to do the many things we want to so badly. Personally, I feel sure of getting back but even then I remember that human beings are so insignificant; they compose such a minute particle of the universe. But as long as we both hold faith in our hearts and trust the proper Person, then we'll have a better chance, I believe. So long for tonight darling. I worship you Ray Ellen. Please believe that my entire soul belongs to you. I cry for you constantly and can hardly bear being away from you. I must admit that your image is slow in coming to me when I am working or in the close vicinity of action. But when I relax and lie in my bunk with my hands behind my head, I talk to you so vividly that it's just like you are here. You *are* here in my heart darling but it's the body I want. God, how much credit I'll give Him when I hold you in these tired arms again. Good night again Darling Baby. Think of me often. I'm going to occupy an awfully large part of your life when I get back. God bless you for being so sweet and such a wonderful wife.

Your devoted husband,
Orvill

P.S. I LOVE YOU!!!

31 January 1945

Hello, Little Darling Baby:

How's it go? Poppie's fine. Except that I'm kinda sad on accounta we aren't sure we'll get our mail here. We arrived tonight and as soon as we get here we go to general quarters and anti-aircraft fire starts floating skyward all around us. We don't fire because we don't see the enemy. It's funny too because up at Lingayen Gulf we went to G.Q. about three times in two weeks I think. And the first thing when we get here, a place we've been in command of for three months, we have an alert. It's like Admiral Nimitz said. The Japs were stupid enough to throw everything they had into the Leyte fight and left the other islands wide open. So ..... they naturally are still fighting here although we have taken the entire island. So much for that.

It's darker than hell tonight. This is the season in the Philippines when the rains come. That is on the east side of the group of islands. It's like the Hawaiian group. It rains like hell on the east side but on the west side it is clear. That's why we had so much trouble with the moon. But we don't have that trouble over here. It's too cloudy. On the way around I noticed that before we came to an island. That is before the medieval "Land Ho" was sounded I could see clouds on the horizon. They would grow higher as we approached and then we'd see the land underneath. It was really fascinating. This morning I saw the most wonderful sunrise. No wonder the Japanese call this and their islands the "Land of the Rising Sun." The sunsets are beautiful but I have the feeling toward sunsets that they are going down in a final blaze after a hard day; expending its last energy in a final effort. Whereas the rising sun is a fresh new day; ambitious and ready to set the world on fire. Well, it sure does. And this morning it was more beautiful than ever. I was standing on the starboard (right) wing of the bridge and watched the first faint glow in the eastern sky. It was behind a huge cloud bank nestled between the volcanic islands. The islands were only mountains, the remains of age old volcanos. At first the glow was silver in the sky. It gradually spread and turned the deep purple of the night sky a firey red. The whole sky soon was on fire. And gradually it began to turn silvery again and then into sky blue. It was truly magnificent and I wished like hell for you. It lasted every bit of half an hour and I vowed then and do now that someday if ever I can afford it, you WILL see it and from the very same spot. I want you to come visit the Philippines with me. I don't care much for your seeing the Solomons or Guadalcanal. They are ugly and unattractive most of the time. But the Philippines are really beautiful.

Boy, everything happens on destroyers. Tonight seventeen men and an officer, what is left of a Navy landing party of forty-five men and three officers, came aboard for transportation. We don't know of course where the transportation is to take us but I will be the first to find out. The men missed their ship some time ago and now are going to rejoin it. At least that means SOMEBODY knows where we are going.

Our mail clerk didn't get to go after the mail tonight. (I was going over with him just to "set foot" on the Philippines.) Maybe he will go over tomorrow. I won't be able to go with him but maybe he'll get our mail. I'm writing this tonight in hopes it will get off for mailing. I want you to know we won't be here long and not expect any mail. Darling, I'm sorry; I've said it so many times. But Poppie does the best he can. And always remember I love you. I worship you. I adore you. I implore you to believe that in spite of all the competition you have in occupying my mind at the moment, you are master of my thoughts. You will be forever and always. God bless you.

Your devoted husband,
Orvill

P.S. I LOVE YOU!!!

The campaign for Luzon dragged on until mid-April 1945. The struggle to liberate the remainder of the Philippines lasted well into the summer. The U.S. 6th Army fought for 173 days to push the Japanese from Luzon and suffered 8,297 soldiers killed and 29,557 wounded. Naval deaths numbered around 2,000, mostly resulting from kamikaze strikes.[11] After her departure from Lingayen Gulf on January 26, 1945, *Howorth*'s involvement with the Philippines campaign was at an end. She would now play a role in the next strategic move against the Japanese empire: the seizure of an island in the Volcano Island group as a base for fighter aircraft to escort Saipan-based B-29 bomber raids against southern Japan.

Iwo Jima was the island selected.

---

11. Morison, *The Two-Ocean War,* 489.

PART THREE

"THE DEVIL'S OWN CREATION"

9

Invasion of Iwo Jima

February 1–March 17, 1945

The Joint Chiefs of Staff originally specified January 20, 1945, for the seizure of an island airfield in the Volcano Islands, with an assault against the Ryukyu Archipelago to follow on March 1. Japanese tenacity in defending Leyte and Luzon forced postponement of the Volcano Island assault to February 19. The month-long delay provided more time for the Japanese to attempt to convert Iwo Jima into an impregnable fortress.

Iwo Jima is 4.5 miles long by 2.5 miles wide. The northern end rises above the sea and is honeycombed with ravines. The narrow, southern end of the island is dominated by a 550-foot, inactive volcano, Mount Suribachi. Under the island's commander, Kuribayashi Tadamichi, the Japanese garrison of 21,000 expanded and connected natural caves into a formidable defensive network protected by concrete and hard volcanic rock. The Japanese constructed 750 gun emplacements, 5,000 cave entrances and pillboxes, and 13,000 yards of tunnels.[1] Although the U.S. 7th Army Air Force began daily bombing attacks on Iwo Jima on December 8, over two months before the marines went ashore, the navy's preinvasion bombardment was scheduled for just three days. The preinvasion bombing and shelling campaign was the most extensive in the Pacific to date yet had little effect in destroying the Japanese defensive positions. Marine General Holland Smith wrote,

> It was plain that Iwo Jima had fortifications the like and extent of which
> we had never encountered. Mindful of Tarawa, where most of the fortifications were above ground and were still standing when the Marines
> landed, my opinion was that far more naval gunfire was needed on an is-

---

1. Manchester, *Goodbye, Darkness*, 339.

land five times the size of Tarawa, with many more times the number of defenses, most of them deep underground. I could not forget the sight of Marines floating in the lagoon or lying on the beaches of Tarawa, men who died assaulting defenses which should have been taken out by naval gunfire. At Iwo Jima, the problem was far more difficult. If naval guns could not knock out visible defenses, how could they smash invisible defenses except by sheer superabundance of fire?[2]

Smith's request for at least eight days of naval bombardment was rejected by Admiral Richmond K. Turner because of "limitations on the availability of ships, difficulties of ammunition replacement, and loss of surprise."[3] Optimistic estimates predicted that the island could be seized in four days. But the marines in the 3rd, 4th, and 5th Marine Divisions were well aware of the miserable, bloody campaign the 1st Marine Division had endured to seize tiny Peleliu the previous September. Iwo Jima turned out to be worse.[4]

Howorth was involved in the Iwo Jima invasion from the first day. From February 19 until March 14, *Howorth* provided gunfire support for the marines, screened the fleet during its nightly retirements during the early days of the campaign, and later kept up day and night gunfire support. The tempo of operations provided little opportunity for rest. The constant firing required regular, backbreaking loading of 54-pound, 5-inch projectiles, powder casings, and boxes of smaller caliber ammunition for the 40mm and 20mm guns. The continual and irregular bang of the 5-inch guns firing starshells all night to illuminate the marines' battlefield irritated *Howorth*'s fatigued crew; each blast shook the ship, causing dust and loose insulation to filter down onto personnel and equipment no matter, it seemed, how many times the overheads were cleaned. Despite the steady movement of the marine front lines on the map in gunfire plot, Iwo Jima seemed to be a campaign that would never end. The stress this placed on *Howorth*'s crew is readily apparent in Raines's letters.

---

2. Holland M. Smith, General, U.S. Marine Corps (Retired), and Percy Finch, *Coral and Brass* (New York: Charles Scribner's Sons, 1949), 243–244. Although Smith had a valid complaint, he overestimated the effectiveness of "superabundant" naval gunfire.

3. Turner quoted in Smith and Finch, *Coral and Brass*, 244. Providing sufficient large-caliber ammunition for five more days of bombardment *might* have been a problem, but Turner's claim that the element of surprise would have been lost was ridiculous given the strategic situation and the two months of daily bombing of Iwo Jima by the army air force.

4. For a description of the marine campaign on Iwo Jima, see Richard Wheeler, *A Special Valor: The U.S. Marines in the Pacific War* (New York: Harper & Row, 1983), chapters 22–25.

2 February 1945

Hello, Mrs. James Orvill Raines:

How goes it this evening? We have been clipping along at a high
rate of speed since darkness last night heading in a direction that leads
us back to the near-clutches of the Japs. But they don't dare try anything because of the power we have thrown at them in recent weeks.

Yesterday was a pretty blue day. And you probably already know
the reason. We didn't get our mail yesterday. Only a few pieces came
in and some official mail. I had to work on the official mail and got
none for myself. Except one letter from Lula. Now I keep saying "no
mail"; that's because, little darling, none came from you. I really "get
mail" with just one little letter from you; when I get a dozen it's "out
of this world." I enjoyed Lula's letter very much (included one page
from Swede). I'm sure glad she wrote that day (Nov. 8th). I would have
been about nuts. As it was we felt damn low. George and I kinda cried
on each other's shoulders; went up on the bridge; brewed a pot of joe;
sat down on the flag bag and drank it and said "Well, maybe at Ulithi
we'll get it." We have to keep saying, "Just a little more ..... it's
rightahead ..... keep punching" in regard to mail and the end of the
war. We don't have such a terrible time of it except when we think
about the longevity of the war. How long before we can go home? It's
something we don't discuss very often because some guy always says
"Three more years" or something and we chase him off the bridge.[5]
George agrees with me that this year will settle it. As it looks now the
Germans may have to give up soon if the Russians keep rolling. May
God in Heaven help them and guide them. It's a terrible thing to wish
one kind of man to kill another kind but somebody has got to whip
the Germans and Japs. They have got to be taught what is right. They
can't run over the little people and kill them for selfish reasons. As it
is, I pray to God that He will help the Russians and Americans, British, French and Canadians and Brazilians and Italians and Australians

---

5. Compare Raines's desire for the war to end, with the Japanese and Germans de-
feated, with Mauldin's characterization of an infantryman named Jack who, according to
the advertising industry, will never want to come home "until the Hun is whipped and
the world is clean for Jack's little son to grow up in." Mauldin disagrees: "Chances are
that Jack, after eighteen or twenty months of combat, is rolling his eyes and making gur-
gling sounds every time the company commander comes around, so the old man will
think he is battle-happy and send him home on rotation. Like hell Jack doesn't want to
come home now"; *Up Front*, 131.

kill the Germans and Japanese. And last I pray that He will teach the Germans and Japanese peace. Peace in their own hearts. There can be no peace for the world until the people of the world feel peace in their hearts. There can be no peace for the world as long as one kind of man has hatred or fear in his heart for another kind of man. Peace, real peace, can come from the heart and only from the heart. Any other kind is not real. It is pretended.

My Darling, all this is brought about by a vile mood I sometimes get into as evidenced by previous letters. Don't let it worry you. I think that sometimes all of us must try to be big thinkers and attempt to shoulder the cross for humanity. Maybe it improves the tolerance we hold in our chests for other men. The news, of course, is still skimpy and I've given my all for this evening. I'm now going up on deck and listen to some of the boys play the phonograph before evening general quarters. I haven't said I love you yet. But I never do forget do I? Nor will I in the future. Always and constantly I love you Baby Darling. I love you so deeply it just about kills me when I think I can't be with you. But perhaps … what little I am contributing now will make a better man of me for the future. God knows I've had my "fling" and now I want my Baby with me forever and always. Good night now precious darling. I'll dream of you tonight if you don't mind. And I don't think you will. God bless you, darling baby.

> Your devoted husband,
> Orvill

P.S. I LOVE YOU!!!

---

3 February 1945

Hello, Baby Darling:

Here's ole Asiatic poppie again. I'm gettin' so tough I just brush my shoulder off to salt my food. The oxidized brine falls off me like dandruff.

We got more scuttlebutt today. A friend of mine, a lieutenant, is my division officer and said when we were in Leyte a few days ago that he saw a dispatch to the fleet post offices out here to send our mail to Ulithi in the Palaus. We get in tomorrow and sure hope like hell it's there. Darling, I know you look down this skimpy page and are disappointed. I'm not writing much because I want to get in the "rack" [bunk]. I promise you that tomorrow or the next day that I will write you a nice long letter. Will that be o.k.? We will be in here a few days we think before shoving off again and I will have time to write. And tonight I'm kinda sick. We haven't had any convoy on this trip and we've been speeding along at a rapid clip. I think I'm kinda seasick. (Was I talking about being "tough" a minute ago?) Anyway, I want to get some sleep. I think I'll feel better when we get into smooth water again. This place where we are going promises to be interesting inasmuch as it is an "Atoll." It will be the first time we get real close to one since being here. I'll give you all the "dope" on 'em. Well, good night Baby Darling. Gosh, I love you. Mommie, if I don't get mail up here, I'm a gonna desert. But that's showing weakness and I don't want to do that. If there's no mail there, I'll just wait until I do get it. So there. Good night again Baby Ray Ellen. Please love me always darling because I love you very desperately.

Your devoted husband,
Orvill

P.S. I LOVE YOU!

---

9 February 1945

Hello, Baby Darling:

Well, my sweet precious, I think I can get a letter off to you tonight if I'm not interrupted. Things have settled down now and not much is going on. We are on the move again of course but don't know where we are going. I will mail this to you from Saipan. We are still cluttered up with work. I have put in fourteen hours steady grind the last four days. Tomorrow, however, I am going to knock off as the biggest top has been knocked off it and I take the watch; Mac can do the rest, with a minimum of help from me.

Well, Baby, I got just oodles of mail over the last four days. I almost got in Dutch a couple of times over it too. In case you are wondering what I'm talking about: I would work like hell in here getting the official stuff straightened out while the other guys read their mail. Late at night I would knock off to read my mail and somebody would invariably come in and ask me to do some "rush job." I got mad a couple of times and told them something like "of course. Any time, day or night." And "I guess I can read my God Damn mail at four o'clock in the morning. Everyone else has sense enough to read their personal mail and THEN work." It resulted in a few clashing words but I wound up doing the work as always.

I'm going to try and read through some of the mail and give you some dope but will save the comment, etc., until I have more time. I just went over to get my letters out of the filing cabinet where I hide them and, honey, I almost have a suitcase full. Boy, it's sure nice after so long a time. But no matter how many I get from you Baby, I'm always sorry and disappointed when I get to the last one. I put them all in order of dates on the outside, open them all with a letter-opener like the one I gave you and then start reading them. Now I have them all in order to answer. I will start with the first one (naturally) and go as far as I can tonight.

Darling, you writing about the cold weather there sure "leaves me cold." I just can't imagine people going through a winter and suffering. I think if I ever get back into cold weather I won't complain one bit. (Yeah, I know it, you'll remind me of those words someday. Just like I'm gonna remind you that you said you would never say "no" again. Let yourself in for something didn't you?) Anyway, rereading it reminds me of a dream I had last night about you. I won't go into details but I was there keeping you warm. I bet its good "curl 'round you weather" but it's that kind all the time. Hey, you tell me your waist is two inches larger than it was when I left! I've been intending to tell you that if I come back and find you with a stenographer's bottom and a bookkeeper's stomach I'm gonna run you to Fort Worth and back to take it off. You are too beautiful being tall and slim and that's just the way I like you. That's the only thing I'm selfish about where you are concerned. You are going to stay just like you are; if you "grow" anywhere I'm gonna take personal responsibility in "spanking it off." Now that's an order. (For you to break, I guess—BOSS.)

Well, Baby, I got through one letter before I was interrupted. I'll have to knock this off until in the morning. I'll come down right after G.Q. and finish up, although there isn't anything else to write; I just feel like I'm "corking off" writing so little. Good night now baby. I hope you can hear my thoughts when I get in bed. They aren't all nice ones but I sure do a lot of thinking about you. Good night now baby doll. God how I love you! I literally worship every inch of you.

13 February 1945

Hello, Baby Darling:

I suppose you are wondering what's happening. Me promising to write the next day and not getting around to it for four days. Anyway we have been fooling around here and now is the first opportunity I've had. First, I'll tell you about our damage. No, not due to action, but to marine perils. Day before yesterday we tried to refuel from a tanker here at Saipan and the ground swells were coming in about twenty to thirty feet high. The Captain was ordered to fuel so we had to fuel. The tanker had huge steel pontoons tied to its side so as to protect its hull from ships banging against it due to the heavy sea. It was unusually heavy. We tied up and started receiving fuel and we banged and banged. It was so disturbing that we in the office gave up trying to work and went topside for air. We were almost made seasick by the lurching and bumping. I went out to watch the boys fight the fenders. (Those things they put over the side to act as bumpers and prevent damage.) First our forward line parted. (Six inch manila rope to you.) Then the forward line again as soon as they put it up. A one-inch steel cable was put over this time and twang it went. The second cable held but we had to have it slack every so often to ease the strain. Next, the midship's fender went to the bottom. It was slung on a large steel davit. It got caught between the pontoons and the side of the ship. (It was 36 inches in diameter.) It broke loose with an awful grinding, tearing, smashing and snapping. The whole business went under and the steel davit was bent double. I was standing next to a kid I stand watch with up on the bridge; he was handling a small fender with a one-inch rope on it. As the ship rose he would let out the rope to keep it between the pontoon and the side of our ship. He was having a tough time and I started to help him; changed my mind as I probably would have been in the way. About two rolls after I decided hands off, the end of the line fouled on an upright stanchion and he couldn't get it loose. The fender got caught in a squeeze between the pontoon and hull and the ship took a heavy roll upward. Naturally it pulled the line downward. He was holding it over a two-inch chain for leverage and got his thumb caught between the rope and the chain. The rope rolled his thumb over the chain and ground it into hamburger meat, bone and all. A second later the strain broke the heavy chain in two. The second roll pulled the whole business over the side except the kid. We took him in Sick Bay and they cut his stub off clear to his hand. He was transferred back to the states today.

The total damage is that our hull is caved in about six to twelve inches for a distance of about 150 feet along the side. All our frames are bent in and the entire port side is weakened tremendously. You understand the principle of "watertight integrity." The ship is divided into several compartments. All watertight and independent of the other. That is to prevent the entire ship taking on water when a hole is put in the side. This way only one compartment gets flooded and the ship will stay afloat. Well, we are no longer that way. We would sink in about one-half minute if we got a fish. We are now tied up alongside a tender and expect to get the damage repaired in the next two days. We tied up about an hour ago. I was kinda worried a while because of the possibility of another operation coming up and us being in that condition. However, we will be back in original shape by the time we depart from the tender.

Speaking of operations, I can't give you any dope of course nor even speak (or rather write) of such things; but I can say that we aren't going to Japan. Everyone is asking "Where do we go from here?" I know, but it will have to wait. No one even knows the time yet. I'll tell you sometime when it is safe and the Japs are covering their graves. Honey, I got the pictures you sent. Those yall made at Mom and Pop's Christmas. They are pretty and I'm glad yall made pictures of the Xmas tree. We do that too every year, don't we? I still haven't had time to read your letters but twice and can't answer any questions yet but will get around to it soon. Oh, yes, please tell Lula and Swede that I got the book. I've been wanting to read that very book too. It is (in case you don't know) "The Robe" by Lloyd C. Douglas. Also got the candy from R.C., Charlene, Robert and Sandra. I'll write my thanks but you tell them I got 'em for me will ya? ...

I just went over to the tender and stood in line about forty minutes for some ice cream and they ran out three men ahead of me. Anyway, I bought two cokes (not bottled) and enjoyed them very much.

Oh, yes, I wanted to tell you. We get better chow now. Since joining this different fleet we apparently rate better stuff. We got some fresh spuds, apples, canned juices and just oodles of other stuff. We have been eating very well the past week. I hope it isn't the fattening of the calf.[6] Just kiddin', Honey. We gotta kid a little, huh?? We always have.

---

6. Moran, *Anatomy of Courage*, 45–46, expressed similar concerns that his division was being "fattened for the fight" by its time away from the front lines: The "animals [soldiers] must be sent to market in good fettle." For the importance of food to soldiers and sailors, and their boredom with their government-supplied rations, see Fussell, *Wartime*, 199 and 291.

Darling, this still isn't what I want to write you. I always have to close the thing. When I'm writing I can't think with people rushing in and out as they are doing now. And I know you are aware of my predicament by the letters you write occasionally from your office. No matter what the situation though Darling, you know that all the outer doings and the cursing, fighting and exhaustion only covers up the real feeling I have inside. I have only one real feeling inside. That's you darling. It sounds and reads so staid and cold when I try to put it down like this. But Darling believe me, inside it is warm and living. I cherish the precious thought of you more than anything in the world. There are so many things happening and I must be on the go so constantly until I am about ready to drop, but never have I climbed into my bunk without laying my head on the pillow and thinking of you just a moment. Sometimes I spend hours lying there thinking of what I am going to do and say when we get together. Other times I just drop down and say "Oh Baby, I'm so tired. God bless you darling, I wish I were there to lay my head on your shoulder." I guess that no matter how long they keep me out here, even ten years, I'll still have my vivid pictures of you and you will be the backbone that keeps me upright and thinking straight. That must be the real kind of love that only is read about. When you can influence my thinking and acting after months of separation and so many thousands of miles between us, it must be the kind of life I've been sure it is for so long. It even tears my heart to know I can't write you more often and longer letters. I'll be going until midnight tonight but I'll be resenting it greatly. One of these days (after a couple of weeks or a month) I'll get my thinking back and will write you a letter that will satisfy me when I seal the envelope. Until then, my Darling Baby, believe this guy that worships you, I'll be your slave forever.

> Your devoted husband,
> Orvill

P.S. I LOVE YOU!!!

---

16 February 1945

Hello, Baby Darling:

Just a line. Unexpectedly we think we are going to get mail off today before leaving this sector. We are heading into a harbor now and may get it off to another ship. We don't know for sure though. There is no news. We are all set to go wherever they want us to go and I expect we'll do a good job of it.

I just want you to know that up to now I am still o.k. and hope to stay that way. I know you had rather have newsy letters but in the case of this kind or nothing, I'm sure you'd rather have this kind. Anyway, I would.

The war is looking better now darling. And from the looks of things out here, we may see a remarkable improvement in the near future. At any rate, I fully expect to be home in the latter part of this year, whether the war is over or not. You can almost depend on that. If they wind up the scrap in Europe within the next two months, I expect Japan to be whipped six months later. She will soon be at our mercy, I believe, and I am thinking that I can see the end already. We can lick her without the aid of the people in Europe but if they come over here it will shorten the strife considerably.

Well, Darling, this is abrupt but the best I can do. I am well and well rested. I get plenty of sleep now and much better food. You remember in Treasure Island where Jim Hawkins the boy hid in the apple barrel and overheard Captain John Silver and his pirates conspiring to overthrow the ship's head and take the treasure? Well, for the first time since we've been afloat, we have an apple barrel. It's a box however but is an "apple barrel" just the same. That indicates that we have plenty of food aboard.

So long for now Baby Doll. Let me repeat that I love and adore you. I will forever; and your sweet face will be before me in all the months to come to help me get over this "hump" of being away from you. Just sit right down now and pray for me. Wait till you get home, on second thought. Tonight say a little prayer for me and all the other guys that are fighting. We'll need it. Bye for now precious, I worship you.

> Your devoted husband,
> Orvill

P.S. I LOVE YOU!
Our "Wagons" are bombarding Japan right now. See what I mean?

18 February 1945

Hello, Baby Darling:

Well, what do you think about things now? Just 750 miles from To-kyo! Poppie's on that highway to the holy (?) empire and boy it seems like we are in Japanese waters all the time. Although this job just about makes the entire Pacific Ocean American Navy controlled. Dar-ling, I believe this is really something. You know, always before we have made jumps of several hundred miles at a time; and before we have made jumps of inches at a time. But this strike means something really good to me. We left Saipan and Tinian Islands a couple of days ago and steam[ed] HALF-WAY to Tokyo. It's 700 miles from Saipan to Iwo Jima and just a little more from Iwo Jima to Tokyo. (In case the kids are wondering why I'm not writing them and answering their let-ters tell them it's awfully hard to write with all this going on. The strain is getting more intense all the time. I'm sure they will under-stand.)

To accent the nearing of Japan itself tonight it is colder than hell up on deck. Our ventilator here in the office is blowing real cold air on my right arm as I type. And just New Year's Day, the aluminum trim on the desks here was too hot to touch in Hollandia. They issued the cold weather jackets today that we wore up in Bremerton and Seattle last spring. (Our latitude is almost as far north as San Diego. Compare that with the Equator that you know as cutting across Ecuador in South America.) All those jumps that we make doesn't seem like much until I think of how far south of Dallas is the Equator over there in the Western Hemisphere. I guess, however, that we have crossed it the last time for a while. Eight times is enough. But damn it honey, we got some new men aboard and I wanted to beat the hell out of them as revenge for my beating the first time over. I suppose you have been thinking I am with the bunch hitting Japan. No, I'd like to be in a way, but we are going in in the morning to make the landing on Iwo Jima. That's why this might read kinda funny. It's hard to concentrate knowing a fight is such a short way ahead. We thought they were pretty well beaten up as a result of 76 days of continuous bombing and three days bombardment but as usual, the "dug-in" devils still have a few guns left and knocked the hell out of a cruiser today. Apparently the cruiser was bombarding and got in too close. We don't know ex-actly what part we will play yet. I don't think we will bombard; just patrol around for submarines. Already on the trip two subs have been sunk by a convoy ahead of us (we will pass it before landing) and one by our destroyers in this convoy. Several contacts have been made but they have yet to get out a fish. (When I write something like that, I can just feel one heading right for the starboard side of the *Howorth* and landing right in my lap. You know how I am at calling my shots.) We probably will hang around this neck of the woods after this operation and hope for the best. Probably give the Nips a *real* thrill next time. We are back eating the four meals a day I told you about, and sleeping in our clothes. We are all keeping our life jackets closer at hand this trip than any we've made.

I told you once I'd explain what an "atoll" is. Well, Ulithi is typical. Many centuries ago, a volcano erupted right in the middle of the Pacific. (Several probably all in line as evidenced by the "strings" of islands.) The earth rose up out of the sea and spurted fire, hell and brimstone, one might say. Since volcanic eruption is molten stone, the lava rolled down the side of the volcano mountain and into the sea. The eruption ended. The centuries pass and the sea pounds away. The earth of the mountain is washed away but the stone remains. Coral feeds on the stone and it gets bigger in size. Through breaks in the lava the sea continues to wash away the earth. Eventually, the inside goes away and leaves a ring of small islands, the inside of which the U.S. Navy uses as a harbor. There is nothing on the "beach" except a place where sailors throw their beer cans on recreation parties. These little islands are not large enough to house any activity so everything is handled on the ships. The islands serving only to keep the sea a mite calmer and furnish a bottom close enough to the surface to hook an anchor into. All clear little Baby? Poppie will explain it real good when I get home. By the way, that "great Naval base of Guam" is one of the biggest examples of overstatement the Navy ever made. That damn harbor isn't large enough to hold the (I bow my head) long deceased Kilocycle. That may have been a "great Naval base" at one time but today the size of the fleet has increased to such an event that the harbor is practically of no use at all. I was certainly disappointed in it, although the island itself is very impressive. (You know I've never received your letter "chewing me out" for trading my watch for the rifle?)

Baby Girl, I got your Valentine Card. And again I bow my head. This time in shame. I didn't even mention it to you. When I should have been writing asking you again to be my little red heart, I was too busy with the Lingayen operation. But I know that you realize the sincerity of my promise I made you long ago. I will *always* be *your* Valentine, whether it's Valentine's Day or not. In fact, all the promises I ever made you still hold good. Particularly the one about giving you a real run for your money when I get back. You are going to have so damn much husband you won't know what to do Baby. You're kinda short now but just remember you are going to catch up pretty soon.

I got a letter from Norval yesterday. (Of all times to receive mail. Right in the middle of the ocean in the middle of an operation.) (A ship in the convoy picked up mail for several ships before leaving Saipan and delivered it at sea yesterday). Anyway, he writes an interesting letter. Says he expects to tie up with LSM's [landing ships medium]. Those are very small beach landing craft. I hate to see him on one. At Mindoro those things had to get in so close, the Japs could have put the skipper's eye out with a sling shot. ...

Darling, I'm going to close for tonight. We will be at general quarters all day tomorrow no doubt but will try and write you the next day. I should get a good amount of reading material collected for you by the time we get mail off again. (Wasn't that damned Lingayen Gulf operation hell on the mail, though?) Good night Darling Baby Girl. When you curl up with yourself tonight try and imagine how very much I'd give to be there holding your precious head on my shoulder tonight. God bless you darling. I worship you.

> Your devoted husband,
> Orvill

P.S. I LOVE YOU!!!

---

19 February 1945

Hello, Mommie Darling:

How's Poppie's little chicken today? I feel fine. In fact very fine. The Japs are having a death struggle over on the beach. I just came down from General Quarters (it's 3 P.M.) which we have been at all day. We secured in order to eat a hot dinner. We came in just before dawn this morning; the island [Iwo Jima] looking like an exclamation point lying down. It is only sixteen square miles (about three miles wide and five long) and lays flat on the water. About 200 feet at its highest point. At the southern tip is a rounded mole-like hill that is almost perfect in circular form. We could just make out the land on the horizon when the wagons and cruisers opened up. Boy, it looked beautiful. The cans did not bombard because it was important to stand far enough off-shore to keep out of the range of the shore batteries. Our little guns take us right up on the beach practically. The big sixteen-inch batteries of the wagons opened up with huge blazes and I watched the projectiles slowly rising out over the water and finally hit the island. They went over in groups of three. Only one turret at a time would fire because all three turrets firing at once causes too much percussion and vibration and that is done only in emergencies. For three hours this bombardment went on. There was a strong wind from the north so the smoke and dust from the island drifted seaward in the direction of the ships. The north end was visible to us as we stood off to westward patrolling. It made a good screen for the bombarding ships and blew the smoke away so the patrol spotting planes could see the terrain and direct the firing. During all this, dozens of planes came in. Honey, they were like flies and flew a thousand miles an hour (it seemed). They were so thick over that little island I couldn't see how they managed to avoid collisions with one another. They bombed and strafed. Only a very few anti-aircraft bursts were visible, attesting to the accuracy of the bombardment by the ships. They held a field day and often dropped to within 100 feet of the ground in order to strafe running Japanese troops. We can't see the troops of course but we get a play-by-play account over the radio circuits.

After three hours bombarding the island, our landing forces went in and took over a beach-head about two miles wide and 100 yards inland. An hour later they were 200 yards and are still going. They are having trouble with mortar fire at the moment and we (the *Howorth*) located two anti-aircraft guns and the planes are working on them right now. While the troops were landing, there appeared numerous splashes in the water in the direction of the wagons. The range was too great for them and the smoke helped hide the ships. They decided the firing was coming from that little mole hill. Everything opened up on the hill. Darling, that damn thing was pounded and riddled and pounded and riddled for two hours until nothing could be seen of it. Only smoke and dust. The enemy fire stopped of course. Although no Admiral or General has announced his own opinion yet, I believe the landing went off much better than expected; and due to the bombardment. (Frankly, I don't see how anything could live through it. The "digging-in" though saves a lot of them.)

The planes are doing a good job. They report such as "I see a tank coming down the road in section _____ . It looks like he is heading for our troops in the western corner of section _____ ." In a moment a couple of fighter-bombers come over and they shift to a new target. One stiff position of mortars and machine-guns was cleaned out by strafing about 11:30 A.M. (one hour before you told me good night officially Sunday February 18th). It was raising hell with our boys and a few minutes after the report, we looked overhead and saw twelve fighter-bombers winging over. They started more hell. An attack by a group of planes is different than you might expect. They come in in beautiful formation, break up and go in scrambling directions, turn and come in from all sides and angles, weaving up and down, left and right, then suddenly streak down like a flash of light straight at the target. Coming from all sides, the enemy is pretty well frustrated. You can't imagine how fast they dive until you see them. They are just a small speck to us but we see the sun flash on their wings as they waggle downward and then see the speck fall like a shooting comet when they straighten out. It's usually a full minute later before you can see the smoke rising from the bomb burst. It takes it a little time to get large enough to see without glasses. I have been watching the proceedings through a "long-glass" which George so generously allowed me to use. (No one else can use them but signalmen and quartermasters.) (And Raines.) The pounding and strafing and fighting has been going on all morning. I think we will be firmly established by nightfall. I don't know yet if we will take a convoy back or stay around here. The way the island is concentrated, I don't believe it will take more than a week to clean out the whole place of Japs. They have a lot of cut up country in the rocky edges of the island and a lot of holes to hide in but you know the Marines and the Army. They just love those new flamethrowers.[7] I do too.

---

7. Flamethrowers were dangerous weapons since their use required close proximity to an enemy. The Japanese army considered them so dangerous that users who returned alive were awarded the Order of the Golden Kite; Harries and Harries, *Soldiers of the Sun*, 356. One option seriously considered for use in the Pacific War was gas. Army Chief of Staff George C. Marshall made a case for the limited use of gas to Secretary of War Stimson, arguing that gas "was no less humane than phosporous [sic] and flame throwers"; J. J. McCloy [assistant secretary of war], "Memorandum of Conversation with General Marshall, 29 May 1945, Subject: Objectives Toward Japan and Methods of Concluding War with Minimum Casualties," quoted on p. 304 of John Ellis van Courtland Moon, "Project SPHINX: The Question of the Use of Gas in the Planned Invasion of Japan," *The Journal of Strategic Studies* 12 (1989): 303–323. Unfortunately for gas advocates within the army, the tests at the Dugway Proving Ground in Utah in summer 1945 were disappointing. It was extremely difficult to build up sufficiently lethal concentrations of gas to inflict an acceptable casualty rate on the goats (masked and unmasked) and rabbits stationed in the caves designed to simulate Japanese-style fortifications; Moon, "Project SPHINX," 306–314.

Well, Darling, I'm going to sign off now. I never thought I'd be calm enough to sit down in the middle of one of the most significant battles of the Pacific and write a letter. (I'm misspelling a lot of words though.) I'll see you later tonight or tomorrow, depending on the "temperature" of things. Bye for now, little precious, is this evidence that I think of you even in the midst of battle? I admit we haven't fired a shot yet but you know—any minute. We never can tell so we are always ready. (We hope.) Bye again my darling, God how I'd love to kiss you right now. I could whip the whole Jap army with the energy from one 400 from you.

22 February 1945

Hello, Mommie Sweetie:

Here's Poppie again. Lots of water has gone under the keel and lots of powder had gone through the barrel since I broke off above. I'll start where I left off. We shoved off that night (let me think, when was it?). The night of the 19th. That's right. Then we came back in before daylight the next morning. (Our reason for leaving was to take a large convoy away from the island to dodge air attacks which did not materialize and to be away from shallow water in case a storm that was brewing came in.) They were still firing when we came back. The star-shells bursting about three thousand feet above the island and in the clouds. It was interesting watching the shells float downward through a thick white cloud. They would burst in the midst of the cloud and cause it to glow like snow and then drift downward through the layers and finally through the bottom and light up the whole island. There were several in the air all the time so the ships could fire. We patrolled around until early afternoon and then received orders to bombard the beach. We went in and fired a few rounds, slowly at first and then it got dark and we commenced firing star-shells for the next night. We stayed at G.Q. until after 10 P.M. and then let the regular sea watch fire the remainder of the night as we only fired about 100 rounds from dark until dawn. I thought I would have difficulty sleeping because each shot rocks and shakes the ship like a mad jelly-fish. But as you have learned from years' experience, I didn't even hear a single one. I was so tired that I slept right through until G.Q. yesterday morning. Then is when the fire-works really started. You might get an idea of how things are by knowing that the island was bombarded heavily for two days before the landing. It had been bombarded two days after the landing when we started firing ourselves. Four days of heavy bombardment and then the *Howorth* opens up! I thought we were going to burn out the barrels (and hoped we would as it means a rest in Pearl or Mare Island! while they get re-bored). You've seen these little walky talkies. Well the Marine on the beach had one and gave us our targets over the radio. He would order so many rounds in a certain place. I noticed that he never repeated his targets and wondered if we were doing as well as that indicated. It developed that we were doing superbly when the Marine on the beach suddenly yelled over the talky: "Look at those bastards run!" Since we can't see the results of our fire (too far away) we were all pleased to hear that and were in good spirits. Especially when the Marine broke in once to say: "It might interest you to know your shooting is very good. The results are very gratifying." It certainly was of interest and we redoubled our efforts to shoot perfectly. And we almost did. It was all due to a junior gunnery officer [Patrick H. Arnold] down in the middle of the ship who couldn't even see the beach. As a matter of fact, during our fourteen straight hours at G.Q. yesterday, he didn't see daylight at any time. He is a "plotting" room officer and has maps and etc. to guide him. Through a series of very complicated instruments and radar business, he put them right where the marine called for them. He is by far our best gunnery officer and everyone is waiting for the senior officer to be transferred so he can take over. It's another case of the Navy's seniority policy gumming up the works.[8] Well, to get on with the story. We fired continuously from daylight until after dark. (No, it was just getting dark.) Our most interesting target of the day was a Jap field artillery position rigged up on tracks and rolled in and out of a cave for firing. They would stick it out of the cave to fire on the troops and then wheel it inside real quick for reloading. Our Marine saw it go off once and started whooping and hollering. He said: "Give it three quick rapid fire five gun salvos when I give the word." He apparently waited for it to come out and then said: "Open fire immediately." We did and immediately afterward he said: "Shift target." Damn it! We knew we knocked it out but he wouldn't give us any dope. Half an hour later he came back with an "incidental" remark that we put all fifteen shells right into the position. We were sure tickled. I remarked over my telephone circuit that there probably was a lot of souvenirs in the cave

---

8. Raines may have been projecting his own frustration over his stalled promotion.

"small enough to carry away in our pockets." One of the guys invited me to go over and pick up enough for the boys, but I declined as gracefully as possible. (You couldn't have dragged me on the beach with a winch.)

Also interesting was watching our tanks and men operate. We got in close to the beach in the afternoon in real shallow water and I used the Executive Officer's glasses to look on. I saw three tanks right up near the front line moving ahead with about thirty Marines running along behind it. They stopped and hit the dirt and everybody began shooting. I couldn't see what they were shooting at of course but shortly they got up and ran a few more yards. The way we were looking at the island, the southern end was to the right and the north to the left. Our forces were on the southern half except for that "mole hill" I told you about. (More about the mole hill later.) About half the island is ours with the rugged country in the hands of the enemy. Over on the left right near the water line I and a quartermaster saw a large enemy tank moving toward the right where our troops were situated. The Captain tried to shift targets and knock out the tank (everybody else wanted him too) but before we could get on it torpedo-bombers went in and blew it skyhigh. When we started firing in the morning (lots of other ships were firing too, directed by other Marines with walky-talkies) we were shooting about the middle of the island. Later, shifted more to the left and then again. We kept moving left all day, stopping several times while our Marines moved up closer to the front. It was like playing checkers. We kept jumping ahead all the time. At nightfall our forces were fighting well past where we had been shooting in the morning. It was gratifying to know we had helped. Planes too worked on them.

God, Honey, the smoke covered the island all day long. It was good too because the wind was still from the north and blew over our forces and they had a natural smoke-screen all day. (Annoying on the eyes no doubt.) But all day long the planes came in. Diving and strafing so much that their fifties [.50-caliber machine gun bullets] bounced off the coral and rocks; it looked like anti-aircraft fire. I thought it was for a while. Then I followed their tracers with my eyes and saw them bounce. They hit numerous fuel and ammo dumps. I don't see how the Nips can stand it any longer. They, the planes, came in dozens at a time. They would break off in fours and come in from various angles to confuse the Nip. Some would level off at 2 thousand feet, others at

2 hundred feet. They bombed and strafed all day long. One raid would hardly be over an hour before they'd start another one. They have mounted rocket bombs on our fighters. They are lots of fun to see launched. They allow the pilots to pull out quicker and do just as much damage as regular bombs. The planes dive in and point the nose right at the target and when about four thousand feet away they let go with a streak of fire. They shoot to the target straight as an arrow and go WHOOM! I didn't see any planes shot down all day.

Now about that mole hill. I got a closer look at it yesterday. I had been so busy on the way up here I didn't get a chance to look at any maps. It is a volcano and solid rock. The Japs have tunnelled back in the lava and really are set up with artillery gun, machine gun nests and rifle pits, block-houses, fox-holes and lava pill-boxes. They are very hard to get at. The Japs still hold the damn thing and as it over-looks our rear position is quite serious. The planes worked on it too as well as cruisers and cans. All day the ships fired on it. Two and three LCIs (small landing craft) shoot all day long right in one area not 100 yards square. I thought they dug up the whole beach but their ma-chine-gun shells just bounced off the hard rock. Like all volcanoes, this one has a hole in the center. (The last time it erupted was in 1919.) The only smoke that comes from it is bombs bursting through. There is nothing inside the thing but sometimes the bombs and shells miss. We aim for the ridges and outer ring. Throughout the day the shelling was very heavy. Many times the ships would be off their aim in elevation and shoot entirely over the island. We received several near misses from big guns (scared the living hell out of us too) and nu-merous machine gun bursts nearby but miraculously nothing hit the ship. Once when in real close to the volcano, I went back to the after head (no, I won't tell you why) and was walking back toward the bridge to my G.Q. station when a string of twenty millimeter stuff started walking up the starboard side about a hundred feet from the ship. Naturally, I was on the starboard side when it started but I walked slowly over to the port side out of the way. (They needed those new hatches right there anyway.) Seriously, though, it was funny. Ev-erybody was hitting the deck with full length belly bursts. The guys seemed to just jump up in the air and throw themselves forward and would hit flat on their stomachs and faces "Splat." I was kinda scared of course but couldn't help laughing. There was just a tiny thin sheet of siding between them and the bursts. I ducked behind it too instinctively I guess and when the string quit I went over onto the other side. I climbed up to the bridge and they were still on their bellies. George was up using his glasses. Now, Baby Honey, you know how cautious I am, don't think I just "casually" walked up to the bridge in the open. It was in the open but I wasn't exactly "casual" about it. There was nothing to be afraid of particularly. Just a Jap who had thrown a quick one at us because our guns were annoying him.[9] He was too busy with the planes to give us much time.

Later in the evening our flame throwing Marines went to work on the volcano. The damn thing is still fighting though and today is the sixth day of intense bombardment of the thing. No wonder the Jap soldier is an insane machine when our troops finally get in close. Our advances were slowed last night (not because the *Howorth* stopped bombarding ENTIRELY). They have pushed the Japs up to the northern end now which is much rougher than the southern end. So far (up to last night) we have lost 3,600 men dead, wounded or missing. That's a lot of men but we are ahead of schedule and the 27,000 Japs will all be dead when we finish. I'm glad, in spite of the sacrifice I feel that you and I are making, that I had something to do with killing some of them. I really feel grand about it. I get a special kick out of killing them. I only wish I were in close enough to see their bodies and parts of bodies go sky high when our shells hit.

Well, last night we retired again. Shoved off several miles from the island and just in time. The Nip planes came in with eleven raids. They were firing on all sides of us; we were trained out many times but fortunately none came in close enough. I was watching a particularly heavy anti-aircraft barrage being put up by a ship just over the horizon off our port bow. It developed into three ships. Then I saw a great flash and a slow dying glow. I saw another in the same spot a few seconds later and then a third off to the left. We later learned that a carrier escort [a CVE, or "jeep" aircraft carrier] had been sunk by Jap bombs and a suicide plane. He must have hit a very vulnerable spot. Anyway the flash and fire was really big. The slow dying glow was caused by suicide planes and some of our destroyers were dispatched to pick up survivors of the sunken ship. Seventeen of our planes were left in the air with no place to land. It was pitiable and I really felt for the boys. The Japs shoved off and all the ships were firing on our own

---

9. This could just as easily have been friendly fire.

planes. It was dark and they couldn't see them to identify them. Several flew over us but we were able to identify them through a means I can't divulge in a letter. They flew quite low and slowly over. We got reports of three being shot down by LSTs. The LSTs do not have the identifying apparatus [IFF] that we do unfortunately. It seems they flew over the convoy not knowing it was there. The whole damn bunch opened up and blew them to hell. I don't know what happened to the rest of them. The usual action is for the pilot to find a destroyer and crash land as near as possible (if the fool doesn't fire on him), hoping he can get out uninjured before his plane sinks. The can then picks him up; feeds him brandy; wraps him in a blanket and puts him to bed; returning him to proper authority later. And incidentally, winter really is at hand. The water is cold as the very devil and Baby, I don't want to be sunk here. That might sound sissy to you compared to the boys sunk in the North Atlantic and Aleutians but coming directly from the Equator up here has wrought a terrific change in climate and we really feel it. It's kinda like you there in Dallas going up to Kansas City or Nebraska. Well, that's about all.

To bring us up to date, we have steamed around all day today in thick weather (rainy and cold) and I saw only one other ship, a tanker, that we fueled from. I don't know when we will get back to civilization or even if we will. We may forge ahead. It seems we are forever in unsafe water. (We get our retiring periods though, it just seems dangerous all the time.) The Jap fleet hasn't shown up yet nor do I expect it. By the way, when you see a movie with all the shooting, zinging bullets and bomb bursts, it is exactly as the sound track records it. I don't know how they do it but those shells that hit the water were just like the noises in war movies. The glancing zing was too damn realistic but accurately recorded on the screen. All the bombing, heavy shooting, etc., is "right on." I felt right at home in a movie until they started coming my way.

Well, darling, that's all for tonight. I don't know what's coming next nor when it will come, but as ever my thoughts are of you and I pray that before long I'll be back there and all this madness will be over. It is madness but I believe that with one look at Commerce and Akard [Dallas streets] will bring everything back to normal; that is if you kinda have your hand through my arm. Oh, yes, before I go. I want to know if you've ever heard the song "Till Then," by the Ink Spots. I know it's corny (but you know me and my Korn) but it quite aptly tells a story. We have it aboard and I heard it several times, the last time just before we got in here and I like to listen to it. Try and hear it sometimes if you can. While I'm thinking about it, give my regards to Roy and Dr. Scanland. I'll give them a chance to meet me one of these days, and until then Darling Baby, I'll do my very utmost to have them meet ALL of me. God Bless You Ray Ellen, I worship you baby girl. I've written that so many times Darling and it seems so weak; but re-member I said it all the time continuously so to speak, when I was with you, so you know it's no imagination of the absent. Good night now. I'm tired and I want to think about how sweet you are before I go to sleep.

> Your devoted husband,
> Orvill

P.S. I LOVE YOU!!!

---

25 February 1945

Hello, Baby Darling:

Poppie must hurry this morning. A small boat is coming out to pick up the mail for a plane back to the states and I want this to get aboard. I was going to write you last night but the sea was so heavy I couldn't even sit in my chair. We have rubber cups on the legs but neverthe-less, they slid all over the galvanized deck. It was so rough that every-thing fell off the desk and the things on the cabinet in front of me fell in my lap. I thought I was hurt once but wasn't when a heavy log book fell on my leg. I thought I was bruised but you know the Navy. It makes men out of boys and corpses out of men. Glad I'm just a boy. (A-hem.) The heavy seas carried away our chemical smoke generators on the fantail sometime during the night. It was by far the roughest it's ever been since we've been at sea. Last night at supper, the deck was filthy and dangerous with food and slippery coffee. I was sitting on a secure bench and escaped being thrown about. There were about eighty men there while I was eating and we took a terrific roll to port. I'd say seventy of them went to the deck with coffee, pie and sandwiches all over them. It was really humorous. I had anticipated such a thing happening and saw where the bench wouldn't overturn. We all had a big laugh at the boys who got more or less scalded. They jumped and hollered all over the place. Last night was another anxious evening. We had twelve air raids within two hours. They weren't exactly raids as you know them. Each "Bogey" (enemy plane or group of planes) is designated as a "raid." It may be one plane or it may be a hundred. We separate them by calling them "raids" because it enables us to keep in touch with all of them on different bearings and ranges. The most at one time was seven raids. And maybe you think it isn't a headache taking care of seven different ranges and bearings at the same time. None of them came in closer than four miles to us. None fired on us or bombed. They were attacking our forces on the island. The anti-aircraft fire was terrifically beautiful going up from the island and ships surrounding it. It was a mile in diameter and looked like an immense golden curtain going up. Like in a theater with the footlights shining on it. They bombed the island and maybe some ships but we have gotten no details yet.

The Marines hoisted the American Flag on the volcano yesterday morning at 10:45. It was truly a victory. The Marines, Army and Navy have all said this has been the worse battle of the Pacific as yet. I can vouch that it has been a very rugged one. Latest reports indicate our losses at about 500 officers and men killed and about 5,000 wounded or missing. At the moment we are engaged in patrol duties and looking for a boat with four wounded men in it. Our lookouts are busy with the task but so far hasn't anyone found them. I don't know where they are from or how anybody knows there are four of them in a boat and wounded. Probably sighted by a plane. At any rate it is still cold and windy. The sea has calmed somewhat but we are still rolling badly. I'd hate to be out in the water now, especially with a hole in me somewhere. This is a bad place to get sunk. Not much land and what there is, is all enemy-held. If you will consult a map, you can see that all we have is tiny dots in a line both northward and southward of us. This is the Japanese Empire proper now and all the more reason we are fighting it out.

The battle on Iwo Jima is now in its eighth day and is just as furious as the first day. I don't know if we will go back to safe territory soon or not. We may stay around here a few more days until this area is declared safe itself. That is our usual method. And o.k. with me. We live from ships anyway, no matter where they are located. Darling, I'm going to close now so as to get this off in the mail. I will write again and mail it as soon as possible. Please be a brave little girl and believe the way I do that "everything will come out in the wash." Now is a very trying time, and as you say, maybe it will improve our character. I don't believe you could be improved but perhaps I'm wrong. I love you so much I can't see any mistakes you might make but am deliriously happy in my "blindness" and want it to stay that way forever. God Bless you Baby Girl, I worship and adore you every moment of my life. (Write Mother that I'm o.k.) (Please?)

> Your devoted husband,
> Orvill

P.S. I LOVE YOU!!!

---

4 March 1945

Hello, My Darling Baby:

Honey, it's been some time now since I've written. Better than a week. A lot has been going on but it's all the same thing. The island is practically ours now with a little fierce fighting left to be done on the north end. We have bombarded the beach five times since the time I wrote you about. Once we fired for twenty-four hours. It was pretty grueling but I managed to live over it. It is now 8 P.M. and we will go to G.Q. in a few minutes to do some more night firing. We were fired on by a beach gun the other day but I don't have time to tell you about it right now. The reason I'm in a hurry is that I think we will get mail off tomorrow and I want this to be ready to go tonight. If we don't stay up all night firing, I will finish this after yep, after G.Q. I was interrupted and just got back down. We didn't stay but little more than an hour. Darling, when I have more time and can think straight again, I'll write you all about it. But I think I have time to tell you about our being fired on. It was the other morning just after sunrise and we were shooting at the beach just prior to an advance by the Marines. We were laying down a barrage ahead of them, covering an area pretty thoroughly. Well, a cargo ship was just off our port bow and practically in the shadow of the volcano on the south end of the island. He had come around on the west side in an effort to land supplies as the east side was too crowded. (Today they landed all day safely on the west side.) Anyway we were wondering at what success he would have so close to the enemy (this was four days ago). He came almost to a stop and just then a large caliber shell exploded in the water about two hundred yards ahead of him. It looked as if it might be a six or eight inch shell burst. Another quickly followed and then another. The cargo ship started turning around as fast as he could and disregarding "making smoke" he really steamed for range. Well they poked them out fast and furious, hitting all around him for about five minutes. Only one came close and that splashed water all over his fantail. We thought he was hit but close observation showed that he hadn't. He rapidly opened range (I didn't know the fat old things could go so fast) and our Captain started hollering at our guns to get on the flashes of the enemy gun on the beach. He started hollering at them shortly after they began firing (as soon as we could identify it) but they were slow. The gunnery officer couldn't find the damn flash with a powerful glass when we guys on the bridge could see it with our naked eyes. We all knew that as soon as the cargo ship was out of range, the enemy gun would turn on us. We were in real close. The reason he hadn't taken us under fire was because the other ship was bigger. So, he trained around on us and we were all screaming for the stupid son-of-a-bitch gunnery officer to get on the target. And honestly, Darling, that damn fool never did fire in the vicinity of the enemy gun. I was never so disgusted with the ship since I've been on it. It was due to only one man however and we all know he knows nothing about his business. Well off our starboard bow another destroyer managed to get the correct range and other mathematical data necessary to fire the complicated firing done nowadays. He was one of our squadron and we just loved him. About ten seconds after the first and only enemy shell burst about two hundred feet astern of us (the Jap is a LOUSY shot) he opened up and fired thirty 5-gun salvos as fast as the sailors could fire them. I'm telling you darling, it was wonderful watching that ship fire those guns; it was almost machine-gun like, they were shooting so fast. Lynch and I just almost hugged each other. We knew we weren't on the target and that ship was probably saving many of our lives. While we were waiting for the enemy to train around on us, George and I huddled on the other side of the bridge, not saying anything, not too afraid, but we jumped each of the three times we fired feebly at the wrong place hoping to "get on target." We expected any moment for a shell to tear through the bridge. After that terrible waiting, we saw this other ship open fire. He put out 150 shells in less than three minutes and that is very fast firing for the big guns. We think he knocked out the enemy gun with the first ten salvos but didn't mind a damn bit when he kept shooting. All we could do was look at that boy shove them out and look at each other with elation and a sigh. We doubly realized our position as the position we occupied had been vacated by us two days before and the three ships that had fired from the same spot before we took over again had been hit. Only once but enough to be hurt. A cruiser also got it in the vicinity. A carrier had been hit the night before (small one) and we felt pretty low when that bastard started shooting at that cargo ship and we knowing it was only a matter of time if we didn't knock him out. The Captain was grateful of course to the other ship. He was as frightened as anyone. But boy, he sure read the gunnery officer off and in no uncertain terms. I know that if the consequences wouldn't have been so great, he would have struck a couple of the dunderheads.[10]

Well, Baby girl, that is about all. We retire from shooting after one day so the crew can get a good night's sleep. (They call five hours a good night's sleep.) At night in here we fire only about every fifteen minutes and it isn't necessary for general quarters crews to man the guns most of the time.

My most pleasant moment came two days ago when our boss radioed over to the ship and said send a boat after mail. We figured it was only official mail and didn't bother but the mail clerk came back with a few bags and I got four from you. One I can't open until April 20th. Dang your hide! Why did you send it two months ahead of time? I'll die of curiosity! No, I know why you sent it so I'd get it in plenty of time. ...

The adage has it that time helps to forget but I know now what I

---

10. This account reflects the stress of being under fire. The supplementary report to the special action report for the March 1–2, 1945, "Illumination and Shore Bombardment Mission" is on microfilm Reel E-108, NPPSO–Naval District Washington Job No. AR-65-78, "*Howorth* (DD-592), Report File, War Diary"; note 25, Introduction above. It noted that the time between the first rounds fired at the AK (cargo ship) by the Japanese shore battery and the beginning of counterbattery fire by *Howorth* was one minute and forty-eight seconds. This was hardly a "slow" response, given the need to locate the target and check it in gun plot to ensure that friendly troops would be safe from *Howorth*'s counterbattery fire. The range to the Japanese gun was over 3 nautical miles (6,050 yards) and at an elevation of 250 feet above sea level. The supplementary report stated that "other ships took this position under fire. The resulting dust and smoke made observation difficult." My recollections from my service as a surface warfare officer in the destroyer *Hamner* are that all my commanding officers liberally chastised gunnery officers, undoubtedly because of their ability to act at great distance, for good or ill, in the name of the ship.

have always felt since I first laid eyes on you. You were meant for me and nothing must ever come between us. Should I never see you again and yet live to be a hundred; the girl in my heart would forever be you. The impression you made there will never be free. If we were to remain on opposite sides of the globe for a century, both in strange country, in strange company, my heart would belong to you. If you cast it out, never to return, it would always be there, waiting for you to summon.

Good night for now, Baby Girl, I worship you and think of you constantly. I'll write again when I can find the time. I am working in the office this week and Mac is standing watch. I hope to answer all your wonderful letters this week before mailing time arrives again. As for my locale—we have the Japs on a narrow strip on the north end now. They are about finished. They [U.S. forces] use lights to unload and work at night on the beach now. Where from here is a mystery. God Bless and keep you safe darling. "Till then,"

Your devoted husband,
Orvill

P.S. I LOVE YOU!!!

7 March 1945

Hello, Baby Darling:

Well, tonight I get a chance to write you again. I am enclosing two bucks honey so you can buy me something I need. I'm not sending the money to keep you from buying it for me but because I need a small penknife and a fingernail file. The reason I'm sending the money is because they both have points and although I'm not superstitious (blackcat) I don't want to take any chance of cutting our love in two. I gave a little girl a fountain pen one time and never saw the dear child again. The penknife I want Baby is a small one to just use for the insignificant things that men usually want them for. I need it for trimming fingernails, peeling onions, picking my teeth, etc. Just a small one and preferably stainless steel if you can get it Baby Girl, because the salt water is so bad about rusting things. Cullam and Boren should have one. For the fingernail file, I can't figure where in the world you might get one; maybe an old one at home. That will do if you can spare it. In fact, I'd rather have one you have used if you have a small one. I can file my nails and think of you filing yours with the same one. Those beautiful precious fingernails of yours. ...

Hey, I haven't gotten the pictures you, Nell and her soldier friend took at Fair Park yet. Guess they haven't been developed yet. Don't forget 'em!

Darling Baby, I've just been re-reading your letters written during that long wait you had while I was up in Lingayen Gulf. Always with your tomorrows. Baby Girl, right now, the time of my return may appear to be away in the future. The tomorrows (although they do help) appear to be many and long. Stop a moment and think that after this eternity is over, the tomorrows will be todays always. This will be over; history must repeat itself and in order to do so it must stop occasionally in order to start over again. I believe this will be our only separation. Some day (and the months *will* pass) we will be together again. And when we are, I guarantee that I will never leave your side again. Only something as huge and important as the war today can pull me away from you. Even as important as our being together seems, the war causes so much strife in so many homes, we must remember that so far we are very lucky and I feel that God is taking a personal interest in us. For the last two weeks I have looked on a tiny rotten little rat's nest of an island and steadily watched the penciled lines on our chart creep from the southern tip to the northern tip. In that area three miles wide (a rifle can shoot across it in any direction) and five miles long ..... three thousand Marines have died ..... six thousand others have been wounded. The bloodiest war and battle in so small a place ever recorded in history. Fourteen thousand Japanese men have died ..... hundreds more dying each hour, burned to a crisp by the flame throwers that flash into their holes and sear them so badly we don't have enough left to bury. Mighty bulldozers scooping giant trenches in the earth to bury the dead by the thousands. And this is only one spot on the globe. There are hundreds of other scenes of battle, like the one that got Doyle Hendrix. Somehow, knowing what terror this kind of death and injury is, I feel very lucky that so far I can look forward to our reunion. I feel very lucky indeed. I haven't told you this yet. It's the only thing I hesitated to tell you. But the other day we were in close to the beach and our amphibious tanks were firing .30 caliber machine-guns into the stubborn rock, trying to feel out the Jap holes. Steel was flying so fast and we were in so close that sev-

eral projectiles bounced off the rocks and flew seaward. One hit a
hatch on the bridge against which I was leaning and chipped the paint
about eighteen inches from my chest. It wouldn't have hurt me had it
hit; but it just occurred to me that a guy could very easily get killed
out here and consequently consider that all the chances we've taken
and still remain unscratched as far as personnel injuries are concerned,
we are pretty lucky. Keep that precious chin up my darling and always
look for your tomorrows. One fine day that one tomorrow for which
we both are looking so intently will arrive. Thereafter they will all be
todays. Right now we just have to sigh and wish and push it out of our
minds. You remain brave my precious Baby and be patient. We are
much better off than those that will never return. We are bombarding
the beach again tonight. Seven times we have come in to help tabulate
the dwindling enemy. In a few days we will be gone and our beer can
be taken onto the beach and we look around for souvenirs. (By that
time of course they shove us off for some other beach and the Army
(who takes over) will find all the little souvenirs we've made out of the
big ones.) (That's supposed to be funny.)

Oh, yes, Baby, a peculiar thing happened the other day. A big beautiful B-29 came back this way from a raid over Tokyo. And believe-it-or-
not, that gigantic thing was flying on ONE engine. The other three
were shot out. She was supposed to crash land near one of the destroyers near the island and we were to pick up her crew. The pilot however, decided the field on the beach would be enough to land on. And
by the old Harry, he did it. I don't think he had an inch to spare when
he stopped rolling but he made it o.k. Several hours later he had another plane's parts inside (don't ask me where he got them) and took
off and winged away for his regular base. It was phenomenal. Honey,
you can't imagine how huge they are until you see them. Their tail as-
sembly alone stands as high as a house. And are they beautiful. Next
to a woman the B-29 and the P51 fighter are the most beautiful fe-
males we have out here. The pretty and mighty *Howorth* is not so
pretty any more. We have banged up her sides and the vibration from
gun-fire has shaken her almost to pieces. (Her crew too.) All the urinals in the heads have been bounced off the bulkheads onto the deck.
Salt water spurting all over the place. We have 48 cups left of our 300
when we got out here. We are drinking coffee out of bowls. Every once
in a while the guns go off as I write this and the typewriter and me
jump about two inches. The bulkhead (wall) behind me is buckled

someway and crunches back and forth like a tub stomped on with a heavy foot. All our clip-boards jump onto the deck. Our supplies in the cabinets do a complete turnover, etc. Boy, it's a mess.

8 March 1945

Hi ya, Leetle Baby:

I hadda quit last night because it was getting late and the gunfire was giving me a headache. Somehow we had to head the ship abeam to the swells and we started rolling. We are still rolling now but it is due to windy sea. We've been struggling to keep on our feet all day. I thought about you and how you'd take the rolling ship. It is worse when we try to eat. Today, for instance, we had soup (good soup) and coffee. Well, we take our trays into the tables and sit down. When we feel a big roll coming we have just enough time to grab one or the other, soup or coffee; the other one must spill. Tonight we had English peas. A very funny thing happened. I had eaten all mine and the guy sitting opposite me had his peas in the tray next to mine. He wasn't paying attention to the roll and a big one came my way. Well, you guessed it, the tray slid over against mine and the peas rolled into mine. We had a good laugh. Of course, he didn't want them back. I even got his pea soup.

We got more mail yesterday. It seems they are sending it up here from Saipan and Ulithi. There are two wide skips in the dates though and we still have some back mail piling up somewhere. Boy, are we getting tired hanging around here. Just shooting all the time. Everytime we look over on the island, smoke and dust is rising. We figure however that there aren't many Japs left alive. There was only 27,000 there to begin and we have accounted for 14,000. Add another 3 or 4,000 for those blown to so many pieces they can't be counted and we have two thirds of them whipped. The fighting is confined to one end of the island now but we can see flame throwers still working on the holes all over the place. About one to two are flaming all the time. We still don't know what the hell is coming next. We have been here long enough to consume most of our fresh provisions and had to re-load yesterday. Everyone but us has either gone away [and] stayed or gone away and [re]turned. (Not everyone, there are still a lot of ships who haven't left yet.) But the turnover has been in the majority. ...

I guess I won't see either Glenn Murray or Glenn Whistler anymore. When we changed fleets, we left them in the old one. We have what we call three classes of fleets. One is slow, one is medium and one is fast. (I'm using the numeral "one" only as a figure of speech. No telling how many there are in fact.) We just came from the slow one. And are now in the medium. We are a part of the fastest fleet out here but not on the "front" line. Just next to it. As far as danger or anything else of that nature is concerned, I see no segregation. One is as bad or good as the other; it is just a different type of operating. I hope you can get it. I can't tell exactly as it is for the sake of security and the spirit of censorship. Norval is getting a new LSM (that's a small landing craft) and probably will be assigned to another fleet than the one I'm in.

Bravo for your finding the Liberty Head Nickel. Finishing those collections won't be my main hobby when I first get back (Heavens no!) but I might later settle down winding them up. Keep those lovely blue eyes peeled for Poppie. Your cooperation is always solicited and appreciated.

Well, excitement just halted things momentarily. We went alongside another destroyer just like us and the sea is so heavy we damn near busted up. Operations must go through under all circumstances to get the job done and boy we tore the hell out of the whale boat on the other ship. The sea was acting strangely and we went way up in the air while the other ship went way down in the trough. Well we went up once and came down on their boat. (It hangs out over the side somewhat.) It broke slap in two, right down the middle of the engine and everything. It looked bad a moment but we came out o.k.

George is down here with me tonight. He was down last night while I was writing. He sits at the desk beside me and uses the typewriter to type up the stencil for our press news. (We run off mimeograph copies and distribute over the ship.) He does it for practice although I have been doing it for work! The radiomen receive it over the air from the states and I help them out by typing the stencil.

Incidentally, I was looking over my beautiful long hair today. It is as long as I could hope it to be. In fact too damn long now. Everybody's is. We have been so busy that the barbers haven't opened up in almost a month. Therefore, all us guys who crowd the dog-catchers anyway are having a rugged time of it. Only yesterday they got to the Captain. He looked like Tarzan (his long hair I mean). Most of us are getting that violin player look about us. George, who spends a lot of time keeping trim is like a shaggy hound himself. I attempted again to raise a mustache but George just won't let me. Our conversations reach the temperature of 180 sometimes. I let it grow just to institute an argument. We enjoy razing about it. I couldn't grow one in five years and even if I did, it would look like hell.

Oh, yes, Baby, I wanted to tell you about Saipan. I think I told you about going over but can't remember if I told you about the island any. Anyway, repeat or not, here goes. It is by far the most beautiful island in the South or West Pacific. It has a smooth clean beach all around it (the south side that I saw also east). The sand is clean and smooth. It rises very slowly from the edge of the water and is beautifully green. It looks like a valley with an altitude of about ten to twenty feet above sea level for five miles inland. Then it starts a gentle rise and gradually slopes steeply up into rolling hills in the background. Looking at it from the sea, one sees the hills about ten miles away through a fine haze unless the weather is unusually clear. On top are instruments of war, but ignoring them you can see the multi-colored farms that checkerboard the entire island. All over the island that I saw the hills rolled. None of the steep cliffs except on the other end where so many Japanese civilians jumped into the sea. It was truly beautiful. George and I went over to get a couple of beers. We drank only one and settled for the cokes that they sold at a stand. We could buy two at a time. We drank two cokes and then two Pepsi-Colas (because they are bigger I guess). I thought about you while drinking the Cokes. And Honey, I didn't forget to take a sip for you. Every other one that I could keep track of with all the happy loud-talking guys spouting off all the time. The 25% of the crew that left the ship and went with us were just like a bunch of kids. Skipping and hopping and raising general Cain like on a picnic. We hadn't been ashore anywhere except at Ulithi where you really don't feel ground but coral reef instead since the first of January. (It was then the middle of February.) Well, naturally, when we had drunk our fill, George and I started wandering about which we aren't supposed ever to do, but always do anyway in spite of regulations. We wandered about inspecting Jap pillboxes and blockhouses and rifle pits. Really a formidable system of defense; as witnessed by the numerous amphibious tanks and landing craft of ours still piled up on the sandy beach. We inspected an unusual gun. It was an eight inch affair (shoots a shell 8 inches in diameter Darling) but only about four inches long. Normally, you would expect them to be about twenty to thirty feet long. We decided it was an anti-landing craft job to help hold the beaches. We wandered on over to where there used to be a sort of village of about eight or ten houses. The only things left were the concrete water supply tanks, concrete flooring and barbecuing outfits. Naturally, no souvenirs. ...

Darling, about our family ideas and my going to school. I'm not going to let anything stand in the way of either one of them. If there is any way possible for us to have any children, I am going to go to work on it as soon as I get back. We want a family and I am done with fooling with it. We may decide from the beginning that it won't be necessary for you to work anyway. And if you do, you certainly can quit to have and take care of a baby. A family is important too and I'm sure I can provide for one and my education too. Maybe I'm too optimistic but the family comes first if a decision MUST be made. As for your being by my side through thick and thin, I have all the confidence in the world in it. If I didn't think you would stick, I wouldn't have chosen you, or rather worked so damn hard to get you to choose me. It's pretty thick right now, beautiful little soldier, but I'll damn sure thin it out for you when they untie my hands.

No, your kisses do NOT embarrass me on your letters. In fact, they make me proud. George and all the guys just beg me for "one little whiff." I've gotten some fresh ones lately (dated early in February, about a month old) and George has to wait so long for his all the smell is out. His girl in Australia sent him her perfumed handkerchief a while back and he came waving it under my nose, in repayment of my many kind acts of letting him smell your lipstick kisses. The strikers (one made Y3/c the other day) (the Jew) always turn handsprings when they see those red lip prints. Your lips are so pretty and formed simply beautiful. I can't help comparing them with their prints and they (theirs) seem so out of shape. Big and thick or narrow and thin. Yours are perfectly formed. By all means don't stop. Even if they did embarrass me, I'd want them to keep coming. I put my lips to them and know that just before it went into the envelope and sealed, your lips are on the exact same spot. It is a good dream baby and a happy thought. Don't quit! Remember? I used to ask you to don't quit when you were administering 400s.

Honey, don't fret when I don't get your mail in a reasonable time. Of course it hurts but the other boys are the same way and certainly it isn't your fault. The day I got Lula's letter and no others, we had about a dozen letters come aboard. Just one of those freak things that happen. Why we had only a dozen letters when we knew of thousands waiting for the ship, no one can figure. The office got only a few letters and usually they bring it up in bags. So don't you worry your little head about it. You most assuredly can't help it. In fact you do very admirably. Much better than 90% of the other wives represented here. ...

About the ribbons. No, honey, I can't buy them out here nor can you find them at home. When I get back to the states, I will know more about what I rate and just pick them up anywhere. On the coast, naturally, every other store is a military establishment. And I promise you now that I won't try for the congressional medal or the purple heart. Glad Buster got something out of his injury though.

15 March 1945

Hello, Baby:

Just a quick one. We will get mail off in a couple of days but I will be too busy to write any other time. If I do, I will do so. We are through with the little rock business up here and are going back to where the little Japanese pond is. Then south again and will write you from there. Can't do more now, Darling. I love you. Believe me!

17 March 1945

Hello, My Sweet Baby Girl:

Well, I didn't get the above off as I expected and bet two to one that it is a good thing I didn't. Boy, writing just that much would have scorched you after all the juicy four, six and eight pagers I sometimes give out with. I would have sent it anyway to let you know that we are "on the road." Well, Baby, they finally "secured" Iwo Jima. I am certainly glad. It took twenty-five days of the bloodiest fighting in history to take it and we were there twenty-four of them. The morning we left, we bombarded the beach on the very tip end of the island. A few of our shells in fact, went right over the tip we were firing on and into the sea, it was so close to the edge. And am I proud to have been there? It was the worst yet for us but I am proud that I had a little to do with it. Of course, the Marines will get and certainly deserve most of the credit. We feel that the Navy did just as much but we didn't have to land on the beach and fight them hand-to-hand like they did toward the last. Honey, we lost more than four thousand Marines dead. That is absolutely terrible! Of course I realize the importance (strategic) of taking the island, but believe me that little piece of rocky hell is worth nothing at all except for sulphur and airfields. There was an additional sixteen thousand Marines wounded. Isn't that terrible too? Boy, I'm sounding like a sissy, but twenty thousand Marines put out of action in twenty-five days is a lot of human flesh and blood. Bet Roy would have had her hands full tending to all those guys. Bet she would have had her hands full for other reasons too after looking at her picture. (More about 'em later.)

Now that we've withdrawn to a more or less safe locale, I look on the map and realize just how close we were to the Jap front door. Honey, we're a' knockin'. And the boys in Europe are doing a right good job too. I'm really proud of them. They are slugging it out and shipping the supermen right on their own damn home ground. Just like we are out here. May the American spirit and ability never decrease. An interesting sidelight: The day before [we] left Iwo Jima, a special ship loaded with turkey put into the "harbor" and all ships, stations and mess kitchens received all it needed to serve every man in the Iwo Jima area. It was a special turkey dinner celebrating the victory. A hard-won victory and I imagine many a Marine had the stuff stick in his throat thinking of some buddy. There were two very neat grave yards on the island when we left. The Fourth Marine Division on the east and the Fifth Marine Division on the west. They were small (due to limited space) but closely knitted in perfect rows. They were still adding the little crosses when we left. Well, so much for that. I will always remember Iwo Jima more vividly than any other place except perhaps Mindoro when I thought maybe I'd be holding up one of those crosses myself. I sincerely pray to God that the people of America will not forget the sons who died there. It was the Devil's own creation.

We arrived here in Saipan this evening and will stay here all night. I will mail this at Ulithi when we get there because no mail goes off here. The most important thing I guess about arriving here is the fact that we passed a hospital ship; the Captain and Executive Officer being garter-snappers of the first water, we passed very close. Luckily three nurses were standing on the main deck in their pretty white starched uniforms looking out over the harbor as we passed. Everybody who could grabbed glasses and binoculars and really looked them over. They watched us come in and finally I couldn't resist the urge (you know me) I waved from up on the bridge. The Exec. and several others waved then and so the girls waved back. Then the whole ship started waving and whistling. The poor girls' arms ached I guess by the time we passed. It didn't matter whether they were good looking. We were too far off to judge but it didn't matter. Oh, yes, another item about Iwo. The cargo planes started coming in there immediately after the first airfield was taken to evacuate the wounded. It was marvelous the way they came in and landed right in the middle of anti-aircraft fire and bursting shells. I think they were the first to land there except perhaps for a very few naval fighting planes who landed for gas, etc., in emergency. There was a steady stream of the evacuation planes after the first one.

We will have a few days at our destination for repairs (not battle casualties just regular upkeep). Honey, did I tell you all our urinals were knocked off the bulkheads due to the sustained gunfire up at Iwo? Well they were and we are having a heck of a time holding ourselves until we get them put back up. No kiddin' though, we are in a helluva mess. Everything is shaken loose and fallen or about to fall. We had a very dangerous trip back as we were the only destroyer with the convoy but I must withhold the details. They can't be put down here. Some planes came over night before last and we couldn't tell who they were. One of the officers said to challenge them with a light and for once an enlisted man told him where to go. It seems that Sid's ship was sunk because of just that. Sid's bridge gang challenged a Jap and got bullets and bombs in their teeth for their trouble. George's signalmen refused and it was commended. (p.s. The officer was embarrassed.)

Honey, there isn't anything else to write tonight except answer your letters and I want to get a good night's sleep tonight (I got off watch today) and will answer them tomorrow. Oh yes, the pictures. Yes, you were right, Roy is a cute girl. In fact, very cute. And what's more, I believe I can read intelligence in her face and posture. By golly, that's so damn hard to find in a girl (wait a minute! Men too now honey). I showed the pictures to a few select personnel and they wanted all the "dope" on you both. I gave it to them but it is hopeless; there's nothing these guys can do about it now. But boy, wait'll they hit the beach in the States again. Boy, I'm going to a USO and stay there. The cops will be rounding up every blue-jacket in town in order to clean out the *Howorth* bunch. They've promised to drink every drop in 'Frisco when they land and these are just the guys to do it too.

Well, darling, good night for now. Tell Roy hello, also all the other guys. I plan to write the kids soon, also Nell and Mom and Pop. I tried to write Mother on March 5th (her birthday) but we were too busy. Bombarding I think and a lot of other things. I couldn't write anyone but you while up there. I finally got off a short one to her though. Good night now Baby Darling. I worship you and really dream so very much about what we are going to do when I get back. I do more damn day dreaming! Speaking of dreaming, last night I was so bushed at midnight that I fell dead in my bunk. A few seconds later I was dreaming and my dream! I dreamed I had just come down from watch and was about to climb in my bunk when I noticed it was full of rattlesnakes, moccasins and cobras. I was so tired, I said to myself, "Hell, this will never do," and started raking them out of it with my hands. Then someone shouted "look out! Raines! and I hollered "OH" when I felt one bite my stomach. Then I woke up. Shaky as hell. I know I shouted out loud because you can tell (there isn't any cotton in your mouth and it wakes you up). Good night baby girl. I love you and maybe before long I will be able to hold you in these aching arms again. God Bless you and keep you safe for me. Darling, how I do worship and adore you!

> Your devoted slave,
> Orvill

P.S. I LOVE YOU!!!

On March 16, 1945, marine Major General Harry Schmidt announced that Iwo Jima was "secured," although marines continued to die fighting entrenched Japanese soldiers. On March 27, elimination of the last vestiges of Japanese resistance was turned over to the army's 147th Infantry Regiment.

The long campaign for Iwo Jima exacted a fearsome toll: The infantry regiments of the 4th and 5th Marine Divisions suffered casualty rates approaching 75 percent; 5,921 marines were killed or declared missing and presumed dead; 19,920 marines were wounded. The navy suffered 881 officers and sailors killed and 1,917 wounded.[11]

After the exhausting Iwo Jima campaign, *Howorth*'s crew received scant rest before pushing on to the invasion of the Ryukyu Archipelago, on the very doorstep of the Japanese home islands.

---

11. Casualty data from Morison, *The Two-Ocean War*, 524. For General Smith's comments on the Iwo Jima campaign, see Smith and Finch, *Coral and Brass*, chapter 13.

10

Invasion of Okinawa Shima

March 18–June 1, 1945

Howorth arrived at the fleet anchorage at Ulithi Atoll on March 19 and spent five days receiving repairs from the crew of the destroyer tender *Prairie*. The daylight hours of March 26 were spent loading ammunition and refueling the ship. Shortly after noon the next day, *Howorth* sortied with the other ships of Destroyer Division 90 to escort one of the transport groups to Okinawa. Heavy weather made the voyage especially uncomfortable.

The Ryukyu Islands were Japanese home territory, and U.S. commanders expected an all-out effort by the Japanese to repulse any assault.[1] The landings on Okinawa were set for Easter Sunday, which also happened to be April Fool's Day. At 3:20 A.M. on "L-Day," *Howorth* joined other destroyers in a sweep of the landing area to ensure the absence of Japanese submarines and to draw fire from Japanese coastal defense guns. At 5 A.M. *Howorth* was ordered to proceed to a patrol area west of Okinawa to screen the invasion force.

At 8:30 A.M. the invasion of Okinawa began with the landings of the U.S. 10th Army and the marine's 3rd Amphibious Corps. After a day on her screening station, *Howorth* joined other destroyers in escorting a transport group westward for the night's retirement to the relative safety of the high seas. The first day of the Okinawa operation was over, and *Howorth* had yet to fire a shot.

The second day at Okinawa was more difficult for Raines and his shipmates. At 12:58 A.M. on April 2, a lone Japanese plane flew down *Howorth*'s port side. The plane had not been detected, and the pilot evi-

---

1. For an overview of the Okinawa campaign, see Spector, *Eagle Against the Sun,* chapter 23.

dently never saw *Howorth* despite a bright moon. It was a frightful experience. After daylight *Howorth* was ordered to a patrol station west of Okinawa and fired on a Japanese plane en route. Suppertime found *Howorth* escorting transport ships on their nightly retirement away from the dangerous waters near the beachhead.

April 3 included a Japanese submarine scare, daytime picket duty, and a night assignment as a radar picket ship 12 miles south of Okinawa. *Howorth* remained on this radar picket station until sent south to rendezvous with and escort a convoy of transports and merchant marine ships back to Okinawa. She returned to Kerama Retto anchorage west of Okinawa on the morning of April 6 and soon thereafter was released from escort duty. While the *Howorth* waited to refuel in the Northern Transport Area, enemy aircraft were reported, and the crew went to general quarters. By 3:34 P.M. it was apparent that waves of Japanese aircraft were approaching Okinawa from Japan; refueling was canceled.

The first suicide attack of the Floating Chrysanthemum was about to hit U.S. naval forces off Okinawa. Ninety-six minutes later, *Howorth*'s last battle would be over and Orvill Raines would be adrift in the sea, mortally wounded.

---

27 March 1945

Hello, Baby Darling:

We got another surprise this morning. We never get much notice when we pullout. We are leaving here today and it will be quite some days before you hear from me again. Just hang on Baby Girl, and pray for Poppie. This is going to be another good one. (They all seem so, but each step takes us closer to our goal and this time we can practically spit on it.) The Japs are threatening us with Kamikaze Corps suicide divers in large numbers when we get close to the Imperial Empire. Well, we can't do anything about it but go on in anyway. We can't win a war by talking them out of it. Some really beautiful ships have been hit pretty hard lately with them and they look a mess. One of them lost 1500 men. That's a lot of guys. (But we are just a LEETLE BITTY ship.) Maybe they won't pick on us if we are in big company.

Darling, you know I hate to sign off this way. I like to have more time. Like at home when I go to work; not hurry and kiss you good bye, but take my time and kiss you a dozen times. Until my legs get like water and my head starts swimming in it. That's a fact Darling.

You know how I feel. Even now I get weak in the knees when I think about holding you and kissing you.

Bye for now Darling. I'll write you as soon as I possibly can. And always remember that I love you more than the world and life itself. I worship you. God bless you and keep you safe for me.

> Your devoted husband,
> Orvill

P.S. I LOVE AND ADORE YOU!!!

---

27 March 1945

Hello, Baby Darling:

Heigh ho (that's supposed to be a sigh), we're at sea again. The jumping, rolling, tossing sea again. With such a short time of 5 days in port gets my stomach settled and when we get underway again, I always suffer a little "land legs" and belly jitters.

My belly isn't the only thing with the jitters this time. They effect my whole body. Okinawa. Just looking at it on the map breaks us out in a cold sweat. By the time you get this it will be old news. (Even to knowing how to pronounce it.) You know? Jap names aren't hard to pronounce. For instance Iwo Jima ..... Jima means Island ..... Yama means mountain or overgrown hill (Remember Suki Yama where all the little lovers go to pitch woo and themselves at some screwy god?). Old Suki Yama will be struggling with a capacity crowd before long. Oh, yes, the pronunciation. You just divide up the words into syllables like English and pronounce the syllables like Spanish and you got Japanese. Follow me? Okinawa is pronounced O ... key ... naw ... waw (leave off the last "w"). Now for the spelling ..... Okinawa spells Kamikaze Corps to us. Hope I don't burden you with all this worry of mine. Of course we worry a little. Somebody's gotta get it and we may be lucky or unlucky. You see the Navy loses a lot of men but you don't particularly hear about it. A few days ago while a task force was working over Okinawa, suicides came down from Honshu (the island of Japan) and seven of them hit one of our big carriers. Fifteen hundred men were killed as a result of the crashes and the subsequent fires.[2]

---

2. This was the aircraft carrier *Franklin*; see ibid., 536.

When those three cans were sunk in the storm a few weeks ago, a few other thousands were killed and more than a hundred million dollars of equipment was lost.[3] (Including damage to other ships.) That will add up to about five thousand including those boys off Iwo Jima and so ..... compare that with the like number of Marines killed on Iwo Jima and what have you got? Iwo Jima was terrible and I'll still take the Navy but the Marines holler pretty loud don't they? You didn't realize the Navy took it so hard did you? Well, we don't get it any harder than anybody else but to always hear the other branches yelling about how tough it is for them, I just like to think that we are ALL fighting this thing. I don't expect any repetition of our disasters in the near future and I grant that it was unusual for the storm to take the boys.

I certainly pray that we won't have as much trouble as we expect up here. If you look on the map you will see that Okinawa is about 310 miles north of Formosa; 360 miles south of Kyushu (the southernmost Japan proper island), and about 400 miles from the China coast (or closer I believe). That takes us right in the middle of their nest and quite susceptible (however you spell it) to air attack by fighters, bombers, etc. I wouldn't tell you all this little baby except that when you get this you will know that the danger is mostly over. Yes, by the time we get mail off again, the job will be practically finished and you can feel comparatively at ease. Everything they can muster and plan to throw at us will already have been thrown. It is amusing to watch all the boys get their knives ready in case they are needed. (I looked up from sharpening my knife long enough to observe this.) And life jackets. Rubber patching for the inflatable kind and testing of all parts of the other kind. I wear the "Kapok" which is the large vest-like thing like the one the sailor wore in the little clipping you sent me a while back ..... the "battle-talker" guy. I have a newer one. A gunnery officer left the ship a little while ago and left his which (naturally) is a perfect job. I stenciled my name on it today and will keep it close to me. My helmet has a new paint job and I'm ready for bear! This is especially significant (I say that every time don't I?). From Okinawa we can support fighter sorties over Japan proper and our cans, pt boats, etc., can give the Japs a lot of hell. A few weeks after we take the place the

---

3. The destroyers sunk in the December 18, 1944, typhoon were *Hull*, with sixty-two survivors; *Spence*, twenty-three survivors; and *Monaghan*, six survivors. For an account of their loss, see Roscoe, *Destroyer Operations*, 448–452.

Japs will find it very difficult to shuttle their supplies over to the Chinese mainland for their troops there. It will aid quite materially to the Chinese cause. Their air activity will be neutralized considerably. Shipping will be as hazardous as smoking on a powder keg. (At the moment there's no room for them on the keg. WE'RE on it!) Well Baby Girl, you precious little doll, Poppie's going to close for now. My right shoulder hurts some. Working on my knife all day did it I guess! Be a sweet girl like you always are and remember that I just worship the hell out of you. Bye for now. I'll add some more tomorrow night if we aren't spending too much time at G.Q. God bless you.

28 March 1945

Hello, Baby Darling:

Well, the sea is so rough this morning we finally had to knock off work altogether. (I welcomed the excuse anyway.) But we did get out some reports. I hate to think how far behind we will be when we finally do get to work on them. I'm having a terrible time. My chair won't stay up to the desk. When I feel a roll coming I grab for the desk or typewriter. I'm afraid I'll bust them up so I have to turn loose and slide. Half the time I'm arm's length from this thing. So you know I'm really interested in writing you don't you.

Baby sweet I hope you don't mind. I just disobeyed an order of yours. I opened the April 20th card you sent me and even read the letter part of it. You understand why I opened it early don't you? There's just a possibility that it might get wet on April 1st when we hit and the ink would run and I couldn't read it. Yes, Baby Girl, you can have a date for 20 April 1946. If the Sylvan Club hasn't burned down, it will be there too. I'll take you out in the car and sit one out too and we can neck a little. You should see me drool over your lipstick "400." I smell it and then kiss it. I smoke so damn many cigarettes that I can hardly smell it but it tastes just swell.

The reason for the heavy sea (our after half of the ship is almost continuously under water) is that there is a storm south of us somewhere and we don't know exactly in which direction it is traveling. It feels like it's already here though. Just to add a little more worry, we are now in the approximate spot where that task force had such a rough time a few weeks back. It's a thrill to stand on deck and watch the huge swells rise on each side of the ship. They rise so high honey that they are above our stacks. Always one coming in and one going out. We rise way up to the crest of one and then way down between it and the next one. I'm going to "secure" now baby girl. Dinner is on but I am not very enthusiastic about it. I was in my rack about 9 hours last night and slept about four I think. But I'm doing fine. I just spent forty-five minutes trying to take a bath; finally succeeded and feel swell. So long for right now sweet darling, I'll try to write more to-night. Did you ever expect to get a letter mailed in the East China Sea? I sure as hell never expected to mail one from there either. Bye little Mommie.

Poppie

29 March 1945

Hello, Baby Girl:

I didn't get to write you last night but will attempt to do so now. It is still rough and that is the reason I didn't write last night. The heavy seas abated somewhat today but this afternoon while I had sneaked down to see the movie "Mrs. Miniver," they passed the word over the speaker that our task force commander had instructed all ships to be making preparations for [an] unusually heavy storm ahead. Of course we can't turn around, we have to continue in order to strike at the right time. Already some of our dare-devil amphibious forces have struck at two small islands near Okinawa. They probably will occupy the flanking islands the night before we strike the large one. (The same way they did at Lëyte.) By the way, did I tell you that I had picked the island of Okinawa as our next strike before we knew where we were going? Well, I did. We were "shopping" around in the office one night just speculating and I advanced the opinion that our next strike would be on Okinawa. Pretty smart, ain't ah? Now for some up-to-the-minute stuff. Last night four cans got it. One sunk with 75 survivors. The scuttlebutt says it was the *O'Bannon* but I believe they confused the name *O'Brien*. The *O'Bannon* and almost all of our old 21st [Destroyer] squadron is supposed to be back in the States by now. (Incidentally, that may be why Glenn hasn't written. He likes his surprises so well he might pull it again. I do know that the *O'Bannon* was SUPPOSED to be back in the States this month.) Don't mention this to LaVerne or anyone. I don't like to put my nose in other people's business even if I don't approve. The other three cans were damaged I believe and not sunk altogether. The Jap fleet has shoved off from Nagasaki (the largest Japanese naval base) and is heading south through the Japan Sea and the East China Sea and is attempting to intercept our forces.[4] I hope they do because that is what Bull Halsey and Nimitz have been crying for for quite a while. And I hope they lick the hell out of them before we get there. There are two reasons why I say that. One: I'm not exactly anxious to tangle with those Kamikaze Corps boys, and second: If we get caught with this slow-moving transport convoy, hell will be to pay. We can't run and we can't fight battleships. Just one torpedo run before we scrape gravel on the bottom. (It would be exciting as hell though and I really would like to get in one of those fights. Probably want out a lot sooner than I got in too.) Anyway, old dried up Admiral [Marc A.] Mitscher was calling all his boys together last night (fast carrier and fast escort vessels) for a look-see today at what the Japs have.[5] If they found them today, the battle probably is about over. If not it will be tomorrow. We arrive the morning of the third day from now. (Forty-eight hours from sunup tomorrow.) I'd hate to see a bunch of Kamikaze boys hit these transports. They are alive with army and marines. ...

I was just out on deck a few moments ago, and if my training under Foree was any good, I see our high pressure front moving toward us from dead ahead. (Barometric pressure.) It has been unusually (never could spell that damn word. Too many "u"s) warm the last two days in spite of the heavy seas. That indicates a low pressure area and when a high moves in on a low, only Foree could aptly describe the results. By the way, did you know Foree had moved down on the second floor and is writing local features for the editorial page? Elmo Luter is taking over the night side of the desk. I'll sure miss Foree but Elmo isn't a bad guy at all. (He's the short fat guy that's always complimenting you.) (When Patton isn't trying to take you away from me.)

Well, Honey, Baby, that's all for tonight. I'll write more in the morning or tomorrow evening. (All depending on the weather.) A

---

4. Elements of the Japanese fleet did not depart Japan until April 6, 1945, when the super-battleship *Yamato*, cruiser *Yuhagi*, and eight destroyers embarked on a one-way mission to attack the U.S. invasion fleet off Okinawa; see ibid., 538.

5. Mitscher commanded Task Force 58, the fast aircraft carrier striking force of the 5th Fleet.

bunch of guys have come in the office and damn, they won't leave me alone. (I'm so popular!) Bye for now sweet heart, I love you to beat all hell.

Poppie

30 March 1945

Hello, Darling Sweetheart:

A year ago today I kissed the most beautiful, sweetest, luscious creature in the world good bye in San Francisco. I've thought about you a lot today Darling Baby. Nice thoughts too. Your soft sweet body and the way you press against me in a good old willing hug. Your lips in a divine 400 kiss. Even the thought almost overcomes me. I sure hope you get the orchid. I ordered it from Mrs. King down on tenth street while still up at Iwo Jima. Surely she has the letter by now. I'm sorry it's Friday night too but maybe you can save it until Saturday night. When you wear it, remember that about 4 P.M. that Saturday afternoon is when we are going in on Okinawa. Can you remember back? If you can, you will know just about where you were when we went in. It will be early Sunday morning about dawn out here. And I'll certainly be thinking about you. Do you know that everytime I learn about another operation the first thing I think of is "Boy, that's dangerous as hell." The second thing is you. Darling, I'm sure I'm not a coward. I realize that I get scared. It's my opinion that it does a little good to be afraid sometimes. (And honest, Baby, I'm not boasting.) But I sincerely believe I'm not afraid of dying. Naturally, I don't want to and it troubles me somewhat at times but really, deep down, my fear is not getting back to you. Perhaps you can't comprehend exactly how I feel. But Darling I worship you so much that the thought of not ever having you in my arms again is more than I can bear. I have searched myself time and again trying to phantom my feelings without prejudice and I honestly know that my real fear is leaving you. I know darling this is a terrible subject, but it is on my mind as a necessity and I will be truthful with you and tell you everything or be damned. Sometimes it's pretty hard to stick by such policies; especially in this case because it makes you uncomfortable and that is the worst pain I can suffer. However, in the long run I believe it is best. I take pride in the strength of our secret obligations to each other. And the strength of our love. I think about not seeing you again and I break out in nervous perspiration. (Baby Darling, I guess you hadn't better let anyone read this one. I wouldn't want people to know you married such a silly husband.) You know what I mean. Not about loving you the way I do but the way I look at certain things. You know me so well that what I say just makes you smile a little and chide me about being a "sweet" little dope. Damn it, what I'm trying to say is that other people couldn't believe that I would worry more about not getting back to you than actually dying. And I know damn well you DO believe it! Simply because I said so. I could have said something else if I hadn't meant it.

Well, to change the subject: my weather training didn't do so much good. The storm apparently went around us. It was calmer today than any other day since leaving port. Tonight however, it is getting bad again. This has been ideal weather for this operation. The ceiling has been not more than four thousand feet, visibility about 4 miles and rain and nasty weather all the way. You see why? Planes can't attack us very efficiently. With low ceiling and limited visibility they can't find us very well. On the other hand, they could knock hell out of us before we could "get on" them. By the way, the ship I was telling about last night was neither one. We got the dope today. It isn't necessary to give the ship's name but it was a can and is now even more so. It struck a mine; exploded its forward magazine. Everything forward of the bridge is gone. The bridge and superstructure practically destroyed. Its stern was backed up on the beach and enemy bombs played hell with the rest of it. Two officers and 126 men survived.[6] I can't tell you how many are aboard these things. Also ten of those suicide boats, I was telling you about up in Lingayen, took out after a DE this afternoon. The DE blew up two of them and turned tail and outran the other eight. That was ironically comical but good headwork. Those devils really tear you up. (This is all happening ahead of us. The destroyer is beached on one of those tiny islands just south of Okinawa.) Well, Baby Girl, this is all for tonight I reckon. More tomorrow. I've run out of news for this time. I'm going to sleep in the office tonight just in case those mines break loose and tag us. (I had to thrash the two kids to win the argument of who is sleeping in here.) I don't

6. This destroyer was *Halligan*, which hit a mine in an unswept area west of Okinawa while steaming to a patrol station. Only two ensigns and 166 enlisted men survived as the ship sank quickly. No survivor could explain why *Halligan* strayed out of minecleared areas. See Roscoe, *Destroyer Operations*, 469.

think anyone else is going to sleep. I've never seen so many life-jackets in the guys arms. Good night baby. I'll already be there. Bye now, God bless you Darling. I adore you.

Poppie

31 March 1945

Hello, Little Sweetheart:

How's my baby this evening? Poppie is fine. I had a very hard night last night. Could hardly sleep. We caught the edge of that storm and boy this damn "ping-pong ball" really hit the high spots. I slept in the office on the deck and rolled all over the place. Finally at midnight I fell asleep and didn't even wake up for general quarters this morning. I told a shipfitter to wake me up and he forgot. I woke up just about thirty seconds before they secured. I could just hear the Captain raving. My station is right under his nose. In fact, I am one of the three people that keep him in touch with the whole ship and I have a majority of stations on my circuit. Mac and Sleeter have the other two circuits. Well, happy day, they're late sounding G.Q. and had it on such a short time that they secured before everybody manned their stations. Of all times to sleep in that was the time. Blind luck. I was really worried. Well, right now Okinawa is about 40 miles ahead. We are steaming right at it and will circle it during the night and then in the morning hit the beach on the west side. (Between the island and China.) We will be the destroyer (one of a few) that goes in close to the beach and sweeps the area for submarines, raise a little hell with the beach with big guns and machine guns and draw any large caliber fire they might have. They would pick us. We ought to get one of our stacks knocked off at least. And tomorrow is Easter. AND APRIL'S FOOL! We are just so uncertain as to who is "it." That's what troubles us. Late plans may not call for us to go in at the last minute, but if we don't go in, somebody will and it may as well be the mighty *Howorth* as anyone else. Besides we haven't had the living stuffin' scared out of us in about six weeks now. Just kiddin' honey. May as well.

Speaking of weeks and time, etc. Have you noticed the steady advances we have been making lately? Ever since I got out here, giant steps have been taken and the Jap is getting his just dues. Our first was Morotai and then we took the very last bunch of Army down to Biak,

New Guinea. Then straight for the Philippines. Then Iwo Jima and now Okinawa. I believe that JAPAN will be next. There is nothing (much) to stop us. We have worlds of Army and Marines and Navy out here. The Limey fleet is out here and pitching in their reserved manner. If we take Okinawa on schedule, two months won't pass before we hit the filthy rat hole itself. And personally, I'm just like everybody else ..... I'd like to see the kill and watch the boys storm ashore on Japan. And then I'd kinda like to be somewhere else too. Honey, our air force is remarkable. It isn't fiction that they are knocking down the Jap pilots as fast as they come up. You should have seen them work on the devils in the Sulu Sea. I saw an article (I can't remember whether Reader's Digest or what) about some correspondent who wrote that the most exciting dog-fight he ever saw was on our run to Mindoro when a Nip came over us and one of our boys got on him. Two P-38s I believe. They were about four miles ahead of us and a little on our port bow. I think I told you about it but if I didn't here 'tis again. They came in on him and the devil was hit badly. He went down in a slow glide and hit the water with a big splash. To our surprise, he bounced up again and sailed away; the P-38s hit again. The guy hit the water a second time and we couldn't believe it when he took the air again. The third time finished him however and he was airborne no more. I hope you see the article, it was so interesting. (Almost as good as I could have done.) I think I told you about it but there were so many at that time, I may have neglected it. At any rate, the flyers are doing a superb job. We just feel like standing up and cheering when they get after one. We lose some, yes, but almost always they tag the Nip just right and literally give him hell. One night our convoy of LSTs shot down a P-38. That is the nearest I've come to running amuck. It was late evening and that's when the Nips like to come in. But even I could tell it was a friendly air cover plane. When the stupid cows opened up on him I almost tore my hair out. It was a beautiful plane and just sailing over to see that everything was o.k. They really let him have it until the boss got them to stop firing. He had to shout in the radio several times before they could quit. And a P-38 mind you! I was almost in a crying rage. But by a miracle the pilot bailed out. He has no one but God to thank. (I'll tell you lots of these stories when I'm lulling you to sleep in the many many years ahead Baby.) (Think you can sleep on those kind?) I bet I bore you with all those tales. But Mommie Darling, that's all Poppie sees. And I love you so much I just gotta write sumpin'.

Well, sweet little baby girl, I'm going to try and sleep now. I go on watch tomorrow and with the operation just getting underway I don't expect much in the coming week. We are in the mine area now and my blanket will be full of needles again. Also "Bogey" reports are coming in regularly tonight. I may not get to sleep tonight. But this letter will get off at the first opportunity Darling. Good night now my sweet child. I worship you very deeply and think of you constantly. I'm gonna work awful hard for you when I get back. And I just think now of every turn of the screws taking us closer to Tokyo. You know? Every time we get farther from home, the nearer home gets. Understand? Yep, I knew you would. Night baby darling, I adore you. God bless you.

Easter Sunday, April's Fool, D-Day.

Hi, Little Baby. How goes it? Poppie's fine. Just lost ten pounds in one of the most magnificent air attack displays I've ever seen. Just at dark, the planes came over and started their eternal diving. Three more ships were hit. Four were hit this morning when we came in. None sunk though. The anti-aircraft fire was simply beautiful. Only one plane came close to us and he was out of range and dived into another ship. So far we haven't fired a shot. Tonight we are "retiring" again. We are heading westward into the East China Sea toward China. At daybreak we will be back for more. Our troops made a very successful landing today. At nightfall they were going ahead on a ten-mile front and had penetrated two and three miles in places.[7] They took an airfield this morning and the only opposition was "one old horse" according to the radio. Apparently the Nip has withdrawn to form a formidable line elsewhere. There are 55,000 Nip soldiers on this island and half a million civilians. The soldiers mostly will be killed by our troops and I hope the civilians commit hari-kari like on Saipan. The sea is calm in here due to it being surrounded by large bodies of land. The island of Okinawa as much as I could see, is the most rugged terrain I've ever beheld. The silhouette (yeah, you know what I mean) is so irregular that I thought it was a cloud bank. Our forces are the strongest I've ever seen and so far we've taken the worst

---

7. For an account of the marine side of the amphibious landing, as well as the subsequent marine campaign, see Sledge, *With the Old Breed*, chapters 7–15.

punishment. However, we (the Navy I'm talking about) can't all be sunk and the boys are on the beach. Honey, I hope your orchid is keeping enough so you can wear it to church today. Won't the gals envy my Baby? They do anyway because of the wonderful husband you have. (Well, I gotta say something nice about me.) Night darling baby girl. I'll write more tomorrow. God bless you and keep you. I worship you more than you'll ever know. Night.

Poppie

P.S. I LOVE YOU!!!

2 April 1945

Hello, Little Baby:

Wow! What a night! It was a nightmare but something I'll never forget. After getting off watch at 8 P.M. I came down and wrote you a little on the preceding page then went to bed. I slept until the moon came up shortly before midnight and then we went to G.Q. We had fourteen raids before daylight. Twice we secured from general quarters but before we had finished smoking a hurried cigarette, we were called back again. It was nip and tuck. As the newspapers have already revealed we have 1600 ships in this operation and it covers a wide area naturally. Only fired at one plane last night and another this morning. But for four hours during the wee hours there was no interval of time longer than five minutes that we couldn't see anti-aircraft fire somewhere within eight to ten miles. It was very interesting to watch as that stuff fascinates me. They had three raids at daylight and then we had cause to worry. I had slept twenty-five minutes from the time we secured from general quarters until I went on watch at 3:30 A.M. I slept on the deck on the bridge with my helmet for a pillow. It was quite comfortable though.

This morning at daybreak the Nip could see what we were escorting around and really opened up on us. It was a large group and most of them attacked on the other side. One guy came over however and got quite close. We opened up with everything, including 20s and when they come close enough for those small guns, he is less than 25 seconds from us if he decides to dive. The firing was heavy and several planes were shot down but no ships were hit. Very fortunate. But the AA barrage was like a solid blanket. I have never seen it so thick. In fact, our second bad scare came when some can was firing large caliber shells at the planes and his fuse settings were off. They first hit close off our port bow and then quite a ways off our starboard bow. Each one got about two hundred feet closer and after six rounds we were really worried. It got to the point that the very next shell (we felt certain) would hit the ship. And miracle of miracles, the guy chose that time to cease firing. The next one did not come. I think the *Howorth* bears a charmed life. I could just feel that shell ripping into our superstructure. It will be interesting to note that only one ship got hit throughout the night and none this morning. I think the Nip must be nervous. Also a contributing factor is that our gunners (on ships) really poke them out. We all know that the only way to stop them is hit with everything, including the galley sink. (We gotta save the stove however, as we are hungry after a good "God-damn" fight.)

I'm really proud of the American sailor. I can't judge the soldier or marine because I don't know him very well. But the sailor is really a fighter. Regardless of what comes, he never leaves his station. Always right in there pitching. It comforts me to know the boys are really shooting it out when I'm confined to the limits of my telephone line. And according to our dope, the army and marines are taking over very nicely on the beach. They have a big job over there and I hope they do it without too much trouble. It's not like anywhere else they've taken over. We have an enemy over here that really hates us and will fight till he dies. I hope they all do too. But I agree with the Jap on one thing. The calling of this land "The Land of the Rising Sun." This morning, in spite of all the firing and conflict and hate, the gorgeous sun came over Okinawa and really splattered the sea and islands with a flood of red glory. It was arresting to see the red glow come up over the very rugged skyline of the beach. Fog and smoke veiled the outer reaches of our visibility but the ships were sharp in outline nearby and the cool breeze was exhilarating (spelling?). Anyway it was good and comfortable. The air is so pure and clean and refreshing. There are many small islands around here (too small to put on the map) and they are rough too. Not many have inhabitants due to the volcanic composition. I suppose I should be thinking of other things with the battle still in its infancy. However, I'm sure the outcome will be favorable and I might as well enjoy as much of it as possible. I don't know how long we will be here. Nor do I know when I can mail this. I expect it will be the same story as at Iwo Jima. We may be here a month. (Which is all right because the time passes faster this way.) If we get

our Army planes situated on the island, the air fight will be different.
We have seen all types of Nip planes here. That indicates that they are
using the dregs of their air force and means either that they are out of
air power almost, or that they are saving the cream for the defense of
the homeland proper. This is their homeland of course but not the island of Honshu which is the almighty imperial holy land. I prefer to
think the latter is true in the case of air power. But if we get our P-61
night fighters out here and the Army P-38s, etc. day fighters, there
won't be much opportunity for the Nip to worry us. They are great
strategists with air power. They come in singly and just often enough
to keep the entire task force alerted at G.Q. I'm sure the same story
will prevail tonight but I have the midnight until 4 A.M. watch anyway. The moon is very bright but the planes are hard to see even then.
One flew over very low last night and no one saw him until he was
past us. We all heard him and had a bad moment. The bad part will be
over in a week though Honey Baby, and Poppie is getting along fine in
the meantime. For instance, this morning after breakfast, I came down
and went to sleep. I slept without interruption, even for dinner, until
3:30 this afternoon. I must have been very tired to sleep through a
meal. But don't worry about me Baby Doll. There are many many
thousands of others just like me out here and we are all getting the
same treatment. So Poppie isn't any worse off than anyone else.
(Maybe a lot better.) I don't let things worry me much and worry
seems to be the principal ailment. Well, so long for now, sweet Baby.
Remember that I love you more than anything in the world and will
forever. God bless you sweetheart. I worship you.

More tomorrow.
"Handsome"

3 April 1945

Hello, Darling Baby Girl:
    Here's Poppie again. We didn't have such a bad time last night. Just
as I put the last word on the above letter last night we went to g.q. due
to air attack. It didn't come near us however and our planes took most
of the sting out of them. I got in a couple hours' sleep and then went
on watch at midnight. An attack started developing at 1:30 A.M. a couple hundred miles out but was still disorganized due to our night air
cover when I got off watch at 4. We went to g.q. again at 5:30 A.M. and
fought off sixteen raids between that time and half an hour after day-

light. We fired at only one plane. The old *Howorth* is really lucky. I hate to think of her luck running out. And speaking of the mighty *Howorth*, today was her first birthday. We had turkey. I swiped a slab of white meat and two pieces of bread and have a sandwich for the 8 P.M. until midnight watch tonight. We came in to refuel this afternoon and I got my first glimpse of the beach close up. I saw dwellings, piers, roads and small communities through the long glass but couldn't make out much else. It will be several days before we are sent in close apparently. We haven't bombarded because the ground forces are doing so well without us. They have cut the island in two now and are fighting northward and southward. We have three airfields set up and the scuttlebutt says that P-61s are here already. I certainly hope so. If they are, the Nips' situation is pretty hopeless. His night attacks will result in disaster. Our Navy fighters can shoot down some of them and chase the rest away, but the P-61 shoots almost all of them down. (Due to 3-man crews and speed and firepower.) It will be interesting when you learn how night fighters operate. I can't tell you now of course. Incidentally, one ship got hit this morning. It suffered some casualties but the only material damage apparently was four of its boats reduced to kindling wood. Darling, Poppie is going to sign off now. I think we might be going to get mail off this evening and I want this to be ready. If so, don't worry about me. Things have been going our way ever since we got here and I don't anticipate any trouble. I will continue to write as much as possible (often) and get it off whenever the opportunity presents itself. Bye for now, precious baby. God bless you. I love you very dearly. With my whole life.

Your devoted husband.

P.S. I LOVE YOU!!!

5 April 1945

Good morning, Little Baby Doll:

It's pretty early, I haven't eaten breakfast yet. We didn't get mail off yesterday (or the day before rather) as I half-expected, so this will be added to the rest. We went down to a patrol station night before last just south of Okinawa and in between all those other little islands you see on the map. There are many other small ones that aren't on the map but they only serve as cover for suicide boats, small subs and PT boats. Our job was four-fold: Subs, suicide boats, PTs and anti-aircraft. We have thrown a screen around Okinawa just like at Iwo. (You can see the weather is rough from the typing.) Well, as a matter of fact, there are THREE screens around this one and we have been in the outer one all the time. This morning at 2 A.M. we were dispatched southeastward and are travelling at high speed to rendezvous with a convoy somewhere east of Formosa. Apparently from out of the Philippines. As we progress southward, I can see evidence of POWER being brought in here and I am enthusiastic about the outcome even more. I learned last night that we took on rations for fifty-three days before leaving Ulithi. That indicates a long siege here. Also indicates that we may go on from here to the next major operation, rather than go back to the semi-safe locales before departing. I am slightly in favor of keeping the bulk of power here and operate out of this neck of the woods. (I'm sure that will be the case because a withdrawal of major units of the fleet would endanger the hold we now have.) We don't contact this convoy until late this evening so it may be a couple more days before we get back to Okinawa. Then, I expect, mail will get off the ship. Also, we may have some for us up there. I'd sure like to hear from you. And I expect if we do, it will be all new stuff too, because it looked as if we'd caught up with the back mail while at Ulithi this time. Well, baby girl, I'm going to close now and run and eat my ration of two eggs. They are sunnyside up and rather tasty. So long for now sweet Darling. Poppie will write again as soon as time permits. God bless you. I love, adore and worship you literally.

Poppie

6 April 1945

Good morning, Mommie:

Just a line. I have to hurry and eat and then go on watch. And this afternoon ..... (had to stop then and eat dinner). This afternoon I hope we get mail off so I'm getting this ready. Be sweet Mommie and remember that I love you with everything I've got. (It isn't much but it's all yours.) We are back up at Okinawa now, we came back very fast. (Can't tell why yet.) Anyway, it's colder than a well digger's seat in Montana but everything is o.k. No sleep last night due to Bogies but things are squared away now. Bye darling. More later.

Poppie

Approximately five hours later, the Floating Chrysanthemum reached *Howorth*. At 4:25 P.M. a Japanese "Val" dive bomber dove at the ship, was hit, and passed between the stacks, severing the radio antennas and one of the guy wires supporting the mast before crashing into the sea close aboard. At 5 P.M. four Zekes were observed flying in and out of the cloud cover on the starboard bow. When the pilots saw *Howorth*, they split into two-plane groups and began a coordinated attack. The first kamikaze was shot down 200 yards shy of the stern. The gunnery team shifted their fire to the next Zeke, which was approaching in a dive. Although hit and smoking, it flew on, scraping its wing across the fantail, ripping lifelines away before hitting the sea. Another group of four Zekes had arrived off the bow and one pilot began a suicide run, apparently hoping to take advantage of the attack under way off *Howorth*'s stern. The 40mm and 20mm guns shot this plane down 250 yards off the starboard side. *Howorth* was boxed in by minesweepers and could not turn to unmask the after 5-inch or 40mm guns to deal with yet another Zeke coming in from the bow. The forward 40mm guns fired only five or six rounds since one gun suffered a jammed firing mechanism and the other had run out of ammunition. At 5:08 P.M. the Zeke flew into the face plate of *Howorth*'s Mark 37 gun director at 200 knots.[8] The airplane's engine traveled through the director, blasting the rear wall loose. In the director, Lieutenant Henry R. Hamner, age twenty-three, and petty officers George F. Nolan, age twenty-three, and Morris E. LeCren, age twenty, were killed instantly. The director radar operator, Fire Controlman 3/c J. W. Stribling, age nineteen, soon died from his wounds. The director trainer, Petty Officer Bernard Murphy, was found lying atop one of the flag bags, horribly burned. Thanks to the initial care provided by *Howorth*'s medical officer, Dr. Ivan Bruce, Murphy survived but faced years of painful burn treatments and skin grafts. A total of sixteen *Howorth* crewmen were burned and survived.

Two members of the crew were never seen after the plane hit. One of the assistant gunnery officers, Ensign Horace L. Bayless, age twenty-three, who served as an air defense officer directing the fire of the 40mm and 20mm guns from the flying bridge, was never found. The remains of Fire Controlman 1/c Julius Cesar Sanchez, age twenty, were never identified in the twisted wreckage of the gun director. Sanchez

---

8. The details of the attack are in "DD592/A16-3 Serial 050 dated 10 April 1945, Special Action Report (Anti-Aircraft Action by Surface Ship), on 6 April 1945," microfilm Reel E-108, NPPSO–Naval District Washington Job No. AR-65-78, "*Howorth* (DD-592), Report File, War Diary"; note 25, Introduction above.

had survived the sinking of his first destroyer, USS *Beatty,* by a German torpedo plane in the Mediterranean in November 1943.

Three men were forced overboard by the explosion and intense gasoline fire. Telephone talkers Orvill Raines and Seaman 1/c Jay V. Grimm, along with lookout Seaman 1/c Russell A. Bramble, ended up in the cold ocean. Grimm was alone, burned, and in shock but was able to blow up his inflatable life vest. Raines saw Bramble enter the water ahead of him and called to Bramble for help. Bramble swam to Raines and found him badly burned and struggling to say afloat without a lifejacket. Bramble put his arms around Raines's waist and held him up as the heavy swells tossed them about and waves broke over them. After an indeterminate time, Orvill Raines died.

As darkness set in two hours after *Howorth* was hit, Bramble and Grimm were rescued by a minesweeping gunboat, *PGM 17.* Grimm was too weak to hold onto the line thrown to him; Boatswain's Mate 1/c Mike La Mar selflessly jumped into the sea to assist him aboard.

The large number of casualties at Okinawa strained the Navy Department's casualty notification process. Ray Ellen Raines did not receive a telegram that Orvill was missing. Her first notice arrived almost two weeks after the attack, when she received a shocking letter from *Howorth*'s captain:

---

7 April 1945

Dear Mrs. Raines:

It is with deep regret that I inform you of the details regarding your husband Orvill who is missing in action following an enemy air attack upon this ship during the afternoon of April sixth. I presume the Secretary of the Navy has informed you so I will try to clarify the picture for you insofar as security allows me.

The ship was at Battle Stations most of the afternoon. Friendly fighter planes were engaged in dog fights with Japanese planes, and were more than keeping the situation under control until the enemy's excess in numbers allowed some to get through. After the ship shot down five dive bombers which fell flaming into the sea nearby, the sixth crashed out of control onto the ship in the vicinity of Orvill's battle station. Several men, including Orvill, were observed to jump or were blown overboard and were seen in the water. It is possible that one of the several ships close by picked him up. We have no information as to whether he was injured or has been recovered as yet.

All of his personal effects are being shipped to you. Please do not expect them too soon as they have a long way to travel. They are being shipped in two packages—one with papers and valuables, the other with clothes. …

Your husband was very popular among the officers and men on board this ship. There certainly was no finer bluejacket to be found anywhere.[9] I only wish I could give you more information but you will receive it as fast as humanly possible from the Navy Department if he is recovered.

If I can be of any further assistance or clarify anything for you, please do not hesitate to write me. …

On June 1, 1945, her fifth wedding anniversary, Ray Ellen came home from work to find confirmation of Orvill's death:

May 27, 1945

Dear Mrs. Raines,

I was a shipmate and friend of your husband James. I feel as if it is my duty to let you know I was one of the men that was in the water with James. I'm sorry to say that James passed away in my arms. That I stayed with him until the very last. I observed that he was badly burned. I was in the water 2 hours before I was picked up. I was one of the men that was listed as missing and was more fortunate to have been wounded. I find it very hard to write this letter to you. I feel that you would rather know one way indifferent. If you want any information you may write to me at my home address. I am going home on leave for a period of twenty-five days. You may get in touch with me at 720 E. 2nd St. Hastings, Nebraska.

Respectively yours,
Russell A. Bramble

9. This same phrasing was used in the letters sent to the families of the other men listed as missing from the attack of April 6.

Ray Ellen Raines received a three-by-six-inch black box containing a Purple Heart Medal. Suspended from a purple and white ribbon was a gold-covered heart with purple inlay under a gold profile of George Washington. On the reverse, in raised letters, was the phrase "For Military Merit."

*   *   *

In July 1946 Commander Edward S. Burns received the Navy Cross, the navy's highest decoration save for the Medal of Honor, for *Howorth's* performance at Okinawa. He was cited "for extraordinary heroism as Commanding Officer of the U.S.S. *Howorth*, in action against enemy Japanese forces while engaged in Transport Screening Operations off Okinawa Shima in the Ryukyu Chain, from April 1 to 6, 1945."

Official appreciation of *Howorth's* war cruise was limited to her captain and to her dead. The gunnery officer, Lieutenant Henry R. Hamner, was awarded a posthumous Silver Star Medal for "gallantry in action." Because Hamner was a scion of an Annapolis family (his uncle, Admiral Alan G. Kirk, commanded U.S. naval forces during the Normandy invasion, and Hamner's father had served with Fleet Admiral Ernest J. King), a destroyer under construction (DD 718) was named in his honor. The five members of the gunnery crew (which did not include Orvill Raines) who were killed on April 6 received posthumous Bronze Star Medals for "heroic and meritorious achievement."[10]

Sailors were the necessary but anonymous proletariat, and the class distinction between World War II white hat and officer precluded widespread acknowledgment.[11] The pistols officers wore during general quarters, to ensure obedience and order, underscored the class difference. Although their accomplishments and suffering under difficult conditions surpassed that of many other destroyer crews awarded the Navy Unit Commendation for service at Okinawa, the men of *Howorth* were never honored.[12] For those who have been in the naval

---

10. Hamner and his director crew manually tracked the aircraft that killed them for almost two minutes, from a range of 8,000 yards to impact. Hamner's last words, spoken over the fire control telephone circuit seconds before he was killed, were "target angle zero," indicating that the kamikaze's line of flight was directly into his fire control sight.

11. For some British opinion on decorations, see Fussell, *Wartime*, 258; for example, "wags ... imputed the award of the OBE [Order of the British Empire] to Other Bastards' Efforts."

12. Scrutiny of Roscoe's encyclopedic *Destroyer Operations* reveals a seemingly sporadic award of unit commendations at Okinawa. Many destroyer crews were cited for saving their damaged ships or for destroying attacking Japanese aircraft. Other ships, whose crews apparently did not destroy a single enemy aircraft or recover from crippling damage, received the Navy Unit Commendation; their only apparent distinction was that they were flagships for a destroyer squadron commodore.

service (navy and marine corps), the lack of an award for *Howorth* will not come as a surprise. The Navy Unit Commendation corresponds to a collective level of bravery equivalent to that which would earn the Silver Star Medal for heroism for an individual.[13] The initial recommendation for any award comes from a senior, and actions deemed worthy of an award by one commander are often viewed as the ordinary performance of duty by another.[14]

Unit commendations were not the only area in which variations occurred. There was considerable disparity between the number of decorations awarded to officers and enlisted men in the naval service during the Second World War. Of the Navy Crosses awarded, only 22 percent went to enlisted men whereas 55 percent of the total number of decorations (Commendation Medal, Bronze Star Medal, etc.) were awarded to officers.

In December 1945 the secretary of the navy convened a board of review under Admiral F. J. Horne to evaluate Second World War decorations. The Horne board justified the high percentage of awards to officers because enlisted men had few opportunities to stand out: "Only in serious emergencies, catastrophes, or battle action do such opportunities occur for them and it is often difficult to 'distinguish' one's self. Heroism is commonplace [!]"[15] With regard to the award of the Navy Cross to commanding officers, the Horne board asserted that "awards are properly made to senior officers in command of large units, ... not only as a reward for their personal responsibility, leadership and gallantry, but in recognition of the gallantry of all hands. Briefly, it is inferred that awards made to Commanding Officers are shared by the crew"—although they are not entitled to wear them, nor is any men-

---

13. The highest unit award, the Presidential Unit Citation, is presented for "gallantry, determination, and esprit de corps in accomplishing its mission under extremely difficult and hazardous conditions. ...The degree of heroism required is the *same as that which would be required for award of a Navy Cross to an individual* [emphasis added]." The Navy Unit Commendation is awarded to any unit of the U.S. Navy or Marine Corps that "has distinguished itself by outstanding heroism in action against the enemy, but not sufficient to justify the award of the Presidential Unit Citation"; quotations from *U.S. Navy Awards Manual (SECNAVINST 1650.1F of 8 August 1991)*, section 3, 3–7.

14. According to one study, a common complaint concerning naval decorations has been that they are awarded to the wrong people and not enough awards are made. See p. 42 of Lieutenant Commander Michael W. Shelton, CEC, USN, "Who Are the Heroes?" U.S. Naval Institute *Proceedings* 104 (August 1978): 41–49. I recall my failed efforts to obtain recognition for one of my machinist's mates who suffered burns on his legs and buttocks when he used his body to plug a leak of 180-degree lubricating oil that would have ruined our destroyer's port main engine reduction gear. Our captain thought his actions "typical" of what was expected of a *destroyer* sailor and not worthy of commendation.

15. *Report of the Board of Review for Decorations and Medals (Serial 105B of 7 April 1947)*, 4–5, quoted in Shelton, "Who Are the Heroes?" 45.

tion of them made in their service records.[16] *Howorth*'s commanding officer was detached from the ship a year before he received his Navy Cross. It is unclear how he could "share" his medal with his crew.

A recent inquiry to the secretary of the navy about an ex post facto award of a unit commendation to the crew of *Howorth*, based upon the extant official records of the ship at Okinawa, the award of the Navy Cross to her captain, and the radio commendation from the commander of Pacific destroyers for "an *unparalleled* 68 minute display of courage and skill," was received coolly.[17] The perfunctory reply from the Office of the Chief of Naval Operations cited a postwar regulation preventing the awarding of a unit commendation five years after the event in order to prevent exaggerated claims substantiated by "blurred" memories. The response from the president of the *Howorth* Veterans Association was pointed: "I refuse to mention ... [this] statement to the families of our deceased shipmates or the walking wounded who are still with us. The only blur they must endure is from the tears they still shed at our reunions."[18]

With no recognition from the navy, the surviving members of *Howorth*'s crew have only their memories, and nightmares, to recall their arduous and dangerous service in the Pacific Ocean War.

---

16. Ibid., 48.

17. William M. McBride to H. Lawrence Garrett III, Secretary of the Navy, July 9, 1991; personal file. This may be one of the last attempts to "get credit" for events in the war; see Fussell, *Wartime*, 159. The radio commendation came in COMDESPAC 252105 April 1945; of more interest to the crew than a ribbon was the message's third sentence: "Beer party for the crew 1600."

18. Rear Admiral R. M. Walsh, USN, Assistant Vice Chief of Naval Operations, to William M. McBride, letter serial 09B33/1U520861 of July 31, 1991; and Harold Middleton, president, USS *Howorth* Veterans Association, to Rear Admiral R. M. Walsh, USN, August 28, 1991.

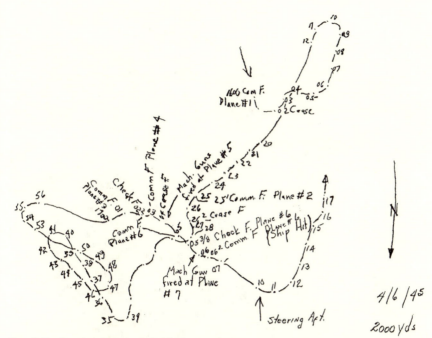

Dead-Reckoning Tracer (DRT) plot made during the fatal kamikaze attack on Howorth off Okinawa. The DRT was an analog device that generated a true representation of the ship's movement. A crewman annotated the track with the time of day and critical events.

Howorth *at Mare Island, California, in the summer of 1945 with most of her Okinawa battle damage repaired. The new Mark 37 gun director (A) is trained to roughly the same bearing as when the ship was hit. Most of the casualties were on the flying bridge (B). Orvill Raines must have been on the port bridge wing (C) when the kamikaze hit. (U.S. Navy photo)*

Howorth's war record: Eleven shore bombardment campaigns and twelve Japanese airplanes destroyed. One of the flags represents the kamikaze that struck the ship off Okinawa. (USS Howorth Veterans Association)

Blown into the sea from the flying bridge, Seaman 1/c Jay V. Grimm was burned seriously and in shock. He managed to inflate his life vest and clung to life in the cold sea.

Boatswain's Mate 1/c Mike LaMar ignored the continuing Japanese air attacks and selflessly jumped into the sea from the minesweeper PGM 17 to rescue Grimm.

Seaman 1/c Russell A. Bramble was also blown off Howorth's flying bridge into the sea near Grimm. Orvill Raines died in Bramble's arms during the two hours Bramble and Grimm were adrift.

Afterword

During the Second World War, approximately 292,000 U.S. servicemen were killed in action. This number includes 36,000 sailors and 19,000 marines. Compared to the *military* casualties suffered by the other warring powers—the Soviet Union with 7 million dead, Germany with 4 million dead, and the Japanese with 1.2 million dead in service—the United States fared considerably better, if one can categorize 292,000 dead as "better." But in a war that killed 50 million people, numbers tend to lose their meaning, and perhaps *better* is as good a word as any.[1]

In the wake of the 1991 Persian Gulf War, government officials and public commentators spoke of "light" U.S. casualties. That characterization falls into the same category of simplistic understatement as does "better" with respect to U.S. dead in the Second World War: Both are meaningless terms to the families of those killed or horribly wounded. On average, 220 U.S. service members were killed in action *every day* during the forty-four months the country was a belligerent in World War II. In terms of U.S. casualties, this translates into fighting a Persian Gulf War approximately every two days for three and a half years.

Canadian historian Tim Travers has chronicled the shift from a qualitative (manly courage, training, esprit de corps) to a quantitative (masses of men and materiel) mentality with regard to war as a result of the European experience between 1914 and 1918.[2] This quantitative mentality was reinforced on a grand scale by the incomprehensible magnitude of the 1939–1945 war. But to those raised in today's mass-media society, which packages and presents violence across its spectrum, what film footage or statistic can begin to transmit the utter waste of that, or any, war? How can one grasp the concept of 50 million dead or "just" 292,000 dead or, in the case of USS *Howorth*, 7 dead? Through his letters, Orvill Raines has provided us with a rare, enlisted man's in-

---

1. Casualty figures are from John Keegan, *The Second World War* (New York: Viking Penguin, 1990), 590–591.
2. Travers, *The Killing Ground*, 76–78.

283

sight into a small piece of a war that bludgeoned the life from 50 million people. Perhaps his letters will help us build the cognitive foundation for an attempt to understand the destructive, personal consequences of modern, impersonal war.[3]

To ascribe rationality to war is delusive, yet students of military history, strategic philosophy, economic history, sociology, and other fields have constructed reasoned analyses of the slices of war they examine. Despite the typically high-minded motives presented as justification for their commencement, wars devolve into irrationality. In *The Face of Battle* (1976), British military historian John Keegan castigated his discipline for its retroactive addition of analytic frameworks to battles.[4] As I constructed my own rational overlay to *Howorth*'s last minutes off Okinawa on April 6 (stimulated by the seductively clear chronology of the ship's records), one of the crew asked me why anyone would be interested in the history of DD 592, as she played no decisive role in the war and his memories of her were not the least bit heroic. To him, the engagement of April 6 was pure chaos. As a participant, he was aware of the narrow focus and pervasive confusion of the battlefield experience and rejected intuitively, as Keegan had intellectually, the application of an artificial, rational construct to the most turbulent of organized human endeavors. The panoramic overview of a battle, so commonly presented by historians and motion-picture makers, is not the experience of those who fight. For battles, like wars, are the accretion of discrete events (including the actions of "small" ships like *Howorth*) so important to those involved, and often (as in the experience of *Howorth*) they end so quickly that surprise and a lack of intellectual closure leads to subsequent depression in the survivors.

The effects of *Howorth*'s war on her crew extended beyond the dead and wounded. Many men were disabled by what today is categorized as post-traumatic stress disorder but in 1945 was simply termed "nervous" in the relatively few cases officially acknowledged.[5] Close to fifty

---

3. For another roster of the human wastage in the Pacific War, see Manchester, *Goodbye, Darkness*, 375–377.

4. John Keegan, *The Face of Battle* (New York: Viking, 1976).

5. See Swank and Marchand, "Combat Neuroses." The other contemporary study previously cited (Weinberg, "The Combat Neuroses") concentrated on 276 enlisted combat branch soldiers withdrawn from the European Theater from the 10 percent of total neurotic patients unable to be returned to duty after initial hospitalization. Of these soldiers, 56.5 percent presented the most common form of neurotic pattern: anxiety, also known as "nervous exhaustion" and "combat fatigue." Neuropsychiatric casualties on Okinawa numbered 26,221; Sledge, *With the Old Breed*, 312.

years after the war, the sound of a propeller-driven plane can still paralyze some former crew members, elevate their pulse, and bring on cold sweat.[6]

In 1949 the recoverable remains of *Howorth*'s dead were brought home from Okinawa.[7] Pete Hamner's were interred at Arlington National Cemetery in his native state of Virginia. George Nolan's came home to Long Island, J. W. Stribling's to Mississippi, and Buck LeCren's to Alabama.

The National Memorial Cemetery of the Pacific is located near the center of the city of Honolulu. Within the cemetery are eight "Courts of the Missing" listing the 18,094 service members missing in action in the Central and South Pacific regions from the Pacific Ocean War. Carved into those walls are the names of *Howorth*'s missing crewmen: Horace Lomax Bayless, James Orvill Raines, and Julius Cesar Sanchez. Between the walls is a broad staircase leading up to a chapel with "flanking galleries containing maps and texts, recording the achievements of the American Armed Forces in the Central and South Pacific regions"[8]—a progressive edifice to assuage the grief of the families of the missing with a logical framework to the struggle that ended the lives of their loved ones.

6. Swank and Marchand ("Combat Neuroses," 241) found that "noises which were associated with danger, i.e., airplanes and gunfire, provoked violent trembling and agitation" among patients evacuated to a rear-area general hospital. Despite receiving initial treatment, the patients suffered long-term nervous disability.

7. See Fussell, *Wartime*, 270–272 and 287–288, regarding battlefield wounds and death. I was told that one family intended an open-casket service prior to internment in 1949, innocent of Graves Registration practices and the damage a 200+-knot aircraft could inflict on the human body. For an introduction to the literature, see Holmes, *Acts of War*, chapter 5. Although he was not a participant, William Manchester's description of the carnage on Iwo Jima is representative: "Often the only way to distinguish between Japanese and Marine dead was by the legs; Marines wore canvas leggings and Nips khaki puttees. ... You tripped over strings of viscera fifteen feet long, over bodies which had been cut in half at the waist. Legs and arms, and heads bearing only necks, lay fifty feet from the nearest torsos"; *Goodbye, Darkness*, 340.

8. "Honolulu Memorial" in *American Memorials and Overseas Military Cemeteries* (Washington, D.C.: American Battlefield Monuments Commission, 1989), 20.

What would those whose names are carved in the cool stone tell us?
Perhaps Orvill Raines can speak for them in his own way, one last
time:

U.S.S. HOWORTH (592)

In care of Fleet Post Office   Pearl Harbor
San Francisco, California   30 July 1944

My Darling Baby Ray Ellen:
    I hope that you never read this letter. I have asked Pop to give it to
you only in the event of my death. If you do read it, I hope to be the
one to read it with you with my arm around your waist and looking
over your shoulder. Whether I am with you or in the sea, please realize
that my love for you has been the greatest that any man has bestowed
upon a woman. I know that my love for you has been great because I
wouldn't deprive myself of certain fundamental animalistic pleasures
that sometimes drive a man near distraction, for any woman except
you. You know my nature and know that nearly all men are on the
lookout for what they can get out of life, especially when they know
they are facing possible death.
    Before you and I married, I told Norval and Red that I would never
marry because I couldn't be true to one woman and that if I couldn't,
marriage wouldn't be what I wanted it to be. But then only a few days
before we married, did I realize just how strong my love for you really
was. It struck me like a physical blow and my chest hurt and I knew
that if I couldn't have you, there was no life for me. It has been that
way ever since. Except that as time went on and you stuck to me so
faithfully and inspired me so greatly, the significance of you being in
my life grew to monstrous proportions. I am grieving that I cannot set
down more aptly how much I love you, Darling Baby. There are so
many things to thank you for. Which is just cause for my being grateful to you as well as love you.
    I look back to my life before we met. I see nothing but ridiculous
emptiness and aimless wandering about. Not even a definite goal was
in sight. Just the desire to stay alive and do what I thought was normal
along the lines of living. I am thankful that I put in my hardest years
before we met because I might have been too withdrawing to tell you

of my love. And Darling, I did put in a hard time. I like to look back now and see what I escaped or climbed out of, which ever way you prefer to put it. (I say it that way because, as always, you will say, "Darling, you did it with your brain. I am proud of you.")

Then a foolish and insignificant thing like a blind date and a class supper came along. I stuck my head inside an automobile and saw something wonderful, fresh and beautiful that smiled. I was smitten in the solar plexus and a curious funny ache has been there ever since. I kissed her a very few minutes later and misjudged her character. A short time later I realized what a mistake I had made and immediately began to love her. She looked at me with shining eyes for many months afterward. When we were together she made me feel like I was the most important person in the world. To her, there was no one else. I FELT like the most important person in the world.

Her lips yielded to mine whenever I wanted to hold her close. Her body belonged to me and by the same token possessed mine so completely that her every desire was like a command to me. A command that I never rebelled against. They were always welcome and a great joy was derived from being permitted to obey them. We were ecstatically happy and so much in love that the only way we could stop kissing at night was to inaugurate a "Good night Officially."

As time went on, almost a year to be specific, I noticed that the person I loved was getting more beautiful. Other people noticed it too. That body that I worshiped was becoming more developed and desirable, until a time came when I couldn't bear to be away from her. I wanted to rush home to her arms and have her tell me everything would be all right. Because at that time, I was laboring very hard to make myself still more important in her mind, and basically, to provide a living for the two of us so that the lack of money would have no opportunity to incite cause for a rift between us.

More years went by, and changes occurred. I did make myself a modest name and became proud of myself and my record. But only because this girl that I loved would often say "Orvill, you are the smartest boy in the world. You are SO much above all the other men we know. You are good-looking too, and I just worship you." (Thanks for saying I am good-looking, although I know better.)

I lived in two worlds. I will try to explain them this way: One world, the one for which I lived, was in the arms of my Darling Baby. The person that God Himself made as a pattern for other women of the universe to impersonate. No wonder I worshiped her. Her beauty, kindness, generosity, and personality were above reproach from heaven itself.

The other world was the one in which I lived to work and protect this one I enjoyed so tremendously. I worked very hard and sometimes extra hours that caused dissention in this world I enjoyed so much. I was willing to risk those minor rifts to insure that all-important life with her.

Finally, my efforts were regarded; no longer was it necessary to put a strain on our love. That was about a year before this world holocaust broke into our lives and brought chaos to our career. Today I am sitting directly over the scene where this conflagration was set off. Beneath me are the decontaminated bodies of many other young men like myself that were betrayed by another group of men who sought to own the world and the country of me and my loved one.

My ship can't distill water from this harbor because of the many unrecovered bodies still lying on its muddy bottom. The many bodies when alive, those that weren't snuffed out immediately, surely cried out in anguished pain "Please, God, help me!"

Somehow our God didn't help. For some reason beyond the grasp of us mortals, He allowed murder. Murder of men and boys who held no recourse with death but sought to make life a happy one. It is pitiable that they did not realize a portion of the happiness they so zealously sought; the kind I so jealously treasured. They couldn't have known what the normal course of life meant because they were separated from their loved ones while so young. Within the space of a very few minutes, they were separated forever. Never will they realize what God intended for them to realize. Their chance is gone; it is wrong to seek revenge; revenge is the privilege of God, so stated by His book. We went into this affair with the intention of "ridding the world" of these fiendish madmen, but in our hearts we are disobeying God's rule for self-satisfaction in revenge. May He forgive us and understand the anger we realize when cowards mistreat the innocent.

Then we were separated, Darling. But just for a short time. We were reunited by a fortunate assignment of duty and for fourteen stolen months we enjoyed an ecstasy ordinarily denied men departing for war. During those months we spent ourselves to the fullest of enjoyment, knowing that sooner or later a permanent separation would come. Never will I forget the complete enjoyment we had of each other's company.

The word came, of course, but we were allowed that last Christmas together. A pitiable Christmas but we both were so deeply thankful for it. Then another brief separation. (Darling, how those separations tugged at my heart!) Reunited again. Then traveling around the country together. Seeing important and unimportant sights and exclaiming our elation over senseless things that only two people insanely in love can enjoy (like that Negro chicken vendor in Alabama; stealing an orange off a tree in Southern California and the cable trolley in San Francisco).

Then the permanent separation came and I suffered the most severe blow I have ever known. The way you clung to me in that San Francisco hotel room is the sweetest thing that ever happened to me, Darling. You wanted me to stay with you so badly. Believe me, I love so much that when we were together I just wasn't responsible for what I did or said to other people. After that wonderful good bye kiss and the extreme bliss of crushing your soft body to mine, that cruel blow struck me time and again as I walked down the hallway. That was the hardest job I ever undertook, Baby. Just walking away from you, maybe forever. Believe me, heaven or hell, God or devil, couldn't strike me one blow more severe. I hope and pray that you never have to read this alone, indicating that the blow has been struck.

That morning was the first time I ever really cried. For the first time in my adult life, tears came. They were choking tears, dry and burning, and I thought my throat was tearing itself out of me. Men and women in the lobby saw my condition, I know. I didn't care. I didn't stop crying until I was a few blocks from the train to Treasure Island. I haven't cried since but my soul has been disintegrating within me. I live only to get back to you. You will know by this letter that I'll never be back. That my life span has been completed, however brief, and our four wonderful years together will have to do us.

For the last four months we have been getting this ship and its men in condition for war and battle. We are almost ready now. We are a precision instrument of death. Going forth like in medieval times to do battle. Searching for a fight and blood and death. We have been operating alone. But now we have joined other units of combat and are part of a huge striking force that can blast a city into the ocean. I went up on the bridge this afternoon and looked over the harbor. Dozens of various types of ships and airplanes and fighting men embraced my view. Gun muzzles pointed at me from all sides and I got the full significance of war. Dynamite, TNT and high explosives are exploded with a crashing roar, its purpose to blast men to hell. It doesn't hurt, I'm sure, just a slight surprise and sting. I hope mine comes as sudden and easy.

I know that I won't be trapped below decks. I have decided to take steps against it. You see if we get hit and a compartment takes water, the nearest man "dogs" down the hatch as tight as he can get it. There are eight "dogs" on each hatch and once dogged down, one man cannot catch up on "undogging" it. He pulls free and goes to another; the man on the other side pulls the one he just left and so on until the man goes almost mad. I have tried to get through them when someone on the other side was playing. That is the nearest I have come to having a fight up to this point. I don't let myself think how horrible it was for all the men who have died with water swirling up and about their neck when life is on the other side of that quarter-inch door; knowing the man on the other side has orders to make him die. It has to be, though, to save the lives of many others.

So you see, Darling Baby, ... life is pretty cheap west of here. Men must go forth to fight and die for a short time in order to have peace for a longer time. Blood and scorched flesh I have already seen. One man has died already. He was scalded to death by the steam from a tank in the engine room. His flesh came off at the touch and while he was on his knees and his eyeballs burning out he kept screaming "Help! Help me! Won't somebody help me?! Come and get me!" Over and over. Until the steam died down and some man went down and got him.

A few days later another man was scalded very near death but we hear he will live. It was discovered that faulty workmanship was responsible for the accidents. It was no accident, however, when we found emory dust in our ventilation system that cost many thousands of dollars and precious time to fix. Nor was it an accident when highly inflammable oil was found in the bilges, waiting for the slightest spark or cigarette to set off the whole ship.

So the war is everywhere. Even at home. We would have killed as readily there as out here had we known who was responsible.

Yes, we have our moments of pleasure. Today out on deck I noticed a group of the crew sitting around looking at papers. Upon closer observation I noted it was a cartoon and leg book someone had brought aboard. They had torn the leaves out and several men were squatting around looking at it simultaneously; handing their finished pages to the man next to him. Then there is wrestling. The younger boys find fun in grabbing each other and tugging for several minutes. That's as it should be for young boys, of course.

Outside of those little things I guess we would be asking too much. You see, our thoughts are all at home. War isn't to the liking of our people. We are a peaceful race and violence does not appeal to us.

Now for the difficult part. It approaches a last will and testament. Now, as always, since I first saw you, everything I own belongs to you. Which, of course, is natural since you stuck your chin up and helped me to accumulate it. By everything (Heaven knows it is so little, but precious to us) I mean the car and my pipes, the house shoes and everything else that I got together to make do until I was able to get you "anything that money could buy."

At last I have arrived at the most difficult part of all; that which inspired this letter and its routing. I am gone, Baby Darling. I am no longer in your life. Orvill stepped into your life five years ago and caused a dozen whirlwind changes. Now I have dropped out and no matter how difficult it is at first, you must adjust yourself to it and continue to live. You must live and be happy to make me happy, wherever I might be.

You are a beautiful woman, Ray Ellen. This time I am having the last word on it. You are a beautiful woman and intelligent. Kind and generous. A wonderful woman to have for a wife. You made my life while it lasted the most happy life a man could have and may God bless you for it.

Now, you must face the facts and make someone else happy, as well as yourself. These are the hardest words I could ever write or say to you but you must allow yourself to be another man's wife. That way, I believe you can be happy and in time forget all about me. I am just a mortal being, My Darling, and a simple one at that. We both have made the other so prominent that we are completely out of focus with the rest of the world. That, I strongly contend, is right as long as we both live. But now things have changed. I am no longer in the picture. Just a blank and you MUST realize that somewhere in the world is another man who CAN make you happy. Impress that on your mind day after day until the pain can no longer be felt. Then you may allow yourself the chance of being happy. I would like to leave that with you: Somewhere there IS a man who can make you happy and cause you to forget. I just ask that you be SURE I am gone before taking any steps.

And be cautious in your choosing Darling. You are a beautiful woman as I said and now you are educated in business and have become more or less sophisticated. I am proud of the job you are holding. "Office Manager." That sounds so important. And I know you are efficient. A business woman with a brain. And with all the advantages you have with your person go forth and seek new worlds to conquer. If you prefer to be a career girl you will be a success, I believe. But I'd rather you make some good man happy because I know he would be a good man if you chose him. That's a left-handed compliment to myself but let me give myself a little credit.

I guess that is all My Darling. If God will be gracious and allow my presence in that place where only people like you can go, I will see you again. You see, I fear that I won't come back to you because I love you so much and your love for me means so much. I have never been so fortunate in anything in my life and I'm afraid it's too good for me. It's too good to last. God knows that I want to live and get back to you. He knows that is the only reason I ask Him for my life.

I suppose He didn't think I was worthy, regardless of my willingness (but failure) to obey His word. I was not really bad, I was faithful to you. I don't know many other reasons why He should condone or deny my requests. Nevertheless, the action is His and such it shall be.

Good bye, My Darling Baby. As I've said before, you gave me enough happiness during our four years together to justify any one man's lifetime. Do not feel that I have been cheated. Think of the many thousands (yes, even millions) of men who have not had even a particle of what you have given me. I had my share. I go feeling content and thankful that Mom and God's miracle created you for me. Had I not had you, I would have cause for remorse. But as it is, I thank you and God for a very wonderful life.

However I get it My Darling, remember that my last breath was drawn in an effort to get back to you. That my last thought was of you and if I cried, it wasn't from pain of wound but pain of not holding you in my arms again.

All the love, devotion and worship that any man can give a woman I give to you in this, my last "Good Bye Officially,"

Your devoted husband,
Orvill

Ray Ellen remarried in October 1947. She subsequently adopted and raised a daughter and a son.

USS *Howorth* was decommissioned in 1946. She was sunk in a torpedo test off San Diego in 1962.

Glossary

Aft	Toward the stern (back end) of a ship.
AK	Navy designation for a cargo ship. The *A* refers to an "auxiliary," that is, a ship other than a warship; the *K* means the ship carries cargo.
Battle cruiser	A type of capital ship that made its appearance in 1908. Battle cruisers mounted guns comparable to battleships but sacrificed heavy battleship armor in order to achieve high speed to serve as scouts for the battle fleet.
Betty	Allied designation for the Japanese Mitsubishi G4M, a twin-engined, land-based medium bomber.
Bluejacket	Navy term for an enlisted sailor.
Boatswain	(Pronounced and often spelled *Bo'sun*.) A warrant officer who is a specialist in deck and boat seamanship and the upkeep of a ship's external structure. Often the term is applied incorrectly to a boatswain's mate.
Boatswain's mate (BM)	Title of the rating of a chief petty officer or petty officer specializing in seamanship and the maintenance of deck equipment (windlasses, ropes, etc.).
Bogey	An unidentified aircraft.
Bridge	The deck on which the pilothouse is located. *Bridge* and *pilothouse* are often used interchangeably. The bridge wings are those parts of the bridge located outside and on either side of the pilothouse.
Bulkhead	In its most general definition, a vertical surface within a ship—a "wall."
CB	Construction battalion; better known as Seabees. Naval units that perform civil engineering duties: the construction of port facilities, airfields, etc.
Combat Information Center (CIC)	The compartment in which intelligence and sensor (radar, sonar, and visual) reports were received and evaluated to maintain an overview of the battle environment. The CIC was developed early in the Second World War and was under the command of the executive officer.

Coxswain   A rating specializing in small boat operation, signaling, and working with canvas. Coxswains were always enlisted pay grade 4 (petty officer 3/c).

Cruiser   A fast warship with relatively large guns but thin armor. Cruisers with guns larger than 6 inches were heavy cruisers (CA); those with 6-inch guns were light cruisers (CL). Cruisers were capable of defeating all ships except battleships or cruisers with larger guns.

CV   Navy designation for a large, combat aircraft carrier.

CVE   Navy designation for an escort aircraft carrier; also referred to as a "jeep" carrier. CVEs carried out antisubmarine air patrols while escorting convoys, transported aircraft, and launched air strikes in support of amphibious operations. Escort carriers were smaller and carried fewer aircraft than CVs. CVLs performed missions similar to CVEs.

DD   Navy designation for a destroyer.

DE   Navy designation for a destroyer escort. DEs were smaller than destroyers and were designed primarily for antisubmarine warfare.

Dog watches   The watches between 4 P.M. and 6 P.M. and between 6 P.M. and 8 P.M. All other watches were four hours long. The dog watches ensured that men did not stand the midwatch (midnight to 4 A.M.) night after night and also facilitated serving the evening meal.

DRT   Dead reckoning tracer. A glass-topped device approximately 4 feet square in which, using analog speed and compass inputs, an electric, motor-driven, lighted "bug" moved in a scale representation of the movement of the ship. The DRT was useful in tracking submarines and provided records of important events.

Executive officer (XO)   The next ranking officer after a ship's captain. The executive officer is responsible for ship's routine, discipline, and administrative matters.

Fantail   The main deck at the stern of a ship.

First lieutenant   The officer who headed a ship's construction and repair department. He was responsible for all damage control and for emergency repairs.

Fish   Slang for a torpedo.

Flying bridge   On *Howorth*, the deck above the pilothouse. *Howorth*'s flying bridge contained the Mark 37 gun director for the 5-inch main gun battery, Mark 51 gun directors for 40mm gun mounts, and torpedo fire control directors. Lookouts were also stationed there.

Forecastle   (Pronounced and often spelled *foc'sle.*) The forward part of
                        a ship's main deck.

Forward   Toward the bow (front end) of a ship.

Galley   A ship's kitchen.

General   A watch condition when all hands man their battle sta-
quarters (GQ)   tions.

Gun, 20mm   The 20mm antiaircraft gun was a close-range, "last-ditch"
                        automatic weapon. Its rate of fire was approximately 450
                        rounds per minute, and its maximum range was around
                        5,500 yards, although it was fired on air targets close to the
                        ship that had not yet been destroyed by the 40mm guns.
                        The gun crew was made up of three men plus a sound-pow-
                        ered telephone talker in some instances.

Gun, 40mm   The 40mm antiaircraft gun was carried on most destroyers
                        in double- or quadruple-barreled mounts. The gun fired ex-
                        ploding shells in either a single-shot or automatic mode.
                        Although it had a horizontal range of 5,400 yards and a ver-
                        tical range of 5,420 yards, the 40mm gun was most effec-
                        tive on targets within 2,000 yards. The automatic rate of
                        fire was around 160 rounds per barrel per minute. Seven
                        men crewed a twin-barreled 40mm gun mount.

Gun, 5-inch   *Howorth*'s main gun battery consisted of five 5-inch, 38-
                        caliber, dual-purpose (antiair and antisurface) guns,
                        mounted singly in gun houses. The gun had a maximum
                        horizontal range of 18,230 yards and could shoot a projec-
                        tile to an altitude of 31,680 feet. The gun normally had a
                        crew of at least eleven, was loaded manually, and fired at a
                        rate of twelve rounds per minute. The projectile weighed
                        54 pounds, the powder case 28 pounds.

Gunner's mate   Title of the rating of a chief petty officer or petty officer
(GM)   specializing in the maintenance, repair, and operation of a
                        ship's guns and ammunition.

Gun plot   The compartment containing fire control equipment and
                        crewmen to assist the gunnery officer in hitting the target.
                        Fuze settings for 5-inch antiaircraft projectiles were gener-
                        ated by an analog computer and transmitted to the fuze
                        setting mechanism in the projectile hoists under the gun
                        mounts.

Handling room   A compartment, located below or adjacent to a gun mount,
                        in which ammunition from the magazines is prepared be-
                        fore being sent to the gun mount.

Head   Toilet compartment. A compartment with showers was
                        usually adjacent.

IFF	Identification—friend or foe. An electronic innovation developed during the Second World War. Shipborne IFF could identify friendly aircraft by the IFF transmissions they broadcast.
JOOD	Junior officer of the deck, the watch officer who assists the OOD.
Kate	Allied designation for the Japanese navy's Nakajima B5N2, a three-seat, single-engined, carrier-based torpedo plane.
Liberty ship	A cargo ship mass-produced during World War II. Liberty ships were manned by civilian crews of the U.S. Maritime Service (merchant marine) but carried naval gun crews to man the defensive weapons.
LSM	Landing ship (medium). A moderately sized amphibious ship (approximately 200 feet long).
LST	Tank landing ship. An amphibious ship designed to ground on a beach and unload tanks or other types of vehicles down a ramp through doors in the bow.
Machinist's mate (MM)	Title of the rating of a chief petty officer or petty officer specializing in the maintenance, repair, and operation of a ship's propulsion and auxiliary machinery.
Magazine	Storage compartment for ammunition. Magazines are located deep in the hull to protect them from enemy gunfire.
Main deck	The highest continuous (bow to stern) deck in a ship.
Mainmast	On *Howorth* this was the ship's only mast and was located abaft (behind) the bridge. The mainmast supported the search radars and radio antennas.
Mess deck	The compartment where meals were consumed. Also used as a gathering place for off-duty sailors at times other than meals. *Howorth*'s large wartime crew meant that some sailors berthed on the mess decks in very uncomfortable conditions.
Minesweeper	A ship, up to destroyer size, equipped to remove (sweep) and destroy mines.
National ensign	Naval term for the flag of the United States.
Nonrated	A sailor, ranking below a petty officer, who has not been selected for a rating. Seagoing nonrated sailors were divided primarily into two groups: deck (seamen) and engineering (firemen).
Officers' country	Officers' living areas, including the wardroom, staterooms, and officers' head and showers—all off-limits to enlisted men.
OOD	Officer of the deck, the watch officer in charge of the ship.

P-38	The Lockheed P-38 Lightning was a distinctive twin-boom, twin-engined, single-seat, land-based fighter aircraft of the U.S. Army Air Force (USAAF).
P-51	The North American P-51 Mustang was a high-speed, single-engined, single-seat, land-based USAAF fighter.
PGM	Navy designation for a minesweeping gunboat.
Pillbox	A reinforced land structure designed to protect a gun crew (usually manning a machine gun).
Pilothouse	Sometimes known as the wheelhouse. Located on the bridge, the pilothouse was the compartment containing the wheel, engine order telegraph, and other ship control equipment.
POA	Pacific Ocean Areas. A geographically defined zone of operations in the Pacific Theater excluding SWPA. POA, under the command of Admiral Chester W. Nimitz, was subdivided into North, Central, and South Pacific areas.
PT	Navy designation for a motor torpedo boat.
Quartermaster (QM)	Title of the rating of a chief petty officer or petty officer specializing in navigation.
Rank	In the navy, *rank* is a term applied only to officers, not enlisted sailors, with regard to their grade (official standing). The following table provides a comparison of navy and army grades (officer and enlisted) during the Second World War:

Navy	*Army*
FLEET ADMIRAL	General off the Army
ADMIRAL	General
VICE ADMIRAL	Lieutenant General
REAR ADMIRAL	Major General
COMMODORE	Brigadier General
CAPTAIN	Colonel
COMMANDER	Lieutenant Colonel
LIEUTENANT COMMANDER	Major
LIEUTENANT	Captain
LIEUTENANT (JUNIOR GRADE, OR J.G.)	First Lieutenant
ENSIGN	Second Lieutenant
CHIEF WARRANT OFFICER	Chief Warrant Officer
WARRANT OFFICER	Warrant (junior grade)
CHIEF PETTY OFFICER	First or Master Sergeant

PETTY OFFICER 1/C (FIRST CLASS)	Technical Sergeant
PETTY OFFICER 2/C	Staff Sergeant
PETTY OFFICER 3/C	Sergeant
SEAMAN 1/C OR FIREMAN 1/C	Corporal
SEAMAN 2/C OR FIREMAN 2/C	Private First Class
APPRENTICE SEAMAN	Private

Rate An enlisted pay grade (rank) within a rating, for example, yeoman 1/c versus yeoman 2/c.

Rating An occupational specialty. Ratings were grouped into branches: seaman branch, artificer branch, artificer branch (engine room), aviation branch, special branch, specialists, commissary branch, and steward branch. The seaman branch, for example, contained boatswain's mates, gunner's mates, torpedoman's mates, quartermasters, signalmen, fire controlmen, and seamen (nonrated).

Signalman (SM) Title of the rating of a chief petty officer or petty officer specializing in the transmission and receipt of visual messages using flashing light (searchlights employing Morse code) and signal flags.

Sound-powered telephone A reliable intercommunication device that requires no external electrical power, making it ideal for use in ships where normal electrical power may be disrupted by an equipment malfunction or battle damage. The user's voice acts on a carbon-filled cell and diaphragm and powers the circuit. Sound-powered telephones are either handset models, which look like regular telephones, or headset models with earphone receivers and a mouthpiece, with an activation button, suspended near the wearer's mouth by a strap around the neck. During general quarters, Raines wore a sound-powered telephone headset as a "bridge talker" in *Howorth*'s pilothouse.

Stateroom Officers' berthing compartment that served as a bedroom and office. With the exception of the captain, who had a cabin for in-port residence and a sea cabin adjacent to the bridge for residence at sea, destroyer officers shared staterooms, usually three or four to a room. Staterooms could include fixed and folding bunks, sinks, fold-down desks, and lockers.

Striker A nonrated sailor who has been selected to serve as an apprentice within a rating, such as yeoman striker. After completing the apprentice training, sometimes in a school, sometimes on the job, the striker would take an examination for promotion to petty officer rank within the rating, for example, quartermaster 3/c.

STS Special-treatment steel. A nickel-steel alloy that provides greater resistance to ballistic penetration than ordinary steel.

Super-battleship Term applied to the three battleships of the Japanese *Yamato* class secretly constructed beginning in 1937 after Japan refused to sign the Second London Naval Treaty limiting naval armaments. Each *Yamato*-class battleship displaced 64,000 tons and featured nine 18-inch guns (compared with 45,000 tons and nine 16-inch guns of contemporary U.S. battleships limited by the June 1938 protocol signed by France, Britain, and the United States). Two of the class (*Yamato* and *Musashi*) were completed; the third, *Shinano*, was finished as an aircraft carrier.

Super-dreadnought Larger, better-armed, and better-armored dreadnought battleships that came into service on the eve of the First World War. The term *dreadnought* derived from HMS *Dreadnought*, the innovative, all-big-gun, turbine-powered battleship introduced by the British Royal Navy in 1906.

Superstructure The part of the ship above the main deck; sometimes referred to as the deck house.

SWPA Southwest Pacific Area. A geographically defined zone of operations in the Pacific Theater that included Australia, New Guinea, the Philippines, Solomon Islands, Bismarck Archipelago, Borneo, and the Dutch East Indies except for Sumatra. The SWPA commander was General Douglas A. MacArthur.

Torpedoman's mate (TM) Title of the rating of a chief petty officer or petty officer specializing in the maintenance and firing of torpedoes.

Val Allied designation for the Japanese Aichi D3A, a two-seat, single-engined, carrier-based dive bomber.

WAC Women's Army Corps. The army organization for women during the Second World War. Created in spring 1942, it was termed WAAC (Women's Army Auxiliary Corps) until late 1943, when equality of pay and benefits came with its transformation into the Women's Army Corps.

Wardroom The shipboard dining and recreation compartment for officers. It also served as a medical operating room and casualty treatment station. On destroyers the captain dined in the wardroom. On larger ships the executive officer presided over the wardroom and the captain dined alone.

Warrant officer   An officer promoted from an enlisted rating. By the end of World War II there were twelve warrant officer specialties: boatswain, gunner, machinist, pharmacist, electrician, carpenter, ship's clerk, torpedoman, photographer, aerographer, pay clerk, and radio electrician.

WAVES   Women Accepted for Voluntary Emergency Service, the navy's version of the WACs. WAVES were limited to duty in the continental United States until late 1944, when the navy allowed them to serve in the Caribbean, Hawaii, and Alaska.

Weather deck   Any deck exposed to the weather, that is, a deck on the outside of the hull or superstructure.

White hat   Slang for an enlisted sailor.

Yeoman   Title of the rating of a chief petty officer or petty officer specializing in administrative and clerical duties.

Zeke   Allied designation for the Japanese Mitsubishi A6M Zero series of carrier-based, single-engine fighter aircraft used by both the Japanese air force and navy.

Bibliographic Note

During the Second World War, U.S. Navy ships were required to maintain a classified "war diary" that was forwarded to the commander in chief of the U.S. Fleet at the end of each month. The war diary was a distillation of the ship's deck log, the legal record of what occurred on the ship and, by necessity, full of details such as personnel actions, disciplinary cases, navigational details, rudder orders, and so on. The diary included the ship's location (latitude and longitude) and a description of each day's events, for example, refueling, provisioning, drills or exercises undertaken, ships nearby, and combat activity in which the ship engaged or observed. If a ship was involved in combat, a classified "action report" was forwarded via the chain of command. The action report allowed operations analysts to assess the efficiency of existing tactical policy (if it was followed) and ordnance personnel to evaluate the efficacy of the ship's weapons, such as the much-touted antiaircraft proximity fuzes in the 5-inch projectiles. USS *Howorth*'s *War Diary* and action reports are held by the Operational Archives Branch of the Naval Historical Center in the Washington Navy Yard. The ship's deck logs are deposited in the Modern Military Records Branch of the National Archives in Washington, D.C.

Anyone interested in a detailed review of U.S. Navy destroyer operations in both the Atlantic and Pacific during World War II will be well served by Theodore Roscoe's encyclopedic *United States Destroyer Operations in World War II* (Annapolis: United States Naval Institute, 1953). Roscoe's prose sounds a little bloodthirsty after four decades, but his study was thorough and based upon classified navy records. Those who have an interest in U.S. destroyers can consult Norman Friedman, *U.S. Destroyers: An Illustrated Design History* (Annapolis: Naval Institute Press, 1982). Although Friedman cites official navy documents, such as design studies, in his bibliography and excerpts appear from time to time in the text, his citations are few, and more often than not questions concerning individual design issues remain unresolved. On the whole, Friedman does provide a generally correct interpretation of why U.S. destroyers followed the design path they did, but the reader should be on the lookout for Friedman's technological determinism.

I found Samuel Eliot Morison, *The Two-Ocean War: A Short History of the United States Navy in the Second World War* (Boston: Little, Brown, 1963), to be a good but compressed overview. This edition is more readily available than Morison's twenty-five-volume study, *History of United States Naval Operations in World War II* (Boston: Little, Brown, 1947–1962), from which *The Two-Ocean War* was drawn. More recently, Ronald Spector has produced an excellent study of the Pacific Ocean War, *Eagle Against the Sun: The American War with Japan* (New York: Free Press, 1985), which is of more value as it is a less celebratory analysis than Morison's. Spector's useful bibliography will guide readers to appropriate starting points for their particular interest in the Pacific War, be it official campaign histories, memoirs, or historical interpretations. For the evolution of the military mentality that resulted in Japan's aggression in Asia, see Meirion Harries and Susan Harries, *Soldiers of the Sun: The Rise and Fall of the Imperial Japanese Army* (New York: Random House, 1991).

In discussing the controversy over the Philippines versus the Central Pacific strategies, I have relied on Michael Schaller's *Douglas MacArthur: The Far Eastern General* (New York: Oxford University Press, 1989). Schaller has made a strong case for his critical assessment of MacArthur as a leader. Also of interest is Carol M. Petillo, *Douglas MacArthur: The Philippine Years* (Bloomington: Indiana University Press, 1981); William Manchester, *American Caesar: Douglas MacArthur, 1880–1964* (Boston: Little, Brown, 1978); and D. Clayton James, *The Years of MacArthur,* 2 vols. (New York: Houghton Mifflin, 1972, 1975). MacArthur's chief adversaries were admirals King and Nimitz, who were defending War Plan Orange, which had evolved during the interwar period. King and Nimitz's side of the issue can be found in Thomas E. Buell, *Master of Seapower: A Biography of Admiral Ernest J. King* (Boston: Little, Brown, 1980), and E. B. Potter, *Nimitz* (Annapolis: Naval Institute Press, 1976). Information on War Plan Orange can be found in a variety of sources, including Russell F. Weigley, *The American Way of War: A History of United States Military Strategy and Policy* (Bloomington: Indiana University Press, 1977), chapters 12 and 13; Edward S. Miller, *War Plan Orange: The U.S. Strategy to Defeat Japan, 1898–1945* (Annapolis: Naval Institute Press, 1991); John Major, "The Navy Plans for War, 1937–1941," in Kenneth J. Hagan, ed., *In Peace and War: Interpretations of American Naval History, 1775–1978* (Westport, CT: Greenwood Press, 1978), 237–262; and in Spector, *Eagle Against the Sun,* chapter 3.

Little has been written about the enlisted "proletariat" of the U.S. Navy during the Second World War largely because the record left by enlisted men has been minimal. Personal naval history has, perforce, revolved around the officers who commanded the task forces and ships and had the time, and often official assistance, to write of their experiences after the war. Until Raines's letters surfaced, the only enlisted man's account was James J. Fahey's *Pacific War Diary: 1942–1945* (New York: Houghton Mifflin, 1963). An officer's memoir is Douglas Edward Leach, *Now Hear This: The Memoir of a Junior Naval Officer in the Great Pacific War* (Kent, OH: Kent State University Press, 1988). A recent anthology is John T. Mason, ed., *The Pacific War Remembered: An Oral History Collection* (Annapolis: Naval Institute Press, 1986). One related background study is Frederick S. Harrod, *Manning the New Navy: The Development of a Modern Naval Enlisted Force, 1899–1940* (Westport, CT: Greenwood Press, 1978). Another recent enlisted man's account of the naval war is Frank Curry, *War at Sea: A Canadian Seaman on the North Atlantic* (Toronto: Lugus Productions, 1990).

More on the Pacific War has come from enlisted marines and soldiers. James Jones's *The Thin Red Line* (New York: Charles Scribner's Sons, 1962) power-

fully delineates the army at war on Guadalcanal. Jones effectively characterized the quantitative mentality of twentieth century warfare discussed in the
excellent study by Tim Travers: *The Killing Ground: The British Army, The
Western Front, and the Emergence of Modern Warfare, 1900–1918* (London:
Unwin Hyman, 1987). Jones conveyed a vivid impression of the magnitude of
the war to emphasize the anonymity and unimportance of the individual soldier, underscoring the necessity for serial numbers. Foremost among marine
recollections of the Pacific War is Eugene B. Sledge, *With the Old Breed at Peleliu and Okinawa* (New York: Oxford University Press, 1989). Having written
his account from contemporary notes secreted in his New Testament, Sledge
presents an unembellished, horrific view of the war; his descriptions of Okinawa are both moving and revolting and reflect the abysmal depths into which
nations cast their young men when diplomacy and statesmanship fail. A moving but often fictionalized marine retrospective is William Manchester, *Goodbye, Darkness: A Memoir of the Pacific War* (Boston: Little, Brown, 1979).

Strikingly parallel to this present study is Martin Middlebrook, ed., *The Diaries of Private Horace Bruckshaw, 1915–1916* (Hamden, CT: Archon Books,
1980), which chronicles the experience of a private in the Royal Marine Light
Infantry from the Gallipoli campaign until his death at Arleux, France, on April
28, 1917. Like Raines, Bruckshaw was the youngest of seven children; both
were older than the majority of their comrades, Bruckshaw being eight months
younger than Raines at their deaths.

The racial component of the war with Japan is treated in John Dower, *War
Without Mercy: Race and Power in the Pacific War* (New York: Pantheon
Books, 1986). The government's efforts to use motion pictures to portray the
Japanese as a subhuman enemy can be found in Clayton D. Koppes and Gregory
D. Black, *Hollywood Goes to War: How Politics, Profits, and Propaganda
Shaped World War II Movies* (New York: Free Press, 1987). Jeanine Basinger,
The World War II Combat Film: Anatomy of a Genre (New York: Columbia
University Press, 1986), is also of interest in understanding World War II films
and their intended effect on home-front audiences.

For those wishing to understand the mentality of those in service during the
Second World War, the first stop is Paul Fussell, *Wartime: Understanding and
Behavior in the Second World War* (New York: Oxford University Press, 1989).
A glimpse into the combat experience also can be found in Bill Mauldin, *Up
Front* (New York: Henry Holt, 1945). Although Mauldin described the daily life
of the European infantry war, much of his work resonates with Orvill Raines's
experience in a different branch of the service, fighting a different type of war
half a world away.

The Second World War was a large, complex undertaking. The majority of its
participants never entered combat and spent most of their time bored and
homesick. For those overseas in combat zones, there was also danger, uncertainty, and fear. For that small percentage of people who engaged in combat,
there was also terror. It was this shared terror that generated what Mauldin
termed "the Benevolent and Protective Brotherhood of Them What Has Been
Shot At" (*Up Front*, 100). For an introduction to the battlefield experience, and
military historians' failure to portray it, see John Keegan, *The Face of Battle*

(New York: Viking, 1976). For a survey of human response to the modern battle-
field, see Richard Holmes, *Acts of War: The Behavior of Men in Battle* (New
York: Free Press, 1985). Authors of several contemporary studies of World War
II neuropsychiatric casualties discuss the effect of the war on its participants.
Notable among these are Lieutenant Colonel Roy R. Grinker, MC, and Major
John P. Spiegel, MC, *Men Under Stress* (Philadelphia: Blakiston, 1945); Roy L.
Swank, MD, and Walter E. Marchand, MD, "Combat Neuroses: Development
of Combat Exhaustion," *Archives of Neurology and Psychiatry* 55 (1946): 236–
247; S. Kirson Weinberg, "The Combat Neuroses," *American Journal of Sociol-
ogy* 51 (1946): 465–478; and Samuel A. Stouffer, Arthur A. Lumsdaine, Marion
Harper Lumsdaine, Robin M. Williams, Jr., M. Brewster Smith, Irving L. Janis,
Shirley A. Star, and Leonard S. Cottrell, Jr., *The American Soldier: Combat and
Its Aftermath*, vol. 2 (Princeton: Princeton University Press, 1949). Less useful
but still of interest is Lord Moran, *The Anatomy of Courage* (Garden City Park,
NY: Avery, 1987).

Within the navy there is a socialization process similar to Mauldin's "brotherhood" in which a familial relation develops among crew members of smaller
ships, such as destroyers. This does not mean that brotherly love abounds or
that the leadership of the family is in good hands. Probably the best representation of the relationship within a ship's crew during the Pacific War can be found
in Thomas Heggen, *Mister Roberts* (Boston: Houghton Mifflin, 1946).

Those interested in a more detailed study of women's roles in the service and
at home during the Second World War should consult D'Ann Campbell,
Women at War with America: Private Lives in a Patriotic Era (Cambridge: Har-
vard University Press, 1984); Susan M. Hartmann, *The Home Front and Beyond: American Women in the 1940s* (Boston: Twayne, 1982); and Judy Barrett
Litoff and David C. Smith, eds., *Since You Went Away: World War II Letters
from American Women on the Home Front* (New York: Oxford University
Press, 1991). The issue of wartime separation has been addressed in Judy Barrett
Litoff and David C. Smith, eds., *Miss You: The World War II Letters of Barbara
Woodall Taylor and Charles E. Taylor* (Athens: University of Georgia Press,
1990).

About the Editor

William M. McBride is a professor of history and Shaeffer Distinguished Humanist at James Madison University. After graduating from the U.S. Naval Academy with a degree in naval architecture, he served three tours of sea duty with the Pacific Fleet, including tours as chief engineer (acting) in the destroyer *Hamner* and as executive officer of the hydrofoil ship *Plainview*. He holds an M.Sc. in aerospace and ocean engineering from Virginia Tech and a Ph.D. in the history of science and technology from The Johns Hopkins University. He is a former Olin Fellow in military and strategic history at Yale University and a recipient of the Society for Military History's Moncado Prize for excellence and the Society for History of Technology's IEEE (Institute of Electrical and Electronics Engineers) Life Members Prize in electrical history. He is also a life member of the Disabled American Veterans.